RELATIONSHIP MARKETING IN PROFESSIONAL SERVICES

A study of agency–client dynamics in the advertising sector

Aino Halinen

London and New York

First published 1997
by Routledge
11 New Fetter Lane, London EC4P 4EE

Simultaneously published in the USA and Canada
by Routledge
29 West 35th Street, New York, NY 10001

Transferred to Digital Printing 2002

Routledge is an imprint of the Taylor & Francis Group

Typeset in Palatino by
Keystroke, Jacaranda Lodge, Wolverhampton
Printed and bound in Great Britain by
TJI Digital, Padstow, Cornwall

British Library Cataloguing in Publication Data
A catalogue record for this book is available from the British Library

Library of Congress Cataloging in Publication Data
A catalogue record for this book has been requested

ISBN 0–415–14607–0

RELATIONSHIP MARKETING IN PROFESSIONAL SERVICES

This is a fascinating analysis of the challenging marketing concept of the decade – relationship marketing. In a five-year 'fly on the wall' case study Aino Halinen explored the relationship between a Helsinki advertising agency and its international client.

Using existing theory and her unique case study, she injects brand new ideas into the creation of a model for understanding agency–client relationships and looks at the most successful way to develop business relationships.

Both the context and content for relationships are described, concept by concept. The roles of interaction style and relational bonds – attraction, trust and commitment – are seen as essential elements in ongoing contacts. Halinen further advances new ideas for understanding the development process by identifying critical events, phases and cycles.

Written with clarity and insight, this book yields a rich topical harvest for advertising and other professional service sectors and will be an excellent source book for business school academics and advanced marketing students interested in processual research.

Aino Halinen (Ph.D.) is Assistant Professor in Marketing at Turku School of Economics and Business Administration in Finland. Her 1994 doctoral thesis discusses relationship development in the advertising sector. She has published articles and chapters in international books on longitudinal research methodology, professional service relationships and service quality. Her current research focuses on the dynamics of international business networks.

ROUTLEDGE ADVANCES IN MANAGEMENT AND BUSINESS STUDIES

CONTENTS

CONTENTS

CONTENTS

LIST OF FIGURES

LIST OF TABLES

PREFACE

This book explores the dynamics of professional service relationships. Relationship marketing has recently aroused considerable interest as a new marketing approach in both the academic and the business worlds. What follows contributes to the current discussion by providing a conceptual analysis of the relationship development process in a professional service setting – with particular reference to advertising.

Relationship Marketing in Professional Services reports on a recent research project involving a thorough theoretical discussion of the content and context of professional service relationships, and substantial case evidence of the relationship dynamics pertaining to a Finnish advertising agency and its international client. Through the comparison of existing theory and the case description, an empirically grounded process model of advertising agency–client relationships is constructed. The roles of interaction style and relational bonds – attraction, trust and commitment – are emphasised as essential elements in ongoing contacts. Furthermore, a number of critical events, developmental phases and cycles are identified in relationship development.

The processual and evolutionary nature of professional service relationships is highlighted with particular care. Marketing academics have on several occasions called for longitudinal studies that would allow a reliable investigation of buyer–seller dynamics, to which end this study leads. It explores the drama of an agency–client relationship over a five-year period. The temporal dimension is taken into account, where concepts are defined and new descriptive devices are advanced to facilitate an understanding of the development process. The richness of the empirical case description, and the theoretical conclusions drawn, offer insights for both practitioners and researchers into the development of service relationships.

ACKNOWLEDGEMENTS

The study reported in this book is the outcome of a long but enjoyable learning process. A number of people and institutions have contributed, to whom I would like to express my gratitude.

I wish to extend my warm thanks to Professors Christian Grönroos, Helena Mäkinen and Kristian Möller for their encouragement and constructive comments in the various phases of the research process. I am particularly indebted to Kristian for his continuing interest in my research efforts and his kind support in getting this book published.

I have had the pleasure of cooperating with two successful companies, Markkinointi Topitörmä Oy and Fiskars Oy Ab, both amongst the market leaders in their business area. I was given the opportunity to follow the management practices of advertising agency–client relationships through the experience of several individuals in these companies. I would like to thank personally all those who participated in the study, for their confidence in the process and the interesting and stimulating discussions that ensued. I would particularly like to thank both companies and their personnel for allowing actual names to be used in this report, a rare feature in business publications.

My appreciation goes to everyone both from the academic community and in my private life, at home and abroad, who has supported me during this study. My sincere thanks to Drs Asta Salmi, Pekka Tuominen, Jan-Åke Törnroos and Pirjo Vuokko for their professional advice and valuable personal support along the way. I also extend my thanks to Alex Frost for his excellent work in language editing and Taru Virolainen for help and assistance in the preparation of the book.

A debt of gratitude is owed to Merita Bank and the persons who initiated their doctoral programme. This study would not have been possible without the Bank's financial support. The grants provided by the following foundations are also gratefully acknowledged: the Foundation for Economic Education, the Dr Marcus Wallenberg Foundation, the Paulo Foundation, the Turku Foundation for Business Education, and several foundations of the Turku School of Economics and Business Administration.

ACKNOWLEDGEMENTS

Finally, my very warmest thanks are reserved for the people closest to me, to Marko and my parents for their continuing encouragement and understanding.

A.H.

1

INTRODUCTION

1.1 RESEARCH AREA

In business-to-business markets, long-term relationships between buyers and sellers are a common form of organising economic exchange. This is the case both where manufactured products and professional or other business services are the object of exchange. Exchange occurs within established buyer–seller relationships, rather than with a new partner each time the need for exchange arises.

In the academic research of marketing, long-term buyer–seller relationships have recently aroused considerable interest. This interest dates back to the late 1960s, when a number of marketing scholars emphasised the role of exchange as the core concept of the marketing discipline (see e.g. Kotler and Levy 1969). Exchange relationships gradually became the focus of discussion. In 1975, Bagozzi argued that the processes involved in the creation and resolution of exchange relationships constituted the subject matter of marketing. Some years later, Arndt (1979) brought up the issue of long-term relationships more explicitly, and argued that their existence should be recognised in the development of marketing theory. Similar ideas were put forward by researchers of industrial and international marketing (see e.g. Guillet de Monthoux 1975 and, for the work of the IMP Group, Håkansson 1982).

During the 1980s, interest in long-term relationships and their development gained ground in different areas of the marketing discipline; in industrial and international marketing (especially in the Nordic countries and Western Europe – see Ford 1990), in distribution channel research (Frazier 1983) and even in consumer marketing (Dwyer *et al.* 1987). This development has challenged marketing scholars to reconsider the concept of marketing and redefine it as the establishment and development of enduring and mutually profitable relationships with customers (see Hammarquist *et al.* 1982; Gummesson 1987b; Grönroos 1990a). The concept of relationship marketing has accordingly been put forward as a new approach for marketing management (see e.g. Berry and Parasuraman

1

1991; Christopher *et al.* 1991; Payne 1995).[1] Relationship marketing has even been regarded as a new, emergent paradigm of the marketing discipline (Grönroos 1994; Parvatiyar and Sheth 1994).

The new relationship approach raises two basic issues for researchers to consider. First, what do we mean by exchange relationships, i.e. how can we define them? Secondly, what do we know about relationship dynamics, i.e. how do relationships develop over time?

First of all, the concept of the exchange relationship should be challenged. According to current understanding, buyer–seller relationships, both in business and in service contexts, are interactive relationships that involve not only the exchange of products and services for money but also, necessarily, social interaction and other interactive processes (see Grönroos 1982; Gummesson 1987b; Ford 1990; Miettilä and Möller 1990; Håkansson and Snehota 1995b). The relationship concept also involves different interdependences between the buyer and seller that are only indirectly related to individual exchange events (see e.g. Håkansson and Snehota 1995b: 12). The exchange relationship concept may thus be misleading when referring to buyer–seller relationships in business-to-business and service markets. In this study the term 'business relationship' is used to indicate the specific nature of buyer–seller relationships in professional business service sectors.

The second issue, the dynamics of professional business service relationships, is the primary focus of this study. Despite increasing research and interest in long-term relationships, research has to date broadly neglected the study of relationship dynamics. The lack of attention to the development of buyer–seller relationships, and to their antecedent conditions and processes, may be regarded as a serious omission in the development of marketing knowledge. With the exception of industrial and international marketing, empirical inquiries into the development of buyer–seller relationships have been rare.

As far as service marketing is concerned, only a handful of studies have even considered the dynamics of buyer–seller relationships. Gummesson (1979) and Grönroos (1980, 1982) have carried out pioneering albeit rather limited work in this area, concentrating on the initiation of customer relationships alone. Besides these efforts a number of empirical inquiries have been undertaken in professional business service industries (for advertising services Wackmann *et al.* 1987; for auditing services see Levinthal and Fichman 1988; for legal and accounting services Yorke 1990). These studies have typically investigated the antecedents and consequences of development or the change of some specific variable in different phases of a professional service relationship. Authors have not been interested in the development process of relationships *per se*, or in its conceptualisation. In the area of service marketing, no attempt has been made to describe the development of business relationships conceptually.

In this study, I concentrate on this neglected research area by investigating the development of business relationships in one specific professional business service sector, namely advertising. A number of empirical studies have shown that long-term business relationships are common in professional business service areas, such as the legal, financial, consulting and advertising professions (see e.g. Levinthal and Fichman 1988; Michell 1988; Yorke 1990; Sharma 1994). Studies in England and the United States have shown that around half of the business relationships between advertising agencies and their clients are maintained for more than five years (Wackmann *et al.* 1987: 22; Michell 1988: 62; see also Twedt 1964: 84). In a Dutch study, the length of agency–client relationships varied from six months to 28 years, at an average of around five years (Verbeke 1989: 23).

Long-term business relationships provide many potential benefits for professional service companies and their clients. It is generally less costly for a service firm to maintain and develop an existing client relationship than to attract a new one (Berry 1983: 25; Grönroos 1990a: 5). The client can also make transaction cost savings by developing a long-term relationship with a service company. In addition, the strategic and social benefits may be considerable for both parties (see Halinen 1989). A long-term business relationship may, for instance, produce strategic benefits for the service provider in its marketing by generating referrals and credentials, or it may create competitive advantage by building barriers to switching the provider. The client, for its part, may enhance the quality of services offered by engaging in a long-term business relationship with a service company (see e.g. Czepiel 1990: 15; Berry and Parasuraman 1991: 148; Halinen 1996).

All this makes it both theoretically and practically interesting to ask how the exchange of professional business services develops into a long-term business relationship, and how such relationships are maintained in changing conditions. For practitioners, a deeper understanding of the development of business relationships will mean a clearer picture of how current clients are kept and current service company relationships maintained. In order to build a mutually beneficial business relationship, it is critical for both the professional service company and the client to recognise changes in their relationship, and to act on them where necessary. In this study, these issues are addressed by using the advertising sector as an example of a professional business service industry.

1.2 THE BUSINESS RELATIONSHIP CONCEPT

While intuitively appealing, the notion of a business relationship may be difficult to grasp. In fact, in marketing literature the concept has rarely been defined explicitly. What makes dealings between two companies in a market become a relationship? Or, in contrast, what makes a relationship cease to exist? Researchers have approached the problem in at least two different ways. They have either tried to classify and characterise different relationships or have sought to identify the necessary conditions for a relationship to exist.

Dwyer *et al.* (1987) and Frazier *et al.* (1988) have separated two principal forms of business relationships: the market exchange relationship and relational exchange relationship. Market exchange relationships arise when the buyer purchases primarily on price, uses multiple sources of supply and tends to switch suppliers frequently. Relational exchange relationships, on the other hand, emerge when the buyer and supplier develop a relationship with a more long-term orientation. Relational exchange is less price-driven and is based on greater recognition of mutual commitment between trading partners than is found in market exchange relationships. Möller and Wilson (1995b: 6) propose another classification of four relationship types or views: market transactions, short-term dyadic relationships, long-term relational exchange and networks.

The debate about the conditions necessary for a relationship to exist has recently become more lively (see e.g. Barnes 1994; Liljander and Strandvik 1995). In business marketing literature, the reciprocal commitment to a relationship is often taken for granted. For instance, Håkansson and Snehota (1995a: 25) define a business relationship as 'a mutually oriented interaction between two reciprocally committed companies'. A relationship indeed requires at least two parties, but it is arguable whether both need to be willing to develop a relationship. In the service marketing area, Liljander and Strandvik (1995) have drawn attention to the existence of indifferent and forced relationships, where the customer feels indifferent towards the relationship or is even willing to terminate it. It is obvious that, in the highly interdependent business markets, relationships are not only positively perceived but also sometimes exist by force of circumstances, e.g. because of the lack of alternative partners. In this study, the starting point is, however, that relationships between professional service firms and their clients are freely and willingly established and maintained.

Most scholars seem to agree that continuity is a key element of business relationships. Each exchange event must be viewed in terms of its history and anticipated future (Dwyer *et al.* 1987: 12). A longer time-perspective is usually considered important (see. e.g. Håkansson 1982; Gummesson 1987b; Frazier *et al.* 1988). Heide and John (1990: 25) have defined continuity as the perceived bilateral expectation of future interaction. Håkansson and Snehota (1995a: 25) and Wilson and Mummalaneni (1986: 52) refer essentially to the same characteristic while emphasising the role of commitment as a key element of business relationships. Commitment involves a future orientation and refers to the stability and durability of a relationship.

4

The idea of frequent or repeated exchange events is often connected with the relationship concept (see e.g. Wilson and Mummalaneni 1986; Frazier *et al.* 1988). In most cases, relationships do indeed include more than one transaction, but continuity is more important in determining whether the companies should be considered to have a relationship. Transactions may occur rarely or irregularly, so that the relationship is dormant over longer time periods. If the companies have expectations of future exchange, however, they should be considered to have a relationship.

Business relationships also exist at a number of levels. At least three levels can be identified: company, departmental or group, and individual (Wilson and Mummalaneni 1986: 46; Möller and Wilson 1988: 11). In this study, the focus of analysis falls particularly on relationships between companies. Other levels are also taken into account, however – at least indirectly. I shall use the term 'business relationship' (or just 'relationship') when referring to relationships between advertising agencies and client companies. The term 'unit business relationship' (or 'unit relationship') will be used to refer to business relationships between an agency and a specific business unit of a client company.

1.3 EXISTING MODELS OF THE DEVELOPMENT OF BUSINESS RELATIONSHIPS

The development of business relationships is a problematic research topic, especially because it explicitly adds the temporal dimension to research design. The inclusion of dynamics typically complicates research and also raises questions that have to date attracted relatively little attention in the discipline of marketing. One has to resolve how the temporal dimension is to be treated at the conceptual level and how it can be grasped through empirical investigation.

In this section, I shall concentrate on these issues by examining how the development of business relationships can be understood in general, and how the existing literature on business relationships has regarded and studied development in practice. I will evaluate the studies carried out in the advertising sector and in other professional business service sectors, but since literature in these areas is in very short supply, I shall also discuss how relationship development has been treated in other areas of marketing – in service marketing in general and in industrial marketing and distribution. Besides analysing the concept of development employed by the studies, I will also examine the focus of their interest; whether it is on the development of the relationship and its description or rather on the drawing of normative implications for strategic marketing purposes. This is also connected with the research tradition from which each study has emerged: from the interaction school, the political economy school, or the marketing management school (for the division see Möller 1992). Finally,

I shall look at the methods of inquiry and how the temporal dimension has been incorporated into research methodology.

Like the strategy process of organisations, the development of business relationships can be viewed from at least three different perspectives: input–output, change and processual (cf. Van de Ven 1992: 170).

In input–output models, the research interest lies in the antecedents and consequences of development, i.e. in the influence of some independent variables on some dependent outcome variables (cf. Van de Ven 1992: 170). The model may focus on the factors that foster the initiation, maintenance or dissolution of a relationship, or it may examine factors that influence, for instance, the success or failure of a relationship in its different phases.

Models and studies using the change perspective tend instead to look at the development process in terms of the changes in a number of specific variables over time (see e.g. Miller and Friesen 1982; Eneroth 1984: 129; Van de Ven 1987: 331). One may examine, for instance, how exchange volume, the experience of the trading partner or commitment change over time, from one point in time to another. On the basis of change models one can usually only say whether a change has happened, not how it happened.

The question of how changes occur is approached by models that take a processual perspective on development. Process models take up the process of development as such, i.e. the nature, sequence and order of events and activities that unfold over time and that describe how things change (see Van de Ven 1992: 170). In terms of Eneroth (1984, 131–2), development is viewed as a change, transition or transformation of something as it flows through the structure of the phenomenon, not as a change of some structural aspect.[2]

Whereas a definition of development indicates the meaning placed on development in relation to other uses in the literature, a theory of development consists of statements that explain how and why processes unfold over time (Van de Ven and Poole 1995). In the context of buyer–seller relationships, two types of theory in particular have been employed: life cycle theories and evolutionary theories.

In life cycle models, the development of a business relationship is divided into phases according to the presumed stages of a life cycle. The use of the life cycle metaphor has been especially common, probably because of its intuitive appeal, neatness and simplicity in consulting and teaching situations in particular. There are, however, some considerable weaknesses in its application.

Life cycle models infer an evolutionary pattern of natural organisms, at least implicitly. They tend to view development as a deterministic, inevitable evolution where the relationship moves progressively from one clear stage to another until decay (Van de Ven 1992: 177). However, it is improbable that companies or relationships between companies will follow this kind of pattern (see Kimberly 1980: 7–11; Ford 1989: 823; Hedaa 1991: 48, 131). The development of business relationships is not intrinsic. Relationships are instead developed consciously or unconsciously by the parties to them.

In addition, the phase divisions of life cycle models are often arbitrary and disconnected from the content of a business relationship. Phasing may have been done *a priori*, for instance, on the basis of the length of a business relationship, which has helped to manage the time dimension and made it possible to study some interesting element in the relationship. Life cycle models typically view development from an input–output or change perspective and tend to treat time as an absolute and linear dimension.[3]

Another possibility would be to describe relationship development more as an evolutionary phenomenon without deterministic phases. These evolutionary models, which are particularly rare, provide rich explanations of development. They are explanatory, not predictive process models (see Van de Ven 1992).[4] It should be noted that these models can also use phasing, for instance as a means of organising data or simplifying the description of development. The underlying theory of development is, however, different from that of life cycle models. Evolutionary models apply the processual perspective to development and try to capture the content of the relationship in dynamic concepts that are themselves defined in relation to temporal modes: to the past, present and future. This releases the models from the absolute time dimension. The development of relationships is viewed in relation to the processes occurring in relationships and events in the context of relationships, not in relation to the mere passage of time (see Halinen and Törnroos 1995: 507).

Finally, relationship development models can also be assessed according to the empirical methods used in their development. In assessing models of dynamic phenomena, one has to ask whether they are grounded on cross-sectional or longitudinal investigations or perhaps on conceptual analyses based on intuition, earlier studies and practical knowledge of the industry. The use of cross-sectional methods may be considered a serious weakness of the models, especially in cases where the description and explanation of relationship development has been the major purpose (Halinen and Törnroos 1995; see also Van de Ven 1992: 172). Longitudinal studies with retrospective or real-time methodology would be more appropriate for studying time-bound phenomena.

I shall commence the evaluation of existing models of relationship development from studies of advertising agency–client relationships. Table 1.1 offers an overview of existing models and frameworks concerning relationship development in advertising or other professional service sectors or in service businesses more generally.

In many studies of the advertising business the long-term nature of

Table 1.1 Models and frameworks of relationship development in service sectors

Author and model	Phase, state or element of development	Focus, conception of development and empirical basis
Gummesson (1979) *Buyer-seller interaction model*	Pre-stage Decision process Decision to select a particular professional Operation of the assignment Post-stage	Describes the stages of buyer–seller interaction in a professional service context Emphasises the decision process that leads to the selection of a professional firm Input–output perspective Conceptual presentation
Grönroos (1980, 1982) *The customer relation life cycle – a three-stage model*	Stage 1: Initial stage Stage 2: Purchasing process Stage 3: Consumption process	Views the life cycle from the marketing planning point of view Builds a corresponding three-stage model for services marketing Input–output perspective Conceptual presentation
Edvinsson (1985) *Service export sales life cycle*	Contact phase Negotiation phase Trial order and delivery phase Maintenance and repeat phase	Applies and extends the Grönroos model to export marketing Input–output perspective Case studies from professional and other business services
Wackmann *et al.* (1987) *The agency–client life cycle*	The pre-relationship phase The development phase The maintenance phase The termination phase	Examines the factors that lead to satisfaction with the relationship in its different phases Input–output perspective Cross-sectional survey data from advertisers
Yorke (1990) *The changing nature of the professional service supplier–client relationship*	Ignorance Interest Initiation Involvement Integration	Examines perceived benefits, range of services offered/purchased, strengths and weaknesses of a supplier and fulfilment of specific client needs in 'young' and 'old' relationships Change perspective Cross-sectional survey data from professionals and their clients

advertising agency–client relationships has been acknowledged. Nevertheless, the studies do not focus on relationship development *per se*. Research efforts have been devoted to factors affecting agency selection (Cagley 1986; Dowling 1994) and relationship vulnerability (Doyle *et al.* 1980; Michell 1987; Michell *et al.* 1992). There are also studies that concentrate on certain elements of agency–client relationships, e.g. creativity or communication strategies (Michell 1984a; Etelä 1985; Beltramini and Pitta 1991). The make-or-buy decision and the structure of advertising markets have been investigated, e.g. by Twedt (1964), Michell (1984b, 1988) and Ripley (1991). But only two studies have purposely treated agency–client relationships as ongoing. Both have approached development from the input–output perspective. The life cycle model of Wackmann *et al.* (1987) and the replication of their study by Verbeke (1989) examine the factors that create satisfaction in different phases of an agency–client relationship.

In the service marketing area, Gummesson (1979) was the first to tackle the dynamics of relationships by introducing the buyer–seller interaction model for professional services. He identified five major stages in a relationship, each of which requires different action from the seller. Grönroos (1980, 1982) proposed a life cycle model of customer relations, which involves three stages. Both the Gummesson and Grönroos models are specially constructed for the purposes of marketing planning: each stage can be viewed as an outcome of marketing activities from the previous stage. The temporal perspective on service relationships is short. The models describe relationships as discrete exchange events rather than long-term relationships, and examine only their early stages.

Yorke (1990) has studied professional services, especially financial and legal services, and compared a number of factors in 'young' (less than five years old) and 'old' (over five years old) client relationships. Drawing on these comparative data and the managerially oriented model of Grönroos (1980), Yorke proposes a tentative model of the changing nature of professional service supplier–client relationships. The age of a relationship is used as a proxy variable for its developmental stage, and the proposed stages are only loosely connected with the empirical study itself. The process of relationship development is not addressed (see Table 1.1).

Edvinsson's model (1985) extends the Grönroos model to export marketing, paying special attention to the interaction between international business partners. The model is a life cycle model constructed for marketing strategy and planning purposes.

As the above review shows, the development of business relationships has attracted only scant attention in the area of service marketing. Academic research has examined the marketing and buying of professional business services from the traditional marketing management perspective (with the 4 Ps), ignoring the nature of professional services as a starting point for marketing planning. Research has treated buyers and sellers as separate actors, and the focus has been on individual service transactions rather than business relationships and their development. The interactive nature of service exchange has been emphasised, but no attempt has been made to conceptualise the process of relationship development in professional business service sectors, or in other service sectors. Consequently, a wide gap has emerged between the received theory of marketing and the reality of marketing within professional business service firms (for further criticism see also Morgan 1990: 291; Edgett *et al.* 1992: 350).

Table 1.2 reviews the models and frameworks of relationship development in industrial settings. Guillet de Monthoux proposed a model of relationship development as far back as 1975, when he described industrial markets in terms of stable buyer–seller relationships and compared relationship development there to a love affair between people. He challenged the prevailing theories of marketing with an inductive study which focused on the change in various elements within a business relationship (see Table 1.2, pp. 12–13).

The development of industrial marketing research later led to the establishment of the Industrial Marketing and Purchasing Group (IMP Group). The group launched a new approach to industrial marketing, namely the Interaction Approach. Ford's model (1982) draws on this tradition and the extensive database collected by the IMP Group. Ford pays special attention to the nature and change of business relationships, but his model also follows life cycle thinking. Regardless of the dynamic phenomenon under study, the model has been constructed primarily on the basis of cross-sectional data.

The study of Ford and Rosson (1982) and Rosson's follow-up study (1986) present the only model of relationship development based on longitudinal real-time data. Ford and Rosson (1982) define and characterise five possible states in business relationships on the basis of the various content elements of these relationships. The study questions the life cycle metaphor by showing that relationships can be at various phases – growing, inert or static – almost irrespective of their age. Rosson's follow-up study (1986) looked at the development of specific relationships from state to state. He made a contribution to the understanding of the dynamics of business relationships by investigating the change in relationships and also the reasons behind the changes in the context of each relationship. The study showed that relationships are vulnerable to termination in every state and especially in the early phases of relationship development. A parallel finding has also been made in the advertising sector. Michell (1988: 64) estimated that a large proportion of agency–client relationships progress only through the earliest stage of the life cycle hypothesised by Wackmann *et al.* (1987).

Frazier (1983) proposed a broadened framework for marketing channel relationships, taking the time dimension into account. On the basis of existing literature, Frazier developed a conceptual description of the processes of channel relationships and of their evaluation in particular. His development perspective can be considered to be processual.

Wilson and Mummalaneni (1986) contribute to the research area by proposing a new conceptualisation of business relationships based on the bonding and investment models of social psychologists. They present an evolutionary model of business relationships, emphasising the processual nature of development. The framework describes how satisfaction, investments and commitment develop in repeated successful interactions, and how commitment in turn leads to continued interactions and further investment in the relationship.

Dwyer *et al.* (1987) have similarly drawn on the work of social psychologists but take the social exchange approach to relationship development. In their model, relationships are supposed to evolve through five general phases – each of which represents a major transition in how parties regard one another (see Table 1.2). The model provides a rich theoretical description of the development process of buyer–seller relationships, but as the authors have stated it is built on conceptual foundations and empirical evidence from social exchange and romantic relations, not from business relationships. The model lacks obvious ways in which to operationalise its key concepts.

Liljegren's model (1988) builds on the IMP Group's Interaction Approach and the Network Perspective of industrial markets. Accordingly, Liljegren also examines the role of the surrounding inter-firm network and the critical events in the process of relationship development. The model is based on a retrospectively conducted case study. Liljegren (1988: 372–4) distinguishes the uncertainty phase as a separate phase in relationship development and shows that new build-up and development phases may also occur in a long-term relationship. This finding lends further support to the earlier proposition that there is no single and inevitable development path that would be common to all relationships (cf. also Ford and Rosson 1982; Rosson 1986).

The most recent contribution in an industrial context is the model suggested by Frazier *et al.* (1988) concerning the development of just-in-time relationships. The model is based on a broad range of theoretical approaches. It concentrates more on the structural aspects and antecedents of business relationships than on the process of relationship development (see Table 1.2).

The overall picture of the existing models and frameworks of relationship development is dislocated and clearly shows the early developmental stage at which the research area rests. There is a lack of cross-referencing between the authors and the models. This can be seen especially between

Table 1.2 Models and frameworks of relationship development in industrial sectors

Author and model	Phase, state or element of development	Focus, conception of development and empirical basis
Guillet de Monthoux (1975) *Model of the mating process of industrial organisations*	Phase 1: Romance Phase 2: Affair, Marriage Phase 3: Divorce Phase 4: New romance New affair, New marriage	Analyses the development of relationships, e.g. with respect to exchange volumes, complexity, formalisation and interdependence Change perspective Cross-sectional interview data
Ford (1982) *Development of buyer–seller relationships*	The pre-relationship stage The early stage The development stage The long-term stage The final stage	Analyses the development of relationships by considering the variables of experience, uncertainty, distance, commitment, and adaptations in the five stages Change perspective Cross-sectional interview and survey data
Ford and Rosson (1982), Rosson (1986) *A model of manufacturer– overseas distributor relationships*	New Growing Troubled Static Inert	Considers relationships to be in one of five possible 'states' of development, which are determined by three factors – stake, experience and uncertainty – and characterised by the level of commitment, adaptation and conflict Change perspective Longitudinal interview and survey data
Frazier (1983) *A framework of inter-organisational exchange behaviour in marketing channels*	Initiation process Implementation process Review process	Describes ongoing channel relationships in terms of three interactive processes and their outcomes, paying special attention to the review and evaluation of rewards and losses from exchange

Table 1.2 concluded

		Processual perspective Conceptual presentation

Wilson and
Mummalaneni (1986)
Framework of
relationship
development
	Need complementarity
	Interactions
	Outcomes
	Satisfaction
	Investments
	Commitment
		Views relationship
		  development as a process
		  where satisfaction,
		  investments and
		  commitment develop
		  between the buyer and
		  the seller in repeated
		  successful interactions
		Processual perspective
		Conceptual presentation

Dwyer *et al.* (1987)
The relationship
development
process
	Phase 1: Awareness
	Phase 2: Exploration
	Phase 3: Expansion
	Phase 4: Commitment
	Phase 5: Dissolution
		Considers relationship
		  development as a
		  process of deepening
		  dependence evolved
		  in five sub-processes:
		  attraction, communi
		  cation and bargaining,
		  power and justice,
		  norm development,
		  and expectations
		  development
		Processual perspective
		Conceptual presentation

Liljegren (1988)
A cyclical model of
relationship
development
	Establishment phase
	Build-up phase
	Development phase
	Maintenance phase
	Uncertainty phase
	Break-up phase
	Settlement phase
		Considers relationship
		  development as a cyclical
		  process focusing on
		  adaptations, uncertainty
		  and conflicts, the
		  surrounding inter-firm
		  network and critical
		  events
		Processual perspective
		Longitudinal case study

Frazier *et al.* (1988)
Just-in-time exchange
relationships
	Interest stage
	Initiation-rejection stage
	Implementation stage
	Review stage
		Analyses why and when
		  JIT exchange relationships
		  are initiated and which
		  factors influence the
		  success and failure
		  of initiated relationships
		Input–output perspective
		Conceptual presentation

service marketing and industrial marketing researchers as well as between American and European researchers. *There is, at present, no agreement on the conceptual language to be used to describe the development of business relationships.* The most significant conceptual contributions have been provided by Ford (1982), Wilson and Mummalaneni (1986), and Dwyer *et al.* (1987).

When considering the process of relationship development in particular, the lack of research knowledge stands out even more clearly. *Studies that examine the development of business relationships from an evolutionary and/or processual perspective have been rare.* Only the models of Frazier (1983), Wilson and Mummalaneni (1986), Dwyer *et al.* (1987) and Liljegren (1988) – which all concern industrial relationships – demonstrate relevance. The use of the life cycle metaphor, explicitly or implicitly, is common. Empirical studies of the process of relationship development have been particularly rare. Liljegren's study (1988) seems to be the only one that has adopted a processual perspective of relationship development and also investigated it longitudinally. *In the professional services area, the lack of empirical research and theoretical models of relationship development is striking.*

2

THE RESEARCH SETTING

2.1 THE PURPOSE OF THE STUDY AND ITS THEORETICAL UNDERPINNINGS

In professional business service sectors, economic exchange has typically been organised through long-term business relationships involving service companies and their clients. The development of a business relationship is an important issue for both parties to the exchange, in their attempts to do profitable business with each other and attain their respective goals through exchange. In order to manage business relationships for each party's benefit, professional service firms and their clients need to have an understanding of the dynamics of business relationships, how they evolve and what factors are likely to affect their development.

Until now, the discipline of marketing has been unable to provide much guidance for practitioners here. The literature review in Chapter 1 showed that no attempt has been made to conceptualise the development of business relationships in the advertising sector or in any other professional business service industries. Empirical studies of the process of relationship development have been particularly rare, in other business contexts as well.

There is obviously a need for empirical research that aims at describing and explaining the development of business relationships between professional service firms and their clients. The empirical focus of this study is the advertising industry. *The purpose of the study is to build an empirically grounded process model for understanding the development of advertising agency–client relationships.*

I will approach the development of agency–client relationships as a processual phenomenon. This entails the examination of relationship development from a processual perspective by studying the nature, sequence and order of events and activities that unfold over the duration of a business relationship (see Van de Ven 1992: 170). The ideas of both change and continuity are inherent to the concept of process (see e.g. Hammersley and Atkinson 1989: 219). In the processual approach it is not, however, change *per se* that is of interest, but rather the process of changing – how changes occur.

Agency–client relationships will also be approached as evolutionary phenomena, without *a priori* phasing or the assumption of a deterministic life cycle. The concept of development will be used in its neutral meaning, referring to the development of business relationships with their ups and downs, not to progressive development alone.

In order to carry out theoretically sound and practically useful research on any processual phenomenon, it is necessary to explore at least three basic concepts and their interconnections through time: the content of the phenomenon, the process itself, and the context in which it occurs (Pettigrew 1990: 268) (see Figure 2.1).

Pettigrew (1987, 1990) and Van de Ven and Huber (1990) have proposed this framework for dealing with processes of strategic change in organisations. These three interconnected concepts can be put to work as an analytical framework for any processual phenomenon occurring in or between firms. Broadly speaking, one may say that the 'what' of relationship development is encapsulated under the label content, the 'how' can be understood from an analysis of the process and much of the 'why' is derived from an analysis of the context (Pettigrew 1987: 5).

On the basis of this general framework I can now express the purpose of this study in the form of three research questions:

1 Which theoretical concepts are the most appropriate to describe the content of an advertising agency–client relationship?
2 What are the processes through which advertising agency–client relationships develop?
3 Which contextual factors have an influence on the development process of advertising agency–client relationships and how does this influence manifest itself?

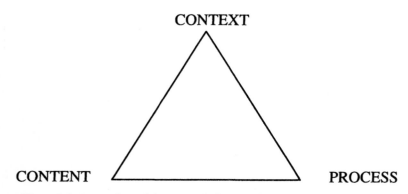

Figure 2.1 An analytical framework for studying processual phenomena
Source Pettigrew (1987: 5)

Advertising services are professional business services that differ in important aspects from most industrial products. It is highly likely that any models developed in an industrial setting will not be directly valid for describing the development of agency–client relationships. Taking the specific nature of advertising services as a starting point, we need to address the question of what concepts are the most appropriate for describing the content of such relationships.

The second question concerns the processes of development and how relationships develop. Answering this question involves the examination of temporal relationships between the different concepts describing the content of business relationships. In building a process model, three types of conceptual relationship should be considered essential: the presence of a relationship between two concepts, the temporal order of the two concepts, and thirdly their logical order. Temporal order means that one concept precedes the other or is simultaneous with the other, and logical order that one concept leads to another or that each of them affects the other (Brinberg and McGrath 1985: 96).

The process of development cannot be understood in isolation from the context of a business relationship. The link between the context and the process is elementary to understanding this issue. Why relationships develop as they do can partly be explained by contextual factors. Processes are constrained by structures, but they also shape structures either in the direction of preserving them or in the direction of altering them (Pettigrew 1990: 270). This means that contextual factors can be a barrier to action in advertising agency–client relationships, but may also be mobilised and activated by the parties to the relationship as they seek to obtain outcomes that are important to them. To understand the development of business relationships, it is necessary to ask which contextual factors affect this process and what kinds of effects these factors have on the process.

This study draws theoretically on the IMP Group's Interaction Approach. Instead of applying the Traditional Marketing Mix Approach, the Interaction Approach will be used as a new theoretical perspective for studying the marketing and buying of advertising services. Besides the Interaction Approach, the study is based on the theoretical developments of services marketing research and on interaction studies of American origin. Figure 2.2 illustrates the area of study and the theoretical approaches used.

The emergence of the Interaction Approach in the investigation of industrial markets and recent developments in services marketing have brought these research traditions into closer contact. Both have emphasised the interactive and processual nature of exchange, starting from their respective research areas. The similarities in these traditions have been particularly emphasised by Nordic researchers (Gummesson 1987b;

17

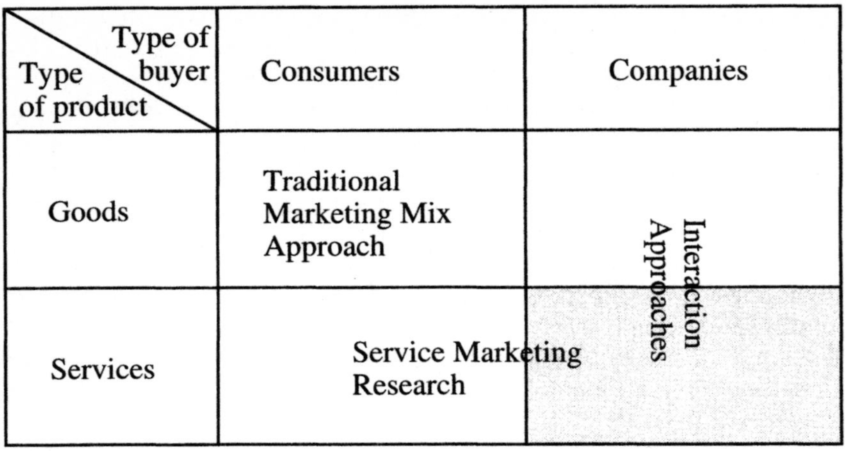

Type of buyer / Type of product	Consumers	Companies
Goods	Traditional Marketing Mix Approach	Interaction Approaches
Services	Service Marketing Research	Interaction Approaches

Figure 2.2 Theoretical positioning of the study
Source Adapted from Gummesson (1987a: 22)

Grönroos 1990a), but cross-referencing and the integration of research results have to date been scarce. In the case of advertising services and professional business services in general, the overlap of the two research areas is particularly apparent.

The IMP Group's Interaction Approach has its roots in Scandinavia and Western Europe. Inductive methodology and a few key constructs guiding empirical research have been characteristic of this approach (Möller 1994). Researchers have carried out important conceptual work in trying to understand the process of relationship development. In considering the specific nature of advertising services, however, the conceptual language of the Interaction Framework seems somewhat weak. I will, therefore, further specify and complement the concepts of the framework by resorting to service marketing research and by borrowing concepts from those American interaction studies that base their models on the theories of social psychology (see especially Möller 1994).

2.2 RESEARCH STRATEGY

First and foremost this study is explorative. It aims at building a model of the development of advertising agency–client relationships and generating ideas and propositions for later empirical tests. In exploring the new model I use an inductive rather than a deductive strategy. I shall employ many of the theory-building principles originally proposed by Glaser and Strauss (1967) in their Grounded Theory Approach, but dissociate myself from their strong inductive emphasis by making broader use of extant models and knowledge of the research topic.[1]

. 18

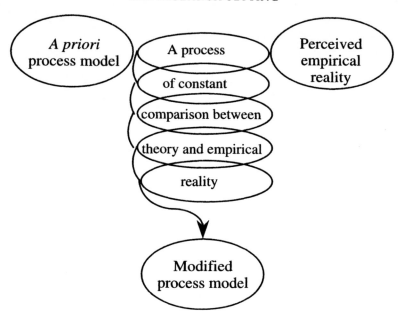

Figure 2.3 The research strategy

The existing theoretical literature and empirical evidence will both be used as sources of knowledge in constructing the model. Figure 2.3 illustrates the research strategy simply. I shall first outline an *a priori* process model of relationship development based on existing theoretical and industry-related literature. This model will then be tried against an empirical case in order to evaluate its applicability to the empirical reality of advertising agency–client relationships. Empirical reality refers here to the image of reality I have been able to build as a researcher by interviewing people in advertising agencies and client companies. The aim of the study is to arrive at an empirically grounded process model via a constant comparison and dialogue between the *a priori* model and the received empirical evidence (see Figure 2.3).

There are many reasons for outlining an *a priori* framework and for making the theoretical perspective explicit. First, it is particularly difficult to study a processual phenomenon without drawing up some preliminary definitions and limits concerning its content and context. A theoretical framework helps to focus the analysis and reveal the links between context and content in a processual study (see e.g. Odén 1989: 138–9, about historical research). Strauss (1987: 222) has also emphasised the role of theory in the construction of case histories. Secondly, it is a matter of scientific credibility. I share the view of Miles and Huberman (1994: 17) that better science happens with an explicit framework rather than by pretending some kind of inductive purity.

Thirdly, the comparison of an empirical case with some existing theory or concept is an important method in creating new knowledge and theory (Normann 1973: 54–5). The *a priori* model is used to guide the empirical investigation but is left open for ideas and reformulations emerging from the empirical data. Delineating a theoretical framework links the study with other empirical settings and theoretical approaches, thus serving theory building. A theoretical framework guides comparisons and the use of theoretical sampling and typologies (see e.g. Layder 1993). Ultimately, it becomes the main vehicle for generalising the results of the case study (see Yin 1989: 40; Norén 1990: 13).

Methodologically the study can be characterised as qualitative, longitudinal and dyadic. I will use qualitative methodology as illustrated via the following features:

1 Different kinds of data will be collected from various data sources during the study (Strauss 1987: 2–3), although most of the data are verbal in nature.

2 Analysis primarily involves the interpretation of words and statements given by the informants. Interpretation occurs at two levels (cf. Strauss 1987: 4; Pettigrew 1990: 280). It aims at providing a description of the empirical case, i.e. giving meaning to things, events and activities in their proper empirical setting. It also aims at building theory from this empirical description, i.e. delineating the phenomenon at a more abstract level.

3 The researcher is seen as the study instrument, as the interpreter of the empirical phenomenon (see e.g. Bonoma 1985: 204).

4 The research process is iterative, proceeding from data collection to data analysis and again to data collection, and so on. Working propositions are drawn from concrete empirical instances and then tried in the subsequent cycles of investigation (see Huberman and Miles 1985: 357).

5 The people involved in business relationships and who will be interviewed during the investigation are regarded as co-operators in data collection. They are experts in agency–client relationships; their experience, conceptions and self-reflection form an important base of empirical data.

6 There are no fixed methodological rules or techniques for conducting a qualitative study (Strauss 1987: 7). Certain methodological guidelines and analysis procedures are, however, available for theory-building research, and these will also be used in this study (e.g. comparative analysis, 'snowball' tactics in selecting informants and open coding of interview transcripts, see Chapter 4).

The study can be characterised as longitudinal, since it investigates the development of business relationships over time and involves data collection from several periods of time. Kimberly (1976: 329), and Miller and Friesen (1982: 1013–14) have defined longitudinal research as 'those techniques, methodologies and activities which permit the observation, description and/or classification of organisational phenomena in such a way that process can be identified and empirically documented'. Several researchers have recently called for longitudinal studies, in order to gain a better understanding of the dynamics of business relationships (see e.g. Anderson and Narus 1990: 55; Crosby et al. 1990: 78; Heide and John 1992: 42).

Longitudinal research provides some evident advantages which are particularly relevant to this study (see especially Kimberly 1976; Miller and Friesen 1982: 1014; Eisenhardt 1989: 542). First of all, it helps to build better, logically consistent models of processual phenomena. Longitudinal research also facilitates attempts to establish causality – or at least local causality[2] – since temporal precedence of events and activities can potentially be shown. Qualitative longitudinal research allows the investigator to acquire a rich understanding of the contextual setting, thus helping us to interpret findings and draw inferences about why things happen. A major disadvantage of conducting a longitudinal study is, on the other hand, that it tends to be extremely time-consuming.

At least three different longitudinal approaches are available for studying the development of business relationships: first, historical or retrospective studies; secondly, follow-up studies that investigate relationships in real time; thirdly, futures studies, which try to conceive of the possible futures of a relationship (Halinen and Törnroos 1995: 510). In this study I shall use a combined approach, where longitudinal data are collected both retrospectively and in real time.

The dyadic or 'two-party approach' is also an essential feature of this study. Business relationships and their development are always a bilateral matter. The smallest meaningful unit for building a process model of advertising agency–client relationships is therefore a dyad of two parties (see e.g. Bonoma and Johnston 1978; Czepiel 1990: 17). Relationship development has to be studied simultaneously both from the agency and the client perspective.

The study will be conducted using a case strategy. Case studies are the preferred strategy, especially when 'how' or 'why' questions are being posed, when the researcher has little control over events (cf. experiments) and when the focus is on a contemporary phenomenon in its real-life context. Case study allows an investigation to retain the holistic and meaningful characteristics of real-life events, such as individual life cycles, organisational and managerial processes, and international relations (Yin 1989: 13–14).

A case study is an especially appropriate strategy for theory-building purposes. Case descriptions often provide important insights into the studied phenomenon and lead to the formulation of hypotheses that can subsequently be more rigorously investigated (Dunkerley 1988: 91). Case studies that aim at theory building are especially relevant in a new research area where little is known about the phenomenon or in an area where current perspectives seem inadequate because they have little empirical substantiation (Eisenhardt 1989: 548). Broad and complex phenomena that cannot usefully be studied outside their natural context, such as dyadic interaction between buyers and sellers, are best approached by case strategy (Bonoma 1985: 202, 207).

In this study, the term 'case' refers to a business relationship between an advertising agency and a client company. One advertising agency–client relationship and its development is investigated intensively. As Miller and Friesen (1982) pointed out, the main advantage of qualitative single-case design is its ability to provide full and in-depth insight into dynamic phenomena in organisations. In this kind of study it is possible to infer causality, to identify critical factors and occasionally to produce new theories and hypotheses (Miller and Friesen 1982: 1022; see also Dyer and Wilkins 1991: 614).

A trade-off is necessary between the number of cases and the depth and completeness of data collection (see e.g. Dyer and Wilkins 1991: 615). This study prefers depth and completeness in a single case, because of the rudimentary level of existing models of relationship development and the processual approach used. The building of a process model requires a deep understanding of both the content and the context of a business relationship. Instead of a set of superficially investigated cases, I intend to provide one thorough description of an advertising agency–client relationship and its development.

A further trade-off is necessary between the number of cases and the generalisability of research results (see e.g. Miller and Friesen 1982: 1024). In this respect it must be emphasised that the aim of this study is not to achieve statistically generalisable results but to build an empirically grounded process model that is created through theoretical reasoning and the comparison of existing theoretical knowledge with the case study description. We are concerned here with analytical generalisation, which occurs at the level of theory (see especially Yin 1989: 38),[3] and contextual generalisation – the transferability of interpretation into other contexts (see Hirschman 1986; Norén 1990). The value of the study depends upon the cogency of its theoretical reasoning and the comprehensiveness of the case description, not upon the sample size and empirical coverage.

2.3 STRUCTURE OF THE STUDY

The structure of the study follows the logic of the research strategy depicted in Figure 2.3. In the next chapter (Chapter 3) I shall first build a comprehensive conceptual framework of the development of advertising agency–client relationships, in order to facilitate a preliminary understanding of the phenomenon. I shall describe the context of a business relationship and delineate the conceptual content of agency–client relationships on the basis of theoretical and industry-related literature and research results. An *a priori* process model of the development of agency–client relationships is presented at the end of the chapter. The model represents the level of knowledge offered by the existing literature, and that possessed by the researcher when starting the empirical investigation. It is therefore tentative and still lacking in a description of the development process, and particularly in the specification of the connections between the context and the process. It is in this area that existing knowledge was and still is most scarce.

Chapter 4 describes the empirical research design and the research process in more detail. The issues of data collection, data analysis and the potential biases and inaccuracies in the empirical data are addressed.

Chapter 5 includes the case description. The case companies are presented, along with the development of their relationship, including three separate unit business relationships, described in chronological order.

In Chapter 6, the *a priori* model is contrasted with the empirical case description. Each concept, its constituent parts, empirical indicators and temporal relationships with other concepts are specified in the light of the empirical evidence. The influence of contextual factors on the process of relationship development is also examined. The emerging theoretical ideas and propositions are linked with the most recent research findings in the area. The results of the study are summarised into a modified process model at the end of the chapter.

Chapter 7 is devoted to the evaluation of the study, to a discussion of its theoretical and managerial implications and an assessment of its validity. A number of avenues for future research are also presented. Chapter 8 briefly summarises the research effort as a whole.

3

AN INTERACTION FRAMEWORK FOR THE DEVELOPMENT OF ADVERTISING AGENCY–CLIENT RELATIONSHIPS

The first major attempt to build a comprehensive framework of business relationships was made by the IMP Group in the form of the Interaction Model (see Håkansson 1982). In this model, business relationships are viewed as interaction processes between buyer and seller companies. The model is composed of four groups of variables that describe and influence interaction between buyers and sellers:

1 Variables describing the elements and process of interaction (e.g. exchange, institutionalisation and adaptation).
2 Variables describing the parties involved, both as organisations and as individuals (e.g. technology, organisation size and strategy, the personality and experience of individuals).
3 Variables describing the atmosphere that affects and is affected by interaction (e.g. power and dependence, conflicts and cooperation, closeness and distance, mutual expectations).
4 Variables describing the environment within which interaction takes place (e.g. market structure, dynamism, internationalisation).

Möller and Wilson (1988) have, since then, extended the model by integrating ideas from other research traditions into it. They have proposed an exploratory contingency framework that particularly identifies those factors that influence buyer–seller interaction, but which also develops conceptual understanding of the content of business relationships. They have separated four broad groups of factors constituting buyer–seller interaction:

1 Contextual factors, defining the environment and situation in which interaction behaviour takes place (e.g. richness of resources, industry life cycle, market concentration, characteristics of organisations).
2 Task factors, referring to the inherent characteristics of the focal tasks of interaction (e.g. complexity, degree of innovation and importance of tasks).

3 Interaction process factors, comprised of the subprocesses necessary for carrying out the tasks (e.g. exchange, adaptation and coordination processes).

4 Outcome factors, defining the intentional and unintentional results of interaction behaviour (e.g. performance and psychological outcomes, bonds, states and changes in the other groups of factors).

The framework built here is based primarily on these two interaction frameworks. The IMP Group and Möller and Wilson frameworks gather the concepts and factors that can be used to describe buyer–seller interaction and its context. They provide, as such, a general framework and the necessary conceptual tools to construct a model of relationship development.

Figure 3.1 provides an overview of the conceptual framework – or, more specifically, of the *a priori* process model that is advanced in this chapter of the development of advertising agency–client relationships. The model's concepts and their relationships are dealt with in detail in the following sections.

Influencing factors in the context of advertising agency–client relationships are divided here into three broad groups. First, factors related to the environment of agency–client relationships; secondly, factors related to the parties to the relationship – to the companies, and the individuals and groups representing them; thirdly, factors related to the tasks that

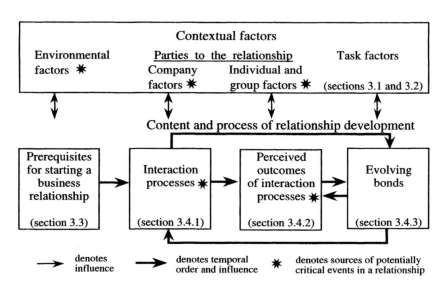

Figure 3.1 Draft *a priori* process model of the development of agency–client relationships

25

are executed in relationships. These groups incorporate the variables describing parties and environment in the IMP model, and contextual and task factors in the Möller and Wilson framework.

The prerequisites for starting a business relationship are added as a new conceptual category, not present in the interaction frameworks. On the other hand, the concept of atmosphere is left out, substituted for mostly by other concepts seen to capture the nature of advertising agency–client relationships more distinctively and in a more measurable way.

The content and process of relationship development are viewed via three conceptual categories: interaction processes, perceived outcomes of interaction processes, and evolving bonds. These categories incorporate the variables describing the elements and process of interaction in the IMP model, and interaction process factors and outcome factors in Möller and Wilson's framework. In order to increase conceptual clarity and distinction in the broad group of outcome factors, evolving bonds are treated here as an individual category separate from other outcomes of interaction. I shall also draw out the link between the process of relationship development and the relationship context. This will be achieved by describing relationship development in terms of events and, in particular, by identifying critical events.

The nature of advertising markets and services is viewed as the starting point for model building and will therefore be examined first, in section 3.1. Other contextual factors are examined in section 3.2. Section 3.3 is devoted to the prerequisites for starting a business relationship and section 3.4 to the content and process of relationship development. Finally, in section 3.5 the relationship development is examined in terms of events, and the nature and role of critical events are discussed. The *a priori* process model is summarised in section 3.6.

3.1 THE NATURE OF ADVERTISING MARKETS AND ADVERTISING SERVICES

The nature of advertising markets and services forms the basis of model building where the development of advertising agency–client relationships is concerned. The type of product exchanged and the nature of the markets are likely to condition the character of business relationships and their development.

Advertising markets are composed of a heterogeneous set of companies including advertisers, advertising agencies, media organisations and a variety of service suppliers such as packaging design firms, photographers, research organisations and different production firms (see e.g. Belch and Belch 1990: 61–3).

The advertisers, or clients, are the key participants in the markets; they have the products or services to be marketed and provide the funds that pay for advertising and promotion efforts (Belch and Belch 1990: 61). Advertisers are private or public sector organisations that use advertising and the mass media to accomplish their organisational objectives (Aaker and Myers 1987: 1). They may choose to perform advertising tasks through their own advertising departments or by setting up an in-house agency which then cooperates directly with media organisations and the suppliers of necessary related services. Alternatively, advertisers may choose to use the services of one or more advertising agencies. (Kerttula 1988: 4; Belch and Belch 1990: 61; Kähkönen 1990: 16)

Advertising agencies are service companies that specialise in the planning and execution of advertising programmes for their clients (see Belch and Belch 1990: 68; Kähkönen 1990: 16). An advertising agency acts on the basis of an assignment placed by the client in which the client also delegates some decision-making authority to the agency (see e.g. Mills 1990). In most cases the agency makes the creative and media decisions. Often it supplies supporting market research as well, and may even be involved in the total marketing plan. The activities undertaken and the amount of autonomy allowed to the agency vary from one relationship to another (Aaker and Myers 1987: 10).

Advertising agencies differ with respect to the range and type of services they offer and the structure of their ownership. In Finland, advertising agencies are usually either full-service agencies or partial-service agencies (see e.g. Kähkönen 1990: 19). Planning agencies and media buying agencies are examples of the latter. Agencies can also be characterised according to their specialisation, which may be concentrated on some part of the advertising and promotion process. Typical examples might be creative work, advertising research or direct marketing, a particular media vehicle (e.g. radio advertising) or advertising to a specific market (e.g. business-to-business marketing). In terms of ownership, Finnish agencies fall under international control, are in-house, or are Finnish-owned – either by private entrepreneurs or organised in privately owned agency groups (see Appendix 1).

Measured against the scale of most industrial enterprises, advertising agencies are small (see Appendix 1). Each agency office services only a small number of advertisers (Comanor et al. 1981: 434; Kähkönen 1990: 20). The clients represent various business areas, due to the common practice of agencies not dealing with more than one advertiser in each product market at the same time – account conflicts are purposely avoided (Ray 1982: 67; Kähkönen 1990: 16).

This also means that advertising markets are highly competitive. Advertising agencies compete with each other but also with the advertisers' own advertising departments and media organisations (Kähkönen 1990: 16). Over the years, interest in undertaking advertising tasks in-house has varied compared with the use of external agencies (Larres 11 January 1990, see Appendix 3; Ripley 1991). The most important competitive tools of advertising agencies have been the range and specialisation of services, price, reputation and the quality of agency personnel (Kerttula 1988: 15–18; Kähkönen 1990: 16). Which factors clients have valued the most has also changed over time. For instance, the Finnish recession in 1990–93 fostered price competition. Advertising agencies have had to adapt to the changing conditions in order to maintain their position in the market.

As to the advertising services, they can be defined as packages of activities that are offered to other companies and which concern the planning, production and/or delivery of advertising. Advertising services are thus activities or processes, not things (Grönroos 1982: 21). They also qualify as professional business services (see e.g. Gummesson 1978: 47–8; Yorke 1990: 348–9). This means that they are provided by qualified personnel, are advisory in nature and focus on problem solving.[1] They are bought and designed to improve the purchasing firm's performance and well-being (Wilson 1972). Advertising is expected to influence the attitudes, intentions and behaviour of the client's customers and thus increase sales and contribute to the growth of the client company.

Advertising may also be described as a knowledge-intensive business service rather than a professional service. The concept of a knowledge-intensive service places less emphasis on the boundaries of professions with their scientific body of knowledge, long formal education and ethical codes, but rather stresses the nature of professionals' work in which various types of knowledge, interpersonal skills and creativity are used (see Alvesson 1993). The core of any service is tied to the benefit it offers the buyer. In buying advertising services, companies purchase knowledge and creativity embodied in individual people.

Creativity is the heart and soul of advertising services and consequently a critical resource in every business relationship. American studies have shown that performance-related factors such as depth of creativity, knowledge and experience in the client's market are important criteria in selecting an advertising agency (see Wackman et al. 1987: 27–8). Creativity and the active presentation of new ideas are also crucial factors in the later phases of a relationship (Etelä 1985: 73; Wackmann et al. 1987: 27–8). In a study in the Netherlands, Verbeke (1989: 22–3) discovered that the quality of creative work was the main predictor of overall satisfaction with an agency. Lack of creativity and a low standard of creative work have been indicated as major reasons for agency switches and conflicts within business relationships (Michell 1984b, 1987: 30; Verbeke 1989: 26).

In service marketing literature, a number of basic dimensions have been used to characterise services and to separate them from each other (see Lovelock 1983: 46; Zeithaml et al. 1985: 34; Normann 1991: 14–18). The following characteristics of advertising services are likely to affect the development of agency–client relationships

1 Intangibility.
2 People intensity.
3 The interactive nature of service processes.
4 Customised character.
5 Ambiguity inherent in the service exchange.

Intangibility is the most commonly accepted characteristic of services (Zeithaml *et al.* 1985: 33). One can consider separately the intangibility of the service act (the process), and the intangibility of the service outcome (see Lovelock 1983: 47). The service acts, planning, production and delivery of advertising are all essentially intangible activities, in spite of the fact that the inherent knowledge and creativity are often translated in tangible form in e.g. written briefs, research reports, commercials and advertising videos, and pictures and text. The outcomes of advertising, their effect on customers, are often intangible as well. The ultimate goal of advertising is usually to produce concrete economic benefits for the advertiser, but it is extremely difficult to assess these benefits. They often remain a matter of belief.

Advertising services, in contrast to capital-intensive services, are people-intensive. In organisations, knowledge may be embedded in individuals, in the organisation itself or in capital equipment (Ekstedt 1988: 179). In the advertising business the core service is bound primarily to the individuals who provide it. The role of facilities and equipment is secondary in the provision of services. This means that the participating individuals significantly influence the perceived quality of the service and the whole business relationship (cf. Normann 1991: 17). In a survey of American advertisers, favourable personal relationships with account service contacts were found to be the most significant predictor of a client's satisfaction with its agency (Wackmann *et al.* 1987: 25–6). In fact, the quality of those people assigned to the account and the compatibility of agency and client personnel are important criteria even in selecting an advertising agency (Cagley 1986; Wackmann *et al.* 1987: 27).[2]

The importance of the human element may imply that relationships between people become stronger than the relationship between the contracting firms. A change in the client's personnel or organisational structure may cause a break-up of the agency–client relationship (Doyle *et al.* 1980: 21; Michell 1987: 32). Where there is a spin-off and the creative team or other key persons leave the advertising agency to establish a firm of their own, some clients may follow the personnel to the new agency. Lindmark (1989) has studied this phenomenon and concluded that it is difficult to make clients change agency, especially if the existing relationship has worked well. If the current agency is unable to manage the change in the team properly, the client may become dissatisfied in the course of time and change to a new agency later on, however. Lindmark's findings show the primary importance of inter-firm relationships in the advertising business, but at the same time point up the significant role of personal chemistry and contacts within the inter-firm relationship.

Service production and consumption are inseparable activities – at least to some degree. While goods are first produced, then sold and consumed, services are first sold and then produced and consumed simultaneously (Zeithaml *et al.* 1985: 33). This is the case particularly when we look at the service process and not the outcomes of a service. The type and degree of interaction in service processes, however, varies from service to service (see e.g. Chase 1978: 138 and Lovelock 1983: 48).

Advertising services are produced – and partly consumed – in an interaction between agency and client. Client participation in the production process is crucial. At the minimum, the client commissions the assignment, negotiates the terms, provides the necessary information for the account team and executes the acceptance of plans and materials. In briefings, face-to-face contact is also needed. The service performance depends directly on the client's needs, its marketing and advertising strategies and its behaviour in the service production process. This calls for coordination in a relationship. In addition, the execution of assignments has to be accommodated to the capacity of the agency. Synchronisation of supply and demand is a critical issue for advertising agencies, since services cannot be stored.

The degree of client participation is also connected with the degree of customisation or standardisation of a service. Customisation increases the cognitive effort required both from the service provider and from the client. Surprenant and Solomon (1987: 88–9) speak about personalisation of the service encounter and divide it into process personalisation and outcome personalisation (cf. also Lovelock 1983: 51). Process personalisation focuses on the way the service is rendered. Outcome personalisation implies that the client has room to choose from a set of service alternatives.

Advertising services are usually highly customised, with respect to both the service options and the service process. It is of the essence of advertising services that they are tailored to the special needs of the client firm. The agency representatives adopt, first and foremost, the role of professional problem-solvers, who are expected to apply their knowledge and creativity to a specific brief. Each client with its marketing strategy, products and individual representatives is different, and expects a creative and distinctive advertising campaign, advertisements, etc. Thus the contents of the 'service package', the appropriate mixture of the agency's service alternatives (Lehtinen 1983: 89), is negotiated separately in each case. The way in which the assignment is organised and the whole planning and execution process are also customised.

The nature of the core service, its intangibility, people-intensity and interactive and customised character, all increase the ambiguity of the service as well, and consequently the degree of uncertainty the parties perceive in exchange situations. As Gummesson (1981: 111) has pointed out, the client is often insecure when buying professional services and wants to decrease his risk. Uncertainty is also one of the major factors explaining the willingness to build long-term relationships (see Williamson 1981).

Drawing on earlier literature on industrial buying behaviour, Cardozo (1980: 273) has identified five types of uncertainty in purchase situations (see also Möller and Laaksonen 1986). For advertising services, one might talk in terms of different types of ambiguities, recognising the fact that ambiguity is an inherent part of advertising services and cannot simply be clarified by gathering more information (see Alvesson 1993).

Need ambiguity implies that the buying organisation lacks a clear understanding of the suitable specification for the product (Cardozo 1980: 273). The need for a certain type of advertising or campaign in some specific market situation can easily be questioned. Ultimately it becomes a matter of opinion. In addition, campaign types and advertising materials can never be specified completely in advance. On the contrary, agencies are often purposely used as experts in suggesting which specifications to adopt.

Technical ambiguity implies that the product may not perform properly (Cardozo 1980: 273). In the context of intangible services it is more appropriate to think in terms of performance ambiguity (see Bowen and Jones 1986: 431). This arises when any dimension of an exchange makes it difficult for either party to evaluate the performance of the other. It is typical of knowledge-intensive services that both the claimed core service, the way professionals work and the results of their work are ambiguous in character (Alvesson 1993). Clients are unable to evaluate service performance before or even after they have experienced it, as they do not – and cannot – possess sufficient knowledge for its evaluation (Bowen and Jones 1986: 431). The problems encountered in the measurement of advertising effects are well known (see e.g. Alvesson and Köping 1993: 276). Even tangible outcomes like sales figures are difficult to measure reliably, because of the multitude of intervening variables and temporal carry-over effects. It is also difficult for the client to control how efficiently the agency works.

Market ambiguity refers to the heterogeneity of offerings and the rate of change in agencies' capabilities (see Cardozo 1980: 273). The client can never know how much better advertising competing agencies could have produced and how much cheaper their services could have been. The capability of agencies can also change rapidly because it is embedded in individuals, who are free to leave their agency and change their jobs.

Advertising services are also politically ambiguous. Political uncertainty (or acceptance uncertainty) refers to the purchase of services which different factions will be for and against. This may be due to disagreement, resistance to change or competition for funds inside the client firm (Cardozo 1980: 274). Advertising services that are intangible, people-intensive and cannot be evaluated objectively can be assumed to be especially liable to political disagreements.

Finally, transaction ambiguity refers to uncertainty associated with delivery dates and other terms of sale, e.g. quality specifications and invoicing (Cardozo 1980: 274). In highly customised, creative and inter-actively executed work it is difficult to estimate in advance how much the project will cost and how long it will last.

3.2 CONTEXT OF ADVERTISING AGENCY–CLIENT RELATIONSHIPS

In this section I will explore the contextual factors that influence the development of agency–client relationships (see Table 3.1). The three groups of factors – environmental factors, those related to the parties to a relationship, i.e. company factors and individual and group factors, and finally task factors – all form a complex set of nested antecedents influencing the buyer–seller interaction process and its outcomes (Möller and Wilson 1988: 11). In order to understand the development process of agency–client relationships, the different levels of context have to be taken into account. These levels are interconnected, which means that events and changes in one level often trigger changes in other levels as well.

Table 3.1 provides an overview of those contextual factors most likely to affect the development of advertising agency–client relationships. These factors will be examined in the following sections.

3.2.1 Environment of relationships – a network

The unit of analysis in this study is the dyadic business relationship between an advertising agency and its client. If we are to understand the development of an agency–client relationship, it has to be related to its environment. Environment is treated here not as an aggregation, but as a surrounding network of inter-firm relationships between customers, suppliers, competitors and other actors in the industrial system (cf. e.g. Liljegren 1988: 106).

According to the network approach (see Hägg and Johanson 1982: 47; Johanson and Mattsson 1986: 247–8), all firms are connected – directly or indirectly – with the global industrial network which stretches across traditional boundaries of markets, industries and countries. Within this total system, it is possible to isolate different subsystems concerning for example geographical areas, products or specific firms. These subsystems

Table 3.1 Contextual factors affecting the development of advertising agency–client relationships

Environmental factors	Parties to the relationship		Task factors
	Company factors	Individual and group factors	
• actors in the primary task environment • actors in the secondary task environment • macro environment: social, economic, political and technological factors • personal contact networks	• size, resources and capabilities • organisational experience • interaction orientation • marketing strategy • organisation structure and extent of centralisation • corporate policy and politics • reputation and price level	• personality • capabilities and experience • motivation • interaction style • inter-firm network of personal relationships • interpersonal inconsistency	• degree of innovation • importance • complexity or breadth • familiarity • exchange frequency

are termed nets. The industrial network of inter-firm relationships and relevant nets together form the environment of an agency–client relationship in this study.

Organisations and their relationships are regarded here as open, interdependent systems which have fuzzy boundaries with their environment (see Mattsson 1983: 6). This means that advertising agencies and their clients are highly dependent on the behaviour of other actors in the network and vulnerable to the various influences mediated through these actors. Nevertheless, the network of relationships is not the only determinant in the development of a specific business relationship. Firms and their representatives are viewed as active participants in the markets, and can deliberately influence the development of their relationships (see Håkansson 1982: 1).

The surrounding network of agency–client relationships may be described in more detail by applying the political economy framework of Achrol *et al.* (1983: 57). This framework depicts the environment and external dependences of the marketing channel dyad and identifies three parts in the dyadic environment: the primary task environment, the secondary task environment and the macro-environment.

The primary task environment of an agency–client relationship includes the most important actors in the advertising production and influence chain. It consists of the agency and client's customers, their suppliers, i.e. media organisations such as broadcasting companies and the press, and suppliers of necessary related services such as market research companies and photographers (see Figure 3.2). It also includes the final consumers of the client's products, since this is where marketing communication is in most cases directed.

The secondary task environment consists of organisations that are horizontally rather than vertically connected with the focal agency–client relationship. It includes competitors and cooperating partners of both the agency and the client, e.g. other advertising agencies used by the client

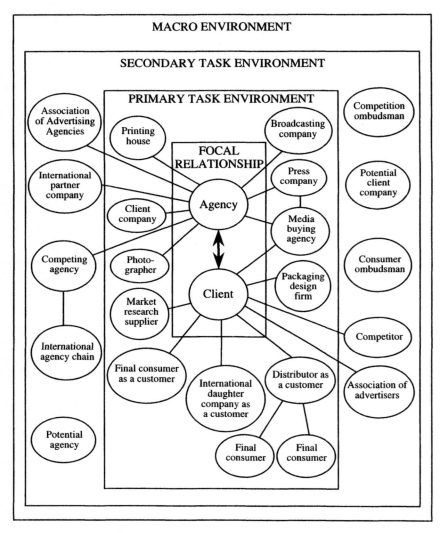

Figure 3.2 A hypothetical net of an advertising agency–client relationship

(which may be competitive or complementary), and governmental and other controlling institutions (see Aaker and Myers 1987: 2).

The macro-environment is comprised of general social, economic, political and technological forces. The parties to the focal relationship perceive the macro-environment and its effects through their interaction with other organisations in the network. Economic fluctuations, internationalisation and consumption trends are mediated for the focal agency–client relationship through interaction. The influence of the environment is also likely to be moderated by many company factors like resources, strategies and organisational experience (Möller and Wilson 1988: 11–12; see also Campbell 1985: 38).

Besides the inter-firm network, the personal contact network of agency and client company employees has to be taken into account when considering a business relationship environment. According to Liljegren (1988: 414), there are a great number of personal relationships that are not clearly related to business relations but which do, however, influence them (see also Cunningham and Turnbull 1982: 308). There is empirical evidence, from advertising and other professional business service sectors, that referrals by existing clients or other business colleagues are important sources of information for prospective clients (see e.g. Wheiler 1987: 194; Yorke 1988: 627; Lindmark 1989: 13–14). In the people-intensive advertising business, personal contact networks are likely to have an important impact on the initiation, maintenance and dissolution of agency–client relationships.

3.2.2 Parties to relationships

Relationship development between the agency and the client also depends on the characteristics of the parties involved. Most of the factors to be considered here are relevant to both the advertising agency and the client company. Nevertheless, their meaning and consequences for the development of an agency–client relationship may be somewhat different.

Company factors

At company level, several factors are likely to influence the development of agency–client relationships:

1 Size, company resources and capabilities.
2 Organisational experience.
3 Interaction orientation.
4 Marketing strategy.
5 Organisation structure and extent of centralisation.
6 Corporate policy and politics.
7 The reputation and price level of the agency.

The size of the agency and client companies is one of the most important factors at company level (see Håkansson 1982: 19). The size and implicit power of the parties set up the basic positions from which they interact. In general, a large firm with considerable resources has a greater ability to dominate its customers or suppliers than a small firm. As typically small companies, advertising agencies may become strongly dependent on an individual client relationship.

The size of an advertiser depends on how much it spends on advertising in general and how large its accounts are. Large-scale advertisers may also have smaller accounts and, conversely, small advertisers may have larger accounts. In a study in the United Kingdom, Michell (1988: 62–3) found that large clients and clients with large accounts more often have long-term relationships with their advertising agencies than smaller clients or those with smaller accounts.[3]

The size of the agency, for its part, may mean greater resources and capabilities to serve the client. Bigger agencies are able to offer a full range of services whereas the smaller ones may have to specialise. Agency capabilities are decisive for the initiation and maintenance of business relationships. Clients require expertise in advertising and in creative planning in particular, but agencies must also have sufficient marketing capability (see Möller and Anttila 1987). This means that they have to understand in what kind of an environment the client operates and how it manages its operations internally. For the planning of successful advertising, agencies need to have market and product knowledge. Similarly, the client's ability to make an informed buying decision (cf. 'buying ability' in Lehtinen and Leivo 1982) is likely to influence interactions and the development of relationships. The buying ability of a firm is dependent on its representatives' knowledge and prior experience of selecting advertising agencies and working with them.[4]

Some sort of balance is often sought with respect to size, resources and dependence. Michell (1988: 64) found that larger accounts are almost invariably handled by larger, full-service agencies. A client may also feel that it grows out of an agency. If the agency is not able to grow and diversify with its client, the relationship may break down (Michell 1988: 31). On the other hand, a small or medium-sized agency may be an especially interesting partner for a large client when it is able to offer some special expertise, flexible operations, personal attention or cheaper prices, for instance. What is important, however, is the balance between control and the freedom to create (Ray 1982: 68). This means that the account must be important enough to the agency for control to be maintained. But the account should not be so important as to stifle new and unusual ideas and creativity in general.

Organisational experience is one of the relevant factors influencing agency–client relationships. It can be interpreted as familiarity with a specific partner relative to other available partners (Håkansson 1982: 19; see also Campbell 1985: 42). It also comprises experience acquired outside the focal relationship, from other similar relationships that have equipped the company with knowledge about the management of that kind of relationship or about a specific industry or a specific type of advertising task (see Håkansson 1982: 19).

Experience and capabilities are both equally relevant in the context of individual and organisational factors. It may be questioned, in general, whether an organisation can have and possess experiences or capabilities, or whether these characteristics are embedded only in individuals. In this study I have chosen to discuss these factors in connection with the company, since the focus of the study is on inter-firm relationships.

Advertising agencies and their clients can adopt different kinds of orientations or strategies towards interaction. Several authors have identified interaction orientation as an important determinant of the nature of business relationships. We have generally identified three types of orientations: cooperative, competitive and command (see e.g. Campbell 1985; Schurr and Ozanne 1985; Wilson and Mummalaneni 1986; Möller and Wilson 1988). The adopted interaction orientation is likely to be based on the company and its representatives' experience of different buyer–seller relationships and the interaction within them (see Möller and Wilson 1988: 20).

Interaction orientation describes how the partners view each other and handle the relations between their respective interests. A cooperative orientation means that the parties perceive common interests in their interaction and, furthermore, intentionally seek them. The firms are aware of each other's interests and demonstrate their interest in each other's well-being. Competitive orientation is, instead, dominated by opportunistic behaviour and self-interest seeking. The parties rely on market forces rather than on close cooperation with each other. Command orientation may arise when one party has a dominant position over the other. (Campbell 1985: 37; Ford et al. 1986: 30; Möller and Wilson 1988: 16)

While a perception of common interests and the adoption of a cooperative orientation contribute to the growth and progressive development of a business relationship, the pursuit of antagonistic goals coupled with a competitive orientation causes the relationship to languish (Wilson and Mummalaneni 1986: 50). Campbell (1985: 36) suggests that parties are likely to become interdependent when they both approach the relationship with a cooperative orientation. Conversely, they are likely to remain independent when they both approach interaction competitively. A dependent relationship results from the dominance one party exerts over the other.

The marketing strategies of both the client and the agency are likely to affect the nature and vulnerability of their relationship. The type of advertising as well as the size of an advertising budget depend directly on the client's marketing function. Every significant change in the client's marketing strategy – in the form of either different marketing objectives or different policies – make the relationship vulnerable, since the current agency is seen to be closely tied to the old and eventually 'failed' marketing policies (Michell 1987: 31). Therefore, any change in the client's marketing strategy is always a challenge for the agency.

The client's marketing strategy is also closely related to the type of product advertised. As early as 1964 Twedt found that relationship stability was dependent on the product category advertised. More recently, Michell (1988: 64–5) has shown that the most loyal accounts are likely to be in mature consumer product categories such as tobacco, food, household stores or appliances. In contrast, many service industry clients, e.g. entertainment, travel, leisure and the charities, have a propensity to switch agency occasionally. Michell gives no explanation for his findings. It could be assumed, however, that the successful advertising of established consumer brands requires consistent communication of brand values and thus continuity of the agency–client relationship.

The advertising agency's strategy may also affect the relationship. In the first place, it determines what kind of clients the agency is interested in acquiring. The perceived strategic importance of a client relationship may dictate how much attention and resources the agency will devote to it. An account conflict or a profitability analysis of existing accounts may make the agency wish to renegotiate its accounts or make itself available to other clients. Respectively, the agency's willingness to extend its expertise to new areas of specialisation may make an individual relationship from such an area especially interesting.

Organisation structure and the extent of centralisation influence business relationships in several ways. This influence is seen in the number and categories of persons involved in the procedures of exchange, in the communication media used and in the formalisation of interaction (Håkansson 1982: 19). The client company may have arranged its marketing organisation according to a centralised functional system or a decentralised brand manager system (see e.g. Ray 1982: 62–5; Belch and Belch 1990: 63–5). The same alternatives are also available to advertising agencies (see Ray 1982: 69–70). Most agencies apply the brand management approach, or account group system. The most critical person in that system is the account manager (or account executive), who organises the agency effort and interacts most with the client's key decision maker.

In the short term, organisational structures can be considered the frameworks within which interaction takes place. In the longer term, it is possible that these structures may be modified by the emergent interaction process (Håkansson 1982: 19). In a series of studies concerning agency–client relationships, researchers have shown that changes in the client's marketing personnel or organisation structure easily lead to a re-evaluation of the agency and a break-up of the agency relationship (see Doyle *et al*. 1980; Michell 1987). Newly elected client managers tend to see the situation in terms of an inability to build ties with the current agency or in terms of the need to shake up advertising to stimulate new ideas (Michell 1987: 31–2). Changes in the agency's organisation or personnel have been shown to be equally critical.

It is important to note that in the case of larger clients and agencies, the organisation structure may actually refer to the structure of a whole agency or client group. As Michell (1987) has shown, either the rationalisation of agency use (which may be seen to be necessary by a client group) or acquisition or merger within the agency group may lead to the break-up of existing relationships. It is probable that the 'intragroup network' of interacting companies also influences the development of agency–client relationships in less radical ways. For example, corporate policy towards advertising agencies or clients, and organisational politics have been noted as determinants of agency–client relationships (see Wackmann *et al*. 1987: 24).

Owing to the intangibility of advertising services agency reputation and price are supposedly important company characteristics. As advertising services are difficult to evaluate, one can assume that an agency's reputation together with referrals play an important role, particularly, in attracting new clients for that agency (see e.g. Belch and Belch 1990: 85). Agencies build their reputation primarily through current and former clients. It is common to use successful campaigns with well known clients as credentials to offer some form of tangible evidence for the prospects concerning an agency's capabilities. Conversely, the loss of an important client may mean a loss of referrals and impair an agency's reputation in the eyes of both current and potential clients. Parallel to credentials, an agency's price level functions as a tangible indicator of its capabilities.

Individual and group factors

A business relationship is ultimately created and maintained in interaction between people. Many clients for professional services do not care about the professional service firm but buy the individual (Gummesson 1981: 111).

The influence of individual factors on inter-firm relationships has to date received precious little research attention. Instead, several individual factors have been identified as important in determining the compliance of buyers and sellers (Bagozzi 1974), the interaction or communication styles of buyers and sellers (Sheth 1976), the likelihood of sale (Evans 1963; Crosby *et al*. 1990), satisfaction with the service encounter (Lehtinen 1983; Solomon *et al*. 1985), the degree of success of a business relationship

(Wackmann *et al.* 1987) and the loyalty of the partners to each other (Morris and Holman 1988). From the perspective of relationship development in the advertising sector, personality, capabilities, motivation and interaction style seem at least significant factors.

As to personalities, many advertising researchers and practitioners have emphasised the central importance of 'personal chemistry' and the compatibility of interacting staff to successful agency–client relationships (e.g. Etelä 1985: 73; Michell 1987: 39; Wackmann *et al.* 1987: 24).

Individual capabilities entail professional skills and work-related knowledge, which are crucial resources in the production of advertising services. The professional skills of the contact people – their expertise and talent – are relevant in building satisfaction into agency–client relationships (see e.g. Wackmann *et al.* 1987: 23–4). The findings of Crosby *et al.* (1990: 76) from the life insurance sector also suggest that relationship quality is enhanced through perceived sales person competence. Individual capabilities may be gained through experience and education. The process of learning from experience is essential for the development of a partner's capabilities (see e.g. Lindmark 1989: 2–3). Experience is made up of familiarity with the specific partner and experience of other agency or client relationships.

Motivation determines the willingness to work with a specific task or relationship. It is based on the perceived importance of a brief or relationship to an individual and on the personal rewards that can be expected from interaction.

The style of interaction is regarded as an important element of personal interaction. However, the concept of interaction style has been used in various meanings in industrial and services marketing literature. Sheth (1976: 593) has studied individual communication styles in buyer–seller interaction and argues that satisfactory interaction will occur if, and only if, both the content and the style of communication are compatible. In services marketing, Lehtinen (1983: 122–3) has distinguished between customers' participation style and that of servicing the customer and concluded that a fit between the two styles is essential to the production of high-quality service. Håkansson (1982: 19) suggests that the varied personalities, experiences, and motivations of each company's representatives mean that they take part in interaction differently. Their reactions to individual exchange events may condition the ways in which the overall relationship builds up. Cunningham and Turnbull (1982: 312) connected the style of interpersonal contacts with firm, market and industry levels and found differences in styles with respect to their closeness, formality and institutionalisation. In this study, interaction style is broadly defined as the manner in which interaction is conducted.[5]

In business relationships, interaction involves groups of people rather than single individuals. Interaction varies in spread from a single dyadic relationship between one salesman and one buyer to situations where several individuals from different functional areas, at different levels in the hierarchy and fulfilling different roles, become involved in interactions. These individuals exchange information and develop personal relationships which influence the decisions of both interacting companies. An inter-firm network of personal relationships emerges between the parties. (Cunningham and Turnbull 1982: 310; Håkansson 1982: 19)

Teamwork is an essential characteristic of advertising service production. Several people from the agency and often from the client company as well are involved in the production process. The size of the buying centre has also been studied empirically. It seems that the number of people who participate in buying professional services tends to be smaller than in buying industrial services or industrial equipment (see Johnston and Bonoma 1981a: 258; Lynn 1987: 122–3). In a survey concerning professional accounting services, buying centres ranged from one to fourteen members at an average of 3.5 (Lynn 1987: 122).

In business relationships, the goals and approaches of individuals and those of the firm are not always consistent with each other. A company can never present a wholly unified approach in its interactions, because of the great number of individuals and departments or other groups involved in the interaction. Ford *et al.* (1986: 36) refer to this as 'interpersonal inconsistency' (see also Comanor *et al.* 1981: 433). People have their own interests with regard to interaction and their own expectations and opinions of their counterparts. Some individuals will also be more capable or motivated in interactions with a particular company than will others, and so on. This poses a fundamental methodological as well as theoretical problem for a study of inter-firm relationships. It raises the question of whose goals, opinions, capabilities or interaction styles are decisive in determining the company's, and how many people are sufficient to determine the company's standpoint.

3.2.3 Task factors

Task factors are embedded in the interaction processes, but in order to enhance the conceptual clarity of the framework I have classified them as a separate group of contextual factors (see also Möller and Wilson 1988: 11). In spite of the fact that task factors have received much attention in the literature of organisational buying behaviour, their role in buyer–seller interaction has barely been explored.

Campbell (1985) has examined task factors in the context of business relationships and identified three product characteristics that influence the interaction strategy (or orientation) of buyers and sellers: frequency of purchase, switching costs due to physical and human investments, and product complexity. Hallén *et al.* (1987: 25) have demonstrated empirically

41

that business relationships are conditioned by the frequency and complexity of product exchange. Möller and Wilson (1988: 18) listed seven task dimensions in their contingency framework for the Interaction Approach: complexity, importance, innovativeness, exchange frequency, exchange dimensionality, substitutability and task familiarity. On the basis of these studies, I have selected five factors that help to differentiate tasks in the field of advertising and that offer most potential for explaining the development of individual advertising agency–client relationships. These five factors are as follows: the degree of innovation, importance, complexity or breadth, familiarity, and exchange frequency.

The degree of task innovation refers to the perceived need to plan and create wholly new advertising. The degree of innovation depends on how much new creativity is required in advertising planning and production, and the degree to which the client's marketing strategy is new (cf. Michell 1984b: 50). Four factors, and the degree to which they are new, are relevant in determining the level of task innovation: the advertised product or service, the marketing strategy (target market, goals and marketing mix variables), the creative strategy and the execution of advertising. An example of an extremely innovative task might be a new product launch campaign, where the product has its own brand name and thus requires a completely new creative strategy and a new execution to go with it. Michell (1984b: 50) has suggested that continuity of current marketing and creative strategies fosters the maintenance of the existing agency relationship, whereas new products, marketing strategies and requirements for a new creative strategy increase the possibility of a switch in agency.

The importance of a task is a multi-dimensional concept that can be defined as the perceived financial and strategic importance of an assignment. In other words, the importance of a task refers to its perceived potential impact both on the company's profitability and on the implementation of its strategies (cf. Möller and Laaksonen 1986; McQuiston 1989). Assignments may incur different costs for the advertiser and have different effects on its sales volumes. Similarly, the cost of an assignment to the agency and its impact on the agency's gross margin also varies. In addition, briefs may be more or less strategically important, depending on their links with the client's marketing or corporate strategy. For example, a company image campaign or the creation of a new brand are seen as tasks of strategic importance (see Iltanen 1986: 11). For an advertising agency, the successful execution of a specific assignment may be important because it helps to maintain an existing client relationship or to acquire other clients from e.g. totally new markets. Based on research results from industrial sectors (see e.g. Johnston and Bonoma 1981b: 153), it seems likely that more people get involved in making the buying decision when the task is perceived to be important. Higher levels of management may also be consulted.

Task complexity refers to the functional complexity or breadth of an assignment. An assignment is functionally complex when it consists of numerous and related tasks (cf. Campbell 1985: 40). A product launch campaign is typically a complex task, ultimately including marketing and advertising planning, creative planning, testing the concepts created, the production of various materials, e.g. brochures, TV commercials and PR material, planning media delivery, testing the results of the media campaign, and so on. In industrial buying behaviour literature, complexity has been linked with various product characteristics (see the reviews of Campbell 1985 and Möller and Laaksonen 1986). For the purpose of differentiating tasks within agency–client relationships, the dimension of functional complexity seems most relevant. The complexity of assignments is likely to increase interaction between parties to the relationship (see Hallén et al. 1987: 32) and to foster cooperative interaction orientation (Campbell 1985: 40).

Task familiarity describes the novelty of the task within a specific agency–client relationship. Thus in contradiction to traditional organisational buying behaviour literature, I have distinguished familiarity from general task-related experience (cf. e.g. McQuiston 1989). Experience is treated as a company or individual factor (see section 3.2.2). As for an innovative assignment, it may be expected that the briefing for a novel assignment will increase the pressure to switch agencies (cf. Michell 1984b: 50). It is also likely that novel tasks will increase interaction and the need for information exchange between the parties. Whether the number of people who get involved with the task also increases is a debatable issue. Research results from industrial and different service settings have been somewhat contradictory, partly owing to differences of conceptual definition and measures of novelty (see especially e.g. Johnston and Bonoma 1981a; Lynn 1987; McQuiston 1989). In studying auditing services, Lynn (1987) could not find a direct relationship between how new a task was and the size of the buying centre.

Finally, exchange frequency is very much linked with company level factors. It varies according to the client's field of operation, the advertised product and the role of advertising in the client's marketing strategy. When advertising is used as a tactical marketing tool in a contemporary competitive situation, assignments are likely to be frequent (cf. Iltanen 1986: 11). The type of task is also related to exchange frequency. Company image campaigns are rare events, whereas media campaigns for an existing brand are likely to be executed more frequently. Exchange frequency will probably have a significant impact on the development of agency–client relationships – at least on the intensity of interaction (cf. Hallén et al. 1987: 32; Möller and Wilson 1988: 8) and the nature of the partners' interaction orientation. Infrequent tasks involving major investments are more likely to be dealt with by competitive tender (Campbell 1985: 38).

3.3 PREREQUISITES FOR STARTING A BUSINESS RELATIONSHIP

Firms and organisations may have various reasons for entering into relationships with one another. Oliver (1990: 245) distinguished six major motives for relationships in his overview of inter-organisational research: necessity based on some authority, potential to exercise power and control over the other (asymmetry), reciprocity of benefits, efficiency of operations, increase of stability and predictability in an uncertain environment, and enhancement of organisational legitimacy. In the marketing area, where exchange theory has traditionally had a strong influence and voluntary exchange has been emphasised, researchers have stressed the reciprocity of benefits as the most critical motive. It has been assumed consequently that the scarcity of resources induces cooperation rather than competition, that relationships are characterised by harmony and mutual support rather than by conflict and domination and that companies expect the benefits of a business relationship to far exceed potential disbenefits.

Starting from these assumptions, researchers have proposed somewhat different lists of the prerequisites of a business relationship (see e.g. Kotler 1986; Wilson and Mummalaneni 1986; Houston and Gassenheimer 1987; and for inter-organisational research Van de Ven 1976). *In the context of advertising services, at least three conditions can be identified as necessary for a relationship to emerge. First, the existence of complementary needs and resources between parties; secondly, personal awareness of the other party's goals, needs and resources and thirdly, a common interest in building a business relationship* (see Figure 3.3).

The buyer and the seller are brought together by their complementary needs and the recognition that each is dependent on the resources of the other (Wilson and Mummalaneni 1986: 50). The division of labour in business markets implies that each company has its own domain, defined in terms of the products or services offered, the clientele served, the functions performed and the time and territory encompassed by each company's operations (Thorelli 1986: 39). Companies enter into business relationships because they need each other's resources to attain their goals in their specific domains.

It is a necessary condition of any exchange such as in a business relationship that the parties are capable of offering something of value to each other (cf. Kotler 1986: 8; Houston and Gassenheimer 1987: 5). Resources and capabilities in the required areas are a prerequisite of exchange which at the same time can and must be developed during a business relationship. According to Ford *et al.* (1986: 31), interaction takes place in the form of continual questioning: What can you do for me? And what can I do for you? Through this process, the essentially passive resources of a company are activated and translated into capabilities for a specific partner.

44

Prerequisites for starting
a business relationship

Complementary
needs and resources
between parties

Personal awareness of
the other party's goals,
needs and resources

Common interest
in building
a relationship

Figure 3.3 Prerequisites for starting an advertising
agency–client relationship

The basic question for an advertiser is whether it needs an outside agency to plan and implement its advertising or whether these tasks could be performed in-house. By using outside agencies, advertisers satisfy their need for specific expertise, new ideas and objective viewpoints concerning their advertising (see Ray 1982: 61; Iltanen 1986: 61; Belch and Belch 1990: 70). Clients have various alternatives in organising their agency relationships, ranging from direct client coordination with the media and suppliers of necessary related services to the use of a full-service agency on a commission basis (see Michell 1984b: 50). The option that is selected depends very much on the existing resources and expertise of the client, on the expected costs of different options and on the earlier practice of the firm (see e.g. Iltanen 1986: 61).

In order to start a relationship, the parties have to be aware of each other's goals, needs and resources. The personal contacts and acquaintances between the representatives of the partner companies provide a necessary mechanism for creating this awareness (see Van de Ven 1976: 31). It is through personal contacts that information is exchanged, knowledge is gained about the market and credibility is established between the participants (Cunningham and Turnbull 1982: 307–9; Wilson and Mummalaneni 1986: 51). Empirical studies have shown that, in professional business service sectors, referrals from independent personal sources and existing personal contact networks play a major role in the initiation of new relationships (Wheiler 1987: 194; Yorke 1988: 627; Lindmark 1989: 13–14).

The third prerequisite, a common interest in building a relationship, arises out of the perceived complementarity between the parties' needs and resources (see e.g. Wilson and Mummalaneni 1986: 50). Whether exchange actually takes place depends upon whether the two parties can settle on terms that leave them both better off (or at least not worse off) than before the exchange (see Houston and Gassenheimer 1987: 5). This is necessary for each individual transaction, but for a business relationship to emerge the parties also have to share – at least to some extent – a common interest in building a relationship. In other words, they have to share common expectations concerning the outcomes of a business relationship (Ford 1989: 825).[6] However, all inter-firm relationships have elements of both mutual and conflicting interests (Ford et al. 1986: 28; Wilson and Mummalaneni 1986: 50).

In advertising, it is important for the parties to share a common view of the client's advertising strategy, since it forms the basis of advertising planning, of the goals set for campaigns and thereby also of the assessment of the results of the exchange (see Cagley 1986: 40). In addition, the parties have to achieve a common understanding about the means of attaining strategic goals. The philosophy of the agency about how advertising and communication work (see Ray 1982: 69) has to fit in with the client's view of advertising and its possibilities. As Mills (1990: 39) has suggested, ideological similarity between the service provider and the client increases the likelihood of quality service.

The situations in which agency–client relationships are formed vary. By applying Frazier's ideas (1983) with respect to marketing channels, at least three situations can be identified. First, the current advertising agency is replaced because it is perceived to be unsatisfactory; secondly, an additional agency relationship is established to stimulate competition or creativity and keep costs down, or, thirdly, a new agency relationship is established in a specific field of activity, geographical market or product line where agency services are not yet used. It is evident that expectations concerning the outcomes of the relationship, and consequently the assessment of the agency and its performance, are influenced by the original situation for which the agency was contracted.

Similar types of situation also exist from an agency's point of view: as a consequence of an account conflict, an agency may have to replace an existing relationship with another, eventually more attractive client from the same market. Secondly, additional clients may be sought from those task areas where the agency already has experience, and, thirdly, agencies may purposely seek new clients from areas outside their current specialisation, in order to diversify their expertise. Agency mergers often create the potential for diversification but may simultaneously also create account conflicts.

3.4 THE CONTENT AND DEVELOPMENT PROCESS OF ADVERTISING AGENCY–CLIENT RELATIONSHIPS

3.4.1 Interaction processes

Business relationships develop over time as a result of inter-firm interactions. Companies interact, react, re-react, etc., with each other both verbally and through other forms of activity such as purchases, deliveries and payments. These interactions may be frequent or infrequent, regular or irregular, explicit or implicit, conscious or unconscious (Ford *et al.* 1986: 27–8).

A fundamental characteristic of interaction is that it is at least bilateral; there are two or more parties involved at each moment. The parties have intentions regarding their interaction and interpret the interaction and intentions of others. Thus in all interactions, there are intentions and interpretation from at least two sides. (Ford *et al.* 1986: 28)

At the most elementary level, a buyer–seller interaction can be described via three basic processes: exchange processes, coordination processes and adaptation processes (Möller and Wilson 1988: 5; see also Johanson and Mattsson 1987: 37). Business relationships are viewed here as results of these processes (Figure 3.4).

Exchange processes form the core phenomenon of interaction. Exchange can be defined as an act consisting of a voluntary transaction and involving a transfer of resources between two actors for mutual benefit (Cook 1977: 64). The key term 'resource' is defined as any valued activity, service or commodity. Exchange thus involves the transfer of a product or service for money but also comprises social, psychological or other intangible entities (Bagozzi 1975: 36).

The concept of an exchange process refers to individual assignments executed in agency–client relationships. Each assignment forms a process which may take weeks, months or even years to accomplish. The exchange process concept encompasses both the time dimension and the different elements of exchange.[7]

Exchange involves four types of elements: product or service exchange, information exchange, financial exchange and social exchange (Håkansson 1982: 16). Somewhat different divisions of exchange have also been put forward. Johanson and Mattsson (1987: 38) divide exchange processes into social, business and information exchange, and Möller and Wilson (1988: 5) divide them into the exchange of resources and social exchange.

Information exchange and social exchange are integral parts of advertising services; the exchange of a service for money cannot be separated

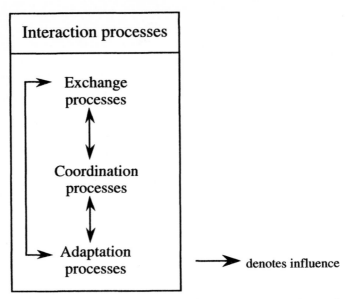

Figure 3.4 The interaction processes of an advertising agency–client relationship

from these elements. Information is the fundamental raw material of professional service firms; it is what the service provider works on in order to generate the service (cf. Mills 1986: 6–7). Much of this information is secured directly from clients. It is exchanged in face-to-face contact but also through technical devices such as telephone, fax and computer networks. Social exchange is essential in communicating values, attitudes and meanings between the firms. It may be purely business-related (e.g. discussing of the effectiveness of different types of advertising) or quite personal (e.g. having a beer with one's colleague after office-hours).

A typical exchange process with a full-service advertising agency is composed of three phases: planning, production and the delivery of advertising. The planning phase begins when a client supplies an agency with a brief. In accordance with the brief, the agency develops an advertising and promotion plan that fits the advertiser's overall marketing strategy. In the creative planning process the agency transforms the advertising message into verbal, visual and audio-visual language. In the production phase the agency produces the planned advertising material, orders parts of its production from suppliers and supervises the production process. In the delivery phase the agency purchases the desired space and time from the media and supervises the publication or broadcasting of the advertising. This is, of course, a largely simplified and generalised description of the process. Varying degrees of the production or media know-how may be bought outside the agency by either of the parties. The process may also include different research activities both before and after production and/or delivery.

Coordination processes are those by which the interacting firms harmonise their actions and decisions, in order to achieve the expected benefits from the business relationship (cf. Tuominen 1981: 4). Coordination processes include decisions on the terms of the exchange between participant firms, the norms and procedures of how the exchange processes are to be implemented, and *ad hoc* responses to conflicts and relevant environmental changes (Möller and Wilson 1988: 7).

In the advertising business, coordination of the parties' activities is essential, since services are created in cooperation between the agency and the client company. As Mills (1986: 49) has pointed out, services emerge from the coordinated efforts of both service employees and clients. In this coordination process the learned service scripts according to which the parties behave (see Solomon *et al.* 1985: 101), as well as mutual adjustments, play an important role (Larsson and Bowen 1989: 225). Coordination involves the everyday work patterns between the parties, i.e. how the agency and client work together to control, coordinate and communicate about advertising that is being developed by the agency (see Wackman *et al.* 1987: 23). It may take some time before the right work patterns are found as the needs and organisation structures of client companies vary.

Decisions regarding the division of work are particularly relevant to advertising services. There are three major options in this respect (see Ray 1982: 61). The most common makes the client company responsible for marketing planning and for research, and advertising agencies responsible for planning and execution in their areas of specialisation. In contrast to this mid-way solution is the 'in-house agency' on the one hand and the 'in-agency marketing department' on the other; in the latter, the agency performs a broad range of marketing activities for the client. In other words, the parties have to decide upon the width of the relationship (Ford 1989: 828) or the size of the role each party is supposed to play in service provision (Larsson and Bowen 1989: 225). Unclear and discrepant role expectations easily cause disappointment with respect to performance and lead to conflict and dissatisfaction in the relationship (see Frazier 1983; Solomon *et al.* 1985: 109).

Coordination processes are closely associated with structural dimensions of business relationships, such as the organisation structure of interacting companies, the extent of centralisation of their decision-making, and the number of units involved and the number of different tasks to be handled in interactions (cf. Van de Ven 1976: 26–7).

Institutionalisation has proved to be an important process in long-term business relationships (see Ford 1982; Håkansson 1982). In this study it is regarded as a dimension of coordination processes. Institutionalisation is the process through which various norms – patterns of behaviour and expectations of behaviour on the part of others – become established (Sills 1972). It refers to the emergence of various rules, customs and standard operating procedures in a business relationship (see Ford 1982: 297–8; Håkansson 1982: 17; cf. also Hajba 1982: 91).[8]

Institutionalisation may occur through contractual arrangements, in the form of contractual norms, or through various other norms – unwritten rules and customs – that are created and learned during interactions (cf. Hyvönen 1988: 12).

Contracts can be seen as devices for conducting and controlling exchange processes in a business relationship. A contract is a mechanism by which the parties project at least part of the exchange into the future (Macneil 1980: 4). It serves as a means of reducing the uncertainty that inheres in service exchanges. However, professional services are complex performances, where contracts cannot be specific (Mills 1986: 50). Although agencies and advertisers generally agree to written statements of fees and charges, there is rarely any agreement as to what constitutes adequate performance, nor is there any time period during which agencies are assured of employment (Comanor et al. 1981: 434). It is likely that the high performance ambiguity of advertising services decreases the usefulness of contracts and emphasises, instead, the role of other norms as control mechanisms in agency–client relationships.[9]

Institutionalisation is likely to reduce the costs resulting from interaction. This is especially important where the 'service package' and problem-solving content itself are, anyway, often customised and expensive. Over a period of time institutionalisation leads to clear expectations on the part of both parties concerning the roles and responsibilities of their counterpart (Ford 1978: 410–11). These expectations eventually become institutionalised to such an extent that they may no longer be questioned by either party (Ford 1982: 302–3; Håkansson 1982: 17). Institutionalisation thus involves the danger that parties become unresponsive to changes in the market and also ineffective in their relationship.

An exchange process also implies that the interacting parties test how well they fit each other. This is a learning process but also *an adaptation process where possible mismatches are eliminated* (Johanson and Mattsson 1987: 38). Should one or each of the parties perceive the relationship to be potentially profitable enough, they can start to adapt function, procedure, capability, and even attitudes, values and goals in order to increase resource exchange and/or to be better adapted to utilise the relationship (Möller and Wilson 1988: 7). Adaptations may be made when the companies start doing business with each other or made more continuously as a result of day-to-day interaction (Hallén et al. 1987: 23). An adaptation process can be started independently, at the initiation of the other party or by mutual consent. It may involve one or both parties (Möller and Wilson 1988: 7).

Through adaptation the firms become increasingly dependent on each other. Mutual functional adaptation may provide considerable benefit in the form of cost reduction or increased revenue, and may thus be viewed as an investment in the relationship. Such investments may lead, in part, to relationship-specific assets[10] that would have no or certainly less value in other business relationships. Adaptations therefore mark a commitment by the agency or client to the maintenance of a relationship. (Ford 1982: 289; Möller and Wilson 1988: 7)

Adaptations may concern different company resources relating to services exchanged, human interaction (to individuals' knowledge, professional skills and attitudes) and finally to the organisation such as to its location, production or marketing procedures.[11]

Advertising services are highly customised, which is to say that some adaptations always concern the service exchanged, both the service process and its outcome. Advertising services are also people-intensive performances so that adaptations and investments are likely to concern individual people rather than physical or other organisational resources. Learning by doing is likely to be an essential part of adaptation processes (cf. Williamson 1981: 555). A certain account team or employee may have to spend a long time and put a considerable effort into acquiring a good knowledge of the client's industry, products and marketing strategies. An account executive may need to instruct a new product manager as to how he is expected to 'play his role' in the service exchange process or, respectively, a client company representative may have to familiarise a new member of the account team with the client's marketing activities. The experience of interacting individuals of the existing relationship and other agency–client relationships is likely to influence the need for making adaptations and investments.

Adaptations related to organisations are likely to be intangible. They may take the form of a common relationship history, including common past experiences, established patterns of behaviour, common values, a sound knowledge of the partner company, and so on. Physical investments are likely to be small or even non-existent compared with the huge investments in production technology that are often required in manufacturing industries. Site-specific investment may sometimes be considerable for the agency, e.g. an agency may have to follow an important client abroad in order to serve the client's international needs more efficiently.

Exchange, coordination and adaptation processes are strongly interrelated activities (see Figure 3.4). Intensive business exchange (i.e. exchange of services for money) requires more social exchange, coordinating efforts and also promotes stronger reasons for adaptation (see e.g. Johanson and Mattsson 1987: 38; Möller and Wilson 1988: 8). Adaptation and coordination, for their part, pave the way to further exchange and are interlinked.

As pointed out earlier, mutual adjustments can be seen as coordination devices (see Larsson and Bowen 1989: 225).

Adaptation and information exchange are the two main processes through which relationships grow stronger. When companies adapt to each other they also become tied to each other, which makes the relationship more durable (Hallén et al. 1987: 25; Möller and Wilson 1988: 8). High contact intensity demonstrates closeness between the parties and the investments the companies make in developing their information exchange make the relationship potentially stable and long-lasting (Hallén et al. 1987: 25).

Business relationships are thus initiated, maintained and dissolved through interaction processes (Möller and Wilson 1988: 7). The IMP Group has in addition identified episodes in an overall business relationship in order to focus on the dynamics of relationships (see Ford 1982: 289; Håkansson 1982: 16). The term 'episode' refers to different acts that are performed to facilitate exchange processes: to every single buyer–seller contact, such as placing an order, negotiating a price or delivering a product (see Ford 1982: 289; Håkansson 1982: 16). In this study, episodes are viewed as elements of all interaction processes. *The episode concept is used to refer to all discernible acts the parties perform within their relationship, whether related to exchange, coordination or adaptation processes.*

It is peculiar to the dynamics of a relationship that every single episode or interaction process may contribute to the deepening of a relationship or its termination (Ford 1982: 289). The interacting parties do not usually have clear, consistent and common views of where they stand with regard to each other or what the other's intentions are. For these reasons each new interaction process is seen as a test of the relationship between the parties and as a way of learning about each other (Ford et al. 1986: 29). On the other hand, each episode and process takes place within the context of an overall relationship (Ford 1982: 289). The parties have memories and thus also interpret current interaction on the basis of previous experience (Ford et al. 1986: 29). The state of the relationship at any point in time determines the nature of exchange and other processes that can take place within the organisations involved (Ford 1982: 289; Håkansson 1982: 16).

3.4.2 Perceived outcomes of interaction processes

During interaction, both the advertising agency and the client are involved in assessments of their relationship, especially the associated reward–cost outcomes (Wilson and Mummalaneni 1986: 51). To begin with, business relationships are developed in order to gain benefits for the interacting companies. However, the perceived reward–cost outcome of a business relationship at any given moment is a multi-dimensional construct. The current outcome of interaction processes can be regarded in terms of economic and functional performance and of psychosocial rewards and costs (Möller and Wilson 1988: 8; see also Ruekert and Walker 1987: 4; Anderson and Narus 1990: 45–6). The rewards and costs of a relationship may further be either tangible or intangible in nature (see e.g. Bagozzi 1975: 37; Frazier 1983; Dwyer *et al*. 1987: 16).

In the most typical case, advertising is expected to increase sales and contribute to the growth of the advertising firm. Advertising may be deliberately designed to satisfy the more intangible needs of the company as well – for example, the need to obtain general social approval for the company's activities. These organisational rewards may mean increasing influence and recognition for the individual representatives of the firm. Growth allows the employees to raise their status and to attain promotion to higher positions. (Comanor *et al*. 1981: 433)

The same types of rewards and costs are also relevant factors for the agency and its employees. The aim of the agency is to satisfy its organisational profit goals as well as its goals for growth and professional development. This happens via client relationships. The agency may further improve its reputation by planning impressive advertising for clients that are well known or recognised as a superior marketing force. Through participation in award competitions, members of creative teams may raise their status and earning potential in the advertising world. A team member may gain personal satisfaction from his work with a professionally interesting client or with a personally attractive counterpart.

In advertising agency–client relationships, where the parties act on the basis of assignments, one may also distinguish between the outcome of an exchange process and the outcome of an overall relationship. *Taking the various rewards and costs of interaction processes into account, three outcome concepts are identified in this study. First, the performance outcome of an exchange process; secondly, the performance outcome of a business relationship and thirdly, the psychosocial outcome of a business relationship* (see Figure 3.5).

Performance outcomes comprise the economic and functional efficiency and effectiveness of exchange, coordination and adaptation processes. Effectiveness involves how well the company meets the needs of the other party and satisfies the criteria of the evaluator. Efficiency is measured by the ratio of resources utilised to output produced. When individuals and firms consider what is being produced, they are concerned with effectiveness rather than efficiency. (Pfeffer and Salancik 1978: 4, 11)

Accordingly, the perceived performance outcome of an exchange process has to be viewed in relation to the goals set for a specific assignment. Depending on whether the brief deals with e.g. a share issue, job advertisement or media campaign for a consumer brand, the communication goals and related target groups vary considerably. For advertising services, the interactive process through which the service is rendered is likely to have an important influence on reaching the desired goals. Service

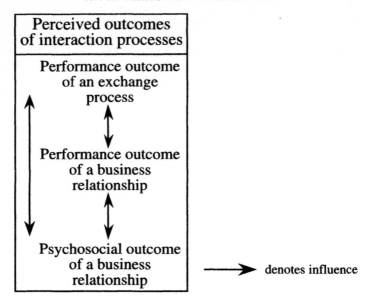

Figure 3.5 The perceived outcomes of an advertising agency–client relationship

quality research, in particular, has emphasised the role of the service production process in the customer's perception of total quality (see e.g. Grönroos 1990b: 37–8; Lehtinen and Lehtinen 1991: 291). The client may thus be deemed satisfied when its goals, needs and criteria concerning the whole exchange process – both the process and its output – are met.

The performance outcome of a business relationship is strongly dependent on the outcomes of exchange processes (see Figure 3.5). There are, however, goals – or at least expectations – that relate to the whole relationship as well, rather than to any individual exchange process. The client may want to build a brand for a whole product family, for instance, or the agency may aim at improving its reputation through the client relationship.

The psychosocial outcome of a business relationship used to refer to perceived satisfaction concerning the relationship in general. It refers to the affective assessment of the relationship (Anderson and Narus 1990: 45) – to the social and psychological aspects of interaction, which cannot typically be evaluated in terms of concrete economic measures. The psychosocial outcome is deeply influenced by such specific dimensions as the perceived fairness of the relationship, reciprocal understanding of and concern for the other party's needs and interests, and interpersonal trust (see Möller and Wilson 1988: 8). Interpersonal appeal and chemistry are also likely to contribute to perceived satisfaction with an agency–client relationship (Etelä 1985: 73; Michell 1987: 39; Wackmann *et al*. 1987: 24).

In advertising, the subjective nature of outcome assessments has to be emphasised. For instance, in four dyadic case studies conducted in professional business service settings, no operational goals in terms of costs and revenues were specified for assignments (Gummesson 1978: 93). Thus it may be suggested that the economic effectiveness and efficiency measures used are mainly implicit and that performance outcomes and the psychosocial outcome are closely related to each other (see Figure 3.5). Solomon *et al.* (1985: 100) have even suggested that in pure service situations with high performance ambiguity, customer satisfaction and repeat patronage may be determined solely by the quality of face-to-face interactions. It is indeed logical to assume that in agency–client relationships the psychosocial outcome is used partly as a substitute for performance measures, and that it plays a major role in the overall assessment of a business relationship.

The parties evaluate the outcomes in terms of satisfaction and dissatisfaction (Wilson and Mummalaneni 1986: 51). In service quality research, satisfaction/dissatisfaction has typically been modelled as a function of disconfirmation arising from discrepancies between prior expectations and experienced performance (see Grönroos 1982; Parasuraman *et al.* 1985; Brown and Swartz 1989). Aside from expected or presumed outcomes, the assessment of reward–cost outcomes can be based on previously experienced, i.e. materialised, outcomes. In consumer satisfaction research Cadotte *et al.* (1987: 313) have proposed that experience-based standards are more appropriate than expectations to serve as a benchmark against which product experiences are compared.

In a relationship context, past experiences from the current relationship and past and current experiences from alternative relationships become important standards of comparison (cf. Anderson and Narus 1984).[12] Knowledge of other companies' similar relationships may also be used as a reference point (see Anderson and Narus 1984: 63; Brown and Swartz 1989: 93). This knowledge is based on other companies' experience and is mediated through personal contact networks and referrals. Finally, the agency's reputation may also be used as a standard of comparison.

Deciding which standards are the most influential depends both on the degree of organisational experience and on the phase of the focal relationship. Referrals and reputation are most decisive for the construction of a standard of comparison when the client has no experience of advertising agencies at all. Referrals and reputation are also likely to have more importance in the initiation of a new relationship. When the parties have some experience of each other, it is most probable that such experience functions as a standard of comparison for forthcoming exchanges (assuming that the experience has been satisfactory).

The assessment of outcomes is essential, since it helps the parties make decisions regarding the upgrading or downgrading of their relationship (Wilson and Mummalaneni 1986: 51). Mutually satisfied interaction experiences are likely to encourage the parties into new interactions and towards actions that strengthen the relationship. Dissatisfied and incongruously perceived experiences, on the other hand, increase uncertainty in the relationship and may eventually lead to dissolution.

3.4.3 Evolving bonds

Interaction processes lead to the development of different kinds of bonds between an advertising agency and its client. Interaction and network theorists have distinguished between technical, planning, knowledge, social, economic and legal bonds and have focused on the strength of bonds in particular (see Hammarkvist *et al.* 1982: 23–4; Mattsson 1983: 3; Johanson and Mattsson 1986: 243). Wilson and Mummalaneni (1986), on the other hand, have proposed a bonding model of buyer–seller relationships based on the theories of social psychology. They identify four types of social bonds – investment, trust, attachment and commitment – but choose to draw only investment and commitment into their model.

Both perspectives seem relevant to the development of advertising agency–client relationships. I have thus integrated the ideas of the two approaches and separated them into two conceptual groups of bonds: operational and relational (see Figure 3.6). *Operational bonds refer to the concrete ties that are created in day-to-day operations between the parties. Relational bonds possess a more abstract character. They incorporate the continuity dimension of business relationships, i.e. the parties' bilateral expectation of future interaction* (cf. Heide and John 1990: 25). Aside from the temporal dimension, relational bonds also incorporate social aspects of business relationships that are particularly relevant in the advertising business.

Bonds may be examined from the point of view of their nature (e.g. social, economic, technical) or strength (e.g. weak, strong) and can also be studied at different organisational levels: company, department or group, and individual. In fact, it is this multi-level aspect that makes the measurement of the ties, and thereby the study of the development of business relationships, so difficult (Wilson and Mummalaneni 1988: 14). The strength of bonds indicates the level of interdependence and stability in the relationship. If bonds are strong, the relationship will not be easily terminated (see Mattsson 1983: 4; Johanson and Mattsson 1986: 247). For instance, an individual, unsatisfactory exchange process is unlikely to break it up. The greater the strength of the bonds and the broader their existence at different levels, the greater the stability of the relationship (Wilson and Mummalaneni 1988: 14).

In practice, bonds are often neither weak nor strong but somewhere in between. It is also common for some bonds to be weak and others strong

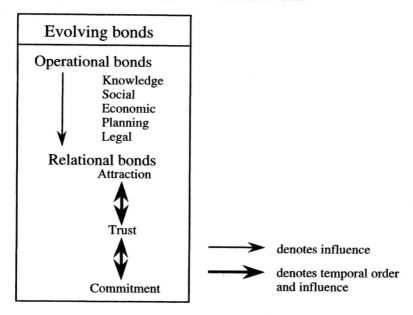

Figure 3.6 The evolving bonds in an advertising
agency–client relationship

within the same relationship (Hammarkvist *et al.* 1982: 27–8). This implies that bonds may develop differently and that the strength of bonds may vary over time within the same relationship. Together with partner-perceived satisfaction, bonds can be used to describe the state of the business relationship at any point in time.

The type of interaction process – exchange, coordination or adaptation – determines what kinds of bonds will most probably develop in business relationships. *Five primary types of operational bonds emerge in advertising agency–client relationships: knowledge, social, economic, planning and legal.*

Advertising services are created through information and social exchange. Consequently, knowledge and social bonds are likely to have an important role in agency–client relationships.

Both the client and agency personnel have to invest time and effort in acquiring and providing each other with the necessary information. Knowledge bonds are created in the process. Knowledge bonds are also closely related to reciprocal disclosure (Crosby *et al.* 1990: 71). Clients often need to provide agency personnel with confidential strategic information (Comanor *et al.* 1981: 432). Another type of knowledge bond may arise where the partners are able to convey important market information to each other, especially when the information is not readily available from other sources. When the parties continue cooperation they have an opportunity to learn to know each other better, which also implies the strengthening of knowledge bonds.

The people-intensive and ambiguous nature of advertising services fosters the development of social bonds. Strong personal relationships sometimes develop between interacting individuals. As Bagozzi (1974: 79) has suggested, the customer-salesman relationship may be interpreted as a social influence process, in which actors mediate a number of positive as well as negative sentiments and activities to the other. Reciprocity is an essential characteristic of these relations. It means that the value of rewards received by one party tends to be compensated for by the giving of rewards by that party (Homans 1958: 606).

Economic bonds result basically from business exchange, i.e. from the exchange of advertising services for money. Economic bonds can be exemplified by special credit agreements or by the intensity of money flows between the parties. In addition, economic risks taken on behalf of the other party and different assets developed during interactions – especially through adaptation processes – are regarded as economic bonds. Relationship-specific investments form particular economic bonds between the firms and increase the perceived cost of switching partners. Switching costs consist of the past investments made in the relationship and of the risks or exposure of making bad choices when changing partner (Jackson 1985: 124–5).

Planning bonds are also important in advertising exchange. Methods of coordinating service operations are included here and may be exemplified by annually agreed budgets, agreed ways of giving feedback to the partner or timetables and cost estimates included in briefs. As to the legal bonds, verbal and written contracts and possible ownership of one relationship party by the other are good examples. Copyright in planned advertising material may also create a legal bond. Technical bonds have tended to be rather less important in the advertising business. This is due to the people-intensive and intangible nature of advertising services.

Different types of bonds are not independent of each other. Social bonds of a minimum strength and of specific content may be necessary for the development of knowledge bonds and economic bonds (see Mattsson 1983: 4; Elsässer 1984: 154–5). For instance, before closing a deal several discussions and meetings may be needed to make sure that the 'interpersonal chemistry' works and that the 'advertising philosophy' of the agency is congruent with that of the client.

Relational bonds, which incorporate the continuity dimension of relationships, are viewed as both economic and social ties that develop between agency and client over time. *I have identified three relational bonds peculiar to advertising agency–client relationships: attraction, trust and commitment* (Figure 3.6).

Attraction is basically an interpersonal phenomenon, which has been studied in social psychology and also in marketing, in the context of personal selling and negotiations (see e.g. Evans 1963; Bagozzi 1974; Campbell *et al.* 1988). Nevertheless, attraction may be viewed as an inter-firm phenomenon as well. For instance Dwyer *et al.* (1987: 16) have identified attraction as one of the subprocesses developing in the exploration phase of buyer–seller relationships.[13] In their view, attraction results from the degree to which buyer and seller achieve – in their inter-action – a reward–cost outcome in excess of some minimum level, i.e. in excess of the economic and social reward–cost outcomes available from other alternatives. Anderson and Narus (1984: 63) view attraction in the same way, emphasising, however, the reward–cost outcome the partner has come to expect from a given kind of relationship as a standard of comparison (see also Kelley and Thibaut 1978: 8–9). To summarise, the attractiveness of a business cooperation partner has typically been viewed in terms of the rewards available from the relationship and in relation to past experiences or alternative relationships.

In this study, I define attraction slightly differently as a company's interest in exchange with another, based on the economic and social reward–cost outcomes expected from a relationship over time. This definition is preferred to that of Dwyer *et al.* (1987) because it incorporates the future orientation of attraction. Relationships may be viewed as investments, where the most attractive business relationship is the one with the highest positive net present value. While entering into a new relationship, attraction can be based only on expected and presumed reward–cost outcomes. In the later phases of the relationship, attraction is also based primarily on future expectations, although the received experiences of the partner, also affect it. The situations of the partners, their needs and resources change over time; those things that are valued by the partners and that create attraction thereby also change. This means that attraction cannot be based on experienced reward–cost outcomes alone.

In the context of business relationships, attractiveness is particularly based on the perceived compatibility of organisational needs and resources. In addition, intangible and personal factors – especially interpersonal chemistry – will probably play an important role in determining inter-firm attractiveness in advertising agency–client relationships. As tangible evidence of performance is limited, potential clients are compelled to base their judgement of an agency's attractiveness on its reputation, on referrals, credentials and discussions with agency representatives. Agencies, for their part, are likely to feel attraction to clients who offer them a high potential to increase their gross margin, expand their client base or improve their reputation.

Attraction plays an important role when parties are initiating a business relationship. A certain level of attraction is a precondition for the commencement of interaction. Attractiveness also has to be maintained in the later phases of the relationship, in order to encourage progressive relationship development and defend the relationship against competitor incursion. The degree of partner attraction increases motivation to maintain the relationship (Dwyer *et al.* 1987: 18). Attraction potentially increases when partners perceive satisfying reward–cost outcomes from their interaction (Dwyer *et al.* 1987: 18; see also Kelley and Thibaut 1978 and Anderson and Narus 1984: 63). Trust is also linked with attraction (see Figure 3.6). A relationship with a trustworthy seller is considered more attractive because the seller's word is thus reliable and exchange obligations may be expected to be fulfilled (Schurr and Ozanne 1985: 941).

Trust constitutes one party's belief that its needs will be fulfilled in the future by actions undertaken by the other party (Anderson and Weitz 1989: 312; cf. Schurr and Ozanne 1985: 940). In other words, trust is a company's belief that another company will act in a way that results in positive outcomes for that company, as well as a belief that the other company will not take unexpected actions that would result in negative outcomes. This belief may lead the company to engage in a trusting response or action, whereby it commits itself to a possible loss depending upon the subsequent actions of the other company (Anderson and Narus 1990: 45).

A future orientation is critical to the concept of trust. Trust is also characterised by reciprocity (see Young and Wilkinson 1989: 112). The tendency to trust or doubt is affected by one's perception of the other's trustworthiness. To trust that a firm (or a person) will act beneficially, one must have confidence that the other has both the ability and the intention to do so.

Trust is assumed to play a central role in the development of advertising agency–client relationships: several researchers have emphasised the importance of trust in service relationships (see e.g. Crosby *et al.* 1990: 70; Czepiel 1990; Yorke 1990: 352). However, it has even more often been studied as an element of marketing channel dyads or buyer–seller relationships in general (see e.g. Dwyer *et al.* 1987; Anderson and Weitz 1989; Anderson and Narus 1990). Grönroos (1990a: 5–6) deals essentially with the same thing when stressing the role of promises in customer relationships. He views the initiation, maintenance and enhancement of a relationship as a process of making and fulfilling implicit and explicit promises of future actions and commitments between the partners.

Trust should form an important bond between the agency and its client, especially because of the intangibility and ambiguity of advertising services. It seems evident, given high performance ambiguity, that service evaluation centres on the trust instilled by the service provider (see Gummesson 1981: 111). In the case of advertising services, it is impossible to draw up specific contracts and also difficult and expensive to monitor a partner's behaviour (see Mills 1986: 50, 1990: 36). Consequently, trust may become a vital supplement to a contract (Thorelli 1986: 41) and also decrease the need for monitoring behaviour (Mills 1990: 39). Aside from the contract, trust and social norms (cf. institutionalisation) also serve as rules and guidelines for ongoing exchange processes (cf. Macneil 1980: 7–8).

There have been few empirical studies bearing on the antecedents of trust in buyer–seller relationships (see Anderson and Weitz 1989, Anderson and Narus 1990, and the review of Young and Wilkinson 1989). *In accordance with the existing findings it is suggested that trust has three basic antecedents: past performance, common clarified interests and, finally, personal relationships and two-way communication.*

Past performance is generally regarded as the most important source of trust (see e.g. Thorelli 1986: 41; Dwyer *et al.* 1987: 18; Anderson and Narus 1990: 54; Crosby *et al.* 1990: 70). This means that trust is based on the perceived reward–cost outcomes of interaction processes that include both economic and social costs and rewards. Past interaction outcomes act as proof of the partner's abilities and intentions. The importance of the said outcomes also accentuates the dynamic nature of the concept of trust. Trust is built up through past experiences but it is focused on the future of the relationship.

Common clarified interests are also introduced here as a source of trust (see Anderson and Weitz 1989: 319; Young and Wilkinson 1989). Common interests involve trust that the other party will provide what is required (Ford 1989: 825). Whether one partner purposely seeks the common interest and the other's well-being or is alternatively self-seeking is another source of trust. Cooperative interaction orientation is associated with a high level of trust, while a competitive orientation is linked with a low level (see e.g. Schurr and Ozanne 1985: 940).

Trust is also built incrementally, in day-to-day interaction, through personal relationships, i.e. social bonds (Thorelli 1986: 40). Trust is particularly enhanced by intensive two-way communication between parties (Anderson and Weitz 1989: 319). Close personal relationships are themselves an important component of confidential exchange (Etelä 1985: 75). Mutual trust, respect and personal friendships between participants allow confidential information to be exchanged between the parties (Cunningham and Turnbull 1982: 307). This is especially relevant to agency–client relationships where the agency has to have access to privileged information regarding the advertiser's strategies in order to provide a service (see e.g. Comanor *et al.* 1981: 432).

In contrast, Ford (1989: 826) claims that there is no basis for trust through social bonds. He states that trust is built through product predictability, which means that the relationship stands or falls on the product. A clear difference between manufacturing and professional service industries may be identified here. While the advertising 'product' is highly dependent on people, their knowledge and creativity, it seems evident that social bonds form an essential basis of inter-firm trust (see Figure 3.6).

Trust may be reposed in the individual or in the corporate entity. This means that one actor may trust another less than she or he trusts the company and vice versa (Wilson and Mummalaneni 1988: 10). In advertising agency–client relationships, it is crucial to understand the extent to which trust is based on personal credibility or the trustworthiness of the firm. Where certain personal relationships are important, changes in them may be decisive for the continuity of the whole business relationship. On the other hand, it is likely that corporate trust develops over time through the concerted actions of the individuals representing the company (Wilson and Mummalaneni 1988: 10). The performance of individuals provides satisfaction and leads the other party to trust in that company's ability to fulfil future needs.

The evolution of an agency–client relationship may be regarded in terms of incrementally increasing trust between the parties involved. Trust develops as the firm or individuals perceive interaction to be positive and beneficial. Rewarded trust begets more interaction and leads to the deepening of trust where satisfying outcomes accrue (see Wilson and Mummalaneni 1988: 10).

Commitment has been treated as an essential construct, especially in models of buyer–seller relationships (see e.g. Ford 1982; Wilson and Mummalaneni 1986; Dwyer *et al.* 1987). *Commitment is defined here as expressed by Dwyer* et al. (1987: 19): *an implicit or explicit pledge of relational continuity between the parties to the relationship.* Commitment represents the most developed state in a relationship, including the idea of increased interdependence between the firms. Committed partners maintain their awareness of alternative partners but do not test them actively and constantly. (Dwyer *et al.* 1987: 19)

The concept of commitment has been used with slightly different meanings, depending on the theoretical perspective adopted, and the level of analysis, whether organisational or individual. However, it seems common to most research that commitment is viewed from one of two distinct but closely related perspectives: behavioural and attitudinal (see e.g. Cook and Emerson 1978: 734; Ford 1982: 289; Morris and Holman 1988: 117).[14] *When commitment is viewed as a function of behaviour, it is postulated that firms and individuals become committed to each other by their actions and choices over time. Attitudinal commitment, on the other hand, refers to the willingness to develop and maintain a relationship in the future as well.* It reflects a long-term orientation to obtaining common results and a willingness to accept restrictions on the potential for switching partners (Hallén and Sandström 1988: 258).

Dwyer *et al.* (1987: 19) have emphasised the behavioural dimension of commitment. They apply the social exchange view to relationships and list three measurable criteria of commitment. First, inputs to the association in the form of economic, communication and/or emotional resources; secondly, the durability of the association over time i.e. a common belief in the effectiveness of future exchanges and, thirdly, the consistency with which the inputs are made to the association. The first criterion refers to the adaptations and investments made in the relationship. The third criterion implies that fluctuations in these investments reflect low commitment to the other party and that the parties have to engage resources purposely in order to maintain the relationship. The second criterion, however, poses a problem. It is very close to the notion of trust used by the same authors (see Dwyer *et al.* 1987: 18), and the conceptual difference – or potential interrelationship between trust and commitment – remains unclear in the proposed framework.

The issue of behavioural commitment leads to the question of what type of actions or inputs potentially create commitment. *The literature suggests at least seven potential antecedents to commitment.*

Adaptations and investments made in the relationship, and especially relationship-specific investments, are commonly accepted as a basis for commitment (see e.g. Ford 1982: 289; Wilson and Mummalaneni 1986: 52). This aspect links economic bonds with commitment (see Figure 3.6). *Contractual terms* may also bind the parties to a relationship (cf. legal bonds). The contract may specify how the relationship will be terminated, making changes of supplier difficult and costly (Wilson 1990: 5). The necessity of exchanging confidential information may also increase commitment (cf. knowledge bonds). From the advertiser's point of view, the fear of conspicuous use of strategically delicate information may create pressure to work longer with the current agency (Comanor *et al.* 1981: 432).

Intensive communication is also a specific type of binding action. For instance Hallén *et al.* (1987: 25) have suggested that the intensive contacts and investments of the parties in developing information exchange link the parties more tightly together and make the relationship stable and long-lasting. Michell (1987: 37) has emphasised the necessity of regular and intensive communication to the continuity of an agency–client relationship. Efforts to stay in touch have also been identified as a key determinant of relationship maintenance in the insurance and banking sectors (Crosby *et al.* 1990: 71).

Social pressures may also exist to maintain the relationship, i.e. those people in an interacting firm who wish to continue the relationship put social pressure on other people not to end the relationship (Wilson 1990: 4). Commitment does indeed embrace both social and economic aspects, as do the other relational bonds. Investments that create behavioural commitment may be emotional and especially directed to personal relationships (cf. social bonds), or they may be economic, resulting in explicit costs or financial or strategic dependences at company level (cf. economic bonds).

Satisfaction with the relationship is often viewed as an important antecedent to commitment (see e.g. Wilson and Mummalaneni 1986: 52; Dwyer et al. 1987: 19; Morris and Holman 1988: 123–4). Nevertheless, a company may also be committed to a relationship despite being dissatisfied with it (Wilson and Mummalaneni 1986: 53). This implies that the current level of satisfaction does not necessarily correlate with the perceived inter-firm commitment. Dependence through relationship-specific investments may eventually lead to worsening terms of exchange and to the loss of better opportunities (Möller and Wilson 1988: 5). Because of the perceived switching costs, the client may feel itself 'stuck' with the agency, which in turn is under no pressure to serve the client efficiently and effectively. Consequently, satisfaction with performance outcome as well as psychosocial outcome decreases.

Trust is a precondition for investment in and increased commitment to the relationship (Wilson and Mummalaneni 1988: 10). Some researchers have also shown empirically the link between trust and loyalty (or stability) (Schurr and Ozanne 1985: 950; Anderson and Weitz 1989: 319; Holden 1990: 251). Trust has further been found to be of particular importance in maintaining stable advertising agency–client relationships (Etelä 1985: 73). On the other hand, commitment may be necessary for the building of trust. In order to establish credibility and gain the trust of the other, parties may have to demonstrate commitment to the relationship by making adaptations (Wilson and Mummalaneni 1988: 9–10).

Commitment is an incrementally evolving bond between the parties to a relationship. According to Ford (1982: 289), commitment escalates slowly over a period of time as both parties make incremental investments in the relationship. Wilson and Mummalaneni (1986: 52) specify that strengthening commitment is the result of multiple interactions involving successful exchanges and incremental investments made at various stages in the relationship. Commitment typically leads to repeated exchange processes with the same partner (Cook and Emerson 1978: 734), which on their part create the potential and sometimes also the necessity for further adaptations and commitment.

A body of empirical evidence exists for the incremental development of commitment (or stability). In the context of auditor–client relationships, Levinthal and Fichman (1988: 365) have estimated what they term the hazard rates, i.e. the probabilities of relationship termination, in relation to the length of the relationship. Their results show that a relationship will not end shortly after it has begun. The hazard rate increases, however, during the initial period and then declines gradually the older the relationship becomes.

3.5 CRITICAL EVENTS IN RELATIONSHIP DEVELOPMENT

In the previous section I described the content and internal process of relationship development between advertising agencies and their clients. The process of development was described in terms of activities – i.e. interaction processes and episodes – and the results of those activities – i.e. perceived outcomes of interaction processes and evolving bonds. However, the process of relationship development can also be described in terms of events that occur within a business relationship and its context. In focusing on events, the content and process of relationship development become linked with the context of a relationship and its dynamics (see Abrams 1982: 192). This linkage is necessary for understanding the development of advertising agency–client relationships.

Events are the principal points of access to the structuring of social action in time (Abrams 1982: 191). An event is a happening, an occurrence, that takes place in time and in a specific setting. Events may arise from different levels of a relationship's context or from inter-firm interaction itself. Events may thus be related to the interacting companies, may be caused by other actors in the companies' task environment or by some major phenomenon in the macro-environment. Exchange processes or specific interaction episodes also form events in agency–client relationships.

Events may be characterised on the basis of their influence over the content and process of relationship development. There are major and minor events, categorised according to their consequences. In this study, I use the term 'critical event' for those events that are decisive for the relationship, and function either as driving or checking forces in its development (Elsässer 1984: 162–3; see also Liljegren 1988: 374).[15]

It is typical of critical events that some types increase perceived uncertainty regarding relationship continuity, while others decrease it (cf. Liljegren 1988: 374). Critical events also place special demands on the resources of the service company, especially on its personnel (see Edvardsson 1988: 434). Uncertainty caused by a critical event calls for new individual and organisational adaptations, if the parties desire to maintain the relationship. In this way, critical events also create situations in which the parties can demonstrate their commitment to the relationship.

A number of researchers have studied and discussed the events that easily lead to break-ups in agency–client relationships (see Doyle *et al.* 1980; Michell 1987; Belch and Belch 1990). Others have investigated success factors in agency relationships (see e.g. Cagley 1986; Wackmann *et al.* 1987; Verbeke 1989). Drawing on these and other research findings, one may list a number of potential critical events in these relationships.

First of all, each exchange process or interaction episode may contribute to the deepening of a relationship or to its termination (Ford 1982: 289).

The most common reason for agency switches seems to be related to agency performance, particularly to the standard of creative work (Doyle *et al*. 1980: 19; Michell 1987: 30–1). Different concepts of creativity quickly lead to disagreement (Michell 1984a). Declining sales and conflicting compensation philosophies have also been cited as potential reasons for relationship dissolution (see Belch and Belch 1990: 82).

Changes in client marketing strategies constitute another important group of critical events (cf. Doyle *et al*. 1980; Michell 1987). Any change in marketing strategy creates pressure for the re-evaluation of the current agency, since it is seen to be closely tied to the old and eventually 'failed' marketing policy (Michell 1987: 31). Confidence in the agency's ability to change its thinking and provide fresh creativity input may be low.

Changes in the account team or in the client's personnel or marketing organisation are also potentially critical relationship events (Doyle *et al*. 1980: 21; Michell 1987: 31). Personal factors are important both in starting up a relationship (see Cagley 1986; Wackmann *et al*. 1987: 27) and in dissolving one (Doyle *et al*. 1980: 21–2). Changes in personnel usually mean that the existing social bonds will be broken, which is apt to undermine the trust between parties and to increase uncertainty. Adaptive measures such as learning to know new people and demonstrating flexibility in changing established patterns of behaviour are required.

Changes in the companies' intragroup nets, e.g. via agency mergers or the rationalisation of agencies within the client group may function as critical events (see e.g. Michell 1987: 32). An agency merger may lead to account conflict and thereby to a dissolution of the current relationship; on the other hand, it may offer a fresh start to a new relationship. In addition, many macro-environmental trends and changes therein may function as driving or checking forces. Economic recession often leads to decreased advertising budgets and in the worst case even to the bankruptcy of either of the interacting parties. Rapidly changing consumption trends and fashions may also create pressure for frequent changes in the products and marketing strategies of the client, leading to subsequent re-evaluation of the current agency relationship.

3.6 SUMMARY OF THE FRAMEWORK – THE *A PRIORI* PROCESS MODEL

In this Chapter I have developed a conceptual framework for the development of advertising agency–client relationships. In defining the concepts and their major interrelationships, I have constructed an *a priori* process model that provides, however, only a preliminary conceptualisation of the development of advertising agency–client relationships (see Figure 3.7). Existing literature is deficient, especially in terms of explicating the relationship development process, and the model thus

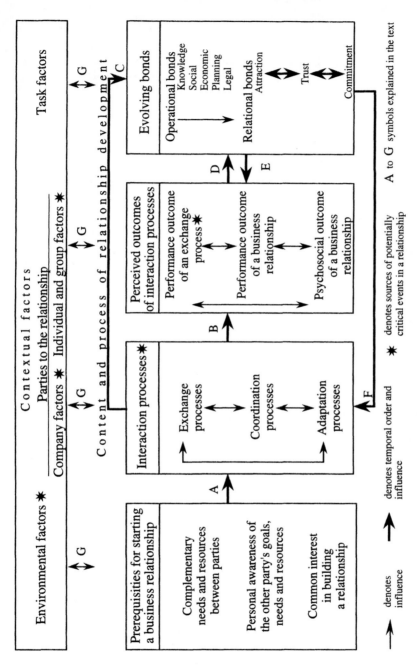

Figure 3.7 An *a priori* process model of the development of advertising agency–client relationships

presents us with a number of blanks to fill in. The role of the case study is to complement and specify the model, especially with respect to the evolutionary aspects of relationships.

An advertising agency–client relationship can start when three pre-requisites are met: the parties have complementary needs and resources, they are personally aware of each other's goals, needs and resources and they can see a common interest in building a business relationship (see arrow A in Figure 3.7).

Business relationships emerge and develop as a result of three basic and firmly interrelated interaction processes: exchange, coordination and adaptation processes. Exchange processes form the core phenomenon of interaction. They refer to individual assignments executed in agency–client relationships. Coordination processes describe how interacting firms harmonise their actions and decisions to achieve the expected benefits from the business relationship. Adaptation processes refer to processes where possible mismatches between the parties are eliminated. Interaction processes are comprised of episodes – of acts the parties perform within their relationship.

During interaction the parties assess their relationship, especially the associated reward–cost outcomes (arrow B). The agency and client representatives evaluate performance outcomes of exchange processes as well as performance outcomes and psychosocial outcomes of the whole relationship. Outcomes are evaluated in terms of satisfaction and dissatisfaction. Performance outcomes refer to the economic and func-tional efficiency and effectiveness of interaction processes, psychosocial outcomes to the affective evaluation of the relationship. The three types of outcome are assumed to be closely related to each other. Psychosocial outcomes are likely to play a major role in the overall assessment of an agency–client relationship.

Resulting from interaction processes, different kinds of *bonds* develop between the agency and the client (arrow C). The level of perceived satisfaction and the nature and strength of the bonds describe the state of the relationship at each point in time. Operational bonds refer to the concrete ties that are created in day-to-day operations: knowledge, social, economic, planning and legal bonds. Relational bonds possess a more abstract character. They incorporate the continuity dimension of business relationships, i.e. the parties' bilateral expectation of future interaction.

Three relational bonds are peculiar to advertising agency–client relationships: attraction, trust and commitment. Attraction refers to a company's interest in exchange with another, based on the economic and social reward–cost outcomes expected from a relationship over time. Trust is one party's belief that its needs will be fulfilled in the future by actions undertaken by the other party. Commitment is defined as an implicit or explicit pledge of relational continuity between the parties to the relationship. All relational bonds have both an economic and a social dimension and exist both between firms and individuals. Trust and commitment are assumed to evolve incrementally over time.

Relational bonds possess temporal interdepedences. Attraction is a precondition for interaction and the evolution of trust. Trust is a precondition for commitment. The reverse effects also exist; actions that indicate commitment are assumed to build trust, and trustworthiness is assumed to create attractiveness. Operational bonds are related to relational bonds. For instance, economic and legal bonds are likely to contribute to the development of commitment and social bonds to the development of trust (see Figure 3.7). Overall, bonds strengthen the relationship and make it more stable and long-lasting.

The recurrent assessment of outcomes helps the parties to make decisions regarding the upgrading or downgrading of their relationship. Satisfaction with perceived outcomes potentially leads to the strengthening of relational bonds, whereas dissatisfaction weakens those bonds (arrow D). Furthermore, existing bonds between the agency and client function as intervening factors in the parties' assessment of the outcomes of interaction processes (arrow E). This means that bonds moderate the influence of the perceived performance outcomes of individual exchange processes on relationship development. A poor performance is not likely to break up a strongly bonded relationship.

The strength and types of bond affect the parties' interaction (arrow F). Some level of attraction is a precondition for exchange. Trust is likely to affect coordination processes by decreasing the need for written contracts. Strong commitment through relationship-specific investments may worsen the efficiency and effectiveness of exchange processes. Strong relational bonds are likely to lead to further interaction between parties, whereas weak relational bonds are likely to decrease interaction, leading eventually to the break-up of the relationship.

Various environmental, organisational, individual and task-related factors in the context of agency–client relationships affect relationship development (arrows G). Each interaction process occurs in a specific situation, determined by different factors in the context of the relationship. The level of satisfaction with perceived outcomes is vulnerable to the effects of contextual factors. The type and strength of bonds are assessed by the parties in the prevailing situation. Changes in contextual factors may transform the situation to such an extent that the prerequisites of a business relationship cease to exist and the relationship dissolves.

The development of agency–client relationships can be conceived of in terms of events that occur in the content or context of a relationship. Critical events are decisive for the relationship and function as driving or checking forces for their development. Critical events particularly affect perceived uncertainty in the relationship and the need to make adaptations. Macro environmental trends, changes in the personnel or organisation of interacting companies, or changes in the strategies or policies of the parties are potentially critical events in the development of advertising agency–client relationships. Performance outcomes of exchange processes or individual episodes in an interaction may also function as critical events (see ✳ symbols in Figure 3.7).

4

EMPIRICAL RESEARCH DESIGN

The empirical part of the study entails a case study, an intensive investigation of one advertising agency–client relationship and its development. The purpose of the case study is to provide the empirical basis for the development of an empirically grounded process model of the development of advertising agency–client relationships. The case description will be used as a reference against which the *a priori* process model that was drafted in the theoretical part of the study may be compared.

In this chapter I first describe the procedure of case selection and present the case selected. Secondly, the research process, data collection methods and the procedures of data analysis are outlined. The quality of the data is discussed at the end of the chapter.

4.1 SELECTION OF THE EMPIRICAL CASE

The strength of a case study is very much dependent on the criteria set for the selection of concrete cases. There are at least two types of case study design that can be used for theory-generating purposes: representative and deviant (Lilja 1983: 348–50). The former refers to the selection of a typical case among the population of research objects, whereas the latter refers to the selection of a case which, according to some logic, is deviant. Both designs require prior knowledge and data about the population of research objects from which the case is chosen. When the essential characteristics of the population are known, it is possible to control the extraneous variation and to define the limits for generalising the findings (Eisenhardt 1989: 537).

Eneroth (1984: 174–5) has paid special attention to the selection of cases in studies that address the dynamics of particular phenomena. By applying his ideas to what I have earlier presented regarding different perspectives on development (see section 1.3), two further types of case design can be distinguished: those that employ the change and those that adopt processual perspectives. When the process of development is viewed from a change perspective, the selection of cases occurs logically

71

by choosing cases that are assumed to be in different phases of the change process. The absolute duration of the business relationships may potentially be used as a selection criterion. In a study taking a processual perspective on development, the cases are logically selected in order to ensure that they have already been through different processes of events and activities. In this option, the age of the relationship may be used as a complementary choice criterion. The primary task, however, is to ensure that certain processes have already occurred in the relationship.

In this study, I have used the representative single case design and the process perspective in case selection. The focal advertising agency–client relationship was chosen so that it would be a typically representative relationship and mature enough for studying the development process. A two-step procedure was followed. First I chose the advertising agency to study and thereafter one of its clients.

The following criteria were used in the selection of the agency:

1 The agency had to be ordinary and average in terms of type, size and operations. In practice it was impossible to define an average agency, since the market is composed of a very heterogeneous set of enterprises. The other problem was to find statistics or generalisable research results on Finnish advertising markets. At the end of 1989, an ordinary agency could have been characterised as a local independent, i.e. an entrepreneur agency, or a part of a national advertising group. Excluding the largest and smallest agencies, the number of personnel employed by an ordinary agency should have been somewhere between 10 and 40 employees and the gross margin between FIM 2 million and FIM 15 million. More than 50 per cent of the agency's turnover should have originated from media advertising, about 25 per cent from the invoicing of purchased production and about 15 per cent from its own work (see Appendix 1).

2 The agency had to be mature enough to have established and positioned itself in the market, and it should already have developed long-term client relationships.

3 The agency had to be big enough to have sufficient long-term clients to choose from.

4 The agency had to be a full-service house, in order for it to have been possible for its client relationships to expand and diversify without having to desert the agency.

5 The agency management and personnel should be willing to participate in the study.

Besides business specific statistics and publications, recommendations of people involved in advertising were used to find a suitable agency. Two potential agencies were approached, the second of which, Markkinointi Topitörmä Oy, became interested in research cooperation and was selected as the agency party for the study. In 1989, Markkinointi Topitörmä Oy (which will from herein be called Törmä) was an independent, full-service agency belonging to the national Advisor Group. It had been operating for 26 years, and with 35 employees and a gross margin of FIM 14.1 million could still be considered a medium-sized agency (see Appendix 1). Moreover, the distribution of its turnover corresponded fairly well with the industry average, even though it was more inclined towards purchased production than media advertising. Media advertising accounted for 49 per cent of turnover, purchased production 32 per cent and its own work 19 per cent. In 1989, Törmä provided services to approximately 36 clients.

The following criteria were used in the selection of the client relationship:

1 The relationship had to be mature enough for me to be able to study several assignments and different events and situations during the existence of the relationship. On the other hand, it could not be too old, because the informants still had to be able to remember what had happened during the relationship and documents about the relationship and its events still had to be available.
2 Typical assignments during the relationship had to concern brand advertising for consumers, which is an area where the services of advertising agencies are traditionally and typically used (see e.g. 'Mainonnan kustannukset . . . '1989; Ripley 1991: 76).
3 The account size had to be average in relation to the agency's other accounts, in order to at least allow the probability that the client had been treated in a 'normal' or typical way.
4 The client company's management and personnel had to be willing to participate in the study.

In order to find a suitable client relationship, I consulted Törmä's account supervisors and collected secondary data concerning the agency's clientele from advertising sector publications. The business relationship with Fiskars Oy Ab was selected for the study. Fiskars is an international corporation operating primarily in the metal and electronics industries. Various types of assignment had been executed during the three and half years of the relationship's existence. The assignments had primarily concerned the advertising of branded consumer products: Fiskars scissors, knives, lawn and garden tools. Some assignments were also being carried out at the point of selection. The agency's management regarded Fiskars as a medium-sized account. It had earlier been larger and ranked among the agency's ten largest accounts.

The selected case relationship includes three unit business relationships. Törmä cooperated with three fairly independent units of the Fiskars corporation: the marketing unit at Billnäs, the Finnish sales unit at Malmi,

Helsinki, and the corporate head office in Helsinki. The case relationship started in November 1986 with the initiation of the business relationship with Billnäs and another relationship with Head Office. The sales unit of Malmi later became involved in cooperation as well.

Altogether, the three unit relationships provide a fairly diversified picture of advertising agency–client relationships. In the relationship with Billnäs, assignments concerned the planning of product concepts and launch materials for international use, whereas in the relationship with Malmi assignments primarily involved media campaigns for these products on the Finnish market. The relationship with Head Office had been dormant for some years but was activated just before data collection began. The client had given the agency a brief concerning a company image campaign, which added yet another type of assignment to the study and also provided a good opportunity to follow agency–client interaction in real time.

4.2 THE RESEARCH PROCESS

The research project began in early 1988 with a search for a theoretically relevant research question in the area of services marketing. I started by going through the service marketing literature and became, quite accidentally, acquainted with the IMP Group's Interaction Approach. There seemed to be an obvious possibility of combining research results from the two areas by concentrating on the development of business relationships in a particular professional service sector.

Figure 4.1 describes the research process as a dialogue between theoretical and methodological knowledge and empirical reality. It depicts the major phases and events of the research project.

The primary motivation for the study emerged from a purely theoretical interest in the topic. I entered the field without any experiential knowledge of the advertising industry. This meant that I had to do a great deal of background work before I could select the case companies, approach them and refine the research proposal. In the winter of 1990 I made a pilot study of the field in order to enable me to define the research problem and outline the empirical investigation. Knowledge related to the line of business allowed me to produce a case study protocol including, in particular, the substantive questions of the inquiry. These questions were posed to myself as an investigator and their role was to serve as reminders regarding the information that had to be collected (see Yin 1989: 76).

The iterative process of data collection and analysis took a year and a half. However, only when all the data were simultaneously available was it possible to play data from different sources and informants off against one another and make sense of the whole development process of the studied unit relationships over time (cf. Simmons 1985: 299). This meant

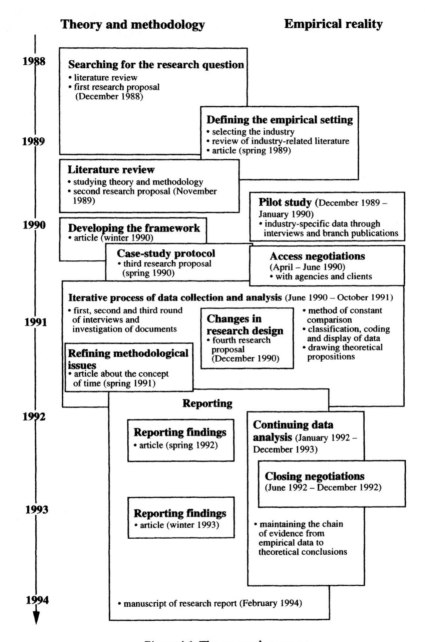

Figure 4.1 The research process

that the writing of case descriptions could be started only fairly late. The data analysis continued parallel with the writing process until all the conclusions were reported.

The research process was, first and foremost, a learning process for myself as the major 'research instrument'. In this respect, two points should be mentioned as being especially relevant to the outcomes of this study. First, during the study my awareness of time and its various dimensions increased, and my perception of time matured from the typical linear and absolute model towards a more relational and cyclical understanding (see Halinen and Törnroos 1995). This concerned both data collection and model construction. I realised that people do not remember *when* something happened; they only remember the event and possibly what preceded or followed it, or what happened at the same time. The linear time conception of the existing models of relationship development had given me a much too idealised and simplistic view of reality. In building the model, temporality gradually became a part of the conceptual definitions and the idea of cycles and break points became emphasised in the description of the development process.

Secondly, the complexity of longitudinal research when conducted as a case study in a real-life context surprised me several times during the project. The problem of gaining access to the past appeared to be the major one. After the first case study interviews I realised how difficult it is to investigate things retrospectively and, in particular, to get accurate accounts of past beliefs and intentions. I had to use my own judgement and apply all my knowledge, skills, intuition and empathy in order to create a comprehensible picture of the past.

In the real-time part of the study the lack of time and resources became a constraint. Real-life events turned out to be so fast-moving that it was difficult to simultaneously keep up with real-time data collection, retrospective data collection and data analysis. In the reporting phase, I was surprised how much effort was required to maintain the chain of evidence, given the overwhelming amount of data.[1] Part of the learning process concerned learning to live with constraints, and finding an outcome which was 'acceptable'.

4.3 DATA COLLECTION

4.3.1 Procedures of data collection

Personal interviews and available company documents were used as primary sources of data to investigate the development of the selected agency–client relationship. Contact persons on both the agency and the client side were interviewed and documents were also collected from both companies. Secondary data sources, especially journal articles and advertising sector publications, were used in case selection and to complement internal data sources in the case description (see Appendix 2). In addition to the data on the chosen business relationship, all other data from the industry's journals, from practically oriented literature and from practitioner interviews were used to support the construction of the model.

The longitudinal and dyadic research design required particular sampling procedures and principles to be used in data collection. Sampling concerned the research period, events studied and informants used.

The research period during which data were collected concerned the period from the early 1980s to October 1991. The period covers the emergence of the conditions that led to the initiation of the agency–client relationship studied, as well as the time during which the relationship, with its three unit relationships, emerged and evolved until the moment data collection was finished. Data were collected partly retrospectively and partly by following the events and activities in real-time (see Figure 4.2). Retrospective data collection concentrated on the period November 1986 to June 1990 – in other words, the period from the initiation of the agency–client relationship studied to the beginning of the real-time part of the study. Real-time data collection concerned the period June 1990– October 1991.

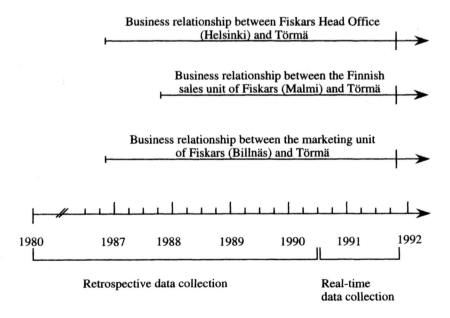

Figure 4.2 Longitudinal research design

Events are the principal analytical tools used in describing the development of agency–client relationships over time. An event is something that can be observed and measured and has empirical meaning (Abrams 1982: 191; Dunkerley 1988: 84). Each explored event can act as an 'in-depth case study' within the overall case study. The investigation of several events within one case provides good opportunities for comparison and insight for theory development. Events in a single unit business relationship can be compared through time, and similar events in different unit relationships can be compared in various contextual settings.

As it is laborious, even impossible, to study all the events in a relationship with the same degree of accuracy, I have chosen the major events for closer investigation; in particular those events that according to existing knowledge can be critical to the development of the relationship. As proposed by Van Maanen (1979: 546–7), it may be fruitful to choose critical events to study, since many 'normal' and everyday events come to the surface only when they can be described with reference to some extraordinary event. In practice, the following events were studied more carefully (the number of events studied is shown in parentheses):

1 Initiation of each of the three unit business relationships (3).
2 All assignments in the three unit relationships that amounted to more than FIM 30,000 of invoicing (24). Special attention was paid to the first briefs of each relationship, to more important briefs or in some way exceptional briefs, for example briefs with exceptionally satisfying or unsatisfactory outcomes.
3 Changes of contact persons on both sides (11).
4 The change in the client company's organisation (1).
5 Changes in the client company's marketing strategy (2).
6 The merger of the advertising agency (1).
7 The economic recession (1).

With regard to informants, I chose contact persons of both companies who were in charge of relationship management and contacts with the other party. The main principle followed in choosing informants was that at least two persons from both companies (or unit) were interviewed in connection with each time period (see Figure 4.3). One was to be from the management level of the unit business relationship and the other from the operational level. In some rare cases this principle could not be followed, since there was, in practice, only one person in charge of the business relationship. 'Snowball' tactics, i.e. information from previous informants, were used to find suitable people for the following interviews.

Altogether 36 personal interviews were carried out during the study (see the list of interviews, Appendix 3). In addition to these, several shorter discussions and telephone conversations were conducted to complement data collection. The number of documents investigated

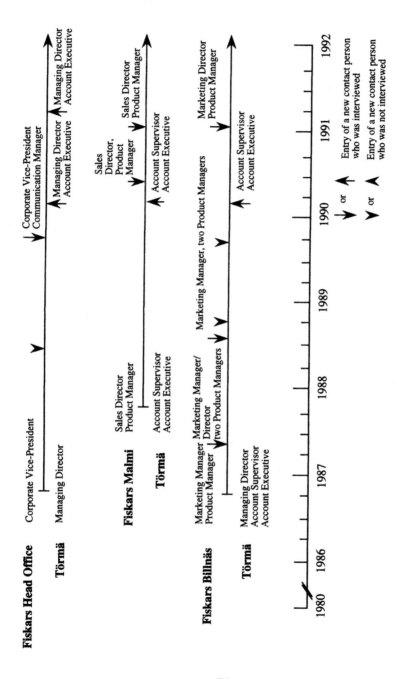

Figure 4.3 Informants from each unit business relationship

79

amounted to several hundred. The interview transcripts and documents have been saved in the case study database (see Appendix 4). Most of the data from original documents have been saved in the form of summaries. Data collection proceeded in six phases (see also Figure 4.1):

1   A pilot study (December 1989–January 1990), included five interviews and data collection from advertising sector publications, statistics and practically oriented literature. The purpose of the pilot study was to assist in problem definition and in the planning of the empirical investigation. The pilot study also provided an opportunity to ensure the practical relevance of the research problem, to become familiar with the field of advertising – its practices and vocabulary – and to practise interviewing. Information was gathered on the following topics: types of advertising agency and competition in the market, major trends in the field in the 1980s, typical length of agency–client relationships, typical problems in the relationships, possible advantages of long-term relationships, situations in which relationships are initiated, maintained and dissolved, and the availability of documents concerning relationships.

2   Access negotiations (April 1990–June 1990), included six interviews and the collection of data about specific advertising agencies and their clients. The objective was to find suitable agency and client parties for the study, and to motivate them to participate by giving information about the study and by getting to know the company representatives personally. Basic information for the study was gathered on agency type (e.g. specialisation, organisation, ownership, company history), clientele type (industry, type of assignments, length of relationship) and about potential client relationships. Negotiations also concerned appropriate data collection methods, available documents, key informants and the companies' requirements for confidentiality and anonymity.

3   The first round of interviews and investigation of documents (June 1990–October 1990) included six interviews, discussions and the collection of briefs, invoices and other documents pertaining to the relationship. The objective of interviews was to build an overall idea of the relationship development and to organise assignments and other major events in chronological order. Documents were used to complement and validate this description. Information was also collected concerning the interacting firms and their development during the 1980s. The real-time collection of data concerning the relationship with Billnäs was started.

4   The second round of interviews and investigation of documents (October 1990–February 1991), included seven interviews, discussions and further collection of documents. The objective of data collection

was to complement and validate the description of the relationship with Billnäs and to extend the study to the relationships with the other two business units of the client company, Malmi and Head Office. Both retrospective and real-time data on these relationships were gathered.

5 The third round of interviews and investigation of documents (June 1991–October 1991) included seven interviews in addition to discussions. The objective was to continue the collection of real-time data about the three unit relationships and to complement and validate the descriptions of the relationships with Malmi and Head Office.

6 Closing negotiations (June 1992–December 1992) included seven personal discussions and six telephone conversations with key informants. The objective was to receive confirmation and feed-back about the case description from the informants and to negotiate for publication rights and use of the data in the future.

4.3.2 Sources of data

In interviewing I used focused or semi-structured interviews. In this method it is usual for the investigator to decide upon a list of themes or general questions for the interviews beforehand, but to leave the exact form or order of the questions unspecified (see Hirsjärvi and Hurme 1991: 35–6). Certain topics were always covered in the interviews. This was achieved not only by question and answer, but by encouraging the informants to 'tell the story' as freely as possible. In some cases the story-telling technique worked fairly well when complemented by deepening and specifying questions. In other cases I had to follow the list of questions that I had separately prepared for each interview more strictly.

Informant-specific interview plans were necessary, since people occupying different posts and with different experience were able to provide information about different things, and also because the questions had to be directed to those periods during which the informant had participated in interactions. Questions for each interview were also formed on the basis of the earlier interviews and information received during them. Appendix 5 provides a list of interview themes and also gives examples of interview questions. The list is by no means complete. It does not include all the topics that were discussed and which affected the construction of the model.

The informants' undirected accounts proved to be useful sources of information about past events and activities, and the contact persons' expectations and evaluations of attraction, trust and commitment to the counterpart. The undirected accounts provided more indications and understanding of factors related to emotions and attitudes than did the more structured and direct questions. On the other hand, the longitudinal research design forced me to collect data about all time periods, which tended to necessitate a more structured interview than was originally planned.

The interviewees were first contacted by phone and then by a letter enclosing a short summary of the research plan and a list of interview themes. During the interviews, I tried to refresh informants' memories by briefly describing what I already knew about the events or by handing out a chart demonstrating relationship events in chronological order. The earlier statements of the interviewee were also used to initiate discussion when the same person was interviewed again. All interviews were tape-recorded, with the permission of the informants.

The investigation of documents involved internal documents that were produced by the case companies and concerned either themselves or their business relationship. The most important data sources were: briefs, invoices, minutes of meetings, a draft of a contract, documents of the correspondence between the parties, notes made by account executives or product managers, account-specific profitability calculations, product brochures, in-house magazines and the companies' annual reports (see Appendix 2).

The role of the documents in the study was twofold. First, they provided a vehicle for triangulation. In order to construct a reliable case description, it was essential to acquire 'competing accounts' of the events and activities and to compare and assess these accounts carefully in order to see whether they supported the same conclusion (see Fielding and Fielding 1986: 23; Pettigrew 1990). In triangulation, one can compare data collected by different methods (technique triangulation) or data collected from different sources (data-source triangulation) (see Fielding and Fielding 1986: 24–5; Hammersley and Atkinson 1989: 198–9). In this study, the data received from documents were contrasted with data received from interviews, and the data from various documents were also compared.

Secondly, documents were also important in complementing the case description, since they provided information about facts that the informants could not remember or express clearly in verbal descriptions. Documents were better data sources than interviews in providing accurate information about the chronological order of events, the specific contents of the briefs, strategies and contracts, the participation of people in inter-actions and the concrete characteristics of the interacting companies.

Data were collected from the documents by copying the original document or by filling in a summary form of it (see Miles and Huberman 1994: 54–5). A document summary form was designed to provide a wide enough range of source critics. It summarised data about when the document was written, who wrote it and to whom, what its main contents were and for what purpose it was written – in other words, what kind of document was involved and to which event or brief it related.

Information was also collected about where and when the document was found. In some cases, summaries were made of several documents at a time. For example, the essential information from invoices was gathered in a summary list and the major events of the advertising agency's history were taken from its annual reports.

4.4 DATA ANALYSIS

The data analysis had two major aims in this study: first, to provide an analytical and reliable description of the selected empirical case and, secondly, to develop a modified and empirically grounded process model of agency–client relationships on the basis of the case description.

The case description is an interpretation of what has happened in the advertising agency–client relationship studied. It has much in common with historical research. Case description is a narration of events in a time sequence which addresses the identification and description of specific events, their antecedents and consequences (cf. Savitt 1980: 53). Interpretation is constructed from a contextual basis (cf. Gillette 1985: 308). The concern is not with reporting exactly when something occurred but in revealing what else occurred at the same time, before or after, and at various contextual levels, in order to show how events came into existence and developed.

Different devices of data display were used to illustrate the flow of events in the business relationships, their connection with contextual factors and with the development of interactions over time (see Miles and Huberman 1994: 11). Various matrices, graphs and charts were produced, not only for illustrative purposes but also for purely analytical needs, for looking for regularities and processual patterns in the empirical data (see Appendix 6).

The second aim, the development of a modified process model, was attained by linking the emerging theoretical ideas that were derived inductively from the case description to the *a priori* model and the most recent debates and findings in the literature (cf. Pettigrew 1990: 280). The case description produced already shows the link between the empirical reality and the conceptual language that seemed appropriate for its description. I took the analysis one step further, however, by discussing the relevance of the concepts in the description of the development process of agency–client relationships, by explicitly describing the indicators of the theoretical concepts, and by delineating the logical and temporal relationships between the theoretical concepts. In other words, the development of a modified process model started with the empirical 'raw data', proceeded to the level of abstract concepts and then to the hypothetical relationships between these concepts.

The process of data analysis proceeded through four partly concurrent

83

activities (cf. Van de Ven 1987: 333–5). The HyperQual program for the Macintosh personal computer was the main tool used in data analysis. First, the primary raw data, i.e. the verbatim interview transcriptions and other notes about interview situations, were saved in the program. Secondly, the data were organised into different files, i.e. into event stacks which allowed chronological order to be established, participant stacks which incorporated information about the interacting companies and specific contact persons, and conceptual stacks where data segments concerning each theoretical concept were gathered. Thirdly, the data segments in the stacks were coded according to the concepts of the *a priori* model and by adding new concepts and respective codes when the data seemed to require it. Finally, connections between the concepts or between empirical phenomena were sought from the data. Pattern codes were used to indicate temporal, logical and explanatory relationships between different concepts and events in the data (see Appendix 7).

Three essential issues regarding the data analysis should be addressed: coding, conceptual tools for mastering dynamics and comparison.

The coding proceeded along the open coding principles suggested by Strauss (1987: 30–2). This means that certain analytical questions were continually posed when coding the transcripts. The transcripts were analysed minutely and the coding was interrupted in order to write theoretical notes on the emerging concepts and the relationships between the concepts. Instead of '*in vivo* codes', which are derived directly from the language of the informants, I preferred to use 'sociologically constructed codes', which are based on a combination of the researcher's scholarly knowledge and knowledge of the substantive field under study (see Strauss 1987: 33–4).

Since the aim of the study was to develop the model, the coding system was kept as flexible as possible. I began first by using a coding list which corresponded to the *a priori* process model, but it soon proved to be inadequate and also partly irrelevant. As data collection and analysis proceeded and new ideas for conceptual categories emerged, the coding list was changed and the text segments coded earlier were recoded accordingly (see the coding list, Appendix 7). During the second round of interviews, I also started to search for core concepts and to clarify the coding system through 'axial coding' (see Strauss 1987: 32). This means that I took each concept separately and studied its dimensions and relationship to other concepts. The validity of the emerging coding list was always evaluated in the subsequent interviews. New data were collected on the basis of earlier data and their preliminary analysis. Gradually, the core concepts and their relationships approached data saturation point, and a logical and consistent process model started to emerge.

A number of conceptual tools were used in the analysis with the purpose of mastering the dynamics of business relationships. Physical time duration, chronological order and simultaneity were used to connect time and events with each other. In addition to these, cycles and break points proved to be useful conceptual tools in the identification of processual patterns. A cycle refers to a recurrent pattern of activities. Break points, on the other hand, represent transitions within and between cycles of activities, and indicate major events or shifts in the development of the phenomenon (see especially Van de Ven 1987: 335)

The role of comparison became accentuated as a method of data analysis. Comparison has been considered a major analytical tool of both qualitative theory-generating research (Glaser and Strauss 1967; Normann 1973: 54) and historical research (Savitt 1980: 53). The entire research strategy of this study was based on comparison. The *a priori* model, its concepts and relationships, were compared with empirical reality in order to see whether the model was relevant and adequate for describing and explaining the development of advertising agency–client relationships, and to see how it should be changed in order to increase its correspondence with this reality.

Comparison was also used in other ways in the study. First, the triangulation of data is based on comparison. Data acquired from internal documents were compared with those from external documents, and both were compared with those gathered from the interviews. Different people's accounts of events were compared. In particular, the accounts given by the agency representatives were contrasted with those provided by the informants from the client company. This was done in order to obtain a reliable description of the relationship development in the past and the present.

Secondly, data from different time periods of each unit relationship were compared to see how the relationship had changed and proceeded. When similar kinds of event were repeated, the data on the events were compared in order to see to what extent the processes, their antecedents and their consequences were similar or different. Temporal comparison was used simply to obtain a better understanding of the process of relationship development.

Thirdly, data from the three unit relationships were also compared. Findings from different contexts increased sensitivity to empirical variation and thus enhanced the robustness of the theoretical conclusions.

4.5 DATA QUALITY

The assessment of the potential biases and inaccuracy of the raw data was an integral part of the data analysis. The reliability and validity of the data were continually assessed during the analysis process, in writing the case description and in drawing theoretical conclusions. In this section I will only touch on the quality of the data collected, discussing, in particular, the weaknesses in retrospective data, interview data and data obtained from documents. The validity of the entire study will be dealt with at the end of the report, in Chapter 7.

With regard to its sources of evidence, the data in a retrospective case study are dependent on the memories of people who participated in the events, as ascertained through interviews and documented materials produced by the participants at that time. In consequence, certain problems are typical of retrospective case studies.

First, the main part of the data is presentational, i.e. the informants' accounts and interpretations of what has happened in the business relationship, not observed facts or behaviour (see Van Maanen 1979). These accounts provide subjective data, which are vulnerable to all sorts of distortions. The data that are stored in the participant's memory about the past have been influenced by his/her opportunity to observe, by selective perception and by personal interpretation. Moreover, with the passage of time, initial perceptions of an event are likely to change because people forget, confuse the chronological order of events, or reinterpret past events each time a new event intervenes and clouds the original interpretation with current dynamics (Simmons 1985: 290).

The only way to overcome these problems was to use the triangulation of evidence in case construction. The subjective accounts and memory loss were corrected and complemented with data from the available documents whenever possible. In many cases a contract, an invoice or an agency brief provided more accurate data than an interview. The dyadic research design also provided opportunities to increase reliability. In accepting data for the case description and for data displays, I used certain decision rules as a measure of reliability (cf. Miles and Huberman 1994: 100). The data were considered reliable if at least two informants or one informant and one document provided confirming evidence. These rules were not, however, used categorically but took into consideration the quality of each piece of evidence (cf. source critics of documents, the experience of interviewees). In some cases only one document could be considered sufficiently credible. For example, the minutes of a meeting were considered reliable evidence of the event, with no informant's reference to the meeting necessary.

Secondly, retrospective data are often inadequate to describe emotions, attitudes, intentions and even overt actions taken by parties to the relationship (Gillette 1985: 314; Golden 1992: 855). Behavioural processes and significant transition periods may remain unrevealed. It proved impossible to ask the informants directly about their expectations, perceived attraction, trust or commitment concerning their counterpart at a specific point in time in the past. It was also difficult to obtain information about institutionalisation and inter-firm adaptation, which appeared to be mostly abstract and to emerge gradually in day-to-day operations. These weaknesses were attenuated by collecting data in real time as well and by encouraging informants to freely describe their personal interpretations of the past.

Both retrospective and real-time data have their strengths and weaknesses (see Pettigrew 1990: 271). The reconstruction of histories over long periods of time makes the identification of continuities, different periods in the relationship development, recurrent cycles and break points possible. Following events in real time on the other hand tends to draw attention to the complexity of real-life events and to minor events and changes in the relationship. The combination of the two types of data can be viewed as a strength from the model-building standpoint. Real-time data added a temporal perspective to my conception of relationship development without which my analysis would have been unrealistically simple. On the other hand, without the retrospective data my understanding of the antecedents of development and the influence of the past on the present and potential future would have remained clearly insufficient. Some temporal distance to the events helped to place them in relation to each other and discern essential changes from incidental and trivial ones.

Certain reliability risks are peculiar to interview data. First, the researcher can be misled, for example because the informants intend to be misleading (Van Maanen 1979: 544). Although emotions, attitudes and accidental events could have considerably influenced the behaviour of the parties to the relationship, they may, nevertheless, explain their behaviour by using rational motives and socially accepted reasons. The informants themselves may also be misled or wrong about matters concerning them, or the researcher can be misled because informants are sometimes totally unaware of certain aspects underlying their own activities (Van Maanen 1979: 545–6). Such risks are particularly relevant in this study, as I have had fairly limited access to the phenomenon. I have not participated in practical decision-making in the industry or in the agency–client relationship studied. As a researcher I have been able to observe reality only from a distance, through documents, interviews and discussions with practitioners.

I tried to take these potential flaws into account in data collection, analysis and evaluation. Those people who were best informed and had direct experience of the unit relationship studied were selected as informants for the study. In addition, competing accounts were acquired from contact persons who had already left the company. This was possible in the relationships with Billnäs and Malmi in particular. Current employees naturally wish to protect their own interests and to act for the benefit of the company. One may form a biased view of reality by relying on either current or previous employees alone.

When evaluating the data I also took into account the informant's experience of advertising agency–client relationships in general. The more experience the informant had of buying or selling advertising services the more I valued the informant's conceptions and descriptions of advertising agency–client relationships in general.

In addition, the informant's experience of the agency–client relationship studied was taken into account. The role of experience was twofold. Those informants who had long experience with the business relationship were more proficient in describing events and changes in relationship development. Those who had only recently joined the company and become acquainted with the business relationship were able, to some extent, to view the relationship from an external standpoint. These informants were also able to see 'normal', routine issues that more experienced informants were not even aware of. The newcomers' previous experience gained from other companies was still fresh in their memory, allowing them to make revealing comparisons concerning institutionalisation and adaptation, for example. I also tried to overcome the difficulty of obtaining information about routine activities by asking blatantly obvious questions about the informant's work and behaviour such as 'What did you do in that situation?' or 'What do you normally do in these kinds of situation?'

Secondly, in the interview method, the researcher is likely to have a strong influence on the reliability and nature of the interview data (see e.g. Miles and Huberman 1994: 265). The dynamics of the interview situation between the interviewer and the interviewee influence the quality of the data in various ways (see especially Hirsjärvi and Hurme 1991). My understanding of the reality of advertising agency–client relationships was formed, to a great extent, during the course of interaction with the informants. My perceptions were dependent on my abilities as an interviewer, the theoretical perspective I used, and the practical experience I had of agency–client relationships. Correspondingly, the attitudes of the informants towards the study and myself as a researcher, and their experience of agency–client relationships and interview situations, influenced my perceptions.

In order to maximise my own sensitivity concerning the quality of the data I documented interview situations, familiarised myself with interview techniques before the data collection and also paid particular attention to the development of my interviewing skills during the data collection process. In order to legitimise my role in the companies, I informed the company representatives about the study and my role as a researcher. In order to facilitate reader assessment of the reliability and validity of the study, I have presented the theoretical framework explicitly in this report. A lack of practical experience can be considered my major weakness as the author of this study. Formal and informal discussions with practitioners in the field helped to overcome the problem to a limited extent.

Documents also posed some reliability risks as sources of data. First, document accessibility formed a practical constraint in the study. The case companies had not produced or saved the documents pertaining to the interaction episodes very systematically. The persons responsible and documentation practice had both changed during the unit relationships. For example, not all the parties' meetings were minuted or otherwise documented, which made it impossible to estimate the frequency of face-to-face communications accurately. The companies were also unwilling to allow me unlimited document access. Some information was provided only on condition that it remained confidential. From the standpoint of the research results this is, however, not a major problem. It was more important to obtain competing accounts to compare with the informants' reports than to obtain a complete sets of records.

Secondly, there is often no way for the researcher to know the meaning attached to a document by the producer (Dunkerley 1988: 88). Documents are always produced by someone for a specific purpose and have to be interpreted correspondingly. Documents also tend to describe a rationalised reality: the reality behind them is much more complicated. I tried to reduce these difficulties by gathering information about the role of different documents in practice and by asking myself the following questions concerning each document (cf. Dunkerley 1988: 88–9). Was the producer of the document able to tell 'the truth'? Was he/she willing to tell 'the truth'? Was the issue accurately reported? In addition to this examination, the reliability of documents was assessed by comparing them with other available sources of data in the process of triangulation.

5

DEVELOPMENT OF THE ADVERTISING AGENCY–CLIENT RELATIONSHIP STUDIED

In this chapter I will first focus on the context of the case relationship and describe the case companies and some major events in their development during 1980–91. The development of the relationship is then examined by separately describing the development of each of the three business relationships between the units of Fiskars Oy Ab and Markkinointi Topitörmä Oy. The descriptions are based on information received in interviews (see Appendix 3) and collected from business publications and internal documents (see Appendix 2).

5.1 THE INTERACTING COMPANIES AND THEIR DEVELOPMENT

5.1.1 The client company – Fiskars Oy Ab

History and background

Fiskars Oy Ab is a multinational corporation based in Finland. It operates in the metal industry with industrial applications in two areas: consumer products and investment products. The Consumer Products Group manufactures high-quality scissors, knives and lawn and garden tools for household and professional use. With regard to investment products, the company manufactures, for example, aluminum boats and hinges for doors and windows. The third area of the company's operations covers real estate business and shareholdings in a number of Finnish companies. The corporate head office is situated in Helsinki.

Fiskars Oy Ab is the oldest industrial enterprise operating in Finland. It started operations as far back as 1649, when a Dutch merchant, Peter Thorwöste, established an ironworks in Fiskars in southern Finland. During the past decade Fiskars has undergone an intense process of internationalisation. At the beginning of the 1980s, Fiskars was still an exporting firm, with only one manufacturing plant abroad. By 1991,

Fiskars had manufacturing plants in nine countries and sales organisations in thirteen, mainly in Western Europe and the United States. The company employed 3,174 people, of whom about two-thirds were employed outside Finland, and the turnover of the corporation amounted to FIM 1,558 million, of which about 80 per cent came from abroad (see Appendix 8). The increase in foreign sales was due to international expansion and the success of the Consumer Products Group in particular. The largest market is North America, which accounted for 32 per cent of the company's turnover in 1991. Finland accounted for 18 per cent, Scandinavia for 16 per cent and other European countries for 29 per cent.

At the time of the study, the Fiskars corporation was managed by the President, Reijo Kaukonen and three Corporate Vice Presidents, Juha Toivola, responsible for finance; Ingmar Lindberg, responsible for administration and real estate, and Wayne G. Fethke, in charge of the Consumer Products Group. The Chairman of the Board of Directors was Göran J. Ehrnrooth.

For the purpose of this study, interest is focused on the company's Consumer Products Group. During the late 1980s and the first half of the 1990s, the Consumer Products Group has developed into the most significant area of the company's operations. Fiskars has achieved a leading position in the scissors market in the United States and Europe. In Finland, Sweden and Italy, knives hold a strong position. In its marketing of garden tools, Fiskars has been most successful in Great Britain and in the Nordic countries.

At the time of the study, the Consumer Products Group was organised into four business groups, which were responsible for their own geographical areas. The Scandinavian Business Group covered all the Nordic countries and Eastern Europe. Most of the business group's activities were concentrated in Finland near the villages of Fiskars and Billnäs, where the company had four manufacturing plants, one for scissors, one for knives, one for long-handled tools for gardening and construction, and one for its own production equipment. The majority of Finnish production was transferred to other units of the Consumer Products Group in Europe and the United States.

Product development and marketing support activities were centred in the marketing unit in Billnäs. The Finnish sales unit was situated in Malmi, Helsinki. Both units were relatively independent profit centres in charge of their own operating profits but jointly responsible for the net profits of the Finnish area.

Development of the company during 1980–91

The economic development of Fiskars stagnated in the early 1980s. This was mainly due to the divestments and rationalisation the company had carried out in its iron and steel industry operations in the late 1970s. In 1983, the centenary year of Fiskars Oy Ab, the company's earnings saw an upturn (see Appendix 8). Internationalisation was the chosen growth strategy for the company.

In 1983–84 several changes occurred in the company's management and in the organisation of the Consumer Products Group. At the beginning of 1984 Göran J. Ehrnrooth was elected Chairman of the Board of Directors and Reijo Kaukonen was appointed Managing Director in his place. The new management placed a high priority on growth and strove to attain it by means of marketing and product development as well as by concentrating the company's resources on selected sectors. A new marketing-oriented approach was introduced into the traditional industrial steel company.

In 1985, Fiskars reformulated its strategy in the following way: 'The company will grow by specialising internationally in select and distinct niche markets, where leadership can be achieved and maintained.' Consumer products were chosen as one of the main areas for future development. The Consumer Products Group strategy aimed at strengthening operations in international markets, especially in Europe and the United States. The group was managed from Finland and its business organised by market area, i.e. *Europe, United States* and *International*.

The increased income of the corporation as well as the recovery of the stock exchange in Finland made new strategic action possible. Within the Consumer Products Group a decision was taken to consolidate the Fiskars brand world-wide. The policy of strengthening the company's own distribution channels and of getting closer to the foreign customers resulted in a series of acquisitions from 1985 to 1989.

The acquisition of Knivman in 1985 gave Fiskars a dominant position in the Swedish market and a leading position as a distributor of kitchen knives and cheese slicers in all the Nordic countries. During 1986, Fiskars entered the US knife and garden tool markets by acquiring the well known knife producer Gerber Legendary Blades in Oregon, and the Wallace Manufacturing Corporation in Connecticut. In 1987, Fiskars participated in establishing a scissors manufacturing plant near Bombay in India. The very same year the company bought the Swedish knife and cheese slicer manufacturer Ergotool Ab.

In 1988, the acquisition of Wilkinson Sword's Home and Garden Division not only strengthened the company's position in Great Britain, but also opened new markets in the Pacific area, in New Zealand. The product range of the group broadened and its distribution channels became stronger in the EC area when Fiskars bought the German company Wilhelm Boos and its 3+ brand in 1988 and Coltellerie Montana s.r.l., the leading Italian knife manufacturer, in 1989. In addition, Gripit became a subsidiary of Fiskars in 1989. Complete ownership was acquired in 1991, when Fiskars also bought Norbergs Redskap Ab, a Swedish manufacturer of hand and garden tools. As a result, Fiskars then manufactured hand and garden tools in Sweden, Denmark, Norway and Finland.

The strong and rapid international growth entailed fundamental changes in Fiskars. The domestic exporting company had become a multinational corporation. Many new and difficult questions had to be answered. How should the expanded Consumer Products Group be managed and organised? Should marketing decision-making be centralised or decentralised? What kind of brand and product range policy should be followed? How should the Fiskars brand be positioned in relation to other well known brands such as Wilkinson and Montana in international markets? In the turbulent years of the second half of the 1980s, the marketing organisation and responsible managers changed frequently.

Since 1987, the company has focused on the consolidation of the acquired business units and the integration of their production, brands, marketing and personnel. The Fiskars brand was to be the premium brand in the Consumer Products Group and, for example, the conversion of the Wilkinson brand into Fiskars was started. For some time the group had derived its income from the famous orange scissors, but it then began investing in new product launches. From 1987–88 the packages of Fiskars branded household products were redesigned and new products, a knife sharpener, Roll-Sharp, and a scissors series, Avanti, were introduced on to the market.

Marketing and marketing materials were planned centrally in Finland. In 1988, however, the Consumer Products Group was reorganised into five operational business groups, each of which was responsible for its own geographical market area and marketing decisions. The management of the group was transferred to the United States, to Wayne Fethke, who had earlier been responsible for the growing American market.

As a result of vigorous internationalisation, Fiskars also experienced considerable growth during the second half of the 1980s (see Appendix 8). From 1986 to 1989 the turnover of the corporation almost doubled, the number of personnel increased by 70 per cent and two-thirds – as against one-third in 1986 – were employed abroad. In 1989, a maximum of 10 per cent of consumer products were sold in Finland. Growth was also rapid in terms of profits (see Appendix 8). Fiskars turned out to be an especially lucrative investment for its shareholders. Demand for its shares was keen, thus allowing the company to increase its share capital by issuing shares each year from 1985 to 1989.

In 1989, the growth trend of earnings shifted into decline. The increase in turnover did not bring in corresponding operational results. Diminishing international demand together with some unprofitable units in the Electronics and Investment Products Groups brought the pre-tax earnings back to mid-1980 levels and led the company to make divestments in these areas.

The capture of new markets through acquisitions also reached a plateau. The efforts of the Consumer Products Group were focused on the consolidation of manufacturing plants, on increasing productivity and on further strengthening the position and distribution of Fiskars branded products. Other brands were developed for lower price categories. In Scandinavia, the focus of marketing efforts shifted from the established markets in household products to the growing market for garden tools. The corporation's major investments were made in this sector.

Instead of making international acquisitions, the Fiskars corporation took a more active role in the companies in which it held shares. In 1990, Fiskars participated in the merger of Oy Wärtsilä Ab and Oy Lohja Ab and in the establishment of the new Metra Group, which further weakened its profitability. In 1991, the deep recession in the Finnish and Swedish markets aggravated the situation and the company incurred losses (see Appendix 8). The Consumer Products Group, on the other hand, was still able to increase its sales and maintain profitability.

In August 1991 the Corporate President, Reijo Kaukonen, resigned. Under his leadership Fiskars had grown into a multinational producer of scissors, knives and garden tools. In other sectors the company's development was weaker. The Managing Director, Stig Stendahl, was appointed President of Fiskars Oy Ab in April 1992. Meanwhile, Juha Toivola acted as Corporate President.

Since 1991, Fiskars has been able to improve its economic results significantly. In 1994, turnover increased to FIM 2,324 million and the company achieved significant profits. In its industrial operations, Fiskars has concentrated even more on consumer products. In 1994, the company decided to dispose of its interests in the production of uninterruptable power supplies and hydraulic access platforms, which had accounted for about a third of the company's turnover. The development of the Consumer Products Group has necessitated the rationalisation of its production plants and brands. Growth has been sought from current markets by making acquisitions and developing new products, as well as by the new business group in fresh geographical market areas.

5.1.2 The advertising agency – Markkinointi Topitörmä Oy

History and background

Markkinointi Topitörmä Oy is a full-service advertising agency operating in Helsinki. It was established in 1963 by Topi Törmä, M.A., together with some other business people. At the time of the study Törmä was a local, independent agency owned by the Advisor Group and independent entrepreneurs Erkki Yrjölä, Managing Director, and Roni Bensky, Deputy Managing Director. Advisor Oy was a holding company, which supported the development of its member companies and provided them with certain administrative services. Together with Törmä, five other agencies then belonged to the group: Turkama & Kumppanit, a full-service advertising agency; Mediapörssi Oy, a media agency; Suomen Tiedotuspalvelu Oy and Oy AC-tiedotus Ab, specialising in PR communications, and Mainoslahja Oy, selling business presents.

During its 28 years of existence (in 1991), Törmä had planned and produced advertising for several international and national brand manufacturers operating in Finland. In addition to package planning and knowledge of marketing channels, Törmä had developed its expertise in product development and advertising research. Törmä's philosophy was proclaimed in its PR materials: 'Anyone can design advertisements. We create long-lasting brands.'

In 1991, Törmä was already among the ten largest advertising agencies in the country. Its gross margin was about FIM 15.7 million and its personnel numbered 43. It provided services to about 50 clients. Raision Yhtymä Oy and Oy Sinebrychoff Ab, which both operate in the food industry, had cooperated with Törmä for more than 20 years. Many of Törmä's accounts concerned imported consumer goods such as the major household appliances of Whirlpool Finland Oy, Lancôme-cosmetics of Finelor Oy and the car marques, Mercedes-Benz and Honda, of Oy Veho Ab. Törmä had also produced export advertisements in cooperation with Fiskars Oy Ab. Although Törmä was clearly oriented towards consumer goods, it also had experience of institutional and services advertising, which it had acquired, for example, with Markkinointi-instituutti and Oy Bore Line Ab. Törmä was organised into three business and planning units, each of which was responsible for its own accounts.

Development of the company during 1980–91

The early 1980s were a period of transition for the company. The ownership of the agency changed radically when the founder members, Topi Törmä, Hellin Törmä and Erik Isomaa, sold their shares, which accounted for 75 per cent, to Advisor Oy Yrjö Turkama. This necessitated far-reaching changes in the agency's management and development. Sampsa Ahokas, who had managed the company since 1977, left operational management and took over the post of Chairman of the Board of Directors. Erkki Yrjölä, the Deputy Managing Director of Turkama & Kumppanit Oy, was appointed the company's Managing Director.

Erkki Yrjölä began the systematic development of the agency. His aim was to make the company grow from a medium-sized agency to one of the ten largest in the field. For this purpose, he introduced a new operating policy for the company in which active marketing, the systematic acquisition of new clients and the development of long-term client relationships played an important role. Some of Erkki Yrjölä's earlier accounts from Turkama & Kumppanit Oy followed him to Törmä. The new policy also included a conscious improvement of the agency's external image and production facilities.

During the following years, 1983–85, the investments in the company's development began to yield good returns. Törmä experienced strong growth in terms of both turnover and gross margin, which resulted in increasing earnings and a stronger market position (see Appendix 9). The favourable economic conditions supported this positive development, which clearly exceeded the industry average. The number of important accounts increased. Personnel turnover remained low, in spite of the large number of people who changed their jobs elsewhere in the industry. Cooperation with the international chain Intermarco-Farner was intensified and concerned, in particular, the acquisition of common Scandinavian clients and the training of Törmä's personnel. In 1985, Intermarco-Farner, which operated in Paris, changed its name to Publicis International.

The year 1986 was a black one for Törmä as well as for the whole advertising industry. Törmä was severely affected by the decline in economic growth and real advertising expenditure. Törmä lost some of its important clients and many others trimmed their advertising accounts. Personnel were reduced from 41 to 34, turnover and gross margin decreased by about 16 per cent and the company incurred losses (see Appendix 9). In addition to existing personal contacts, international partnerships and speculative offers were used to acquire new business and to make up for the losses.

The short recession was succeeded by a new period of growth, which lasted until 1990. During these years Törmä increased its gross margin every year and the owners earned a good yield on their investments. The turnover of personnel increased, however. Around a quarter of Törmä's personnel changed their jobs both in 1988 and in 1989. Some changes also occurred in the management of the company.

During the second half of the 1980s no major changes occurred in Törmä's market position. Törmä remained well known and ranked among the 15 best-known agencies but, on the other hand, did not achieve any particular reputation as a creative, interesting, expensive, pioneering or internationally experienced agency. Törmä's market share remained constant in this period – Törmä continued to rank among the twenty largest advertising agencies in the country (see Appendix 9). Törmä also followed the common trends in the industry with respect to turnover distribution. The share of media advertising continuously decreased while company planning as well as purchases from suppliers increased.

International cooperation in the advertising sector increased considerably in the late 1980s and several acquisitions were made by international advertising agencies in Finland. In 1988, Törmä's partner, Publicis International, took an important step towards establishing a worldwide service network and formed a joint venture with the American company Foote Cone & Belding. Publicis-FCB thus became the largest advertising chain in Europe. Törmä also had a share in this development. A take-over bid mounted by Publicis in 1988 did not succeed and Törmä managed to maintain its independence. Cooperation intensified, especially with the Scandinavian partners of Publicis-FCB, which brought new international clients to the agency.

In 1989, the management of Törmä decided upon concrete measures to turn the company's market share into growth. A medium-sized agency such as Törmä risked becoming too dependent on international partners or on a few large accounts. In order to maintain its independence, to be able to attract big clients and to safeguard objectivity in servicing them, the company wanted to grow. A project for acquiring new business was initiated, which included special personnel training. In September 1990, Törmä acquired its sister company, Markkinointiryhmä Oy Mary, which increased the number of clients from 38 to 50 and the number of personnel from 36 to 46. New clients and new business could not, however, compensate for the paralysing effects of the strong and sudden recession in the Finnish economy. The results of these efforts were not be seen until 1991, when Törmä was one of the few agencies able to increase its gross margin in the sharply declining advertising markets. Törmä succeeded in increasing its market share and ranked among the ten largest advertising agencies in the country.

At the time of writing (in 1994), Törmä was already the fourth largest agency in the country, with a gross margin of FIM 27.4 million. In the first half of the 1990s, strong growth, ownership changes and internationalisation had been characteristic of the agency's development. In the spring of 1992, Advisor Oy went into liquidation and the entire ownership of Törmä passed to the management of the agency. A year later, Törmä finally relinquished its local independence and sold a minority share to its long-term international partner, Publicis-FCB. The importance of international clients to the agency's business and the pressure of international competition have since increased.

5.2 DEVELOPMENT OF THE BUSINESS RELATIONSHIP BETWEEN THE MARKETING UNIT OF FISKARS OY AB AND MARKKINOINTI TOPITÖRMÄ OY

5.2.1 Before the relationship (1980–October 1986)

Situation in the client company and in its marketing function

In 1983, the Fiskars corporation was already an international but primarily export-oriented company. Internationalisation had been an essential feature of the company's development during the previous two decades, but was now adopted as a more purposeful growth strategy for the coming years. In 1985, the strategy was further specified as specialisation in select and distinct niche markets, where leadership could be achieved and maintained. The Consumer Products Group, comprising scissors, knives and lawn and garden tools, was selected as the main area for development efforts.

After several years of poor profitability, the company result improved in 1983. The positive result together with an increased capital supply afforded improved opportunities for the Consumer Products Group to invest in marketing activities. The new management placed a high priority on marketing, product development and customer orientation. In 1984, a marketing unit was established in Billnäs. The purpose of the unit was to provide marketing services and different sales back-up materials to sales units all over Europe. New products were developed and brought to the market by Billnäs. The unit was also responsible for exports and contacts with the European distribution network. Marketing decision-making was concentrated at the corporate head office in Finland.

At the time, Fiskars scissors already had a good position in the Finnish, French and Scandinavian markets. As much as 90 per cent of Fiskars scissors were sold abroad. The awareness of Fiskars brand name was high, but the name was connected only with the familiar orange scissors. The Consumer Products Group practically lived off this single product, which had been on the market since 1967. Sales of knives and other consumer products were low, both in Finland and internationally. The newly renovated production plants in Billnäs and Fiskars had increased production capacity and thus created pressure within the company to increase marketing effort.

Under these circumstances, the company decided to invest in developing a global Fiskars brand. Its purpose was to serve as an umbrella brand under which other consumer products – including new ones – could be positioned. This meant that the brand needed a consistent appearance. Packaging and other marketing materials should conform to a consistent visual line in all European countries. Since Fiskars itself did not have enough qualified personnel, an advertising agency had to be contracted for the task (see Figure 5.1[a]).[1]

Situation at the personnel level

The management team behind the new ideas comprised Reijo Kaukonen (joined 1981 and appointed Managing Director in 1984), Kimmo Käyhkö (Consumer Products, Europe), Wayne Fethke (Consumer Products, United States), Ingmar Lindberg (extensive experience in advertising, appointed Director of Corporate Development in 1985) and Thommy Hellberg (employed by Consumer Products in 1985, first in charge of lawn and garden tools but soon appointed Marketing Manager for scissors).

While still working in the advertising business, as a Deputy Managing Director of Oy AC-mainos Ab, Ingmar Lindberg had got to know Erkki Yrjölä, the Managing Director of Markkinointi Topitörmä. As a consequence of the take-over of AC-mainos by the Advisor Group, Törmä and AC-mainos became sister companies. Over a period of time the men became good friends (Figure 5.1[b]). In 1983, because of a disagreement about ownership, Ingmar Lindberg left AC-mainos, where he had been in charge of the Fiskars accounts, and started at another advertising agency, Anderson & Lembke Oy. Some of the Fiskars accounts were transferred there with him.

Situation in the client company's advertising agency relationships

At the beginning of the 1980s, Fiskars was cooperating with Womena Oy and Oy Liikemainonta-McCann. When the strategy of internationalisation became more pronounced, it was necessary to organise an agency contest for the company's international consumer products account. Womena, with its domestic orientation, declined to take part; McCann and AC-mainos, on the other hand, did participate. AC-mainos won the account and from 1982 onwards designed packaging and materials for Fiskars consumer products.

The situation changed when Ingmar Lindberg was appointed to Fiskars in 1985. The agency relationships had to be reconsidered. Cooperation with AC-mainos had not been entirely satisfactory; the agency charged too much and contact persons changed frequently. Moreover, it did not seem suitable for the future needs of the Consumer Products Group. The agency had to be able to execute the new plans for a consistent appearance for Fiskars branded products and to act as a coordinating agency in Europe. As a friend of Erkki Yrjölä, the Managing Director of Törmä, Ingmar Lindberg informed him of the situation and about the company's need for a new agency (Figure 5.1[c]).

The Marketing Manager, Thommy Hellberg, had recently begun to

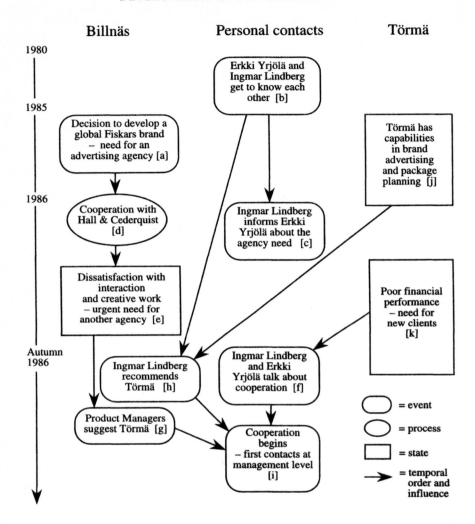

Figure 5.1 The flow of events before the relationship between Billnäs and Törmä began

work in scissors marketing at the marketing unit in Billnäs. He had hardly any experience of advertising agencies and was badly in need of an executor for the new brand strategy. Several agencies were interested in the Fiskars account. Interplan Oy marketed itself actively, but the period of cooperation remained short. For Törmä the situation was delicate. Several units of Fiskars were already doing business with AC-mainos, Törmä's sister company. This made it impossible for Törmä to market itself actively to Fiskars. Finally, Ingmar Lindberg recommended Hall

& Cederquist, a big Swedish agency of good reputation. Contacts were initiated (Figure 5.1[d]), but it soon turned out to be too laborious, time-consuming and expensive to travel back and forth to Stockholm. The marketing team in Billnäs was not satisfied with either the working process or the creative proposals for the packaging design (Figure 5.1[e]). Thommy Hellberg, who had never thought highly of advertising people and their working style, became more and more sceptical about cooperation with Hall & Cederquist and about advertising agencies in general.

After a year of trial and error, an urgent need for a satisfying agency relationship was apparent (Figure 5.1[e]). The agency changes had required time and personnel effort from the marketing team in Billnäs. These experiences, together with the strategic importance and urgency of the task, contributed to the team's willingness to engage in collaboration with one capable and cooperative agency.

Events leading to the start of the initial phase

In autumn 1986, Ingmar Lindberg informed Erkki Yrjölä about the new turn of events in the marketing unit's agency situation (Figure 5.1[f]). Erkki Yrjölä and Ingmar Lindberg both enjoyed hunting and were in the habit of elk-hunting together at weekends. At the same time the Product Managers, Hans Carlander and Pekka Havupalo, collected information about potential agencies in Billnäs. On the basis of referrals from business acquaintances and other information, they finally suggested Törmä (Figure 5.1[g]). When Ingmar Lindberg also recommended Törmä (Figure 5.1[h]), the choice was clear. Ingmar Lindberg and Thommy Hellberg visited Törmä, where Erkki Yrjölä presented the agency (Figure 5.1[i]).

Törmä was an attractive alternative for Fiskars in many ways. First of all Ingmar Lindberg knew Erkki Yrjölä and trusted him and his potential to manage the Fiskars account in the best possible way. Törmä was known for its capabilities and long experience in packaging design and in advertising high-quality branded products (Figure 5.1[j]). Moreover, Thommy Hellberg, who did not know Törmä beforehand was ready to try it. At least day-to-day cooperation seemed easier with Törmä, whose office was situated in Helsinki.

From Törmä's point of view, Fiskars was especially attractive. Fiskars was the kind of company that many agencies sought as a client. Fiskars scissors were said to be the best known Finnish brand abroad. It would be a challenge for the agency and its creative personnel to plan advertising materials for such a successful and international company. Moreover, the Fiskars brand was the oldest Finnish consumer brand, which fitted in well with the agency's capabilities as well as with its philosophy. In addition, the whole year had been very unfavourable financially for Törmä. The agency had lost important clients and was now actively seeking new ones to replace the losses (Figure 5.1[k]). Fiskars, as an expanding company, had particular potential from the standpoint of future business.

Summary of the pre-relationship phase

The prerequisites for starting a business relationship were fulfilled between Billnäs and Törmä. First, Billnäs had a clear and urgent need for advertising services, which Törmä could provide. The decision to invest in a global Fiskars brand and the lack of human resources created this need. Following the unsuccessful trial of the Swedish agency, the need for a new agency was already urgent. Törmä was known for its capabilities in brand advertising and packaging design. Its poor financial performance in 1986 made it actively seek new clients.

Secondly, the personal awareness of potential partners, their needs, goals and resources also played an important role in the initiation of the business relationship. The favourable personal relationship at top management level considerably affected its establishment. Referrals from business acquaintances and friends were also used in agency selection. Thirdly, the parties had a common interest in building a business relationship; they could both expect to benefit from the relationship. Fiskars with its old and well known consumer brand fitted well with the philosophy of Törmä of creating long-lasting brands. Future business possibilities with the internationally expanding Fiskars were promising. The new brand strategy of Billnäs required uniform visual planning and, preferably, a stable agency relationship. The attraction felt between the parties was strong, particularly that of Törmä for Billnäs.

5.2.2 Starting the relationship (November 1986–March 1987)

First assignments and interaction

After the initial contacts, the marketing unit of Fiskars invited Törmä's team to Billnäs for the first briefing in November, 1986 (Figure 5.2[a]). Törmä had appointed the Account Executive, Gunnel Falck, the Art Director, Reijo Rautanen and the Copywriter, Curt Boucht, to the account team. Deputy Managing Director Roni Bensky acted as account supervisor. At Billnäs the Product Managers, Hans Carlander and Pekka Havupalo, handled the operational contacts. The first assignment concerned the design of a sales folder for dealers, in which different types of Fiskars scissors and point-of-sale materials would be presented. The schedule was tight. The team was informed that same kind of folder pages for knives and some tools would be produced later.

The tasks were not economically very significant but included plenty of

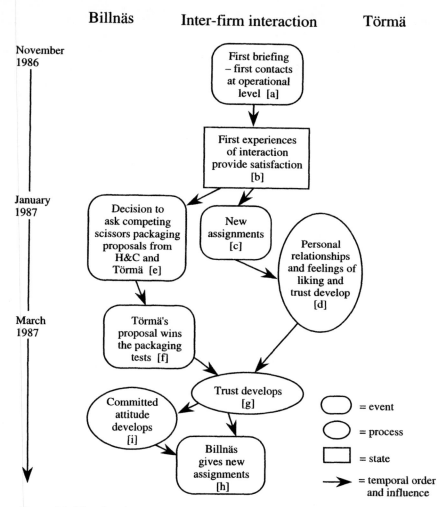

Figure 5.2 The development of the relationship between Billnäs and Törmä in the initial phase

planning work – for example, the design of display materials that had to be ready before the sales folder could be completed. The contact persons on both sides formed an initial picture of their counterparts. The account team learned about the client's products, packaging and display requirements. The client's marketing team, on the other hand, gained their first experience of the agency's creative work. The first impressions of interactions were positive on both sides (Figure 5.2[b]). An urgent assignment concerning a brochure for the French market was given out a couple of days later. Another brief, the design of sales folder pages for knives and a knife promotion, was offered within six weeks (Figure 5.2[c]). Gunnel Falck and Hans Carlander were in contact almost every day.

It was clear that Thommy Hellberg and his marketing team wanted to test Törmä and its team. They wanted to be convinced of their abilities and compatibility with the people in Billnäs. The relationship was strategically important for Billnäs. They needed an agency for a longer period and for important international tasks. At the same time as he was starting the business relationship with Törmä, Thommy Hellberg still continued cooperation with Hall & Cederquist. He could not be sure of Törmä's suitability until he had some experience of the agency. Quite soon, however, he became convinced of Törmä's creative ideas and style of working (Figure 5.2[b]). In particular, acquaintance with Roni Bensky, and his willingness to act in the client's interests, increased Thommy Hellberg's trust in Törmä (Figure 5.2[d]). There was considerable pressure for the new scissors packaging to be designed as soon as possible and so a decision was made to request proposals from both Hall & Cederquist and Törmä in order to determine which of the two agencies should receive the assignment and any future briefs (Figure 5.2[e]).

The account team was excited about the opportunity offered to it. Both agencies drafted their own proposals for scissors packaging, which was then tested in France and in Finland. Törmä's proposal, which was primarily designed by the Art Director, Reijo Rautanen, was successful both at home and abroad (Figure 5.2[f]). Hall & Cederquist were naturally disappointed with the result. They would have liked to keep the Fiskars consumer products account. They sought to challenge Törmä's proposal with another of their own, which was then tested, but Törmä won again.

This was a turning point in the business relationship. When the packaging had been tested, cooperation started at full speed. The personnel at Billnäs were now convinced of Törmä's capabilities and trusted the agency enough to give it new assignments (Figure 5.2[g] and [h]). During the six-month period of collaboration the personnel at Billnäs and Törmä's team discovered that they got on well with each other. Törmä had won the marketing team's confidence and secured its position as the Fiskars Consumer Products Group number one agency for the time being (Figure 5.2[i]). However, at this point in time, Törmä's team had yet to realise how important a client Fiskars would become.

Summary of the initial phase

The perceived outcomes of interactions were satisfying, which created trust between the parties. During these interactions personal relationships also had the opportunity to develop. The contact people liked each other and felt that they could have confidence in each other's capabilities and reliability. The client's emerging trust in the agency led to the briefing of new assignments. Moreover, attitudinal commitment developed early in the relationship, which was partly due to the client's urgent need for advertising services. Billnäs promised new assignments even at the beginning of the relationship. Both corporate management and contact staff at Billnäs participated in the selection of Törmä, which strengthened committed attitudes.

The success of Törmä in the package test against Hall & Cederquist was a critical event in the relationship. Business exchange intensified considerably thereafter. The dissolution of the relationship with Hall & Cederquist was a clear sign of the willingness of Billnäs to maintain and develop its relationship with Törmä. Attitudinal commitment between the parties became stronger.

5.2.3 Growing relationship (April 1987–March 1988)

New assignments and interaction in 1987

After the package tests in spring 1987, Billnäs's new assignments provided the account team with ample work. Three important assignments were given within a month (see Figure 5.3[a]). Törmä had to plan and produce new packaging for the entire range of scissors, which was called the Fiskars Classic series. Some weeks later, Billnäs presented a brief for the packaging design of cheese slicers and cheese knives. The goal was to create a new Fiskars Cheese series, which was composed of a range of products formerly belonging to Swedish Knivman Ab, which was bought in 1985. With regard to external appearance, the packaging was to have a strong visual connection with the Classic concept. These two assignments were neither economically significant nor broad in scope compared with the third one, which concerned a totally new product – a knife sharpener – the Fiskars Roll-Sharp (see Figure 5.3[b]).

Roll-Sharp was the first complete marketing concept Törmä was to plan for Billnäs. The task was to plan a name, packaging, leaflets, point-of-sale materials, an in-store video and a TV commercial – all for international use. The Marketing Manager, Thommy Hellberg, had earlier given a hint of a new and particularly promising product that would soon be launched. The team awaited the brief eagerly and was actually quite disappointed when it heard that the product in question was a knife sharpener. It was always a pleasure to create advertising for good-quality products which offered consumers a clear benefit, and which would also provide opportunities for impressive advertising. But a knife sharpener! It hardly corresponded to the team's idea of a promising product. The build-up of the team's expectations resulted in disappointment.

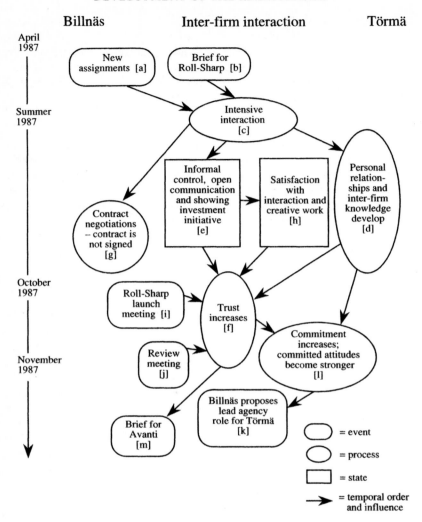

Figure 5.3 The development of the relationship between Billnäs and Törmä in the growth phase

Nevertheless, the disappointment was soon turned into enthusiastic teamwork. Thommy Hellberg was convinced that the sharpener would be a success and quickly encouraged the team with his trust in the team's know-how. The product characteristics were, actually, quite convincing. The product was unique on the market, it was efficient, long-lasting and easy to handle. The strategic goal of the Consumer Products Group was to transfer the positive reputation of Fiskars scissors to other products with the help of a uniform style for all products sold under the Fiskars brand name. Roll-Sharp was planned as a spearhead product that would increase the sales of all products in the same family. This necessitated a uniform appearance consistent with Classic scissors and heavy advertising. The price was set relatively low to make the product available to every household. The aim was to move rapidly to automated mass production, to achieve high sales volumes and to pay off the advertising investments within a short time period. Not everybody was easily convinced, however. Scissors and knives were the main products of the company, and if the aim was to strengthen the market position of knives, the launching of a successful knife sharpener did not seem logical. The risk of declining knife sales was evident.

There was an enormous amount of work to do during the rest of that year, 1987 (Figure 5.3[c]). In addition to the Roll-Sharp project and the package redesign projects for Classic scissors and the Cheese series, there were yet other assignments going on at the same time. A new knife concept, Function, was created for young urban consumers. The products were in fact the old Fiskars knives slightly modified in accordance with contemporary trends in interior design. Billnäs had taken on a new Product Manager, René Österman, in the spring and he was now in charge of the Function project. The other two Product Managers, Hans Carlander and Pekka Havupalo, worked primarily with packaging redesign and the Roll-Sharp project. Pekka Havupalo handled the European contacts and Hans Carlander the logistics side of package planning and production.

Communication between Törmä and Billnäs was very intensive during the rest of the year (Figure 5.4). Thommy Hellberg initiated the projects, which meant that he was always present at the briefings. He also visited Törmä and Roni Bensky, the Account Supervisor, every now and then and informed him of the internal situation of the Consumer Products Group, of new product concepts and also of conflicting views among marketing management inside the corporation. Roni Bensky had won Thommy Hellberg's confidence both professionally and personally. The confidential information exchanged between them helped Bensky to understand the decisions of the client firm better and to manage the account team at Törmä appropriately. Personal relationships and inter-firm knowledge developed (Figure 5.3[d]). The favourable personal relationship between the Managing Director, Erkki Yrjölä, and Deputy Managing Director, Ingmar Lindberg, was also used as a link to reconcile differences in views and to keep the projects going.

The other members of the marketing team, Hans Carlander, Pekka Havupalo and René Österman handled the operational contacts with Törmä. Meetings with the Account Executive, Gunnel Falck, or other members of Törmä's team were frequent, and fax, telephone and post were used almost daily. People from management and operational levels met each other in different gatherings almost weekly (see Figure 5.5).

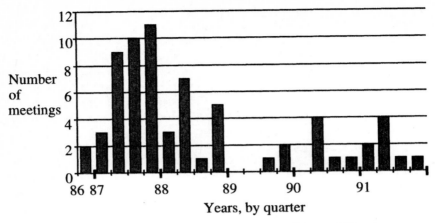

Figure 5.4 Documented meetings between Billnäs and Törmä

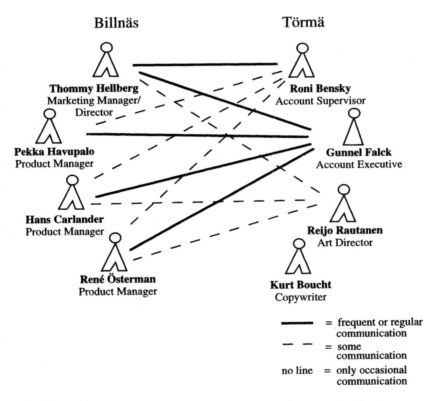

Figure 5.5 The interacting teams and the frequency of communication between Billnäs and Törmä in the growth phase

The style of interaction was informal and characterised by trust rather than formal control (Figure 5.3[e]). Briefs were relatively open and often verbal. The responsible team members from Billnäs as well as from Törmä were usually present. No strict budget limitations were imposed at the beginning but the schedules were usually tight. Thommy Hellberg, who was not an expert in advertising himself, put his effort into clarifying communication concerning assignment goals and maintaining a continuous dialogue between the parties. When the goals were clear and accepted by everyone, he could trust that the teams of Törmä and Billnäs would do their best to execute the task. An unwritten rule of professional trust characterised the cooperation. The team members considered each other professionals, which meant that there was no need to intervene in the minor details of one another's work. During the projects, meetings were organised to maintain open and critical discussion and to check that everything was in line with the stated goals (Figure 5.3[e]). Törmä's team welcomed this way of working. The team members were especially happy about the trust and respect Thommy Hellberg showed in them and their professional abilities. It increased the attractiveness of Billnäs as a client and motivated the team to work harder for it. Mutual trust was gained in the process (Figure 5.3[f]).

The distribution of work between the parties was soon regularised. Billnäs delivered translations of leaflets and package texts in the appropriate languages for Törmä and coordinated and informed Törmä about orders for leaflets and other materials from the subsidiary companies. Hans Carlander at Billnäs ordered the printing and production of display and sales packaging, and Törmä negotiated and ordered the printing of leaflets and some point-of-sale materials. It was also clear that all the materials were planned for international markets, not just for Finland. This meant that the preferences and feedback from the subsidiaries of the Consumer Products Group had to be taken into account. Billnäs took care of product planning, possible product tests and marketing research. Törmä took part in the strategy discussion by making proposals concerning the marketing concepts. The personnel resources of Törmä and their know-how were also used by the client. Roni Bensky presented the Roll-Sharp campaign as well as the subsequent Avanti scissors campaign to the representatives of the European subsidiaries at the launch meetings.

In the summer of 1987, when cooperation began to be economically significant, Törmä suggested a written contract to Billnäs (Figure 5.3[g]). Törmä was accustomed to draw up written contracts with its clients for the purpose of determining the main guidelines of collaboration concerning invoicing, relations with competitors, copyright questions and the termination of the relationship. The contract was negotiated at the highest level between Ingmar Lindberg from the corporate head office and Erkki Yrjölä from Törmä but was never signed. In the organisation of the Consumer Products Group at that time it was not clear who should sign the contract or whom it would bind. Ingmar Lindberg, who knew the advertising business well, did not feel the need for a written contract. From his point of view it was a useless document, because it could always be evaded. In order for things to run smoothly, favourable personal relationships, which were based on reciprocal trust, were much more important. On this point Erkki Yrjölä concurred and the contract remained unsigned (Figure 5.3[g]). The draft was, however, followed in practice. In invoicing, for example, the proposed fee system was established as a standard between the parties.

Satisfaction with the business relationship

The cooperation proceeded smoothly from both parties' point of view (see Figure 5.3[h]). The style of interaction was informal, open, and demonstrated investment initiative, and people got on well with each other. It was teamwork at its best. Billnäs was an easy client for Törmä in the sense that the team did not have to invest much effort in studying the client's field, competitors, products or logistics. There were several assignments in progress and new ones were to be expected, which meant that Törmä's team and managers did not have to actively seek new business opportunities. On the contrary, the account was growing so quickly that the adequacy of the agency's personnel resources had to be considered. Many members of Törmä's team were ready to say that Billnäs was an ideal client.

The feeling of satisfaction was mutual. For the marketing team at Billnäs it was wonderful to see how the briefs stimulated the account team and how it was able to deliver good work and also meet the tight deadlines set for the projects. The team was especially pleased with the Art Director, Reijo Rautanen's, creative performance. His visual planning and packaging proposals were often accepted unaltered (Figure 5.3[h]).

The cooperation with Törmä was closer than anything the Billnäs team had experienced before. At the time, they not only bought the necessary advertising services but showed investment initiative in cooperation and also activated the agency to do so. Törmä's role was to serve as an extension of the marketing team. Both parties also felt that they were learning from each other, which made cooperation rewarding. The account team was able to improve its capabilities and achieved good results in creative planning. For the Billnäs marketing organisation the new brand strategy and cooperation with Törmä meant a gradual shift from traditional product based marketing to a genuine customer and market orientation. Softer values and appeals became part of the client's marketing communication. Both parties considered the relationship beneficial, thus forming a sound basis for a cooperative orientation on both sides.

At the end of 1987, after the intensive period of work and the launch meeting of Roll-Sharp for the European subsidiaries (Figure 5.3[i]), the parties felt a need for a joint review meeting (see Figure 5.3[j]). Mutual satisfaction with the business relationship was affirmed. However, some problems were also discussed. The invoices for the projects had aroused some discussion during the year, which was, however, regarded as a normal point of disagreement in any agency relationship rather than something especially critical. Billnäs also criticised the texts and Törmä the tight timetables set for the projects. Both parties agreed that there had been too many contact people in Billnäs and that from then on they would name project leaders, who would maintain contact with the Account Executive, Gunnel Falck.

Situation in the business relationship at the end of 1987

During 1987, the relationship between Billnäs and Törmä had developed into intensive and economically significant cooperation. The somewhat insignificant exchange at the beginning of the year had gradually developed and increased both in economic value and in strategic importance (see Figure 5.6).

The package redesign of the Fiskars branded household products was an important and long-term project for Billnäs. The launch of Roll-Sharp was a major project as well. As it was a strategically important spearhead product, Billnäs had focused and planned to continue focusing considerable sums of money on advertising. In consequence, the relationship with Billnäs had become significant for Törmä as well. At the end of 1987, Billnäs ranked among the ten largest accounts of the agency. The parties had gradually become more committed to each other (Figure 5.3[l]). The solid international reputation of the Fiskars brand and the account's growth potential increased the attractiveness of the client. Achievements with the Fiskars Consumer Products Group could be cited as credentials in Törmä's own marketing – in raising Törmä's status in the eyes of its then current and prospective clients. As a multinational company Fiskars also provided opportunities for Törmä and its personnel to develop their capabilities in the area of international marketing communication, packaging design and international agency cooperation.

At that time, the Fiskars Consumer Products Group was divided into three divisions: Europe, the United States and International. Marketing operations were managed centrally from Finland. When the time came for Roll-Sharp to be launched on the European market the position of Törmä as the company's main advertising agency came under discussion. Törmä had successfully planned marketing materials for the whole of Europe. From the point of view of the Fiskars Consumer Products Group it now seemed economically efficient and appropriate to apply these

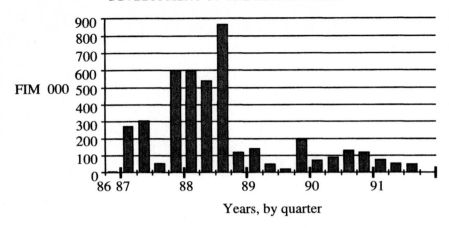

Figure 5.6 Invoicing between Billnäs and Törmä, adjusted by the wholesale
price index (1985 = 100)

materials directly to Finnish, Scandinavian and other European markets
as well. The European consumer products division needed a lead agency
to coordinate international marketing communication and to maintain
contact with the local advertising agencies in the foreign markets.

As the designer of the new visual line for Fiskars branded consumer
products, Törmä had achieved an important position as the single agency
for Billnäs. In November 1987 the Billnäs team presented the idea of using
Törmä as the lead agency for the Fiskars brand (Figure 5.3[k]). This was,
of course, a fascinating proposal for Törmä, but also a great challenge that
would require investments on the agency's part. The proposal was a
display of trust by Billnäs and a sign of the company's willingness to
commit itself more strongly to cooperation with Törmä (see Figure 5.3[l]).
The performance of both companies' teams, the compatible style of interaction as well as the favourable personal relationships at all levels from
top management to operational level had built up trust between the
parties. The economic and strategic importance of their business relationship meant that they had already become more dependent on each other.
Billnäs's proposal was a sign of the company's willingness to continue the
relationship with an even closer degree of cooperation in the future.

New assignments and interaction in 1988

Cooperation between Törmä and the marketing unit at Billnäs continued
to be intensive during the end of 1987 and the first half of 1988. There
were regularly four or five assignments in progress at the same time,
some at the briefing phase, some at the phase of planning or production
and some at the invoicing phase (see Figures 5.6 and 5.7). The planning

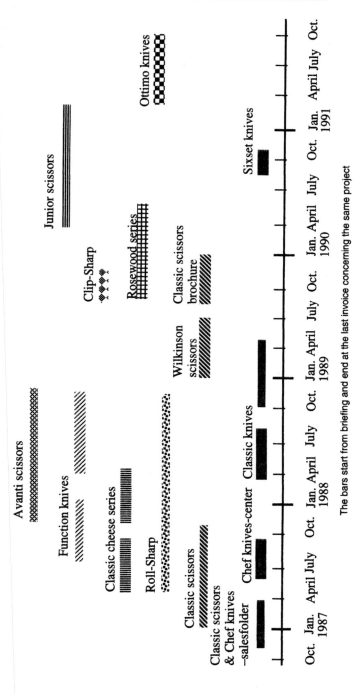

Figure 5.7 Assignments executed between Billnäs and Törmä.

113

and production of marketing materials for the international launches of the Roll-Sharp and Fiskars Cheese concepts were well under way in the winter of 1988. Diminishing knife sales also required marketing activity; Billnäs presented a brief for a package redesign for Chef knives, which were to be renamed Classic knives. The packaging layout had to be streamlined with the new Fiskars Classic look, and consumer and trade brochures had to be planned accordingly. On completion of this project, Billnäs would have a complete product family designed with the same look. In addition, the new Function knife concept needed marketing materials. Billnäs presented a brief for the planning of a TV commercial and other consumer advertising materials but soon suspended the project. Sales of the Function knife did not develop as expected, and the concept was later withdrawn.

The most important and innovative of the assignments handed out was, however, the new scissors series, about which Billnäs hastened to brief Törmä immediately after the European launch meeting of Roll-Sharp (Figure 5.3[m]). Törmä's task was to develop a marketing concept in the same way as it had done for Roll-Sharp. According to the established strategy, the concept should be clearly connected with the Fiskars brand visually but at the same time differentiated from the Classic concept. Instead of positioning by hard criteria (e.g. durability, quality, ergonomy) which had been used in scissors marketing up until that point, the new Fiskars Avanti scissors were positioned by soft life-style criteria and planned to appeal to young consumers. The earlier projects, the creation of the Classic concept and the launching of Roll-Sharp and Function knives, had paved the way for a new kind of marketing approach in the client organisation. The marketing unit also considered the possibility of introducing other products under the same concept umbrella later on.

The launch of Avanti scissors was, strategically, an extremely important event for the Fiskars Consumer Products Group. Since 1967, the Classic orange scissors had been the only scissors series marketed by Fiskars and now another series was to be launched. In spite of the different target markets, it was uncertain to what extent the products would cannibalise each other's markets and to what extent Avanti would manage to create new demand or to capture competitors' market share. The two hot topics concerning marketing strategy were the brand name of the series and its price. Törmä took an active part in this strategic discussion and argued for higher pricing than for the Classic series and for the use of Avanti as the key name of the series instead of Fiskars. The client's aim, on the other hand, was to price Avanti clearly lower than the Classic series in order to gain new markets. The results of price elasticity research also supported this option. Moreover, Billnäs wanted to support the number one brand, Fiskars, in this launch. In the final decision, Törmä had to adapt to the client's point of view. The price was set somewhat lower than for Classic scissors and the product was named Fiskars Avanti.

Communication between Törmä and Billnäs was intensive and open. The planning of Avanti advanced smoothly, and the goals of the task under discussion were clarified for both teams. At the end of the year, some changes had taken place in the companies' personnel. The Marketing Manager, Thommy Hellberg, was promoted to the position of Marketing Director of the European scissors division. At the beginning of the Avanti assignment a new copywriter, Pirjo Virola, was appointed to Törmä's account team and in the spring of 1988 the Product Manager, Pekka Havupalo, left Billnäs. These changes did not significantly affect co-operation, which continued in a positive atmosphere.

Satisfaction with the results of the projects

From Billnäs's point of view, the two most important indicators of the success or failure of agency cooperation were the subsidiaries' acceptance of the concepts created, and the sales figures in different markets. The new Classic look was regarded as a long-term investment, which was expected to produce returns within a period of five to ten years. The final success of the concept could therefore be assessed only over a period of time. The first results from the markets were, however, considered as important signs of the concept's viability. These results began to be visible during the spring of 1988, when the packaging of the new scissors was introduced on to European markets. The concept was commended by the subsidiary companies and was well received among consumers. Roll-Sharp advertisements supported the sales of scissors as well; the strategy of brand extension seemed to work. As a result of the increased demand, Fiskars decided to extend the scissors factory in Billnäs in 1987. The success of the package redesign was especially rewarding not only for the marketing team responsible at Billnäs but also for Törmä's creative team (see Figure 5.8).

The results of the Roll-Sharp project were also positive. The product itself was well received among the European subsidiaries and it received design awards in several countries. The entire marketing concept seemed to work well. The sales volumes exceeded expectations in many countries and the launch costs were already covered during 1988, which was considered a remarkable achievement. The Roll-Sharp project was developing into a success story in the business relationship between Törmä and Billnäs. It deepened positive feelings and trust on both sides and was remembered several years later as the most successful project of all. The good results consolidated Törmä's position as the single advertising agency used for Fiskars branded consumer products. The materials for the cheaper brands such as the Swedish Knivman and later the German 3+ were planned in-house.

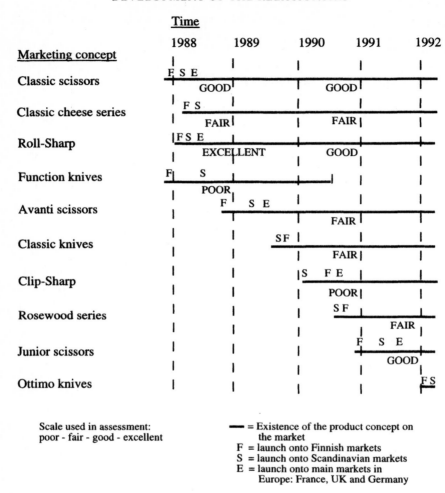

Figure 5.8 The success of the marketing concepts over time, as assessed by the client

The cooperation of the European subsidiaries and sales companies was decisive for the success of the new concepts. In this respect, Roll-Sharp was not easy to launch. The European subsidiary and sales companies were not as experienced in launching new products and they had difficulties in accepting an outside authority deciding and controlling their marketing activities. The centralised decision-making system was still taking its first steps in quickly expanding international corporation. The marketing materials and TV commercials planned by Törmä were not accepted as such in all countries. What was 'not invented here' seemed not worth using. Swedish managers were especially critical, whereas the English and French were more accepting. For the European consumer products division this meant that the cost savings expected from the internationally standardised marketing materials were not fully achieved. Furthermore, the basis of the proposed lead agency idea began to break down when the European subsidiaries became increasingly unwilling to integrate their marketing.

The feedback from the international network of the Consumer Products Group was diverse and affected the relationship between Törmä and Billnäs in many ways. The European subsidiaries expressed their own requirements for the planned materials, for example for the Roll-Sharp package design. As a result, new packaging for several markets was planned with Törmä during 1988 and 1989. Criticism of high prices in Finland and information about cheaper film producers and other service suppliers spread easily to Billnäs from the Swedish subsidiary company. As a result, the in-store video for the Cheese series was filmed in Sweden, where the copywriter Curt Boucht supervised the production.

Summary of the growth phase

This phase was characterised by intensive and increasing interactions, in terms of business exchange, communication, coordination and adaptations. Unwritten rules and other social norms began to be established during interaction. Both parties were satisfied with the business relationship. This was due to the open and informal style of interaction, to investment initiative and to the high standard of creative work and good sales results achieved by the products in their markets. The parties' interaction orientation was cooperative. During interactions, the anticipated common interests materialised into benefits for both parties. Törmä in particular realised the potential of this business relationship, which strengthened its attraction to the client. Attraction was strong on both sides, especially because of favourable personal relationships, involving interpersonal appeal and trust.

Trust developed along with the strengthening personal relationships, open communication and satisfaction with assignment outcomes. The result of the contract negotiations showed that interpersonal trust was more highly valued in the relationship than a formal contract. Strongly committed attitudes also characterised the relation; the lead agency proposal of Billnäs was a concrete manifestation of this. In intensive cooperation, the parties gradually formed a behavioural commitment towards each other. Törmä had achieved an important position as the single agency used by Billnäs. Billnäs, for its part, had developed into one of the ten largest clients of the agency. Billnäs had also committed itself to the new brand strategy and its implementation, which bound it to

Törmä even more firmly. Favourable personal relationships and invest-ment in inter-firm knowledge also increased commitment.

5.2.4 Troubled relationship (April 1988–December 1988)

Situation in the client company

The three years from 1985 to 1988 were a period of strong and rapid growth for the Fiskars corporation and its Consumer Products Group. Growth was achieved primarily through the numerous international acquisitions made by the Consumer Products Group. As a consequence, power conflicts and disagreements inside the group began to become more serious. The head office and subsidiaries, as well as the group's two divisions – the United States and Europe – had different opinions regarding the management of the group. The organisation of product development and the issue of centralised versus decentralised marketing decision-making divided the opinions of the group's management (see Figure 5.9[a]).

During the winter and spring of 1988, the turbulent internal situation at Fiskars began to influence the relationship between Törmä and Billnäs to a greater extent. The conflicts within the corporation sometimes disturbed cooperation. Törmä's team could not always understand the decisions of the Consumer Products Group, particularly as it did not know enough about the situation inside the client company. The favourable personal relationships at top management and management level turned out to be valuable channels of information in these circumstances. It also became clear that the German subsidiary would not accept Törmä's international partner, Publicis-FCB, as a cooperator but decided to use the local subsidiary of McCann in Germany instead. The European sales units and subsidiary companies showed their willingness to be independent in marketing decision-making (Figure 5.9[b]). As a result, the reorganisation of the group seemed inevitable and supporters of the lead agency idea inside the Fiskars corporation dwindled.

In this uncertain situation, Törmä's management felt it too risky to invest in the lead agency position offered, even though it would have been extremely interested in improving the agency's capabilities in inter-national assignments (Figure 5.9[c] and [d]). Billnäs was regarded as an attractive client, particularly as it was expected to offer opportunities to develop the international capabilities of the agency. The prerequisites for acting as a coordinating agency seemed, however, to be disappearing. With regard to the Billnäs team, its expectations in this respect did not materialise. Thommy Hellberg, who had particularly supported the lead agency idea, was disappointed at Törmä's passivity when it came to marketing itself as a potential lead agency and concretely working to achieve it. In addition to the parties, individual managers had conflicting interests in the matter.

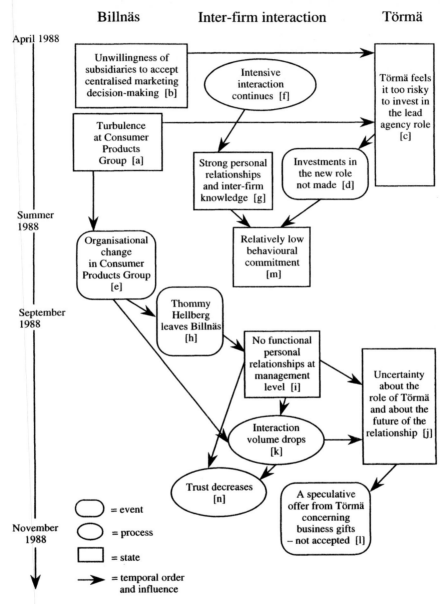

Figure 5.9 The development of the relationship between Billnäs and Törmä in the troubled phase

During the spring of 1988, the Consumer Products Group finally achieved a decentralised organisation structure (Figure 5.9[e]). The previous three divisions, Europe, the United States and International, were replaced by five independent business groups responsible for their own areas: two groups for the United States, Canada and the Pacific Area, one for Scandinavia and Finland, one for Continental Europe and one for Great Britain. The product group-based organisation in Europe, including the knife and scissors divisions, was dissolved and a market area-oriented organisation was established instead. Each group made independent decisions about product range, marketing plans and marketing materials. It also became clear that the leadership of the Consumer Products Group would be transferred to the United States, to the manager of the American consumer products division, Wayne Fethke. This meant extensive changes in the organisation and management style of the Consumer Products Group.

Situation at the personnel level and in interaction

Meanwhile, interaction continued to be intensive between Billnäs and Törmä (Figure 5.9[f]). The planning of Avanti was finished in a friendly atmosphere at the operational level. The teams very much enjoyed working together. After the European launch meeting of Avanti in June 1988, the parties were keen to celebrate the success of seven months' rewarding cooperation by dining together. Personal relationships between the teams became stronger (Figure 5.9[g]).

As a result of organisational restructuring, however, certain changes occurred in the personnel of Billnäs. The Marketing Director, Thommy Hellberg, left the company in September 1988 (Figure 5.9[h]) and Jan Ekwall from Sweden was appointed Marketing Director of Scandinavian Business Group. At the same time, the Product Manager, René Österman, was promoted to the position of Marketing Manager. The Product Manager, Tuija Rajamäki, who had joined Billnäs earlier in the summer took charge of the operational contacts with Törmä and communication with the company's European subsidiaries. Hans Carlander continued as Product Manager and handled contacts with production and the logistics of consumer products.

These turbulent times also affected the assignments in progress. The packaging redesign of Chef knives was suspended in the summer of 1988 because the future of the concept was unclear. Fiskars had plans to move its knife production to Sweden. Moreover, the need for a Classic knife series was questioned, as the company had already taken on a large knife range as a result of the acquisitions it had made. There were also disagreements about the packaging design itself. As a result, the packaging was partly redesigned and photographed again in the autumn. At that time, Billnäs also gave Törmä two other assignments, which were, however, cancelled at an early stage.

The organisational change in the Fiskars Consumer Products Group marked a major turning point for the relationship between Törmä and Billnäs. Until then, Thommy Hellberg had been in active contact with Roni Bensky, the Account Supervisor, and informed him about new assignments as well as about the situation inside the Consumer Products Group. In autumn 1988, Törmä's team suddenly found itself without functional information channels to the management of Billnäs (Figure 5.9[i]). For a time, the team was unaware of who was actually in charge of the international marketing of consumer products and ignorant of the future plans of Billnäs concerning concept design and international advertising. There was considerable uncertainty about the future of the relationship (Figure 5.9[j]).

Interaction between the parties decreased (Figure 5.9[k]). Törmä had based its future expectations on the frequent assignments and considerable invoicing of the past. Its expectations turned out to be completely wrong. Until then, the client had acted progressively and demonstrated market leadership by being visible and by introducing new products on to the markets. All this activity seemed to have ceased. The 18 months' period of cooperation had been exceptionally active from Billnäs's standpoint. As the team members saw it, Billnäs had completed several years' work during these months. Törmä was not aware of this, as it had no previous experience of Billnäs. In addition, Fiskars had become an important client for Törmä. In 1988, it was the agency's third largest client in terms of gross margin. The shrinkage or complete loss of the Fiskars accounts would have cut a significant portion of Törmä's activities and earnings.

In this situation, Törmä's team felt an urgent need to develop new contacts with the client company and to get new assignments in order to maintain the client relationship. Fiskars had already established a marketing unit for business gifts in Sweden, in Eskilstuna, in 1986, and now had plans to intensify Nordic marketing cooperation in this growing area. The brochures and direct marketing materials for business gifts did not at that time have a uniform look in the Nordic countries. Törmä's team felt they did not communicate the high quality of Fiskars products. This was considered a good opportunity to put Törmä's expertise at the client's disposal. Roni Bensky contacted Stig Måtar, the Director of the Scandinavian Business Group, with the purpose of suggesting new business and also in order to clarify the confused situation in the relationship between Törmä and Billnäs (Figure 5.9[l]).

As a result of this meeting, Törmä was brought into contact with Jan-Henrik Clevberger, the Managing Director of Fiskars Kundservice Ab in Sweden, who was also in charge of business gift operations. Contacts were established and basic information about the business gift markets exchanged in a meeting at Törmä in November 1988. Jan-Henrik Clevberger was not, however, interested in collaboration. Törmä's attempt to extend the Fiskars relationship did not succeed (Figure 5.9[l]).

The events of the previous year had shown that neither of the parties was ready to invest seriously in the relationship. The plans for more committed cooperation at the international level did not materialise (Figure 5.9[m]). Towards the end of the year, Törmä's position as Fiskars's advertising agency became increasingly unclear. The parties' trust in each other and in future exchanges decreased considerably. The awareness of being one of Törmä's largest clients in terms of gross margin annoyed the managers of the business group, who themselves had not been in personal contact with Törmä. They began to ask whether Billnäs had paid too much for Törmä's services in previous years. In the absence of a long-term personal relationship at managerial level distrust easily gained ground in the business relationship (Figure 5.9[n]).

Summary of the troubled phase

The developments at company level created a troubled phase in the business relationship. The strong international growth and the resulting power conflicts within the client company created uncertainty both at Billnäs and in its relationship with Törmä. Törmä had to decide whether it would invest in the lead agency position that was available. The turbulent situation at Fiskars made it hesitate and finally the whole idea was rejected when Fiskars decided to reorganise the Consumer Products Group.

The change in the organisation turned out to be a critical event in the relationship between Törmä and Billnäs. It caused various rapid and unexpected changes in the relationship. Business exchange diminished, the types of assignment changed and some assignments were even terminated. The management changes at Billnäs increased the effect of the organisational shake-out. Törmä's team lost its favourable personal relationships with Billnäs's management, which increased uncertainty concerning the future of the relationship. The role of Törmä had changed, but Törmä did not know what its future role in the relationship would be, nor did it now have information about the client's international activities. Personal relationships, the level of inter-firm knowledge and the role of the agency had weakened. Törmä tried to change the situation by forming new personal relationships with management and by proposing new business to the client. It could not persuade the new management, however. Attraction decreased and the bond of trust between the parties weakened.

5.2.5 Declining relationship (January 1989–February 1990)

Situation in the business relationship at the beginning of 1989

The troubled phase and the organisational change in the client corporation were followed by a period of low interaction in the business relationship. The number of briefs and their economic value decreased considerably, as did the intensity of communication between the parties (see Figure 5.4 and Figure 5.6, pp. 108, 112). Only a few meetings were organised and the number of people meeting each other diminished on both sides. Moreover, the types of assignment changed: the briefs were not so broad or innovative as before. In comparison with the previous two years' intensive interaction the relationship languished (Figure 5.10[a]).

Billnäs's need for advertising agency services changed primarily because of the organisational change. The independent European units made independent decisions about marketing and advertising. Billnäs still developed new products and concepts but it no longer had the authority to make decisions regarding European market launches. Its business area was restricted to the Nordic countries and even there it had to sell its ideas to the local business units. After the two important product launches and the implementation of the new look for Fiskars branded consumer products, Billnäs no longer needed Törmä's services to the same extent. For Billnäs, these projects had been long-term, seldom undertaken investments. Instead of new investments it was time for Billnäs to put more effort into the international distribution and marketing of the existing concepts.

From the beginning of the relationship, Törmä's role had been to plan and produce marketing materials for international use. Törmä then had to adapt to the changed situation in the client corporation and accept a minor role as an agency for the Finnish and Scandinavian market area (Figure 5.10[b]). As a result of the organisational change there remained a difference between the parties' expectations concerning Törmä's role that lasted for some time.

As a result of the organisational change, Törmä also lost direct personal contacts in the management of the Consumer Products Group. Personal relationships between the parties weakened and narrowed (Figure 5.10[c]). The new management was situated in the United States, much too far from Finland. Without such contacts Törmä had insufficient information about the client's international activities on which it could have based its proposals concerning consumer product advertising. Törmä had lost the investment initiative opportunity at international level. Moreover, the nature of collaboration with Billnäs changed to project-based cooperation, in which long-term marketing or advertising strategies were no longer discussed (Figure 5.10[d]).

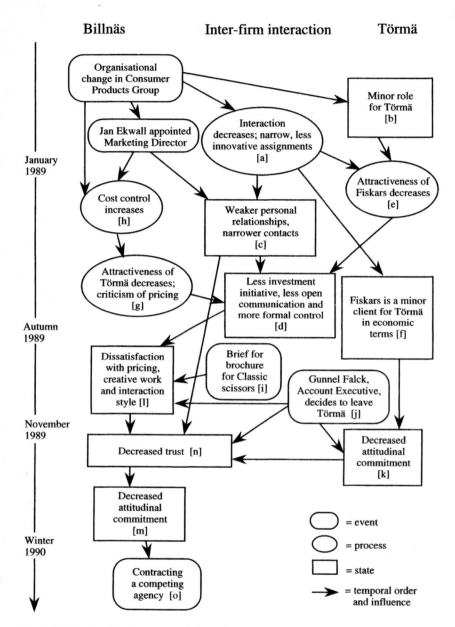

Figure 5.10 The development of the relationship between Billnäs and Törmä in the decline phase

The minor role, the diminishing account and the changed nature of assignments and the client's marketing activities were disappointments for Törmä's team. Billnäs had lost a large part of its attractiveness as Törmä's client (Figure 5.10[e]). The account team realised that it was not worth putting special effort into the business relationship, and in order to ensure the agency's profitability had to direct their investment initiative towards other clients (Figure 5.10[d]). The decrease in the number of assignments and their economic significance also meant that the position of Fiskars as Törmä's client changed markedly. The economic significance of the Fiskars accounts (both Billnäs and Malmi) decreased considerably (Figure 5.10[f]). In 1988, Fiskars was still one of the three largest clients, but by 1989 no longer ranked even amongst the ten largest, either in terms of gross margin or in terms of turnover.

Moreover, the perceived attractiveness of Törmä as a business partner had decreased slightly at Billnäs (Figure 5.10[g]). The need to cooperate with Törmä had simply become less. The new company policies and the preferences of the new directors also influenced the attractiveness of Törmä. The new American management had introduced new operating policies into the Consumer Products Group. Wayne Fethke set tight, short-term profit goals for all functional areas of the group. More control was exerted over production and marketing costs, and external competition was welcomed when choosing suppliers of traded products and marketing services (Figure 5.10[h]). The management also placed more emphasis on dealers as target markets instead of the final consumer.

As a result of the increased cost control within the company, critical voices were raised against Törmä's prices. The new Marketing Director, Jan Ekwall, who had experience of Swedish agencies, considered Törmä expensive and started to issue invoice limits for creative planning in new briefs (Figure 5.10[d]). Jan Ekwall was not personally committed to using Törmä, but accepted the agency, as the company's earlier choice. He lived in Sweden and was seldom in contact with Törmä's team (Figure 5.10[c]). At Billnäs, the Product Managers Hans Carlander and Tuija Rajamäki oversaw cooperation to an increasing extent (see Figure 5.11).

Assignments

In spite of the temporary decline in activity and effort on both sides, cooperation continued. International briefs did not immediately end. During the previous spring, Fiskars had bought the Wilkinson Sword Home and Garden Division in England, together with the right to use the famous Wilkinson brand name for some years. During the winter and spring of 1989, Fiskars had new scissors packaging designed for the German market with a connected brand name 'Classic Wilkinson Sword by Fiskars.' The aim was to gradually convert the scissors brand name from Wilkinson to Fiskars Classic.

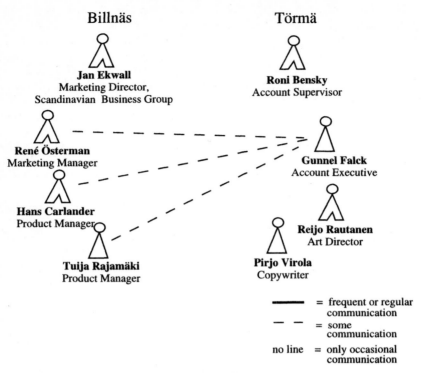

Figure 5.11 The interacting teams and the frequency of communication between Billnäs and Törmä in the decline phase (up to summer 1989)

After the quiet summer season, Billnäs gave Törmä three small briefs (see Figure 5.7, p. 113). Jan Ekwall had left Billnäs during the summer and the Managing Director, Jan-Henrik Clevberger from Eskilstuna, succeeded him as Marketing Director of the Scandinavian Business Group. As the Roll-Sharp knife sharpener had sold well, the new management decided to extend the product range with a completely new product, a scissors sharpener, Clip-Sharp. Törmä's role in the project, however, was modest. The team designed a trade brochure and packaging in accordance with the Roll-Sharp look. In the Roll-Sharp and Avanti projects, Törmä had invited tenders from printing houses and supervised the printing of brochures but in the new project the marketing team at Billnäs handled such matters. The distribution of work between the parties had changed, assignments become narrower.

The other assignment dealt with a packaging redesign and a brand conversion for the old Knivman knives, which had lost their position in the distribution channels of the Nordic countries. Törmä's team, which had remained unchanged during the last two years, successfully designed a new look for the knives, which were named Fiskars-Rosewood. The appearance had to differ clearly from the Classic look of the Fiskars brand. From an economic and strategic standpoint the project was small.

The third task, the planning of a new brochure for Classic scissors, was not as successful (Figure 5.10[i]). Gunnel Falck had decided to seek another position (Figure 5.10[j]) and Reijo Rautanen was engaged in other projects. Their efforts were directed elsewhere, a fact that was remarked upon by the marketing team of Billnäs and interpreted as decreased attitudinal commitment (Figure 5.10[k]). The standard of creative work did not please the client, and new versions of the brochure were required. Negative feedback also exacerbated problems in personal relationships for a while. Dissatisfaction with the creative design and the account team's style of interaction increased among the personnel at Billnäs (Figure 5.10[l]).

Situation in the business relationship at the end of 1989

During 1989, the relationship between Törmä and Billnäs acquired a different dimension. Both parties had gradually become committed to the relationship but they did not put much effort into it in practice (Figure 5.10[k] and [m]). Billnäs had committed itself to the new look of the Fiskars brand in marketing and, as far as this brand was concerned, it would have been too troublesome to change the agency and start all over again with a new partner. Part of the marketing team had been cooperating with Törmä almost from the beginning and were willing to continue the relationship.

The parties had common experiences of past successful cooperation that inspired mutual confidence in each other's ability. Everybody remembered the Roll-Sharp project, which continued to bring good returns to the Consumer Products Group. The personal relationships within the teams were also favourable and the parties knew each other well, even though information about marketing strategies, future assignments and internal events at Fiskars was not exchanged as openly as before. Neither the organisational change nor the two changes of Marketing Director had been able to destroy the companies' confidence in the profitability of their relationship, although the confidence had weakened (Figure 5.10[n]).

During 1989 dissatisfaction towards Törmä had increased, however, and the client's attitude began to tend towards a more competitive orientation. The number of people in the marketing team dissatisfied with the pricing or creative results of Törmä's work was increasing. Moreover, Gunnel Falck's departure from Törmä was a great disappointment to the team. Certain people began to think that Törmä were taking the Fiskars relationship for granted and wanted to see some competition. As a result,

Billnäs started to seek a less expensive alternative for the advertising needs of other brands such as Knivman and 3+, which had a lower price premium. On the basis of referrals, a small advertising agency, Adastra Markkinointiviestintä Oy, was contracted to design a campaign package for Avanti scissors in the spring of 1990 (Figure 5.10[o]). The sales volumes of Avanti scissors had not been satisfactory and new ideas were required for their promotion.

Summary of the decline phase

The effects of the organisational change manifested themselves significantly during this phase. Business exchange diminished; assignments became less important, less innovative and narrower in scope. The intensity of communications and the number of people involved in interaction decreased accordingly. The style of interaction developed towards more formal control and reserved communication. The degree of investment initiative was low. Dissatisfaction with the business relationship increased on both sides. Billnäs was especially critical of Törmä's pricing and the poorer standard of its creative work. Törmä was dissatisfied with the changed style of interaction and particularly disappointed with the minor position it now occupied with respect to Billnäs and its international intra-group nets. The future of the relationship did not seem as attractive as before.

The decreased attitudinal commitment, dissatisfaction with the creative output for a smaller assignment and the change of account executive all weakened the trust Billnäs had earlier felt towards Törmä. Dissatisfaction and weakened trust also diminished Billnäs's willingness to maintain the relationship. Billnäs contracted a competing agency in addition to Törmä. In practice, the parties were committed to each other by many ties formed during their interactions. A common history and the client's commitment to the Fiskars brand kept the parties together.

5.2.6 Growing relationship (March 1990–December 1990)

Interaction

The winter of 1990 began to show some signs of recovery in the business relationship. Since Gunnel Falck had left Törmä in November 1989, Roni Bensky once more played an increasing part in cooperation (see Figure 5.12[a]). In February, a new Account Executive, Marja Tuunanen, joined Törmä and started to work with the Fiskars accounts (Figure 5.12[b]).

The attractiveness of Billnäs as a client increased again when Tuija Rajamäki informed Roni Bensky of the company's decision to launch a new product, children's scissors (Figure 5.12[c] and [d]). It was the first

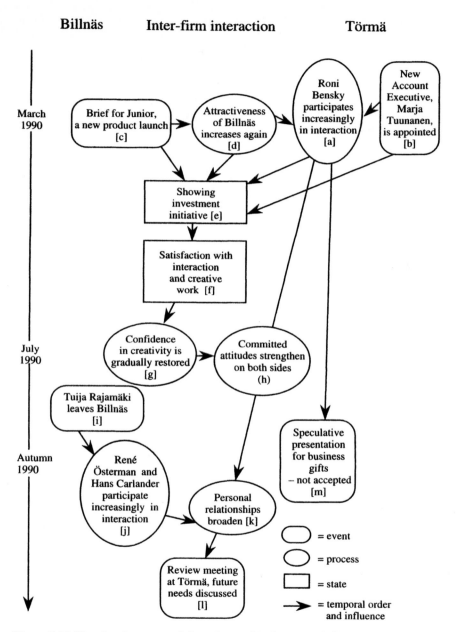

Figure 5.12 The development of the relationship between Billnäs and Törmä in the new growth phase

large project since the launch of Avanti scissors in 1988. Törmä's task was to plan the concept: packaging, leaflet, display and PR materials, but no advertising materials at that time. The task was innovative. It dealt with a new product, the first scissors that were ergonomically designed especially for children, including the left-handed child. The concept also required a fresh look that would appeal to children. Both the Törmä account team and the Billnäs marketing team were motivated and ready to invest time and ideas in the project (Figure 5.12[e]).

During the project, communication between the parties became intensive again (see Figure 5.4). On Törmä's side, the old team of Roni Bensky, Reijo Rautanen and Pirjo Virola continued, with the addition of the new member, Account Executive Marja Tuunanen. On the client's side, Tuija Rajamäki, the Product Manager, was particularly active in cooperation. Hans Carlander and René Österman were also in contact with Törmä. Jan-Henrik Clevberger, on the other hand, had never been actively in touch with the account team. He put a high priority on effective selling and paid less attention to advertising issues (see Figure 5.13).

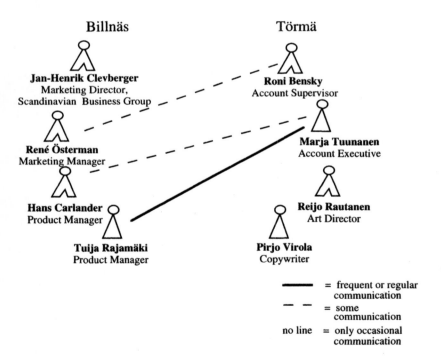

Figure 5.13 The interacting teams and the frequency of communication between Billnäs and Törmä in the new growth phase (up to July 1990)

Cooperation proceeded smoothly. Tuija Rajamäki and Marja Tuunanen appreciated each other's competence and style of running things. The brief was clear and inspired Törmä's team to make suggestions of its own about the marketing concept. They proposed the name Fiskars Junior for the product and a direct marketing campaign to promote its sales. Both ideas were accepted by the marketing team at Billnäs. The team also liked the creative design and so did the Nordic subsidiary companies to whom the concept was presented in August 1990 (see Figure 5.12[f]).

In spite of the change of account executive, working practices remained almost the same. Reijo Rautanen and Roni Bensky, who had worked with the client from the very beginning, conveyed the essential information about the common history and accustomed habits to Marja Tuunanen. The unwritten contract established during the previous years was already taken for granted. Neither was there any need to discuss the invoicing system, the right to use planned materials internationally, the composition of the account team, or any working practices. The distribution of work in the execution of the assignments had also become established. Billnäs took care of the necessary translations and increasingly handled planned materials production such as the printing of leaflets. Törmä, on the other hand, produced the original texts in Finnish and concentrated on the creative development of the concepts.

The fresh visual ideas of Reijo Rautanen and the team's investment initiative restored the marketing team's confidence in Törmä's creativity (see Figure 5.12[g]). Their willingness to continue cooperation and to invest in the business relationship strengthened correspondingly (Figure 5.12[h]). René Österman and Hans Carlander began to take a more active role in cooperation again, after the departure in July of Tuija Rajamäki, who had been almost solely in charge of agency communication (Figure 5.12[i] and [j]). The web of personal relationships broadened in the business relationship (Figure 5.12[k]). In August, a meeting was organised to discuss the current state of affairs as well as Billnäs's plans for the coming spring [Figure 5.12[l]). The garden tools business was developing into an important product line within the business group and Billnäs also informed Törmä of the possibility of advertising services being needed in this area. During the autumn season, the direct marketing campaign for Fiskars Junior and packaging for a block of six knives were planned in cooperation with Törmä.

Contact with the corporate head office also intensified when Fiskars decided to brief Törmä about the planning for company image advertising in the winter of 1990. The activated contacts with the top management of Fiskars presented Törmä with a good opportunity to try to extend the cooperation to other units of the client corporation. The earlier idea of planning new materials for Fiskars's business gift marketing in Scandinavia was brought up again. This time Törmä's team prepared a concrete proposal, including direct marketing materials, a leaflet and a leaflet folder, and presented it both to Vice President Ingmar Lindberg and to the marketing team of Billnäs. Subsequently, Törmä's management was informed that the person responsible for business gift marketing was Jan-Henrik Clevberger. In September, he visited Törmä, where the proposal was presented to him. The idea pleased the Billnäs team but did not convince Jan-Henrik Clevberger, who turned down the offer of cooperation for a second time (Figure 5.12[m]).

Satisfaction with the results of the projects

In 1989–90, Fiskars Consumer Products Group had launched Classic knives on the Nordic market and Avanti scissors and the scissors sharpener Clip-Sharp on both the Nordic and the European markets. Gradually, the marketing team at Billnäs formed some idea of how consumers from different geographical areas had received the concepts designed by Törmä. Until that time, the marketing team had been fairly reticent in giving information about the sales volume of its products or about the value of different markets, but was now ready to let Törmä know the current sales figures. Törmä's team appreciated this information, even though it was brought home to them that their estimate of the size of the business had been optimistic.

The redesign of the old Chef knives into the Classic Fiskars look had succeeded fairly well (see Figure 5.7, p. 113). Sales of Classic scissors had also been satisfactory, even though the volume had decreased in 1990. The Classic concept had proved to be a good investment for the Consumer Products Group over the years, and it still seemed viable. Quite obviously it was one of the best concepts that Törmä had created. The attention of Billnäs was already shifting, however, to the creation of completely new concepts and visual solutions both for old products and for potential new products.

During 1991, there was a clear but expected decrease in the sales of Roll-Sharp. During its three years on the market the product proved to be a major source of revenue for the Consumer Products Group and was clearly the best single product concept designed by Törmä. Avanti scissors, on the other hand, did not sell as expected either in the Nordic countries or elsewhere in Europe. The new marketing concept had not been realistic enough. Packaging redesign and changes in pricing policy were considered in several markets, including the Scandinavian Business Group. The expansion of the product group by the addition of Clip-Sharp had not been successful either. The expected spin-off from using the Fiskars Classic look did not work in this case. Consumers were not enthusiastic about the innovation, although it had received several design awards.

Summary of the growth phase

The growth phase involved a slight increase in business exchange. The increase in communication and the strengthening of the relationship in terms of attraction, trust and attitudinal commitment were, however, even more important. They were partly due to the new, innovative assignment and the change of contact persons, which also fostered investment initiative in the relationship. More people became involved in interaction and the attitudes of the parties became more committed. The inertia and the declining trend developed into more enthusiastic cooperation again; satisfaction with the relationship increased. The client's trust in the agency's capabilities was restored and information was exchanged more openly than before.

5.2.7 Declining relationship (January 1991–)

Situation in the client company

At the end of 1990, the Finnish economy drifted into a deep recession. The growth of the Fiskars corporation had also ceased and profitability was declining (see Figure 5.14[a]). In spite of this, the Consumer Products Group continued to increase its sales and its profitability also remained good. The management of the group placed a strong emphasis on cost effectiveness, which also created pressure to increase the work done in-house (Figure 5.14[b]). Billnäs invested in computer software and personnel resources in order to design packaging and leaflets itself. It was also able to use the services of an internal design group from the United States. As a result, Billnäs did not need a full-service advertising agency as much as before.

During 1990, the focus of activities in the Scandinavian Business Group had shifted from household products to garden tools (Figure 5.14[c]). In 1989, Fiskars had acquired a Norwegian garden tool company, Gripit, and consequently become an important manufacturer of garden tools in the Finnish and Scandinavian markets. Garden tools thus became a major part of the group's business, and the consolidation of Gripit required considerable internal effort. During 1990, the marketing staff of Billnäs had been considering how to produce advertising materials for this product group in the most economic way. Eventually, they decided to manage with the marketing unit's own resources and to supplement them with the services of smaller agencies. Törmä was also considered but was thought to be too large and expensive for the purpose. The marketing of garden tools fell within the sphere of the traditional ironmongery business, where marketing efforts were focused on trade partners and employees were not used to customer-oriented thinking or to the use of

133

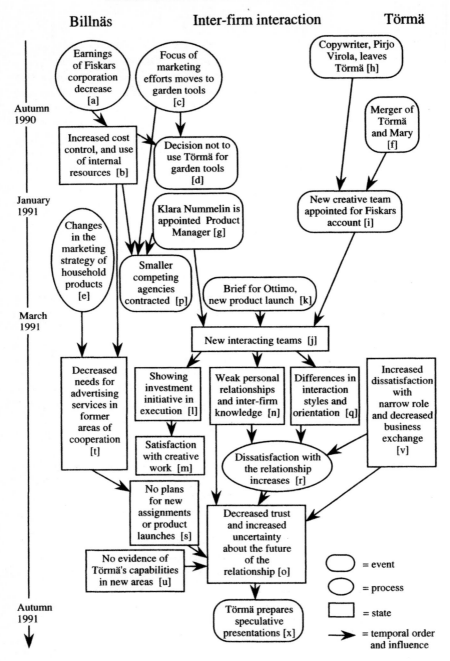

Figure 5.14 The development of the relationship between Billnäs and Törmä in the new decline phase

full-service advertising agencies. Furthermore, it seemed reasonable to select a new partner for garden tools, which formed a separate product group and required a different marketing approach (Figure 5.14[d]).

The acquisitions of foreign competitors, well known trade marks and new market areas stabilised with regard to household products during 1990 and 1991. Effort was focused on the consolidation of the companies acquired, on strengthening sales forces and on improving the visual presentation of the existing Fiskars products in retail outlets. In addition, competitive action was planned against the producers of low-priced and low-quality products, who had increased their share of the scissors market in Europe (Figure 5.14[e]). Since 1990, Billnäs had already produced and marketed low-priced scissors under brand names other than Fiskars. The gross margins of these products did not allow heavy advertising investment or the use of full-service agencies. Packaging and other marketing materials were planned in-house, instead.

Situation in the advertising agency

In September 1990, Törmä's policy of growth and the increasing financial problems of Advisor Oy led to the acquisition of Markkinointiryhmä Oy Mary, the sister agency from the Advisor Group (Figure 5.14[f]). Through this acquisition, Törmä expanded its area of expertise to services advertising and grew to rank among the ten largest advertising agencies in Finland. Törmä was organised into three business and planning units, and the old teams of Törmä and Mary were merged.

The depression in the Finnish economy also affected Törmä's earnings, which after three years of positive development declined. In spite of the merger, the company's turnover and gross margin remained at the previous year's level. Neither the increased number of accounts nor the new business could compensate for the cuts in advertising made by the majority of clients. However, in relation to many other agencies, Törmä seemed to be succeeding well in the struggle against recession.

Interaction and situation at the personnel level

At the end of 1990 and the beginning of 1991, a series of changes occurred in the interacting teams (see Figure 5.15). Early in 1991, René Österman succeeded Jan-Henrik Clevberger as Marketing Director of the Scandinavian Business Group. Klara Nummelin was appointed Product Manager for household products taking the place of Tuija Rajamäki, who had left the company the previous summer (Figure 5.14[g]). At the same time, Hans Carlander, who had been involved from the beginning, started to work with traded garden tools and so was no longer in contact with Törmä.

135

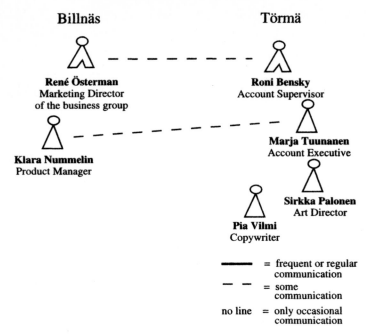

Figure 5.15 The interacting teams and the frequency of communication between Billnäs and Törmä in the new decline phase

Since the summer of 1990, Törmä's team had managed without a permanent copywriter, as Pirjo Virola had left the agency in June (Figure 5.14[h]). Finally, the merger of Mary and Törmä brought a new copywriter, Pia Vilmi, to the account team. The regrouping of Törmä's teams also meant another change for the team. Reijo Rautanen, the renowned designer of the Fiskars Classic look, moved to another team and was succeeded by a new Art Director, Sirkka Palonen (Figure 5.14[i]). With the exception of the Marketing Director, René Österman, and the Account Supervisor, Roni Bensky, the interacting teams changed completely (Figure 5.14[j]).

After the acquisition of the Italian knife manufacturer, Coltellerie Montana s.r.l., in 1989, the launch of Montana knives on the Scandinavian market became a reality for Billnäs. In the United Kingdom and Germany the new knife series was launched under the brand name Fiskars Avanti, but did not do well. Discouraged by the experience, the Scandinavian Business Group decided to design a completely new marketing concept for Montana knives. In March 1991, Billnäs was ready to present Törmä's team with a brief which included the planning of a name, packaging design, trade brochures and PR materials (Figure 5.14[k]). The Scandinavian Business Group wanted to broaden its range of knives with a high-quality and high-priced knife series, which it was not yet marketing in the Nordic countries. The market for the new product was not expected to be large and, therefore, heavy promotional activities were not planned.

The execution of the Montana assignment was the first mutual project for the new interacting teams, and consequently a test of their compatibility. Klara Nummelin was responsible for maintaining contact with Marja Tuunanen, and the new creative team eagerly began the planning work. The task was challenging and inspired the team to show initiative and invest their time and energy in the project (Figure 5.14[l]). The team took photographs of the packaging in the actual purchasing environment of department stores and prepared an advertising plan for the knives on their own initiative. They suggested the brand name Fiskars Ottimo, which the marketing team accepted straight away. However, several visual proposals of the concept were needed until the client was fully satisfied. The look of the concept was in the end highly commended by the other Scandinavian and even by some of the European subsidiary companies (Figure 5.14[m]).

As the individuals in the relationship were new, much effort on both sides was put into the execution of the project. Less attention, on the other hand, was paid to building personal relationships and inter-firm knowledge (Figure 5.14[n]). For some time, the interpersonal relationships between the respective teams remained distant, which resulted in increased uncertainty and distrust on both sides (Figure 5.14[o]). The replacement of the trusted art director made the marketing team somewhat insecure until the convincing creative proposals of Sirkka Palonen reassured them. At the same time, the change of the primary contact person at Billnäs increased uncertainty at Törmä.

The style of interaction and the client's orientation towards interaction changed as well. Fiskars Consumer Products Group's tight cost control manifested itself in invoice limits and in growing concern about the costs of cooperation. The dialogue between the parties was no longer as open and intensive as it had been previously. Marja Tuunanen had become used to cooperative interaction, where information and ideas were exchanged freely and the agency could actively make suggestions concerning the client's advertising. Klara Nummelin, on the other hand, was used to requesting tenders via agency contest, and was therefore not ready to immediately trust Törmä's efforts. She would have liked to invite competing proposals from other agencies, and she did in fact introduce a small agency, MacAD Oy, to the marketing team working on lawn and garden tools (see Figure 5.14[p]). The parties' interaction styles and orientations differed from each other (Figure 5.14[q])

Situation in the business relationship

After the Ottimo project, communication between the parties dwindled. There was no basis of regular contact, as Billnäs had not given Törmä any new assignments. Economic and social ties between the parties had both been weakening after the changes in the teams at the turn of the year. The web of personal relationships had become thinner. Fewer people knew the other party well and less information was exchanged between the parties. Dissatisfaction with the relationship also increased (Figure 5.14[r]). Törmä's team was not aware of the marketing team's latest plans and Billnäs knew less and less about what was going on at Törmä. The relationship had become more distant. In addition, the economic recession had increased uncertainty in the business environment and also affected the parties' expectations concerning future cooperation.

In the light of the modifications made to the company's policies and strategy, the marketing team could not be sure how much it really needed Törmä's services in the future (Figure 5.14[o]). No plans for new product launches were made (Figure 5.14[s]). Some old concepts might sometimes be redesigned, and growing ecological concerns in the world at large may necessitate the replacement of certain old packaging with environmentally safer new versions. Nothing was decided, however.

The attractiveness of Törmä as a business partner had decreased primarily because of the changed needs of Billnäs. The increased internal resources of the unit, together with the changed focus of its marketing activities, had decreased the need for the kind of services Törmä had provided in the past (Figure 5.14[t]). Moreover, Billnäs had no evidence of Törmä's capabilities in the new focus areas such as point-of-sale marketing and the marketing of lawn and garden tools (Figure 5.14[u]). Törmä was known to be very capable in the area of concept planning and brand advertising for consumers, but also had one major disadvantage in that area: Törmä was considered far too expensive, particularly when the client was following a tight cost control policy. During previous years, Törmä had successfully planned high-quality brand image concepts and that of Avanti scissors. While considering the packaging redesign for Avanti, the marketing team began to question whether Törmä was the right agency to plan the new package. Would it be able to reject the previous visual ideas and modes of thinking after so many years?

The marketing team at Billnäs trusted Törmä, considering it an experienced producer of marketing concepts and brand advertising. This confidence was founded on a common history. Billnäs was also committed to following the current visual strategy for Fiskars branded household products and to using Törmä for the planning tasks needed for the brand. If an agency contest was organised for the possible redesign of the Avanti packaging, Törmä would naturally be invited to participate.

Good reasons would be needed to break this kind of long-term, reliable partnership.

Törmä's team, however, was not satisfied with the narrow role Billnäs offered it (Figure 5.14[v]). In addition to concept planning, the team would have liked to become involved with the launch process at an earlier stage, and to take part in strategic discussions and client product planning. Törmä's team also hoped for a more important role in the client's international advertising. During 1991, the economic significance of Billnäs as a client decreased further, accounting for only a tiny proportion of Törmä's gross margin. Nevertheless, Fiskars Consumer Products Group was still regarded as a very attractive client, especially in terms of its future potential. Billnäs was a challenging partner because of its innovative, high-quality products and its strong interest in foreign markets. Any agency would have been happy to plan advertising for Fiskars consumer products. No information about new assignments was forthcoming, however. The situation was frustrating for the account team. In order to acquire business, it had to concentrate its efforts on more lucrative potential clients.

In the autumn of 1991, Törmä's narrow role and the increasing uncertainty of future business activated the team to make a new effort in order to maintain and expand the relationship. It invited the marketing team to Törmä for the purpose of gaining information about the client's future plans and of making new business proposals to the client. The account team had previously been informed about the client's plans to improve the visual presentation of its products at retail outlets. Törmä decided to take the initiative in this matter and prepared a speculative presentation concerning the in-store displays of Fiskars household products and hand tools (Figure 5.14[x]). With this presentation, the team wanted to show that Törmä was both able and willing to expand the relationship into new areas. The traditional domain of cooperation was not forgotten, though. The team also had new suggestions for the consumer marketing of the new Ottimo knives. The marketing team listened to the presentations with interest, but decisions were left to a later date.

Summary of the decline phase

The business exchange between the parties decreased further because of changes in the client's marketing strategy and operating policies. More use was made of internal resources in the planning and production of advertising materials. Several changes occurred both in the client's marketing team and in the agency's account team that weakened personal relationships and inter-firm knowledge between the parties. As a result of differing interaction styles and interaction orientations, dissatisfaction with the relationship increased on both sides. This created distrust and uncertainty in the relationship. Trust and committed attitudes were, however, still strong with respect to the familiar tasks in the traditional area of cooperation. In the new areas such as the marketing of garden and hand tools, the client did not have confidence in the agency's capabilities. The speculative offers signalled Törmä's willingness to continue the relationship and show its abilities in new areas.

5.3 DEVELOPMENT OF THE BUSINESS RELATIONSHIP BETWEEN THE FINNISH SALES UNIT OF FISKARS OY AB AND MARKKINOINTI TOPITÖRMÄ OY

5.3.1 Starting the relationship (August 1987–April 1988)

Situation in the sales unit and in its marketing function

In 1987, Fiskars Oy had a sales unit in Malmi which was responsible for the sales and marketing of consumer products in the Finnish market. The unit was led by the Sales Director, Matti Ranta, and it employed about ten people who handled the marketing activities, orders, deliveries, and invoicing for the two product lines: household products and the lawn and garden tools, including tools for construction, forestry and snow clearing.

Product distribution took place primarily through the Finnish group wholesalers and larger department stores. In its advertising and sales promotion, Malmi placed a high priority on cooperation with these dealers. Sales of household products were usually supported by joint advertising campaigns with the group wholesalers. Malmi's products were included, for example, in direct marketing catalogues or TV commercials. In addition, Malmi organised media campaigns of its own, although their importance was diminishing during the 1980s. The unit had invested in point-of-sale marketing instead. It employed several demonstrators, who circulated on sales promotion duties in larger stores all over the country.

Situation in the unit's advertising agency relationships

The Sales Director, Matti Ranta, had been cooperating with AC-mainos Oy since the contest for the Fiskars consumer products account in 1982 (see section 5.2.1). At that time, marketing decision-making for the Consumer Products Group was concentrated at corporate head office in Helsinki. Fiskars did not have a separate marketing unit in Billnäs at that time. Most of the advertising for the Finnish market was planned in direct cooperation with advertising agencies, and Matti Ranta took an active part both in the selection of agencies and in cooperation with them. In addition to AC-mainos, other agencies were occasionally used, e.g. Interplan Oy in 1985.

In 1986, AC-mainos Oy was merged with Suomen Ilmoituskeskus Oy Ilmo, its sister company from the Advisor Group. The Managing Director changed and the new agency was named Oy AC-Ilmo Ab. Several people left the agency, and the Malmi account team also changed in 1987 when the creative team started their own agency, Teamac Oy. As a result, the Buster boat account of the Fiskars Investment Product Group was transferred to Teamac. The marketing unit at Billnäs had ceased cooperation with AC-mainos at an earlier date and started working with Törmä. Malmi, on the other hand, continued cooperation.

Events leading to the start of the initial phase

By the autumn of 1987, the planning of marketing and advertising materials for the new knife sharpener, Roll-Sharp, was almost completed between Billnäs and Törmä (Figure 5.16[a]). The Fiskars Consumer Products Group had decided to follow a standardised marketing strategy, according to which the same marketing concepts and advertising materials would be used in all European markets. One year earlier, Törmä had been selected as the group's advertising agency for the planning of these materials (Figure 5.16[b]). From the point of view of the Consumer Products Group, it was natural that Malmi should also use Törmä's services to launch Roll-Sharp in Finland (Figure 5.16[c]). Consequently, the Deputy Managing Director, Ingmar Lindberg, from Corporate Head Office, and the Marketing Manager, Thommy Hellberg, from Billnäs, discussed the matter with Matti Ranta and recommended Törmä (Figure 5.16[d]). Matti Ranta decided to adapt to the company's choice. This meant that cooperation between AC-Ilmo and Malmi had to end and as a result a new agency relationship with Törmä was started.

Törmä had not been marketing itself actively to the sales unit of Malmi, and was unaware of the unit's role in the Consumer Products Group's organisation. All materials and media planning had been ordered by the marketing team of Billnäs. Furthermore, Malmi was cooperating with Törmä's sister agency AC-Ilmo, which made the situation delicate within the Advisor Group. It was not appropriate to compete with a sister company for the same client. Finally, in dealing with Billnäs the Account Supervisor, Roni Bensky, received information about the Malmi unit, and that Matti Ranta was responsible for marketing in Finland (see Figure 5.16[e]).

In August 1987, Törmä's team and the Billnäs marketing team invited Matti Ranta to a common meeting at Törmä in order to discuss the launch of Roll-Sharp on the Finnish market. Roni Bensky and the Account

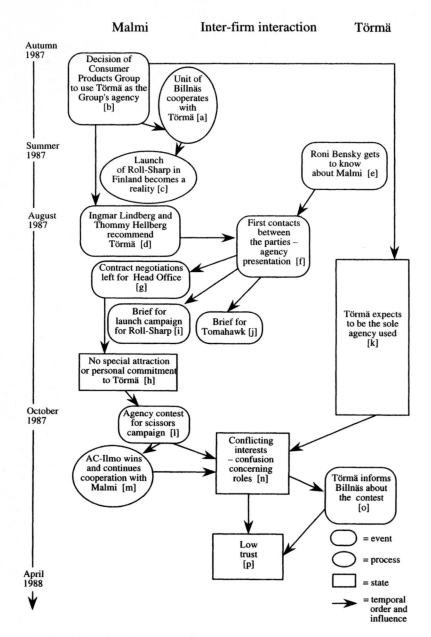

Figure 5.16 The development of the relationship between Malmi and Törmä in the initial phase

Executive, Gunnel Falck, organised an agency presentation (Figure 5.16[f]). The terms of cooperation were also negotiated. Matti Ranta wanted the same fee arrangement as had formerly existed with AC-Ilmo. Roni Bensky agreed to this, and the parties also decided that quantity, material and other discounts granted by the media would be directly credited to the client's account. Everything was agreed to verbally. Only the contract remained to be concluded between Head Office and the agency (Figure 5.16[g]). At a later date, Erkki Yrjölä also invited Matti Ranta to visit in order to convince him about the new agency relationship.

Törmä's team was happy to have responsibility for Consumer Products' advertising in Finland. The Fiskars accounts as a whole were thus expected to become larger. The experience gained with Billnäs concerning advertising and marketing, and the intensive cooperation associated with it, also seemed to promise an interesting and lucrative business relationship with Malmi. For Malmi, on the other hand, Törmä was 'a choice by force of circumstances'. Matti Ranta relied on the selection made by Head Office and expected Törmä to be a modern and capable agency. Nevertheless, he did not feel any special attraction to the agency. He had not taken part in the selection of Törmä and felt no personal commitment to it either (Figure 5.16[h]).

First assignments

The first assignment concerned the launch of Roll-Sharp on the Finnish market (Figure 5.16[i]). Törmä's task was to design the media plan and to order and supervise the production of the Finnish versions of the existing campaign materials. Törmä's team also planned some PR materials and a campaign bulletin for dealers. In the winter of 1988, an impressive launch campaign was organised in order to get the new product quickly known on the market. The sales target for Finland was ambitious and a considerable amount of money was spent on television and magazine advertising. The project was significant for Malmi, from both the economic and the strategic point of view. Certain risks were associated with the launch of the knife sharpener: the product deviated from the company's traditional range of products and the possibility existed that the new product launch might jeopardise knife sales – knives were one of the main articles in the household cutting product line.

In addition to the Roll-Sharp campaign, Malmi also gave Törmä another assignment which dealt with Fiskars tools. The brief included the planning of a marketing concept for a new axe: the name (Tomahawk), PR materials and a leaflet for consumers and dealers (Figure 5.16[j]). The task was innovative and inspired Törmä's team but it remained, however, small in terms of invoicing. Matti Ranta briefed Törmä himself but he soon delegated the operational contacts to the newly appointed

Product Manager, Eija Kalliala. Eija was invited to Törmä to hear about the earlier projects Törmä had realised with Billnäs and to discuss the launch of Roll-Sharp. At Törmä, the same account team that had been responsible for cooperation with Billnäs also started to cooperate with Malmi.

Situation in the business relationship

The execution of the initial assignments proceeded smoothly. Nevertheless, the relationship began in the shadow of distrust and conflicting interests, which resulted primarily from disagreements within the client company. On the basis of the information Törmä's management and the account team had received from Corporate Head Office and from the Billnäs marketing unit, they assumed that Törmä would be the only agency cooperating with Malmi (Figure 5.16[k]). Törmä's team was used to cooperating with Billnäs as sole supplier and had just been told about Fiskars Consumer Products Group wanting to use Törmä as a coordinating agency in the European markets (see section 5.2.3). Consequently, cooperation with Malmi was taken almost for granted.

Malmi, in turn, did not like a situation where it could not choose its own advertising agency. It was willing to use other agencies besides Törmä, particularly for minor tasks, which could not justify the hourly fees charged by Törmä. Malmi's advertising budget was relatively small and, in addition, it had to be divided between the major distributors and advertising agencies. Matti Ranta and Eija Kalliala would rather have seen at least two agencies competing with each other, in order to keep costs down. In October 1987, they invited both AC-Ilmo and Törmä to an agency contest concerning a scissors campaign for consumers (Figure 5.16[l]). AC-Ilmo's pitch won and so they continued cooperation with the agency at the beginning of 1988 (Figure 5.16[m]).

Evidently the use of competing agencies did not correspond to Törmä's expectations of its role with regard to Malmi (Figure 5.16[n]). The account team also informed the management in Billnäs about the agency contest (Figure 5.16[o]), which resulted in tough discussions both inside the Consumer Products Group and between Törmä and Malmi. Agency contests ended but the personal confidence between the Product Manager, Eija Kalliala, and the Account Executive, Gunnel Falck, was lost for a while (Figure 5.16[p]). Distrust overshadowed the relationship for about six months until the roles of the parties were accepted and the contact people on both sides began to understand each other's situation.

Summary of the initial phase

The relationship between Malmi and Törmä was initiated not completely voluntarily but at the request of the Consumer Products Group, which had selected Törmä and decided to use it in the implementation of the standardised marketing strategy. Malmi had a need for an advertising agency but it did not have a special attraction towards Törmä, which it considered too expensive. The parties had difficulty in finding a common interest in building a relationship. Matti Ranta, in particular, could not expect any special benefits from the relationship. The originally strong attraction felt by Törmä was weakened when Törmä realised its small role in the relationship and the competitive orientation of the Malmi team.

The parties' awareness of each other's needs, goals and resources was formed in the few meetings that were organised on the initiative of Billnäs and Corporate Head Office. Matti Ranta had not been in contact with Törmä earlier. Neither had he participated in the selection of Törmä, which decreased his commitment to the initiation of the relationship. Personal relationships and inter-firm knowledge started to emerge between the new parties. Trust was, however, low and was further weakened by the feeling of betrayed confidence at the personal level.

5.3.2 Constant relationship (May 1988–April 1990)

Assignments and interaction

By the summer of 1988, the situation between Malmi and Törmä had improved and the formation of an independent and separate business relationship began. At the end of May, Malmi briefed Törmä about basic planning of media advertising for the rest of the year (Figure 5.17[a]). The marketing team at Malmi wanted to support knife sales by organising a TV campaign during the autumn. Advertising for Roll-Sharp also had to be continued.

In June, the new scissors concept, Avanti and its marketing materials were presented to the European subsidiaries, including the unit of Malmi (Figure 5.17[b]). This meant that the launch of Avanti on the Finnish market also came on stream. Malmi gave Törmä a brief (Figure 5.17[c]). As in the Roll-Sharp campaign, the existing international marketing materials were used in the launching of Avanti. The assignment was, however, much smaller in economic terms and also narrower in scope. It consisted of the planning of a television campaign and printing a dealer brochure for the new product. The campaign was scheduled for October 1988 (see Figure 5.18). Television advertising for Roll-Sharp was broadcast simultaneously, and the launch was further supported by a separate campaign organised in cooperation with the group wholesaler, Kesko Oy. The television campaign for knives, on the other hand, was cancelled.

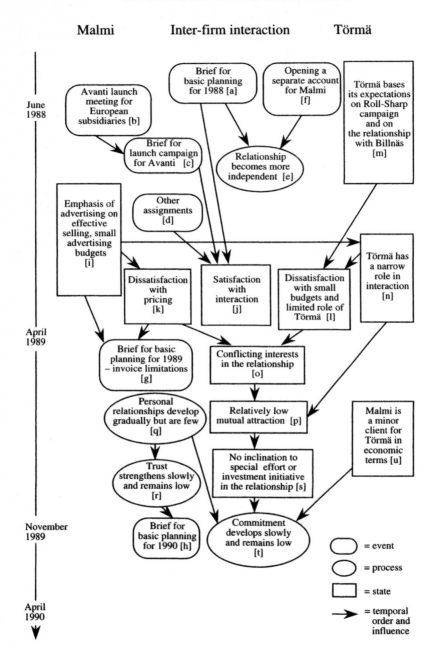

Figure 5.17 The development of the relationship between Malmi and Törmä in the constant phase

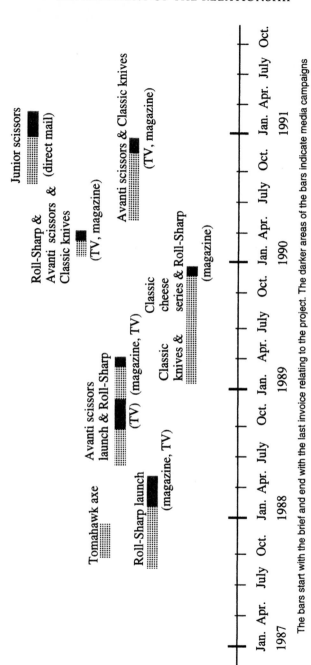

Figure 5.18 Assignments executed between Malmi and Törmä.

The bars start with the brief and end with the last invoice relating to the project. The darker areas of the bars indicate media campaigns

As a strategically important product, Avanti and its marketing provoked lively discussion inside the Consumer Products Group and also between Törmä and Malmi. Diverse opinions revolved around the pricing of the product in particular. For the marketing team of Malmi, the main question was how much lower the price should be set in order to safeguard sufficient gross margins and the existence of Classic scissors on the market.

Törmä also received other assignments from Malmi (Figure 5.17[d]). A media campaign was organised in March to promote the sales of Avanti scissors and Roll-Sharp (see Figure 5.18). Malmi also presented a brief for advertising planning for garden cutting tools, with the aim of promoting them as high-quality Fiskars products in the same way as Classic scissors. The project was, however, cancelled for lack of marketing funds.

During 1988, the relationship between Malmi and Törmä developed into an independent exchange relation (Figure 5.17[e]). The launch campaigns for Roll-Sharp and Avanti had been commissioned by the Fiskars Consumer Products Group but Malmi then began to brief Törmä independently. Moreover, Törmä had opened a separate account for Malmi (Figure 5.17[f]).

In the spring of 1989, Malmi presented a brief for the basic planning of media campaigns for the rest of the year (Figure 5.17[g]). Malmi's team also decided to launch the Fiskars Cheese series on the Finnish market. As expected, knife sales had decreased after the launch of Roll-Sharp and thus required some advertising support. In this situation, Eija Kalliala organised a sales promotion campaign in cooperation with Oy Valio Ab and TLK, the manufacturers of cheese and meat products. A new Fiskars cheese slicer guide as well as a Fiskars Classic knife guide were produced for consumers with Törmä's support. Törmä's team also planned magazine advertising and dealer bulletins for the campaign, which was scheduled for November 1989 (Figure 5.18). A certain amount of magazine advertising for Roll-Sharp was realised at the same time. The entire campaign of late 1989 became significant in terms of invoicing.

The basic media campaign planning for 1990 was already complete by the end of 1989 (Figure 5.17[h]). A television campaign for Roll-Sharp, Avanti scissors and Fiskars Classic knives was organised in March with the purpose of stimulating the declining sales of the knife sharpener and of reminding consumers of the Avanti scissors. The old Chef knives were advertised as Fiskars Classic knives for the first time on television, which necessitated minor changes to the old TV commercial. Existing materials were used for the rest of the campaign. For autumn 1990, Malmi had planned a reminder campaign for Avanti scissors and Fiskars Classic knives.

The Törmä and Malmi teams remained unchanged for a long time. At Malmi, the Product Manager, Eija Kalliala, oversaw operational contacts with Törmä. Matti Ranta made the more important decisions concerning the marketing of household products but delegated the operational tasks and advertising agency contacts to Eija Kalliala. Matti Ranta himself concentrated on cooperation with the group wholesalers and on the marketing of hand tools, in particular. In previous years, Malmi had extended its business activities to the area of hand tools, which kept Matti Ranta busy. With regard to the relationship with Törmä, he negotiated the discounts and invoicing principles with Roni Bensky. This occurred on an annual basis, which also meant that Matti Ranta met Roni Bensky or Gunnel Falck only seldomly. The network of personal relationships remained narrow (Figure 5.19).

Briefs, future plans and other information were exchanged between Eija Kalliala and Gunnel Falck. They usually organised the briefings and other appointments at Törmä, in the centre of Helsinki. The briefs were verbal but accurately defined. In most cases, briefing was simple because campaign materials already existed and creative planning was not required. The distribution of work was clear as well. Törmä's primary task was to handle the media planning and buying and also to provide Malmi with any media information required.

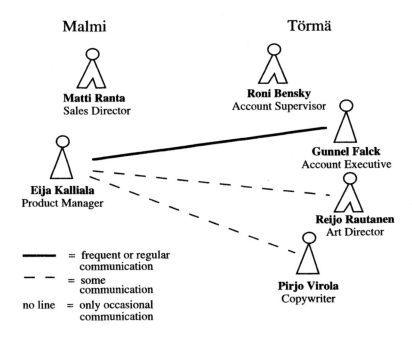

Figure 5.19 The interacting teams and the frequency of communication between Malmi and Törmä in the constant phase (up to November 1989)

The basic plans for media advertising were made once or twice a year. Malmi's marketing efforts were planned in good time, about six months in advance, because this was the time schedule on which the group wholesalers planned their buying. For Malmi, the media campaigns were, primarily, devices which facilitated product distribution. It was crucial to inform the distributors about supportive marketing activities, because most of the unit's turnover was realised by means of these campaigns (Figure 5.17[i]). Certain campaign times, the late autumn and early spring, had proved to be most advantageous from a sales standpoint. This also guided the scheduling of marketing activities and, consequently, the business exchange with Törmä (see Figure 5.20). It was also in the interest of Törmä to know about future assignments in good time, so that it could plan its own budget and reserve the necessary media time.

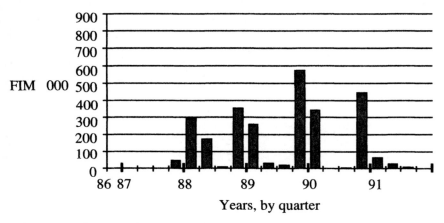

Figure 5.20 Invoicing between Malmi and Törmä, adjusted by the wholesale price index (1985 = 100)

Satisfaction with the business relationship

Cooperation between Eija Kalliala and Gunnel Falck proceeded smoothly (Figure 5.17[j]). They got on well with each other and sometimes also had lunch together. Although communication between the parties was neither frequent nor very open, it was sufficient for the execution of tasks. Information about short-term advertising plans and budgets, about sales trends, market shares and marketing measures were exchanged between Eija Kalliala and Gunnel Falck. From Malmi's point of view, Törmä showed sufficient investment initiative in interaction. It was clear, however, that Törmä paid more attention to the business relationship with the marketing unit of Billnäs, with which the business had first started and which also offered the account team more innovative assignments.

Matti Ranta and Eija Kalliala appreciated the quality of Törmä's work but considered it too expensive (Figure 5.17[k]). It seemed that there was plenty of 'air' in Törmä's invoices, which was not in congruence with Malmi's restricted advertising budget (Figure 5.17[i]). Invoicing constantly led to unpleasant discussions between the parties, even though they always arrived at a satisfactory solution. After the initial experiences during 1988, Eija Kalliala started to set invoice limits for media planning, and to demand accurate cost estimates for all work in order to keep costs under control (Figure 5.17[g]). Moreover, she would have liked to use cheaper agencies for minor tasks.

The careful control of costs, the small advertising budget and the role of advertising in the client's marketing did not please the account team (Figure 5.17[l]). In particular they were disappointed with the relationship to the extent that expectations had been based on the impressive Roll-Sharp campaign and on experience of cooperation with Billnäs (Figure 5.17[m]). Törmä's role in the relationship remained narrow (Figure 5.17[n]). Malmi's assignments were not especially inspiring or challenging, as no new materials were planned and the media budget was relatively small. Under these circumstances, Törmä's team had nothing to show for its efforts. It had no opportunity to contribute to the client's marketing success in any visible way. Cooperation was smooth and satisfying in those assignments Malmi gave Törmä but opportunities to broaden the relationship to other product groups or tasks other than media planning and buying were fairly limited. All this was frustrating for the account team, both personally and in the light of the agency's business possibilities. Nevertheless, the team tried to offer Malmi new services and to make further suggestions for the client's marketing every now and then.

Satisfaction with the results of the projects

The Roll-Sharp launch in 1988 had gone well in the Finnish market. The sales target was not quite achieved, but the costs of the campaign were covered during the first year, which was considered exceptional. Any misgivings about launching this type of product and how it would fit into the range of Fiskars branded products were mostly forgotten. Both Matti Ranta and Eija Kalliala were satisfied with the results. Classic scissors also sold well but the sales of knives had dropped as a result of the Roll-Sharp launch (see Figure 5.21).

Avanti scissors, on the other hand, had been a slight disappointment – the sales volumes did not develop as expected. The whole launch project and the profile of the product and its marketing policy had not been as clear as in the case of Roll-Sharp. The advertising budget had also been tighter. The pricing of Avanti at about 10 per cent below the price

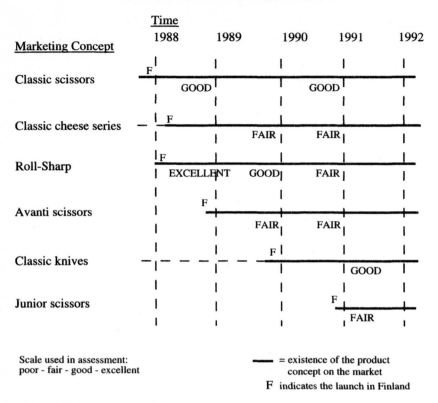

Figure 5.21 The success of the marketing concepts in Finnish markets over time, as assessed by the client.

of Classic scissors turned out to be too cautious. Avanti's advertising seemed to support Classic scissors' sales rather than its own; the latter maintained its important position in the market (Figure 5.21). By the end of 1990, the sales of Roll-Sharp had dropped considerably from the volumes of 1988 and remained at a relatively low level.

In general, it was extremely difficult to assess the role of the media advertising realised with Törmä. Malmi had simultaneously organised in-store promotion and joint campaigns with the group wholesalers. The overall effect of the campaigns in sales figures was easier to see and, indeed, it had been positive. With regard to media advertising, Matti Ranta believed in the Fiskars brand and in its spin-off effects: the advertising of one Fiskars product would draw attention to other articles of the same brand and increase their sales as well.

Situation in the business relationship at the end of 1989

It was evident that the interests and expectations of Malmi and Törmä with respect to their business relationship differed (Figure 5.17[o]). In the first place, the parties did not entirely agree about the role of advertising in the marketing of Fiskars household products. For Matti Ranta, advertising was primarily a device for increasing sales to distributors and for acquiring shelf space in retail outlets. When advertising was used this way its effects could also be seen and measured, at least to some degree of accuracy. Törmä's team, on the other hand, saw more options and potential for Malmi's advertising. They would rather have seen Malmi investing in brand and image advertising, for example. In addition, the parties' expectations concerning the economic significance of their business relationship were different. Törmä expected more impressive campaigns and bigger advertising budgets. Malmi, on the other hand, economised on advertising and was not willing to pay the prices Törmä charged for its services.

The difference in interests was clear but, however, understood by the parties to the relationship. It was seen as normal disagreement between any client and agency and not as a severe conflict. Attraction between the parties remained low, however (Figure 5.17[p]). The difference in views necessitated adaptive measures from both teams. As Fiskars was an important client for Törmä with future potential, the agency wanted to give way in invoicing and adapt to the client's situation. Malmi's marketing team also understood that Törmä had been used to intensive and more economically significant cooperation with the marketing unit at Billnäs. Eija Kalliala did her best to make the account team realise that the situation was different with Malmi.

Matti Ranta and Eija Kalliala relied upon Törmä's capabilities and respected their opinions and knowledge of media planning. The distrust at the beginning was forgotten; personal relationships gradually strengthened (Figure 5.17[q]. Nevertheless, the relationship did not develop into a close, confidential partnership (Figure 5.17[r]). The Malmi team continued to have misgivings about Törmä's invoicing. The turbulence and risk of organisational change within the Consumer Products Group kept the team cautious. The situation did not encourage confidential communication or investments in an independent and strong agency relationship (Figure 5.17[s]).

As Malmi's advertising budget was relatively small, it was more or less immaterial which agency handled it. As Malmi was an attractive client, it was occasionally approached by competing advertising agencies. The marketing team visited some of them but ultimately it was always Törmä that executed the assignments. During the previous two years, Matti Ranta had gradually become more committed to Törmä, as was manifested in his reluctance to change agency. He was less interested in alternatives than he had been at the beginning of the relationship. He had become particularly aware of the risks as well as the costs in time and effort that a switch would involve. The level of commitment remained low, however (Figure 5.17[t]). Malmi used a small agency, Grafiala Oy, in addition to Törmä for economic reasons. It was used for minor work, particularly for the marketing of garden tools, which formed a distinct product group.

From a strategic and economic point of view, the relationship with Törmä had never been especially significant for Malmi. During the 1980s, Malmi had continuously increased its advertising expenditure. Meanwhile, however, the role of group wholesalers had also become increasingly powerful. Competition for position in the distribution channels had become harder. As a result, the share of wholesalers in the advertising budget had increased at the expense of the unit's own advertising and simultaneously to the detriment of Törmä. Malmi had also planned to start advertising at sports events, which would not be organised through Törmä. Matti Ranta devoted more of his time and effort to cooperation with group wholesalers, department stores and other distributors instead of direct advertising agency contacts (Figure 5.17[s]). Previously, there had been no basis for strong commitment to the unit's own agency (Figure 5.17[t]).

Neither of the parties showed any special commitment to their opposite number. Both Matti Ranta and Roni Bensky remained in the background with regard to cooperation and delegated the execution of the assignments to a lower hierarchical level – to Eija Kalliala and Gunnel Falck. From Törmä's point of view, the Malmi account had never been particularly important (Figure 5.17[u]). Malmi's advertising budget was always quite small and both Matti Ranta and Eija Kalliala had been careful in using it. During 1989, the importance of the Malmi unit in the Fiskars–Törmä relationship had, however, become more pronounced. Malmi accounted for 1.3 per cent of the agency's gross margin, which was slightly more than Billnäs's share. The media campaigns organised by Malmi partly compensated for the decline of business exchange in the relationship between Billnäs and Törmä, but they could not completely fill the economic loss that the diminished exchange with Billnäs had caused.

Törmä's tasks in the relationship were not very innovative; almost all advertising was based on the use of existing materials. Törmä's role in the interaction remained narrow (Figure 5.17[n]). It did not offer opportunities for initiative, for making suggestions about client marketing, for planning speculative offers or for investing in the relationship in any special way. The business relationship worked well at a basic level – with a narrow scope – but it did not provide any special benefits for Törmä.

154

The relationship with Malmi formed part of Törmä's business with Fiskars, which was an important and attractive client on the whole. As long as Billnäs cooperated with Törmä, the account team could also have confidence in a common future with Malmi.

Summary of the constant phase

During the constant phase, the relationship between Malmi and Törmä became established as an independent unit relationship. There were no large variations in the intensity of business exchange or communication between the parties. Certain norms or patterns of behaviour in interaction emerged. Personal relationships strengthened gradually, but the network of personal relationships remained narrow. Attraction was fairly low because of the conflicting interests of the parties in their business relationship. Neither of the parties could expect any special benefits from the interaction. Neither's experience of each other had been very satisfying, but the relationship worked sufficiently well for the parties to be willing to continue it. When contact people changed, efforts were made to build new personal relationships. The business relationship was not especially close, trusting or committed.

5.3.3 Declining relationship (May 1990–)

Interaction and situation at the personnel level

By the summer of 1990, the changes of contact staff on both sides had disrupted the *status quo* in personal relationships; new people became involved with the business relationship (Figure 5.22[a]). The Account Executive, Gunnel Falck, had left Törmä in November 1989. The new Account Executive, Marja Tuunanen, replaced her in February 1990 (Figure 5.22[b]). In April 1990, Eija Kalliala left Malmi, which broke Törmä's strongest personal contact with the client (Figure 5.22[c]). Tuija Rajamäki from the Billnäs unit handled her duties until July when she also left the company (Figure 5.22[d] and [e]). Personal relations had to be rebuilt.

During the summer of 1990, the volume of interaction between the parties was low (Figure 5.22[f]). The redesigned knife series, Rosewood, was launched in Finland in August and the new scissors sharpener, Clip-Sharp, in June. Hardly any advertising was planned to promote their sales, however. Malmi organised a TV campaign for Clip-Sharp with the group wholesaler, Kesko Oy. Törmä, however, played no part in the project. Activity decreased on both sides, until the new projects, in particular the launch of Fiskars Junior scissors in Finland, were realised in the late summer of 1990 (Figure 5.22[g])

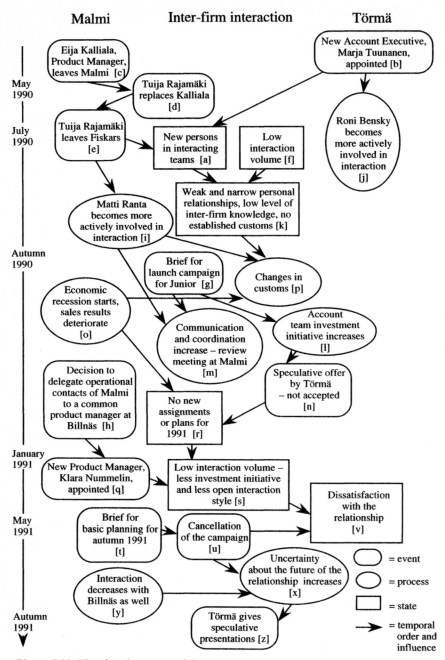

Figure 5.22 The development of the relationship between Malmi and Törmä in the decline phase

After Eija Kalliala and Tuija Rajamäki had left, the marketing organisations of Malmi and Billnäs changed slightly. It was decided that the two positions of Product Manager should be integrated and the office would be in Billnäs (Figure 5.22[h]). This new Product Manager would be responsible for household products and would handle contacts with Törmä on behalf of both Billnäs and Malmi. The decision to employ a new Product Manager for the marketing of garden tools at Billnäs and another for business gift marketing at Malmi was also made. With the help of the new staff, Matti Ranta hoped to be able to acquire a greater share of the advertising work done in-house in the future. This was in accordance with the Consumer Products Group's tight cost control policy.

Malmi remained without a Product Manager for the rest of 1990. As a result, the Sales Director, Matti Ranta, became more involved with the agency relationship (Figure 5.22[i]). Roni Bensky, the Account Supervisor, also devoted more time to cooperation than before (Figure 5.22[j]). Personal relationships between the parties were both weak and narrow (Figure 5.22[k]). It required effort from both parties to rebuild working contacts. Gunnel Falck, Eija Kalliala and Tuija Rajamäki, who had had almost sole responsibility for operational contacts during the previous two years, were no longer available, and neither were their mutual knowledge, customs or the common ways of working established between Törmä and Malmi (Figure 5.22[k]). The account team, especially the new Account Executive, put their effort into activating the business relationship (Figure 5.22[l]).

During the autumn, a couple of meetings were organised to discuss the launch of Junior scissors (see Figure 5.23). Some materials also had to be renewed for Malmi's media campaign in the autumn. Törmä and the Billnäs marketing team had planned a direct marketing campaign for the Junior launch, to be offered to the Nordic subsidiaries. The execution of the project in Finland was negotiated with Matti Ranta. The campaign was scheduled for the winter of 1991 and magazine advertising was planned for its support (see Figure 5.18, p. 147). In August, Matti Ranta invited Törmä to Malmi in order to go over the current projects and discuss the future needs of the sales unit (Figure 5.22[m]). Törmä made a speculative offer for the launch of a new shovel, which did not result in any concrete cooperation, however (see Figure 5.22[n]).

The internal coordination between the units of Fiskars once again began to have more effect on the relationship when the new product, Fiskars Junior, was launched. The division of work and costs in both projects had to be negotiated between the units (Figure 5.22[m]). These decisions directly influenced cooperation, particularly questions such as: Who would the responsible contact persons be? Who would accept cost estimates, and where should the invoices be sent? Törmä and Malmi also

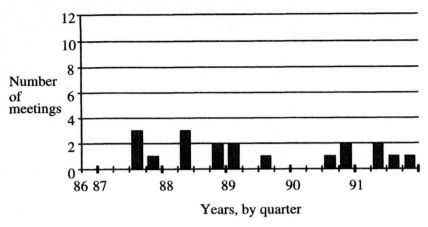

Figure 5.23 Documented meetings between Malmi and Törmä

independently negotiated transferring part of the autumn's invoicing to the coming year. Matti Ranta was satisfied with the behaviour of Törmä's team and appreciated their flexibility over invoicing arrangements.

The deep recession in the Finnish economy also started to influence the relationship between Malmi and Törmä (Figure 5.22[o]). In the uncertain market situation, Matti Ranta decided not to run a media campaign in the first half of 1991. He did not give any brief for basic planning for the new year, which was unusual, as this had been the custom in the relationship to date (Figure 5.22[p]). The planning period of exchange shortened.

At the beginning of 1991, a new Product Manager was finally appointed to the marketing unit of Billnäs (Figure 5.22[q]). Klara Nummelin started as Product Manager for household products and also began to deal with agency contacts on behalf of Malmi. During the first half of the year there was, however, no need to talk about advertising in Finland; there were no plans for new campaigns or other assignments for 1991 (Figure 5.22[r]). The continuing recession and the deteriorating sales results had made Matti Ranta cautious. The whole retail sector was wary of making marketing decisions until the last minute. The direct marketing campaign for Junior scissors was organised in the winter, but it did not require much communication. Interaction volume was low between the parties (Figure 5.22[s]). Only a limited amount of follow-up information was exchanged between Marja Tuunanen and Matti Ranta (see Figure 5.24).

Finally, in May, Matti Ranta visited Törmä and briefed the team about basic planning for the autumn of 1991 (Figure 5.22[t]). He was planning to run the old Avanti scissors TV commercial in November. He also briefed Törmä on the planning and production of a magazine advertisement for Fiskars Classic knives, the Cheese series and the Roll-Sharp knife

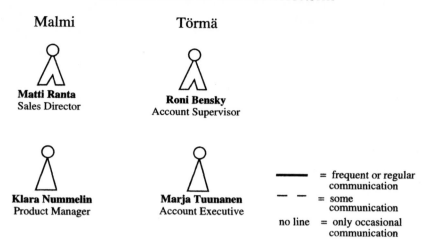

Figure 5.24 The interacting teams and the frequency of communication between Malmi and Törmä in the decline phase (up to 1991)

sharpener and the media planning for it. Törmä's cost estimates showed that the budget was insufficient for an effective magazine campaign, and it was therefore decided to spend the money on a campaign for Classic scissors instead. Classic scissors had not been advertised on television for years, and a Danish commercial was available for the purpose. This plan also turned out to be futile. Some days later, Malmi decided to cancel the whole campaign and postpone it for a year (Figure 5.22[u]). Klara Nummelin informed Marja Tuunanen of the decision and promised to return to the matter later.

Situation in the business relationship at the end of 1991

The cancellation of the campaign was naturally a disappointment for Törmä's team. During the entire year, there had been no active communication between Malmi and Törmä. Since the introduction of the new arrangements between Malmi and Billnäs concerning the Product Managers' duties, it had not been clear who was the primary contact person in Malmi's advertising affairs. Matti Ranta had not been as active in cooperation as during the previous year. It was in his interest, as far as possible, to delegate the responsibility for maintaining contact to Billnäs, so that he could concentrate on other things. Moreover, Klara Nummelin was new to the business relationship and inexperienced in her duties at Malmi. The account team was dissatisfied with the relationship and felt that Malmi was not committed to cooperation (Figure 5.22[v]). The relationship had almost ceased to exist as a separate business relationship.

In the absence of annual planning and active communication, Törmä's team felt uncertain about the future of the business relationship (Figure 5.22[x]). The situation was worrying, the more so because interaction with Billnäs, which formed the backbone of the whole Fiskars relationship, had recently decreased as well (Figure 5.22[y]). The account team naturally understood the client's changed market situation, but the silence had lasted rather a long time. It seemed necessary to take the initiative and invest in the relationship in order to stimulate business, and so Roni Bensky invited Matti Ranta to a joint meeting with the Billnäs team.

At this meeting Roni Bensky and Marja Tuunanen made a speculative presentation concerning the in-store displays of Fiskars household products and hand tools (Figure 5.22[z]). The improvement of the visual presentation of Fiskars products in retail outlets was an important project for the whole client company and required investments and acceptance from all units. Törmä also made new suggestions for advertising Ottimo knives in Finland. By means of these proposals, Törmä wanted to show that it was willing to broaden its relationship with Malmi. The client's market situation and the sales prospects of different products and product lines were also discussed at the meeting. The parties found themselves surprisingly able to state that 1991 had been exceptional with respect to media campaigns. It had been the first year since 1980 that Malmi had not arranged the customary spring and autumn campaigns (see Figure 5.18, p. 147). In spite of the fact that the outlook for the Finnish market already seemed more promising, Malmi's team was not yet ready to inform Törmä about its advertising plans for the following year.

Summary of the decline phase

During the decline phase, the relationship between Malmi and Törmä had become particularly weak. The personnel changes had broken the established personal relationships, changed the norms and patterns of behaviour and also decreased the level of inter-firm knowledge between the parties. The parties had almost no behavioural commitment to each other. Matti Ranta was still attitudinally committed to the relationship, but at that time he did not see any potential for exchange. The recession had almost put an end to all interaction between the parties, which created dissatisfaction among Törmä's team and a strong feeling of uncertainty about the continuity of the relationship. From the standpoint of future potential, the Fiskars Consumer Products Group was still an attractive client for Törmä, and it was therefore in its interest to invest in the relationship with Malmi as well. The speculative presentation signalled Törmä's willingness to continue the relationship and broaden its role in interaction.

5.4 DEVELOPMENT OF THE BUSINESS RELATIONSHIP BETWEEN THE HEAD OFFICE OF FISKARS OY AB AND MARKKINOINTI TOPITÖRMÄ OY

5.4.1 Starting the relationship (November 1986–)

The role of Head Office in the relationship between Fiskars and Törmä

In 1986, the Corporate Head Office and the management of the Consumer Products Group were situated in Helsinki. In November 1986, the Consumer Products Group initiated cooperation with Markkinointi Topitörmä (Figure 5.25[a]). Its intention was to use Törmä internationally as a lead agency in the implementation of its standardised marketing strategy. The Finnish sales unit started cooperation with Törmä a year later. Agency selection was strategically important and top management from Corporate Head Office was therefore involved, particularly Ingmar Lindberg, the Director of Corporate Development (Figure 5.25[b]). He had considerable experience of the advertising sector and offered his knowledge and contacts to the Consumer Products Group (see section 5.2.1).

In practice, the marketing unit at Billnäs and the sales unit at Malmi handled cooperation with Törmä. The role of Head Office and Ingmar Lindberg was decisive in the initiation of both unit relationships. Ingmar Lindberg also handled contract negotiations with Törmä's Managing Director, Erkki Yrjölä (Figure 5.25[b]) (see section 5.2.3). The units subsequently managed their relationships with Törmä independently. The role of the Finnish Head Office in decision-making regarding consumer product marketing diminished considerably after the organisational change in the summer of 1988 (Figure 5.25[c]). The leadership of the Consumer Products Group was transferred to the United States. As a result, the influence of the American management and the established Scandinavian Business Group on the marketing activities of Billnäs and Malmi grew stronger.

The active role of Head Office in initiating the relationships meant that corporate management had positive attitudes towards Törmä. The parties had in fact started a relationship, although it remained inactive for some time. Contact was maintained at top management level between Ingmar Lindberg and Erkki Yrjölä. The management of Fiskars kept Törmä in mind as a tried and trusted partner of the corporation's two units, and listed it among its preferred advertising agencies (Figure 5.25[d] and [e]). The attraction was mutual, since Törmä also considered Head Office an important potential partner. Cooperation with Head Office actually occurred through the personnel responsible for corporate communication.

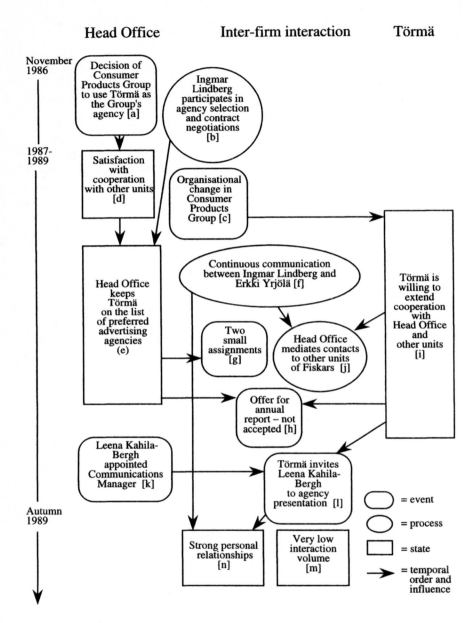

Figure 5.25 The development of the relationship between Head Office and Törmä in the dormant phase

The communications department at Corporate Head Office

The communications department at Corporate Head Office was responsible for the company's internal and external communication. It was responsible for corporate image and design, press releases, annual reports and in-house magazines. A Communications Manager was employed for these tasks. During the second half of the 1980s, the Communications Manager changed twice. In the summer of 1989, Kimmo Linkama left Fiskars and Leena Kahila-Bergh was appointed in his place in August 1989.

With regard to communication, Fiskars consciously followed a reserved rather than an open policy. During the 1980s, it had not invested in any extensive image campaigns, despite their great popularity among Finnish companies following the increased trading volume on the Finnish stock exchange at the end of the 1980s. The company graphics and logotype were nevertheless redesigned in 1983 and a new promotional corporate video was produced in 1987.

Situation in the department's advertising agency relationships

During the second half of the 1980s, the communications department had been cooperating with a number of advertising, design or communication agencies. From 1983, Head Office had been working with Anderson & Lembke Oy and in particular with Ingmar Lindberg's team. One year later, A & L established a design agency, Alform Oy, which planned the new logotype and corporate graphics for Fiskars. Cooperation with Alform continued in 1991. The communications department had confidence in its capabilities, particularly in its ability to handle the production of the company's annual reports.

When the marketing unit of Billnäs had already ceased cooperation with the Swedish company Hall & Cederquist, Head Office briefed it on the planning of a promotional corporate video in 1987. Since then the parties had not been linked in active cooperation, but in 1991 Fiskars still remembered Hall & Cederquist for the quality of its work and kept the agency on its 'shopping list' for future service needs. The communications department used two small agencies for the writing and layout of the in-house magazine.

Interaction and situation in the business relationship in 1986–89

During the late 1980s, Ingmar Lindberg and Erkki Yrjölä met each other every now and then in private. These meetings provided an ideal framework for exchanging company and industry-related information (see Figure 5.25[f]). This contact also provided occasional business opportunities for Törmä. The agency handled a few job advertisements on behalf of Fiskars in 1988 and designed a logotype in 1989. Both assignments were, however, very small – economically and strategically almost insignificant (Figure 5.25[g]).

In 1988, the communications department invited Törmä to participate in competitive bidding for the production of the annual report (Figure 5.25[h]). For Fiskars, the competitive bidding was primarily a means to promote investment initiative in Alform Oy and to check its price level. Törmä made an offer but failed to wrest the assignment from Alform. It was in Törmä's interest to extend cooperation to other units of the corporation as well – particularly after the organisational change of 1988, when the strategic management of the Consumer Products Group was transferred out of reach (Figure 5.25[i]). The Corporate Head Office did in fact mediate some important business opportunities for Törmä but for one reason or another they did not result in concrete cooperation (Figure 5.25[j]). In the autumn of 1988, Törmä was given the opportunity to put forward a proposal for a company name, logotype and company brochure for Rahkola, a manufacturer of hand tools, which was also a subsidiary of Fiskars. The same autumn, and also in the spring of 1990, Head Office mediated contacts and added momentum to the negotiations between Törmä and the business gift unit in Sweden (see sections 5.2.4 and 5.2.6).

In 1989, Leena Kahila-Bergh was appointed Communications Manager of Fiskars (Figure 5.25[k]). In order to broaden personal contacts with Head Office, and in the hope of future business opportunities, Roni Bensky invited her to an agency presentation in the autumn of 1989 (Figure 5.25[l]).

The initial phase from the end of 1986 to the end of 1989 can be viewed as a dormant period in the relationship between Head Office and Törmä. Interaction volume was very low in the relationship: from a business exchange standpoint the relationship hardly existed (Figure 5.25[m]). Only two very small briefs were executed. Head Office simply did not need Törmä's services or preferred to use other agencies instead. A framework for cooperation had, however, been established. The parties had built strong personal relationships, which also increased their knowledge of each other (Figure 5.25[n]).

Events leading to the active phase in the relationship

From 1989, the management of the corporation was organised through two executive bodies: the Corporate Executive Committee and the Management Board. The former comprised Reijo Kaukonen, who had been President of the corporation from 1984, and three Vice Presidents, Wayne Fethke, Ingmar Lindberg and Juha Toivola. The Management

Board included representatives of personnel and of different business sectors of the corporation. Ingmar Lindberg was in charge of real estate business and administration and thereby corporate communication. Leena Kahila-Bergh acted as Communications Manager.

At the beginning of 1990, management decided to take measures in order to adjust and improve the company's image in Finland. During the 1980s, Fiskars Oy had gone through a vigorous internationalisation process, in which the company's size, branch structure, degree of internationalisation, range of manufactured products and brands and many other things had changed considerably. Consumers as well as many potential investors had no knowledge of this development. The public still knew the company primarily for its famous orange scissors. The company had in fact developed to such an extent that international company image advertising had become a reasonable possibility. Moreover, the strengthening of the company image in the eyes of potential investors was especially important with respect to the company's future financial needs (Figure 5.26[a]). The strong growth of the company and its foreign acquisitions had required a considerable amount of capital. Fiskars had been both a promising and a lucrative investment for its shareholders and, consequently, had been able to increase its share capital through share issues each year from 1985 to 1989. The weakening financial performance of the company had, however, changed the situation.

In the winter of 1990 Ingmar Lindberg informed his friend Erkki Yrjölä about the company's plans to organise an image campaign (Figure 5.26[b]). The actual briefing of the account team was not arranged until the end of April (Figure 5.26[c]). During this period, the idea matured both at Fiskars and at Törmä. The account team was the same as that which had cooperated with Billnäs and Malmi. It was composed of the new Account Executive, Marja Tuunanen, the Copywriter, Pirjo Virola, and the Art Director, Reijo Rautanen. Rather unusually, both Erkki Yrjölä and Roni Bensky acted as account supervisors. The primary contact person at Fiskars was Leena Kahila-Bergh (see Figure 5.27).

Törmä was more or less an automatic choice for the image campaign. The management of Fiskars did not seriously consider any other alternatives, although they were available. It felt no need to brief other agencies for this kind of complex assignment, which also included strategically and legally sensitive information. An agency contest would have been too laborious to organise and could by no means have guaranteed any better results than a single agency could provide. Moreover, Törmä had been working with the Billnäs and Malmi units for several years and was expected to already have a good knowledge of Fiskars as a company. Törmä was also a particularly attractive alternative because of the favourable personal relationship between Erkki Yrjölä and Ingmar Lindberg. Ingmar Lindberg considered it very important to have a trusted

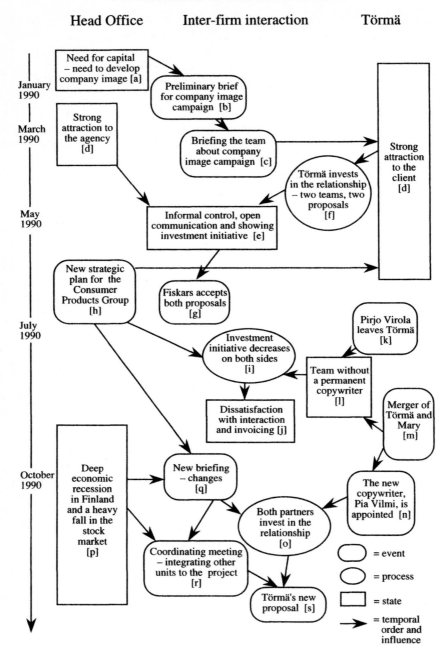

Figure 5.26 The development of the relationship between Head Office and Törmä in the active phase

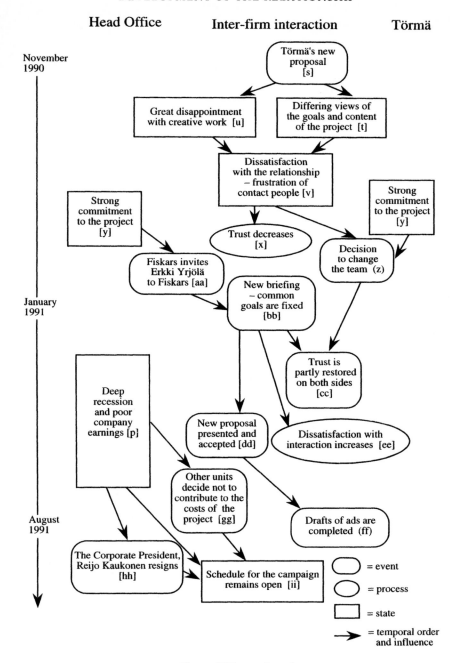

Figure 5.26 continued

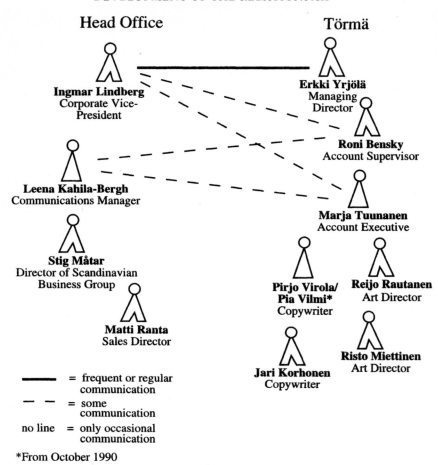

Figure 5.27 The interacting teams and the frequency of communication between Head Office and Törmä in the active phase (1990).

person in the management of the agency. This way it was more probable that cooperation would proceed smoothly and the performance of the agency would correspond to the client's requirements.

The management of Törmä was happy to be finally able to activate its relationship with Head Office. Attraction was strong on both sides (Figure 5.26[d]).

Interaction in the spring of 1990

At the beginning of the project, the parties did not discuss the terms of cooperation. In 1987, Erkki Yrjölä had negotiated a gentleman's agreement with Ingmar Lindberg, which the units at Billnäs and Malmi had followed in their cooperation with Törmä. The invoicing principles that had been established as norms between the parties during the previous years were also accepted as a tacit contract between Törmä and Head Office. The discussions therefore centred on the assignment itself.

The primary goal of the image campaign was to support a probable share issue initially scheduled for the end of the year. Management had not yet made any final decisions, but wanted to prepare a supporting campaign in the event that the share issue was realised. Accordingly, Fiskars chose both potential and existing investors as the target group for the campaign, which was simultaneously aimed at the larger public. The task of the account team was to discover a simplified and appealing way of presenting the essence of the Fiskars corporation and to communicate it to the target group. The internationalism of Fiskars and the many opportunities it had to conduct profitable business all over Europe was the basic message of the campaign.

The brief was open in the sense that it left room for creative thinking and set no invoice limits on planning. Formal control was not emphasised (Figure 5.26[e]). The deadline for planning was set for midsummer. Resolving the nature of 'Fiskars' and the content of its image, in terms of what the company wanted to communicate, required insight from the account team and also sound knowledge of the client company. The task was innovative for both parties. The Fiskars 'product' had to be defined in a new way. It was also a question of changing the company's existing, somewhat reserved, communications policy, for which the new stock exchange regulations set new requirements. Organising an image campaign was a rare event for the client as well as for the agency.

Evidently, the brief was both strategically and economically important for the client. It was also important for Törmä, as it provided an excellent opportunity to extend cooperation with Fiskars and to do some good business. Consequently, Törmä's management was ready to invest in the relationship and engaged a further creative team for the planning work (Figure 5.26[f]). The team was composed of the Copywriter, Jari Korhonen, and the Art Director, Risto Miettinen (see Figure 5.27).

At a meeting in May, Törmä presented two proposals to Fiskars: one was domestically oriented, the other took a more international perspective. The Fiskars team, Ingmar Lindberg and Leena Kahila-Bergh, liked both suggestions and accepted them for further development (Figure 5.26[g]). It was decided, however, to work on the domestic project first. Törmä had previously showed initiative and suggested a company image study, which would help to measure the effects of the campaign. The team introduced the offer at the same meeting but Fiskars decided to reject it later on.

The project proceeded by designing and refining a couple of

advertisements for the domestic version. At this stage, the Fiskars team also asked Törmä for cost estimates and media plans. The account team, in turn, wanted more information about Fiskars for the development of the advertisements. Communication between the parties was relatively open (Figure 5.26[e]). The Fiskars team was ready to share confidential strategic information with the account team. The parties, Roni Bensky and Marja Tuunanen, Ingmar Lindberg and Leena Kahila-Bergh, also met each other a few times.

The state of the business relationship in late spring 1990

The innovativeness of the assignment, its economic significance and its strategic importance in extending cooperation with Fiskars all increased the attractiveness of the client in the eyes of the account team. Fiskars had always been an attractive client for Törmä, but cooperation was not very active at that time with any of its units. The image campaign drew the team's attention back to Fiskars again.

The Consumer Products Group had recently drawn up a new strategic plan for the coming years, which provided the account team with new information and ideas (Figure 5.26[h]). The new strategy seemed promising. Törmä could expect challenging briefs in the future and new opportunities to use its capabilities on the client's behalf. Törmä ranked Fiskars among its most attractive clients, because the company gave inter-national assignments in which the agency could also develop its own capabilities. It was worth investing in such a potential client. The manage-ment of the agency and the account teams were personally committed to the planning of the campaign.

In turn, the Fiskars team had confidence in the capabilities of Törmä and in its willingness to offer quality work. The participation of Erkki Yrjölä as an account supervisor in the project increased their peace of mind. The proposals presented by the agency to date had been convincing.

Interaction in the summer and autumn of 1990

The summer holidays caused a natural break in the interaction. However, as early as June, the parties began to realise that cooperation was not advancing as well as expected. Communication had decreased and the planning process had begun to stagnate (see Figure 5.28). The account team felt that Fiskars was not willing to give them the information they needed to plan the advertisements. Other Head Office projects seemed to be taking precedence over the image project and the account team felt that it had to push the process forward. The decreased investment initiative aroused dissatisfaction on the agency side (Figure 5.26[i] and [j]).

170

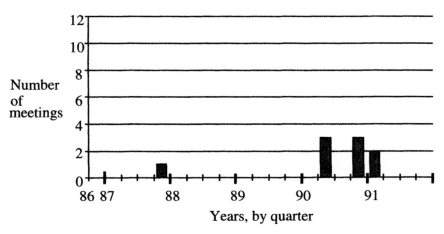

Figure 5.28 Documented meetings between Head Office and Törmä

A new problem arose when Pirjo Virola, the creative team's copy-writer, left Törmä in mid June (Figure 5.26[k]). Consequently, the account team did not have a permanent copywriter for four months (Figure 5.26[l]). Törmä was planning the merger with Markkinointiryhmä Mary Oy and it was not reasonable to employ new personnel at that point (Figure 5.26[m]). As a result, the planning of the advertisements and particularly the development of the international version did not proceed. The Fiskars team felt that Törmä was not being enterprising enough in acquiring the information it needed from Fiskars (Figure 5.26[i] and [j]). When the new Copywriter, Pia Vilmi, finally started in October, she had to be informed about the image campaign (Figure 5.26[n]). Both Leena Kahila-Bergh and Marja Tuunanen invested their time and energy in giving her the necessary information about Fiskars and the project (Figure 5.26[o]).

During the autumn, the situation had also changed at Fiskars. The Finnish economy fell into a deep recession which spoiled the company's sales prospects in the home market (Figure 5.26[p]). Several other countries in Europe were also suffering from recession. Fiskars's earnings had been in decline during 1989, and that trend seemed set to strengthen. In addition, the stock exchange had slowed down in Finland. In this situation, Fiskars had to reconsider the needs as well as the goals of the planned image campaign.

All these events in the economic environment and in partner companies caused delays in the image project. Marja Tuunanen sent media plans and cost estimates to Fiskars, but the Corporate Executive Committee was not yet ready to make any decisions. Törmä had also invoiced Fiskars for the planning work carried out so far. Head Office was not satisfied with the

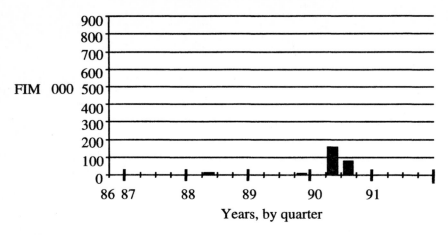

Figure 5.29 Invoicing between Head Office and Törmä, adjusted by the wholesale price index (1985 = 100)

invoice, however (Figure 5.26[j]). The agency had already invoiced them
for a considerable sum of money, even though they had nothing concrete
to show at that point, not even a single advertisement (see also Figure
5.29).

Finally, in October, the project moved on but in a rather different form.
The parties met each other again at a couple of meetings in which the
primary goals and target groups of the campaign were renegotiated
(Figure 5.26[q]). Törmä's team wanted to know the possible launch date
of the campaign in order to include it in its budget but Fiskars had not
yet decided on the schedule. The new deadline for the advertisements
was set for the end of the year. The message of the campaign had to be
changed so that it would appeal to the average consumer more and also
increase sales of consumer products. The company management wanted
to take the new strategic ideas of consumer product marketing into
account. This implied that Fiskars should include Stig Måtar, the Director
of the Scandinavian Business Group, and Matti Ranta, the Sales Director
for Finland, in the project.

A coordinating meeting was organised in the village of Fiskars at the
beginning of November (Figure 5.26[r]). The client wanted to inspire and
motivate the account team by inviting them to the historical surround-
ings of the old ironworks. In addition to the teams of Törmä and Head
Office, Stig Måtar and Matti Ranta were present at the meeting. The
account team had listed a couple of open questions, which it considered
important for the campaign and which needed to be answered. The
parties held a broad discussion which touched on the current company
image, the wishes and goals of the different units, the marketing policy

of the different product families, the importance of in-store displays of Fiskars products, and so on. One of the questions was how could the costs of the campaign be divided between the units.

On the basis of this meeting, the account team presented a broad proposal for the image campaign at the end of November (Figure 5.26[s]). This meeting turned out to be a big disappointment for both parties and a turning point in the long planning process. Ingmar Lindberg and Leena Kahila-Bergh realised that Törmä's team had not understood the goals or the content of the campaign as they saw them (Figure 5.26[t]). The proposal, including a campaign for company personnel and ideas for product marketing, did not correspond to the original ideas of the Fiskars team. It was a far cry from the three advertisements Fiskars required, which should have appealed to the general public and potential investors, at image level only, without incorporating selected facts (Figure 5.26[u]). Moreover, the entire proposal would have cost the company a fortune. The resultant feeling of resentment and irritation was mutual.

Satisfaction with the relationship and the situation in December 1990

During ten months of working together, the teams at Head Office and Törmä had not been able to fix clear and common goals for the image campaign. A number of events in the economic environment as well as in partner companies had caused delays and changes in the project and increased its ambiguity. Confusion increased when the Malmi unit and the Scandinavian Business Group were integrated into the campaign as informants and payers. The parties also had different views concerning the content and style of the image campaign. Törmä took the initiative and made proposals for broadening the campaign, but these ideas did not please Head Office.

Cooperation had not proceeded as expected. Both interacting teams were disappointed in some respects with the cooperation and with each other's working styles (Figure 5.26[v]). Head Office complained about Törmä's lack of initiative in asking for and acquiring the information they needed about Fiskars. From their perspective it seemed that Törmä had been more enterprising in selling its own ideas than in effectively executing the brief. Törmä's team, in turn, was annoyed about the lack of clear briefing and clear vision about what should be communicated to the public. It was obvious that both parties were somewhat inexperienced in this kind of exceptional assignment but, nevertheless, Törmä's team would have expected more effort from Fiskars in the briefing. In these turbulent circumstances, the management of Fiskars seemed not even to know what they wanted themselves. In the absence of a clear brief it was easy for the team to become confused and also to cling to their own ideas of the project.

Fiskars had supposed that the account team already knew Fiskars well as a corporation when starting the project. In fact, only some of the team members had been cooperating or were in active contact with the client. Marja Tuunanen was newly employed at Törmä and, unfortunately for the project, the copywriter also changed during the process. The personal contact between Marja Tuunanen and Leena Kahila-Bergh did not work out as well as they had hoped, either. Considering the importance and the nature of the project they met rather rarely.

Both operative teams had great confidence in the personal relationship between Ingmar Lindberg and Erkki Yrjölä. They supposed that information about the project and knowledge of the company would be transferred through this channel during the process. However, such seemed not to be the case. Erkki Yrjölä and Ingmar Lindberg only occasionally discussed business matters. Internal communication at Törmä did not work particularly well either. There were two account supervisors on the project, which obscured the boundaries of responsibility. Neither the management of Fiskars nor that of Törmä participated actively in cooperation. Erkki Yrjölä, who had developed the original idea for the image campaign, did not take part in the process personally in its later phases. Other matters seemed to be more important to Fiskars.

The account team interpreted the difficulty in obtaining the requested information from the client as unwillingness and therefore as a display of distrust on the part of the client. The Fiskars team also began to have doubts about Törmä's capabilities and willingness to offer a solution to the client's needs. The feeling of trust had decreased on both sides and aroused uncertainty about the outcome of the project (Figure 5.26[x]).

The project was still being worked on and both Fiskars and Törmä were strongly committed to completing it (Figure 5.26[y]). The parties had adapted to the changing situations, invested time, money and thought in the project and naturally wished that it would reach a satisfactory conclusion. Marja Tuunanen and Leena Kahila-Bergh, in particular, had put personal effort into cooperation. A common vision and understanding of the project had not emerged, however. They felt frustrated and their willingness to work with each other decreased. It was particularly difficult for the account team to change their ideas about the campaign at this stage and to find the motivation for a fresh start. New faces were needed in order to provide the client with what it wanted. Consequently, Törmä selected a new team for the project (Figure 5.26[z]). At the same time the Fiskars team decided to invite Erkki Yrjölä to Fiskars (Figure 5.26[aa]). It was time to discuss what had gone wrong and how the project could be brought to a satisfactory conclusion.

At this stage, the parties were not ready to say anything about the future of their business relationship or their willingness to continue cooperation after the project had been completed. It would have meant progressing in advance of events. The most important thing was to bring the image project to an end. The future essentially depended on it. If the relationship later broke down it would not cause any particular economic or social loss for the parties. Fiskars Head Office was not committed to Törmä in any concrete way. An alternative partner could easily be found, even though it would require some time and effort to start a new relationship. For Törmä, the loss of Fiskars would primarily mean the loss of attractive business opportunities in the future.

Interaction during 1991

Erkki Yrjölä did not meet Ingmar Lindberg and Leena Kahila-Bergh until the end of January. With the help of favourable personal relationships the parties reached a mutual understanding. They both agreed that the content of the project had been transformed during the process and had moved away from the original idea. They then decided to put the original idea into a concrete form. Erkki Yrjölä promised that Törmä would plan the required three advertisements as soon as possible without charge (Figure 5.26[bb]).

The visit of Erkki Yrjölä restored the confidence of the client in the possibility of attaining a satisfactory result from the project (Figure 5.26[cc]). The meeting had shown that the agency was willing to provide quality work and that the parties could still agree on common goals for the project. The process could thus continue in a cooperative spirit. The prospects of economic recovery also seemed more promising again. At that time, neither party had any idea how deep the recession was to become.

Erkki Yrjölä mediated the task to the new team, which included the Account Supervisor, Rolf Hällfors, the Account Executive, Asser Kaksonen, and from the earlier competing team the Copywriter, Jari Korhonen, and the Art Director, Risto Miettinen. Cooperation started in a positive atmosphere at a personal level as well, since Asser Kaksonen knew both Leena Kahila-Bergh and Ingmar Lindberg from previous acquaintance (see Figure 5.30).

It was most important for the new team to redeem the promises that the client had been given. Asser Kaksonen met the Fiskars team, which informed him about the planning of the advertisements. The brief was now carefully considered but also tight. It did not leave much room for innovation. As a result, Asser Kaksonen found it difficult to motivate his team to do their best in creative planning.

Asser Kaksonen and Erkki Yrjölä presented the team's ideas to the client in March. Ingmar Lindberg and Leena Kahila-Bergh were satisfied with the planning work and accepted the advertisements as such (Figure 5.26[dd]). Nevertheless, the working style of the new team, as had been

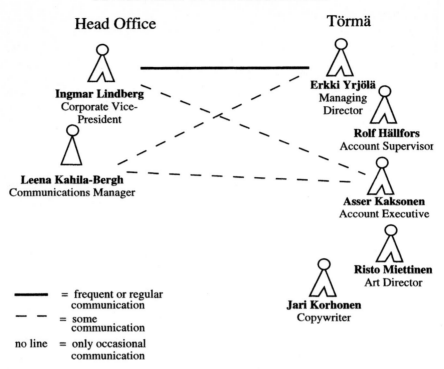

Figure 5.30 The interacting teams and the frequency of communication between Head Office and Törmä in the active phase (1991)

the case with the previous one, did not correspond with their ideas of investment initiative or innovative agency work. The process started to stagnate again. In order to finish the planning work, Törmä had to get in touch with certain foreign clients of Fiskars whose statements could be used as testimonials. The account team also needed some information about Fiskars. The advertisements were to be ready before the summer, but it seemed that the client's effort in pushing the process forward had decreased again. Dissatisfaction with cooperation increased (Figure 5.26[ee]).

At the beginning of the autumn, the drafts of the advertisements were finally ready (Figure 5.26[ff]). The account team waited for the right time to plan and start the campaign. In the light of the feedback received, the team had confidence in the client's willingness to brief Törmä on the media campaign whenever the time was ripe. However, it seemed evident that the campaign could not be launched for a long time. Matti Ranta and Stig Måtar were not willing to participate in the costs of the campaign, at least during that year, and under the prevailing economic circumstances (Figure 5.26[gg]). The Corporate President, Reijo Kaukonen, had resigned in August, which increased uncertainty among the corporate management and in decision-making (Figure 5.26[hh]). It was not yet clear who would succeed him. The economic recession continued, the stock exchange was totally stagnant and the company's profitability had further deteriorated from the previous year. For the time being there was nothing to do but wait (Figure 5.26ii]).

Summary of the initial phase

The initial phase from the end of 1986 to the end of 1989 was a dormant period in the relationship between Head Office and Törmä. Business exchange was minimal, as the client had no clear need of Törmä's services at that time. The parties communicated with each other, however, and left the door open to possible future exchange. They both felt attraction to each other. They built an infrastructure for their relationship, i.e. favourable personal relationships at management level and knowledge of each other. The relationship thus existed more at a potential than at an active level.

In 1990–91, the parties finally executed a larger assignment. As a major and challenging project, the company image campaign further increased the attraction the agency felt towards the client. Cooperation started in an enthusiastic atmosphere and inspired the agency, in particular, to invest in the relationship. Gradually, however, various events in the economic environment and in the partner companies prevented the smooth advance of the project. The new strategy of the Consumer Products Group, the deep recession in the Finnish economy, the substantial fall on the stock exchange, and the contracting earnings of the corporation put pressure on the partners to change the goals and content of the project. The merger at Törmä and the change of copywriter also led to stagnation.

The expected growth of the relationship turned out to be a continuation of uncertainty and investment typical of the initial phase. Dissatisfaction and disappointment characterised the relationship. They concerned not only the interaction style, its openness and investment initiative in particular, but also the personal relationships between contact persons and the lack of inter-firm knowledge. Problems that arose during the project resulted in decreased trust between the parties. The change of team, new creative work without payment, the new briefing by the client and new efforts on the part of management all showed commitment to the project and a willingness to see it through. In spite of these efforts, trust could not be fully restored. The simultaneous negative impact of several contextual factors negated the efforts of the contact persons. The planning phase of the project was finally finished but nobody was really satisfied with the whole experience. The future of the relationship remained completely open, since the parties had not become behaviourally committed during their relationship.

6

A MODIFIED PROCESS MODEL OF ADVERTISING AGENCY–CLIENT RELATIONSHIPS

The purpose of this study is to build an empirically grounded process model for understanding the development of advertising agency–client relationships. Three broad questions were set to answer the research question:

1 Which theoretical concepts are the most appropriate to describe the content of an advertising agency–client relationship?
2 What are the processes through which advertising agency–client relationships develop?
3 Which contextual factors have an influence on the development process of advertising agency–client relationships and how does this influence manifest itself?

In this chapter I answer these questions by confronting the *a priori* process model with the empirical case description. In accordance with the chosen research strategy, new ideas and theoretical modifications are sought in this comparison. A modified process model of the development of agency–client relationships will be developed discussing each concept, conceptual relationship and processual pattern in detail.

Besides the case description, all advertising sector-related information gathered in the pilot study and during the research process will be used as empirical evidence in the development of the model. Recent findings of other empirical studies of the advertising industry, of other professional service industries or of other buyer–seller contexts will also be used as supporting evidence for the emerging process model.

Figure 6.1 describes the form of the emerging model. Prerequisites for a business relationship are distinguished as a separate conceptual category in the model. Four conceptual categories are identified within the content of agency–client relationships: interaction processes and related interaction styles, the evolving relational infrastructure, the perceived outcomes of interaction processes, and evolving relational bonds. Each concept belonging to these categories will be examined in the light of the

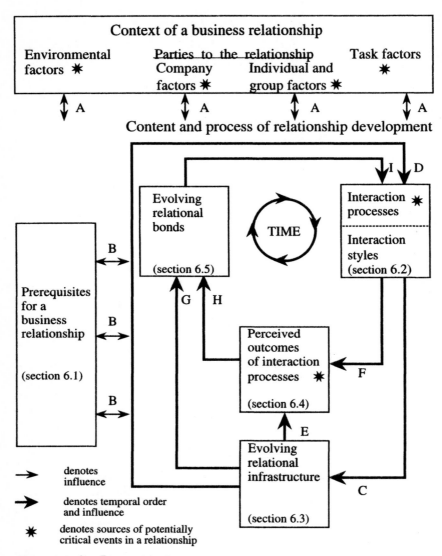

Figure 6.1 The emerging process model of the development of advertising agency–client relationships.

empirical evidence. The meaning of the concepts, and their dimensions and indicators in the empirical data, are specified. Some old concepts are dropped and new ones – viewed as descriptively more powerful – are introduced, in their place.

The development process is addressed by investigating the temporal and logical relationships between concepts. A number of propositions are put forward concerning the new concepts and the new conceptual relationships between the concepts of the emerging model. In addition, the development process is examined in terms of events. Critical events are identified in the content and the context of relationships. As a result of critical events and the subsequent development processes, different phases and cycles are identified in the development of relationships.

Agency-client relationships emerge in a context comprised of various environmental, organisational, individual, group and task-related factors. The link between contextual factors and the content and process of relationship development will be considered throughout the analysis.

The model's concepts and their relationships will be discussed in detail in the following sections. In section 6.1, I shall first examine the pre-requisites for a business relationship. In sections 6.2–5, I concentrate on the conceptual content of advertising agency–client relationships and the relationships between the concepts. Sections 6.6–8 discuss the process of relationship development more explicitly. Finally, in section 6.9 the research results will be summarised in the form of a modified process model.

6.1 PREREQUISITES FOR A BUSINESS RELATIONSHIP

In the *a priori* process model I identified three prerequisites for an advertising agency–client relationship: complementary needs and resources between parties, personal awareness of the other party's goals, needs and resources, and finally common interest in building a business rela-tionship. These three factors were also identified as elementary for relationship development in the unit business relationships studied between the agency and the client. The study revealed, however, that the prerequisites were not only relevant to the initiation of a relationship, but that *there is a continuing requirement for the existence of the prerequisites for a business relationship, and that they are continually assessed by the parties to the relationship.*

Several informant statements in the data referred to the existence and assessment of prerequisites. Table 6.1 illustrates the nature of these statements and lists a set of inductively derived indicators that were considered empirical manifestations of the three prerequisites.

The complementarity of needs and resources between the parties was manifested in all three unit relationships studied. When starting the

Table 6.1 Indicators of the prerequisites for a business relationship

Indicator	Concept
Estimate of the degree of complementarity between the client's needs and the agency's resources, based on the client's perceptions of - the nature of its needs for the advertising agency's services - the fit of the agency's resources and capabilities to the client's needs Estimate of the degree of complementarity between the agency's needs and the client's resources, based on the agency's perceptions of - its need for the client - the fit of the client and its resources to the agency's needs	Complementary needs and resources between parties
Estimate of the degree of personal awareness, based on - efforts to build awareness (agency presentations, creation of personal contacts) - existing personal relationships with the personnel of the other party - referrals from friends and business acquaintances	Personal awareness of the other party's goals needs and resources
Estimate of the degree of mutual interest, based on the parties' statements about - their potential to materialise their own interests through the relationship while also benefiting the other party - lack of potential to materialise their own benefits through the relationship	Common interest in building a business relationship

relationship with Törmä, Billnäs had a clear and urgent need for advertising services. Törmä, for its part, was actively seeking new clients (see section 5.2.1 pp. 101). The decision of the Consumer Products Group to use the same advertising materials internationally, and the need to launch the new product Roll-Sharp on the Finnish market, created a need for Malmi to use Törmä's services (see section 5.3.1, p. 141). In the relationship with Head Office, the need for Törmä's services arose fairly late from the company's concern to strengthen its image among investors (see section 5.4.1, p. 165). The match between the needs of the client and the resources and related capabilities of the agency was pronounced. Informants on both client and agency sides brought up the issue of compatibility:

> The most important issue is definitely that it's a quality agency, that it does a good job. Because we're seen as a quality company with quality products, and so on, there has to be quality and brand thinking at the agency as well.

> The agency knows what it can do best, and so we try to find the right clients to match our know-how. Clients who are large, demanding and who could be lucrative from our point of view.

It also became clear that the parties' needs and resources change over time. *Every time a change occurs, the parties need to create a new fit between their needs and resources in order to maintain the relationship.* Changes may happen during individual assignments or over longer time periods during the relationship's existence. Once the marketing unit of Billnäs, for instance, had implemented the new look for the Classic products, its needs for Törmä's services diminished (section 5.2.5, p. 123). Various contextual factors also affected the client's needs for advertising services. Changes in the client's marketing strategy shifted its emphasis to the advertising of new product groups, e.g. lawn and garden tools, and to new types of tasks, e.g. the planning of point-of-sale materials (section 5.2.7, p. 133). Changes in the client's policy towards outside agencies – the change in emphasis on cost effectiveness and the use of internal resources, for instance – relocated the client's preferences and reduced its needs for Törmä's services (see section 5.2.7, p. 133). Environmental trends, like recession, and changes in the parties' intra-group nets, such as the organisational change in the Fiskars Consumer Products Group, also influenced the needs the parties felt it necessary to satisfy through exchange.

The parties purposely acquired new resources for themselves, and their resources also developed through interaction. As suggested by Ford *et al.* (1986: 33), interaction does not only employ the resources of a company, but also translates the resources into capabilities, and leads to change and development in resources over time. As a consequence of changing client needs, the maintenance of a business relationship required continual resource adaptation on the part of both parties, and for the agency in particular. The agency had to grow with the changing needs of the client (see Michell 1987: 31). Törmä, for instance, tried to demonstrate its capabilities in new areas by making speculative presentations. Interaction with a capable partner was perceived as an opportunity to develop one's own abilities in marketing and advertising. Several contact persons mentioned that certain assignments had been important personal learning processes.

Personal awareness of the other party, its goals, needs and resources, was constructed through agency presentations in particular. Existing personal relationships and contact networks were actively used to find new business opportunities. *Personal relationships were indeed revealed to have a significant role in creating the necessary awareness of the other party, particularly of its resources and capabilities* (see also Van de Ven 1976: 31).

In the case study and pilot study interviews, I was able to identify several cases where favourable personal relationships had a decisive influence on the initiation of a business relationship. In the case of Törmä and Fiskars, the strong personal relationship at top management level provided an impetus for starting the business relationship (see section 5.2.1, p. 101). This personal relationship, together with the earlier decision to use Törmä as the company's agency, later contributed to the establishment of the relationship with Malmi and also activated the relationship with Head Office (see section 5.3.1, p. 141 and section 5.4.1, p. 161). By that time awareness of the agency's resources had also developed amongst other people in the client company.

Earlier research results lend further support to these findings. Studies of agency selection have shown that agency presentations and personal contact with agency personnel are the major sources of information in agency selection (e.g. Dowling 1994: 236). Cagley (1986) and Marshall and Bong Na (1994) further suggest that the quality of people assigned to the account is an important criterion in agency selection. It is evident that personal contact is necessary for convincing the parties of the potential of the relationship. In the case studied, favourable personal relationships were regarded as a resource or a means of achieving satisfying exchange outcomes. A client representative put it this way:

> Yes, sure, social relations, that you know somebody [in the agency] has a lot to do with [establishing the relationship]. But I wouldn't call it doing business because of a friendship. Of course it's a fact that if you know somebody you know how he works and you trust that he'll do the job just right. If you give the job to him it's much easier . . . It's a distinct benefit . . . At least I know that it'll be done as well as they can do it there and that it'll be finished, and that he won't have the heart to ask me quite the top price for it.

In addition, referrals from friends, business acquaintances or employees who themselves had experience of a potential agency played an important role in the initiation of new business relationships. Billnäs, for instance, used referrals as an important source of information in the choice of Törmä (see section 5.2.1, p. 101) and when it later selected other smaller agencies (see sections 5.2.5, p. 128 and 5.2.7, p. 137). These findings are congruent with other studies of professional business service sectors, which also emphasise the role of referrals in relationship establishment (see Wheiler 1987: 198–9; Yorke 1988: 627; Lindmark 1989: 13–14).

The study also showed that parties need to find at least some common interest in building a business relationship, if they wish to get it started and make it develop (cf. Houston and Gassenheimer 1987: 10; Ford 1989: 825; see also Cagley 1986: 40; Marshall and Bong Na 1994: 224). Each party needs to feel that it benefits from building a business relationship. The following extracts from agency interviews give examples of the importance of common interests:

> We had this client for just over a year and it was certainly a short-term relationship . . . Our worlds were so different. The client had a surprisingly short-term approach though they represent a world-wide brand. They wanted the job done very quickly and cheaply, and we really couldn't work with so little thought and money.

> It's obvious that it isn't worth practising a 'take-the-money-and-run' system. But we specifically set out to build really long-term client relationships. And that means that we have to give so much that the client is really satisfied and that we have a positive impact on the client's business. But at the same time of course we want to make money – I mean, that's what we're here for!

A client representative stated:

> The agency's got to understand which hat the client is wearing at any particular moment, or what's realistic. And I think that this agency has got it pretty right: they don't try to sell us the sun and the moon at the same time.

It also became obvious that some differences of interest are inevitable in any business relationship (cf. Ford *et al.* 1986: 28). Differing interests hindered the progressive development of business relationships only when they became considerable. The necessary conflict between advertisers as buyers and agencies as sellers manifested itself in the clients' willingness to obtain the necessary services at the lowest possible price, and in the agencies' willingness to sell more services and at higher profit margins.

The differences and similarities in the parties' interests were clearly manifested when the three unit relationships were compared, and when changes of interests were investigated separately in each relation.

At the beginning of the relationship with Billnäs, the parties clearly had parallel conceptions of advertising; the strategies of the client were discussed and the goals of the tasks became clear for both parties. In addition, the client and its well established consumer brand were a good fit with the agency's philosophy of creating long-lasting brands (see section 5.2.1, p. 98). When cooperation advanced, Billnäs also discussed its expectations concerning the role of the agency within the client's international marketing units. During this interaction, expectations of mutual benefits emerged and the relationship developed into a close partnership (see e.g. section 5.2.3, p. 110). Later the distance between the parties' interests increased. Business exchange reduced, the role of the agency became narrower and the types of assignment changed. The parties' conceptions of the right type and quality of advertising also began to differ. The client decreased its investment in advertising and started to control its advertising costs more carefully (see e.g. section 5.2.5, pp. 123–5). In consequence the relationship became weaker.

The relationship with Malmi provides another kind of example. In initiating the relationship, the parties had different expectations about the role of Törmä and about an appropriate price level for the required services. The settlement of expectations was necessary to the establishment of an independent business relationship (see section 5.3.1, p. 142). Even in the later phases of the relationship, the parties could not reach full consensus about the role and economic importance of advertising in the client's marketing (see better section 5.3.2, p. 153). As a result, the relationship never developed into a strong and close partnership.

In the relationship with Head Office the client's unrealistic expectations concerning the agency's knowledge about the client company caused problems and dissatisfaction with the interaction (see section 5.4.1, pp. 173–4).

To summarise, the study revealed that the existence of common interests fosters the establishment and progressive development of a business relationship. Some degree of mutual interest is always required to maintain a relationship.

6.2 INTERACTION PROCESSES AND INTERACTION STYLES

Three types of interaction process were separated in the *a priori* model as processes that form business relationships: exchange processes, coordination processes and adaptation processes (see Möller and Wilson 1988: 5, 1995a: 27).

These three processes also seemed to cover the various episodes that could be identified in the agency–client unit relationships studied (see Figure 6.2). *Exchange, coordination and adaptation processes could be identified in the data, but it also became evident that they were strongly connected with each other.* They were interwoven in a continuous process of actions, reactions and re-reactions between the parties, where it was difficult to discern any temporal order between the processes. In the relationships studied, coordination often required adaptation on the part of the parties and information exchange was often related to coordination or adaptation. In fact, coordination and adaptation processes can be regarded as integral parts of exchange processes, or, conversely, when either coordination or adaptation is the focus of investigation, the remaining two can be seen as integral parts of that process. For instance, mutual adjustments and the exchange of information can both be seen as means of achieving coordination between the parties (see Larsson and Bowen 1989: 227; Anderson and Weitz 1992: 21).

It is the essence of interaction that it is also a continuous process of interpretation (see Ford *et al.* 1986: 27–8). In the case study, the importance of interpretation for understanding the development of business relationships was pronounced. The parties interpreted each other's actions and intentions, and based their own actions and assessments of the business relationship on these interpretations.

The interaction style turned out to be an important element of agency–client relationships. Interaction style has typically been viewed as a characteristic of individual people or interpersonal interaction (see Sheth 1976; Lehtinen 1983; Lehtinen and Lehtinen 1991), but the case study showed that it can also be seen as a characteristic of inter-firm interaction. *Interaction style is thus specified here as the manner in which inter-firm interaction is conducted.* Three types of interaction style were identified in the study: openness of communication, formality of control and investment initiative (see Figure 6.2). The three interaction processes, and types or dimensions of interaction style, will be examined in more detail in the following sections.

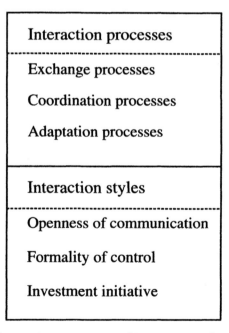

Interaction processes

- -

Exchange processes

Coordination processes

Adaptation processes

Interaction styles

- -

Openness of communication

Formality of control

Investment initiative

Figure 6.2 The interaction processes and interaction styles in an advertising agency–client relationship

6.2.1 Exchange processes

The exchange process concept

In the *a priori* model, the exchange process concept was used to refer to individual assignments executed in advertising agency–client relationships. In the light of the strong interdependence of exchange, coordination and adaptation processes this definition no longer seems logical. The execution of any assignment involves episodes of exchange, coordination and adaptation – not only episodes of exchange.

In advertising agency–client relationships, individual assignments play an important role. Exchange is not only a flow of exchange episodes between the parties as proposed in the IMP Group's Interaction Model (see Håkansson 1982: 16; see also Johansson and Mattsson 1987: 37), but rather a series of individual assignments. When the emphasis is on describing relationship development over time, the concept of assignment is useful. Assignments are processes or events that can be distinguished and studied empirically. By contrast, when the emphasis is on describing the types of episodes and processes that occur in agency–client relationships, then the concepts of exchange, coordination and adaptation processes are relevant.

As a consequence, I prefer to use *the term 'assignment process' when referring to individual assignments executed in an advertising agency–client relationship. The exchange process concept is used to describe the flow of exchange episodes and the type of these episodes in an agency–client relationship.*

The processual nature of assignments was found to be pronounced in this study. The time duration of an assignment process ranged from about three weeks to 16 months. Assignments were characterised by several phases, recurrent meetings and contacts, eventual changes in plans, delays in time schedules, and 'second rounds' of creative planning and materials production.

Table 6.2 illustrates the nature of the data that were interpreted as manifestations of assignment processes and exchange processes in the study. An assignment process was defined empirically to start from the brief and to end at the last invoice concerning that assignment. Within the three unit relationships, I investigated 24 assignments in more detail and further identified several smaller ones. Several types of assignment were studied: concept planning and packaging design for consumer brands for markets both at home and abroad, product launch campaigns, media campaigns for old products and company image planning. The value of the studied assignments ranged from FIM 30,000 to around FIM 1.3 million. Assignments also varied clearly in terms of importance, degree of innovation and breadth.

Exchange processes form the most elementary content of advertising agency–client interaction. They incorporate two major types of exchange:

Table 6.2 Indicators of assignment and exchange processes

Indicator	Concept
Period from brief to last invoice	Assignment process
Estimate of the intensity of business exchange per three months • Volume of invoicing • Number of ongoing assignments	Business exchange
Estimate of the intensity of communication per three months • Number of documented meetings • Number of meetings × number of people present • Number of people in face-to-face contact • Qualitative estimation of contact frequency, including all modes of communication (face-to-face, letters, telephone calls, fax messages, etc.)	Communication

business exchange, which refers to the exchange of the service for money, and communication, which includes the social and information exchange necessary for the execution of advertising services. *In order to make the model more straightforward, social and information exchange are integrated here into one concept – communication.* More sophisticated divisions (see e.g. Håkansson 1982: 16; Johanson and Mattsson 1987: 38; Möller and Wilson 1988: 5) seem unnecessary here and are in practice difficult to make. The concept of communication is also commonly used in channel relationship models (see e.g. Anderson and Narus 1990; Anderson and Weitz 1992) or buyer–seller relationship models (Dwyer *et al.* 1987; Crosby *et al.* 1990).

I define communication here as the sharing of information and meaning between parties to the relationship (see also Anderson and Narus 1984: 66). Parties pass information to each other through communication but also convey meaning and evince their values and attitudes, which is necessary for service provision and a working relationship.

The intensity of exchange is an elementary characteristic of a business relationship. Changes in exchange intensity often indicate major changes in the whole relationship, as could be seen in the case descriptions. Two indicators could be used for the intensity of business exchange: invoicing in Finnish marks and the number of ongoing assignments, each per quarter (see Table 6.2). The intensity of communication, for its part, was assessed by using four indicators that reflect the frequency of contact between the parties through various modes of communication and the number of people involved in communication.[1]

Temporal considerations of exchange processes

The case study revealed that assignment processes were often dependent on each other over time. The influence of the adopted marketing strategy on assignments, and especially on the recurrence of assignments within the current unit relationship, became clearly apparent in the study. In the relationship between Billnäs and Törmä, everything started from a new internationally standardised marketing strategy. The decision to create a new look for household products led to a series of assignments with the same agency. The renewed concepts and new products had later to be launched on the Finnish and other European markets, which increased business exchange between the companies and led to the establishment of a relationship with the Malmi unit. Thus within the limits of the new strategy, one assignment process created the logical need for another and led in this case to the expansion of interactions in another unit. It should be remembered, however, that single-execution assignments also exist that are independent of other assignments.

The timing of assignments may also be relevant to the development of relationships. It appears from the data that timing is dependent on the marketing and advertising strategy, and consequently on the type of brief. The redesign of the creative strategy and the perceived urgency of its execution led to assignments piling up and consequently to intensive interactions in the growth phase of the relationship with Billnäs. This created favourable conditions for building a strong relationship within a short time period. In the relationship with Malmi, on the other hand, the briefs concerned media campaigns organised primarily for the purpose of supporting distribution channel supply. The peaks in market demand and purchases by distributors determined the timing of briefs and campaigns. They were organised on a fairly regular twice-yearly basis. This appears to have secured regular communication between the parties but no period of intensive interactions. The relationship also remained weak.

Similar contextual factors that changed the client's needs for advertising services also affected the intensity of business exchange. For instance, economic recession significantly decreased exchange intensity in the relationship with Malmi (see section 5.3.3, pp. 158). The organisation change and the client's new policies decreased the intensity of business exchange in the relationship with Billnäs (see section 5.2.5, pp. 123; section 5.2.7, p. 133).

It appears that critical events in relationships foster more communication between the parties. For instance, in the organisational change, personal contacts between the companies increased temporarily. A parallel situation was identified in the relationship with Head Office when conflict arose in the planning of the company image campaign (see section 5.4.1, p. 175).

These results also get support from earlier findings in industrial settings, according to which unforeseen interruptions and crises affect the intensity of contact between the parties (see Cunningham and Turnbull 1982: 315). In this study, increased communication was particularly prevalent in the increased participation of management, which also reflects increasing investment in the business relationship.

6.2.2 Coordination processes

Coordination turned out to be an especially important element in the interaction between agencies and clients. Harmonisation of actions and decisions between the parties necessarily constitutes a significant part of interaction, since advertising services are created in the interaction between agency and client (cf. Mills 1986: 49). The case study also revealed that *the control of assignment processes, and the development and use of mechanisms that facilitated the monitoring of exchange, formed an integral part of coordination processes.*

In the agency–client unit relationships studied coordination involved various elements of the business relationship. It influenced the perceived outcomes of interaction processes as well as relationship development. On the one hand, coordination concerned individual assignment processes and on the other, the whole business relationship (see Table 6.3).

First of all, the parties have to agree upon the division of work within assignment processes. This means that they decide, for instance, who will contract and control the various producers of film, packaging and other materials, who will take responsibility for translations, and whether the agency will take part in campaign presentations to dealers, and so on. When similar tasks recurred, as in the relationship with Billnäs, the parties did not then need to discuss their duties each time; certain norms in the distribution of work became established between them. However, the distribution of duties did sometimes change as well. At the beginning of the relationship, Billnäs issued broad assignments, since there was a great deal to do in the implementation of the new strategy; time was tight and Billnäs's personnel had limited experience of product launches and the planning of new product concepts (see section 5.2.3, p. 109). In later phases of the relationship, briefs became narrower as the client's own resources and capabilities increased. Billnäs no longer used Törmä's resources in international launch meetings or in the printing of brochures (see section 5.2.5, p. 126 and section 5.2.6, p. 131).

Coordination also involved the temporal harmonisation of assignment processes. This refers to the continuous negotiations regarding what should be done, and especially when. Because of the processual nature of assignments, three temporal issues emerge in interactions, i.e. the need for time schedules, the need for synchronisation of activities and the need

191

Table 6.3 Indicators of coordination processes

Indicators	Concept
The nature of coordination as manifested in	
- arrangements concerning the division of work within assignment processes - temporal harmonisation of assignment processes - arrangements concerning contact people - contract negotiations - invoicing and cost negotiations - future assignment negotiations	Coordination

for time allocation (see Hassard 1991: 116). The parties decided upon outline timetables and activity plans in briefings, but detailed plans and agreements were finished in day-to-day operations. A client informant described her requirements for an agency relationship:

> The tempo of our operation is often very hectic. That's just the way the business is. You've got to react really fast: sometimes there are sudden changes. I need an agency like this which does what's required almost overnight and an account executive who runs like dry skin when we're in a hurry.

Continuous synchronisation was necessary, since each assignment process is composed of a chain of activities that need to occur partly concurrently and partly consecutively, and which require attention from either one or both of the parties, depending on the activity. What is more, both parties also had to decide how to allocate their time most efficiently to different tasks inside their companies as well as within the framework of interactions. Time was indeed perceived to be money for the inter-acting firms. This was partly due to the fee system applied in the unit business relationships studied.

Coordination was clearly manifested in the arrangements concerning contact people, which also reflects the people-intensive nature of advertising services. In the execution of an assignment it is essential to know which individuals are responsible for what, and with whom one should make contact with reference to each specific detail. In the unit relationships studied, the agency appointed a 'permanent' account team, but the client mostly named responsible contact persons from case to case. The need for personnel arrangements and communication regarding interacting staff showed a particular increase when some of the contact persons changed (see e.g. the relationship with Malmi, section 5.3.3, p. 155), but also when the operation of the business relationship itself required modifications of individuals' responsibilities or new contact persons (see e.g. the relationship with Billnäs, section 5.2.3, p. 111 and the relationship with Head Office, section 5.4.1, p. 175). Nevertheless, it became apparent that the parties expected each other to take the initiative in naming and changing contact people. These things were rarely negotiated; decisions seemed to be taken independently rather than together.

The parties arranged the maintenance of contact so that representatives of each hierarchical level worked mainly with their opposite numbers, and so that several levels were involved. In other words, 'the matched status, multi-level contact pattern' was used (see Cunningham and Homse 1986: 16). Besides this custom, it was typical that, at least for briefings and presentations of bigger campaigns, people at different hierarchical levels, and sometimes from different functional areas, met each other. Contact patterns of this nature are fairly common throughout the sector. Advertising is typically team work, which implies that several people are involved with service exchange.

Coordination was manifested in contract negotiations as well. Neither party had signed a written contract in this case. Negotiations were, however, conducted between Törmä and Billnäs, mainly at the initiative of the agency, which aimed at more security and control over the increasing volume of business exchange (see section 5.2.3, p. 109).

In business exchange, coordination always implies negotiation of invoicing and costs. The parties have to negotiate which compensation system they are to apply in their relationship: fee, commission, project-based, outcome-based, or some combination thereof. In the relationship with Billnäs, the compensation system remained the same throughout once it had been negotiated. It was even taken for granted when Head Office activated its relationship with Törmä, demonstrating the extent to which it had become a norm in the companies' interactions. With Malmi, the compensation system was renegotiated annually.

The study also showed that the exchange of money may require its own coordinating actions. Cost estimates were typically given in the early stages of an assignment process and their contents and amount were usually discussed. Cost estimates helped the client to control the agency. Perhaps the client would set an invoice limit for planning when giving the brief. In later phases the agency sometimes informed the client about the amount of an impending invoice. Which unit should pay the invoice and the timing of the payment were also discussed. Last, but far from least, the final invoices often caused argument between the parties, especially where Malmi was concerned, and also in later phases of the relationship with Billnäs.

Negotiation of future assignments and their timing were emphasised by the agency side in particular. This is to be expected since the synchronisation of demand and supply is always a problem for agencies:

The way it is in our business is that it never comes in steadily. That's one of our problems. If we knew that there's always work coming in like this it'd be really easy to budget and to get people and so on. But that's not the case. Sometimes it's really quiet and other times very busy, and we often wish that clients would tell us what they're planning and when it's due and so on. Then we could prepare ourselves a bit.

In the studied case the agency also preferred early discussion of future assignments because it wanted to extend its role *vis-à-vis* the client by getting involved with concept planning in its earlier phases.

6.2.3 Adaptation processes

The adaptation process concept

Adaptation was revealed to be an important part of interaction in the agency–client unit relationships studied. The existence and importance of adaptation processes did not, however, show up as clearly in the data as did the existence and importance of exchange and coordination processes. This is due to the nature of adaptation in advertising agency–client relationships, and to the research method used, rather than to any potential lack of significance in relationship development. Adaptations seem to be very much connected with people and to come about, on the whole, gradually in day-to-day operations. The process character of adaptations and the retrospective research method made it difficult to pinpoint when major adaptations actually occurred, or indeed whether they occurred at all. Adaptation processes were revealed to be strongly related to coordination processes between the firms as well.

In the adaptation process, companies eliminate potential mismatches between their needs, resources and interests, their functions and procedures, and even between their attitudes and values (see Johanson and Mattsson 1987: 38; Hallén *et al.* 1991: 30; Möller and Wilson 1995a: 27). On the basis of the studied case, adaptations seem to include two dimensions: first, *investing – the firm purposely adapts or changes its resources in order to make the relationship more beneficial,* and secondly, *adapting – the firm adapts itself to the requirements of the other party or to the demands of the contextual setting and eventual changes in it.*

Investing shows activity; it involves the idea that has usually been linked with the concept of inter-firm adaptation (see e.g. Ford 1982: 289; Möller and Wilson 1988: 7). Adapting, on the other hand, is passive by nature. It implies the idea that the firm abides by the current state of affairs and that it probably misses some business opportunities. Both forms of adaptation require resources. When investing, the party may expect some future gain, whereas, in adapting, costs occur in the form of lost opportunities and social and economic sacrifices. The two dimensions can actually be seen as different sides of the same phenomenon. By investing in the relationship the partner may eventually avoid the necessity of adapting to unfavourable conditions.

In the interviews I brought up the issue of adaptation by asking the informants directly whether they had adapted and changed their organisation, marketing strategies, production processes or working habits in some way because of the other party, and also whether they had devoted effort to getting to know or teaching the partner (see Appendix 5). On the basis of the answers, adaptations seemed relatively low or even non-existent in the unit relationships studied. However, by listening to the informants' free descriptions of their relationship a broader understanding of adaptations emerged. The importance of passive adapting became clear. Finally, seven indicators emerged from the data as manifestations of adaptation processes and their intensity; five for active investing and two for passive adapting (see Table 6.4).

In the theoretical framework I suggested that adaptation processes can be related to the service exchanged, to human interaction and to the organisation. In the light of the empirical data it seems, however, simpler to distinguish between the foci of adaptation and the type of resources that are used in adaptation processes.

I was able to identify several possible foci of adaptation in the study. Adaptations were related to specific assignment processes, i.e.:

1 To the content of assignments.
2 Their outcomes and payment conditions.
3 To the marketing and advertising strategy of the client, including the advertised product or service, or
4 To the execution of the assignment process (see Table 6.4).

They could also be related to the whole business relationship:

5 To personal relationships and inter-firm knowledge, or
6 To inter-firm roles and positions. *Adaptations concerning the content of assignments, their outcomes and payment conditions, the execution of assignment processes, and inter-firm roles were the most accentuated in the case study.*

It was typical of all three unit relationships that final invoices and payment conditions were discussed and adjusted by mutual consent. Client representatives described adjustments as follows:

> Yeah, we've been able to discuss the payment details as well. We moved some of December's costs to January and it worked out then. So the agency has been able to be flexible in things like this.

Table 6.4 Indicators of adaptation processes

Indicator	Concept
Estimate of the intensity of purposeful individual investments in - learning and building knowledge of the other party - teaching, i.e. building knowledge of the other party in oneself - building personal relationship Estimate of the intensity of organisational investments, based on • Number of people in face-to-face contact on each side • Participation of different management levels in interaction on each side • Purposeful investments in organisation and personnel on each side • Purposeful investment in changing – the content of assignments – marketing and advertising stategies – the execution of the assignment process – inter-firm roles	Investing
Estimate of individual sacrifices the contact persons felt they had to make in interactions Estimate of the intensity of organisational adapting by each party, based on their perceived need to adapt - in the execution of assignment processes (e.g. to changes in initial plans, to tight time schedules) - to payment conditions or assignment outcomes (creative output, final price, personal rewards) - to inter-firm roles and positions	Adapting

Well, let's say when you go to a shop and buy licorice it's the bag that costs seven marks. When you go to an advertising agency there are general costs and then there are always costs created along with the project. The assignment itself may change as well, it's a kind of a process which changes a little – you get new ideas, and everything that's done, it costs money. Then the one who presents these ideas, well he forgets that originally it was said that it costs 100,000, now the bill is 150,000. Then you've got to figure out where the 50,000 came from. Well, the advertising agency then tells you and then there's discussion about it and then something small is written off [the bill] and then everything is OK again. That sort of thing – no, they aren't crises, but there are always this kind of [negotiations]. But it hasn't led to any kind of dead end, we've been flexible on both sides.

Sometimes the agency also managed to broaden the assignment by proposing additional ideas for or changes in the assignments and subsequently also in the client's initial marketing strategies. An agency representative expressed this in the following way:

This is what we quite concretely seized on, that in our view you're far too modest. As it is that you're out with such a good product and innovation, you're making a mistake by not inputting. And on our own initiative, though we weren't given a brief for it, we proposed an advertising schedule and timing for the direct mail campaign. And they'll probably buy both.

A client representative gave another example:

The agency's ideas certainly did change our marketing view, but not the product as such. They didn't . . . well, perhaps on the colour, they had a viewpoint which sort of half got through, but . . . I think it's always been quite clear that the product comes from us and the agency won't get involved with it. [But for instance with children's scissors] first we had an idea that it would be sold without any of this kind of sub-brand . . . But they kind of got it through in the end, and it became Fiskars Junior . . . which was actually a good idea.

The execution of assignment processes typically required mutual adaptations. The parties had to adjust to changes in the initial plans and usually also to tight time schedules. Changes in personnel, in the intra-group nets of the companies, in market conditions and in the original brief all required adaptations, which became clearly evident, for instance in the progress of the company image project between Törmä and Head Office (see section 5.4.1, p. 171). The effect of tight timetables could be seen especially at the initial and growth phases of the relationship with Billnäs. The parties had continually to adjust their actions to each other to get things done in the agreed time frame. Messages often included requests for a quick response: 'We need it urgently' or 'We are already in a tearing hurry to . . . '

Adaptations concerning the business relationship as a whole are also considered to be elementary. The building of a business relationship means, first of all, investing in personal relationships and inter-firm knowledge. Working personal relationships are necessary for the communication of crucial information and for the interactive production of advertising services. The need for investing in personal relationships and inter-firm knowledge was remarked on by both parties:

> But we should invest more in people, too. We should build a kind of team spirit. The time for that would be right now as the new people there have just worked themselves in.

> But for our part there is room for improvement in that . . . let's say, as we actually did do last time when we were there briefing, that we told them the size of this market. So that they'd understand our pressures better. And they were amazed that 'Oh, [the market] is that small.'

> Well, yes we do maintain a relationship continuously. There's no way how it could work so that you do one job and then that's over and then you start again. It has to be pedalled all the time like a bicycle. You keep in touch all the time and think. Because the earlier the agency has the information about the client's needs, the better it can take into account what the client wants.

The importance of adaptations relating to the parties' roles and positions *vis-à-vis* each other were sharply manifested in the data. The parties' roles emerged from the data as a relevant concept for understanding relationship development (see section 6.3.4). The role of a company determines the extent to which it is involved in the business relationship and how much responsibility it has, which is naturally a function of the parties' needs, resources and capabilities. In fact, some researchers have viewed inter-firm adaptations primarily as a process whereby the companies try to bring about a fit between their needs and capabilities (see Hallén *et al.* 1991: 30).

Passive adapting to a given role and purposeful investing in that role were both identifiable in the interviews. Adaptations with respect to inter-firm roles were manifested on the agency side in particular, where informants from different hierarchical levels described the phenomenon as follows:

> Well, the message that we've been getting recently is probably that they see us as developers of concept . . . Never in my time has there been discussion of marketing strategy and joint objectives of advertising, it hasn't been dealt with at all . . . I would wish that of them. But on the other hand, I've accepted the explanations that they've given about the present situation . . . but now would be the time for it, and I've talked about it [internally at the agency] many times, that this is an issue that should be attended to carefully.

> We saw this [speculative offer] as important in the sense that we wanted to point out to the client that we don't just make new packaging and perhaps an odd ad or TV commercial every now and

then for them but that we want to be involved in a wider sense in thinking and reflecting and ideating with them.

Yeah, we did talk about [our international role] and it was discussed [internally at the agency] so that we should actually invest in it now. We wondered if we have the right people here who could tour Europe and . . . and who could go there and build a contact organisation . . .

Adaptation processes required both individual and organisational resources from the interacting firms. As expected, the role of individual adaptation – learning by doing – turned out to be the most relevant type of adaptation. *The resources used in adaptation processes were typically intangible rather than physical or economic, with direct cost implications for the organisation concerned.* These results are also in keeping with the recent study of auditor–client relationships (Seabright *et al.* 1992: 153).

Certain assignment processes were important learning experiences for the interacting staff. The parties in all three relationships seemed to invest actively in learning and building knowledge of the other party on their own initiative (see Table 6.4). The experience of other employees involved in the business relationship helped significantly. Sometimes the parties felt a need 'to teach' the other's personnel, but this was not easily achieved. The need for learning and teaching effort was clearly dependent on individuals' experience of the existing relationship and on their previous experience of agency–client relationships. New entrants naturally had the most to learn and also caused new adaptation requirements for those already involved with the relationship.

Passive adapting required individual resources as well. Contact people might feel they had to make individual sacrifices by working with people they didn't like, or by being compelled to work on tasks that didn't offer personal satisfaction or potential for professional development (see Table 6.4).

Broader organisational adaptations were rarely made in the studied relationships. Adaptations at organisational level mostly meant occasional increases in the number of people involved in face-to-face contact and the participation of different management levels in interactions (see Table 6.4). In the unit relationships studied, no new people were hired by the agency for the client's sake, although some organisational arrangements were made, especially in the relationship with Head Office. The agency allocated an exceptional two teams to the planning of the campaign and later changed the team in order to provide the client with what it wanted (see section 5.4.1, pp. 169, 175). An agency representative described the investments thus:

I think that it's obvious that we want to invest [in this relationship] and the fact that we changed the team here and tried to organise things internally in such a way as to make them happy shows that we're prepared to invest in them. The fact that we've done quite a lot of work and not charged for it also shows that we input to this client.

Temporal considerations of adaptation processes

The foci and intensity of adaptations varied over time in the unit relationships studied. In competitive advertising markets agencies have to be especially active in attracting new clients. When a relationship is initiated, special effort is required from both the agency and the client. The parties have to learn to know each other's needs, resources and interests, as well as the contact people and their style of working. *In the early phases of a relationship, adaptations are made to create inter-firm fit between the parties' needs and resources and build up the relationship* (see also Hallén *et al.* 1991: 35).

At the beginning of the relationship with Billnäs the client clearly tested the agency, its capabilities and its compatibility with Billnäs's staff (see section 5.2.2, p. 104). The relationship with Malmi could not start life as an independent business relationship until the parties had clarified their roles and positions and modified their original expectations concerning the interaction (see section 5.3.1, p. 144). The inter-firm fit was created in role negotiations internally within each firm, between the firms and especially through adapting to the required role. Some agency informants described the initiation process this way:

> The beginning of each relationship sure is difficult and painful each time. You have to invest time, money, transformation . . . With it, a stage starts in which you really learn to know each other as people, businesses, ways of thinking. And that is a very interesting point for the client to see, how interested this agency really is in our business . . . So this means if the agency is prepared to invest their time, work input etc. to learn the client's business, because that is important.

From the case study, it also seems evident that in a relationship that is already established, adaptations are basically made to support and expand current business (see also Hallén *et al.* 1991: 35). Continual adaptations are needed from both parties in order to maintain a business relationship and also to develop it towards a stronger and broader partnership. For instance, inter-firm knowledge and personal relationships had to be rebuilt each time people in the account team or in the client's marketing team changed. These changes were always demanding, as personality, individual experience and working style could alter interaction styles and the interaction orientation of the whole business relationship.

It also became apparent that agencies may make a considerable investment when they perceive the risk of losing an attractive and important client (see e.g the efforts of Hall and Cederquist, section 5.2.2, p. 104). The need for adaptation became especially clear in connection with certain critical events, for instance, when the client company's organisation was changed and the agency lost its personal contacts with the client's marketing management. Törmä was already committed to the relationship with Billnäs and when uncertainty about the future of that relationship increased, account management felt that it had to invest in the maintenance of the relationship (see section 5.2.4, p. 121). Agency representatives described the situation and subsequent investments as follows:

> Well, after the organisational change it was a bit like that. There were fewer assignments and we were quite uncertain of what was actually going on in the client's organisation. And we did have an internal meeting at the agency, trying to figure out what we could do about it. There we decided that we'd try to contact the client's bosses, and decided to suggest this business gift idea to them.

> We wondered why nothing was happening, just some very small jobs, and we'd budgeted the year at just the same rate as before, and then we started to see that, oh dear, our budget isn't holding up at all! Then we started examining what it's all about and who makes the decisions. We had as our starting point that surely this client won't stop its activity just like that, but that's exactly what they did. And nobody was making any decisions there. We had a chat with [the Deputy Managing Director] and he said, go and talk to [the Director of the business group], and I did, and he said, go and talk to [the Marketing Manager] and that's the way it was . . . And that of course was because they didn't have a stable organisation, but they were changing it all the time and that meant that these project opportunities were trampled on.

As already mentioned, the needs and resources of the parties also changed over time and required frequent adaptations from the parties. This meant that a new match had to be found between the parties each time changes occurred and a new assignment was given. Adaptations were required on the part of the agency in particular.

6.2.4 Interaction styles

During the empirical investigation, interaction style turned out to be an important element of inter-firm interaction. *The manner in which agencies and clients conduct their interaction was found to be a key determinant of mutually satisfying interaction processes. Two types of interaction style – openness of communication and investment initiative – appeared to be especially relevant to understanding the dynamics of relationship development.*

The three types of interaction style – openness of communication, informality of control and investment initiative – are closely related to their respective interaction processes: exchange, coordination and adaptation.

Openness of communication

Openness of communication refers to how candidly and over how wide an area the parties exchange information and meaning with each other. Openness proved to be an essential element in the development of relationships and an important determinant of mutually satisfying interaction processes. The importance of open communication was highlighted by both parties and in clearly different situations. Both its existence and absence were remarked upon:

> And of course, if you [work] with an advertising agency or some other outsider, you have to be open, tell them what you're after. You've got to lay all your cards on the table – you can't expect them to read your mind.

> [The reaction at the other end of the phone was] 'Oh dear, he's asking me these questions which he shouldn't really be asking me. I'm the one who should be telling him these things. So why is he asking?' I think our channel of communication has been so very narrow, we've met so rarely that ... I've got used to us knowing more about each other ...

Various types of data segment were interpreted as manifestations of openness in a business relationship (see Table 6.5).

Some degree of openness seemed to be essential for the execution of assignments as suggested earlier. This is due to the specific nature of advertising services. The agency works first and foremost with information when generating the service (see Mills 1986: 6–7). The client often needs to provide the agency with confidential information concerning its strategies (see Comanor *et al*. 1981: 432), future plans and sometimes also its internal politics. The study further revealed that open communication is conducive to creativity, especially to constructive differences of opinion and the testing of new ideas, both of which are particularly necessary in advertising planning (see also Michell 1987: 38). In an open relationship the client can expect the agency to criticise its advertising, which typically produces novel insights.

Open communication about assignment goals was found to be essential

Table 6.5 Indicators of interaction styles

Indicators	Concept

Estimate of the openness of communication based on
• Openness concerning assignment processes, e.g.
  – discussion of marketing stategies and future plans
  – exchange of confidential information related to internal politics
  – criticising the client's advertising
  – discussion of goals, means, etc., during an assignment process
  – exchange of feedback information concerning the success of earlier campaigns in the target markets
• Openness concerning the relationship, e.g.
  – discussion of inter-firm roles and positions
  – exchange of feedback information concerning the relationship
	Openness of communication

Estimate of each party's willingness to control interaction in formal ways based on
• Formality of control in assignment processes, e.g.
  – use of invoice limits
  – giving strictly defined briefs instead of open ones
• Formality of control in the relationship, e.g.
  – existence of a written and explicit contract
  – negotiating annual budgets
	Formality of control

Estimate of the parties' investment initiative based on
• Initiative in advancing assignment processes by, e.g.
  – making suggestions for client's marketing
  – motivating the account team
• Initiative in advancing the development of the relationship by, e.g.
  – making proposals for new assignments or for a broader role
  – keeping communication channels open
	Investment initiative

for providing satisfaction from assignment processes. It is crucial that the parties achieve a common understanding of the goals and means of advertising. The company image campaign with Head Office provides an example where the constantly changing situation and lack of open communication between the parties hindered mutual understanding of the project goals (see section 5.4.1, pp. 173–74). Particular campaigns in the growth phase of the Billnäs relationship, on the other hand, provide examples of the reverse, where the parties valued open communication and were also able to arrive at a common view of the goals (see section 5.2.3, p. 109). Tailoring the advertising service to the needs of the client requires that the client opens itself up to the account team concerning its market situation, advertising goals, and the extent of the success of earlier campaigns in the target markets (cf. Czepiel 1990: 16). Reluctance on the part of the client to reveal critical business-related information may block or severely delay satisfactory service performance (Crosby *et al.* 1990: 71). The following citation nicely describes the necessity of openness in achieving a satisfactory assignment process:

> [What makes an assignment successful is] that perfect understanding is reached of what we both want to achieve. It has to be gone through in such a fashion that we both understand it. And it may be that you've got an idea and this kind of goal somewhere and then it has to be made concrete and that can only be done through talking about it . . . 'We've understood it this way. Is that [how you understand it]?' . . . It may be that the idea in your mind is slightly different. Then you've got to evaluate the idea that's come up, to see whether it's better than your original and . . . So it's this kind of interaction that's happened along the way. And it's bloody important. And it can only be formed in an environment that's completely open . . . That's exactly what it takes, that you can openly give this [brief and feedback].

Open communication seems necessary for satisfaction not only with an assignment but also with the business relationship as a whole. Through open communication the parties are better able to find common interests and expectations of the business relationship, which are in turn prerequisites of relationship development. Without good communication of the inter-firm roles and positions and sufficient feedback information about the relationship as a whole, expectations may move out of line with reality, which may lead to disappointments and frustration. This was the case at the initial phase of the relationship with Malmi as well as of that with Head Office (see section 5.3.1, p. 144 and section 5.4.1, p. 174). Openness helps to maintain the relationship over time (cf. Spekman and Wilson 1990: 1004).

The study revealed that reserved communication soon caused tensions and misunderstanding in the relationship. When the parties had working communication channels, through which negative feedback could also be passed, many potential barriers to smooth interaction could be eliminated and conflicts resolved constructively. The freedom to share information permits the parties to delve beneath the surface and accurately examine the underlying problem they are confronting together (see also Spekman and Wilson 1990: 1004).

In a recent study concerning the evaluation of architectural and engineering firms, good communications were also found to be important to a mutually satisfying business relationship (see Day and Barksdale 1992: 89). In the context of distribution channels, open communication was investigated as a separate variable, and was shown to be correlated with trust and commitment (Anderson and Weitz 1989, 1992), which are also central concepts in the model advanced here. As Dwyer *et al.* (1987: 17) put it, a relationship seems unlikely to form and progress without bilateral communication of needs, interests, priorities and eventual changes in these.

The need for open communication became particularly evident when changes occurred in the partner companies – in their personnel, organisation or strategies – or in the companies' environments. The parties change over time and their respective environments exert various demands, which subsequently change the parties' needs and their valuation of outcomes (Dwyer *et al.* 1987: 17). Thus I propose that *open communication is an important medium in building an agency–client relationship and maintaining it through changing situations.*

Formality of control

Coordination in its various forms provides devices for controlling interaction and the partner company. Control may be seen as an essential dimension of the coordination process (cf. Möller and Wilson 1995a: 27). The parties control their relationships in order to safeguard satisfaction with the outcomes of interaction and to secure future assignments. The high performance ambiguity and the degree of uncertainty related to advertising services increase the parties' need to monitor exchange (Mills 1990: 36).

Controlling interaction was considered to be meaningful in the unit relationships studied, although not to a great extent. The study showed that the *formality of control – how formally and strictly the parties controlled each other and their relationship –* could vary. Clients, in particular, may have different styles in monitoring the assignment process and the agency's working. Some emphasise the freedom to create and informal ways of working with an agency, while others feel a strong need to control the agency's activities in order to secure desirable outcomes. The latter can be achieved through more formal control mechanisms such as the use of invoice limits, or by giving strictly defined briefs, e.g. by dictating in detail what the agency should do (see Table 6.5). The following extracts from client and agency interviews illustrate this:

We did perhaps test the agency a little in this project. We said, 'This is the amount of money available – you've got to do it with this.' We gave maybe tighter instructions than before, so that they couldn't wriggle. This is not a volume product that could take large marketing costs.

The way it should be is that the client willingly brings the agency expert into their problem-solving, to actually do the job. So that there'll be this tone of interaction, appreciation and cooperation. If, on the other hand, the client says, 'We want an ad for next Sunday, size 180 mm, this is what it says in the heading, and we use two colours and . . . ' well, fine, if it's good, boss, then go ahead, but it's not a question of cooperation then. Then there's a big chief and a minor actor. The performance will be nothing but routine and the agency won't have a chance to ideate or use their expertise.

The agencies' need to control interaction was also manifested in the data. Their willingness to sign a written contract and have a budget for the coming year indicates a wish to secure the future of the relationship and avoid unpleasant surprises and potential economic losses in the future. The preference for a written and explicit contract can be seen as an indicator of a formal style of control (see Table 6.5). Clients may also prefer written contracts, as the following shows:

Yeah, we had a contract with this client. And very tight it was, too. It had all the possible details on it, of what could be done and what not. I've never seen a contract with so many pages, I'm sure it was one of the masterpieces by the lawyers of the client company.

Tight client company cost control and invoice limits used by both Billnäs and Malmi in certain phases of their relationships were not perceived positively by the account team (see section 5.2.5, p. 128; section 5.3.2, p. 151). Agency informants were, in general, critical towards clients who wanted to specify every detail in the planned advertising and were not ready to trust the account team's capabilities in their area of specialisation. On the basis of the case study evidence, I propose that *formality of control is a meaningful dimension of interaction style in agency–client relationships.*

Investment initiative

During the empirical investigation a need emerged to introduce also investment initiative as a new concept for the model. The data showed through many instances the importance of initiation and efforts aimed at advancing assignment processes, and maintaining and developing of the relationship. *Thus by investment initiative I mean that the firm and its representatives take the initiative and make an effort to develop the relationship in the form of ideas, action, time or money.*

Investment initiative was especially indicated in the parties' efforts to advance assignment processes, e.g. the agency's suggestions for the client's marketing and advertising and the client's efforts to activate and motivate the agency (see Table 6.5). Agency proposals for new assignments and a broader role, and both parties' activity in keeping communication channels open, indicated initiative in the development of the business relationship. The emergence of the concept of investment initiative was a logical consequence of the two dimensions of adaptation processes identified. When one partner demonstrates investment initiative, it shows its willingness to invest in the relationship. In the absence of this activity the relationship languishes, potentially leading to passive adaptation.

The concept of investment initiative is particularly important in understanding the dynamics of relationship development. The intensity of adaptation processes in a specific phase of a business relationship incorporates the static aspect of the phenomenon. It indicates the achieved and required level of commitment, whereas the investment initiative shows the current positive attitude and willingness to develop the relationship further. It indicates who takes the initiative and how the relationship is advanced. Investment initiative is an important means by which to demonstrate commitment to the other party and create possibilities of new assignment processes.

Investment initiative may be especially relevant to agency–client relationships, owing to the difficulty of evaluating service performance. Where it is difficult to establish standards of quality, the perceived effort displayed by the service provider is used as a substitute (Mills 1990: 38). In fact, in the unit relationships studied, the client seemed to appreciate and expect initiative on the part of the agency personnel. The importance of investment initiatives for the client was manifested, for instance, in the client's efforts to motivate the account team (see section 5.4.1, p. 172). By contrast, a low level of investment initiative was perceived negatively, which was more generally visible in client informant interviews:

> It was just at the time that this business relationship with them wasn't in the best possible shape. It had got this feeling of routine and we felt that they didn't have their best possible resources taking care of us. And there were faults on our side, too, that we couldn't be critical enough. But there was this feeling of boredom, we'd worked together a long time, we weren't happy . . . And then we decided, we just had a new product coming to the market . . . a kind of independent project, and then we just decided that we'll give it to a different agency, just for tactical reasons.

It is also important for the client to show investment initiative, as the following shows:

> Now we've actively invested more, in that we've also sold this product more to advertising agencies, so that they know everything about the product and so on. It's more important to us than it was. Earlier it was more like we bought certain services, but now we actively try to get the advertising agency along to develop this idea.

Investment initiative has also been found to be relevant in other studies in the field of advertising. In a case study of four advertising agency–client relationships, the client representatives expressed their desire to see more activity and initiative on the part of the agency, e.g. in the form of putting forward new ideas, suggestions and opinions (Etelä 1985: 73). *Thus I propose that investment initiative is an important medium in advancing assignment processes and developing agency–client relationships.*

6.3 EVOLVING RELATIONAL INFRASTRUCTURE

In the *a priori* process model I distinguished between operational and relational bonds, drawing on the two theoretical approaches proposed by network and interaction researchers (see Mattsson 1983; Johansson and Mattsson 1986; Wilson and Mummalaneni 1986). Operational bonds were defined as concrete ties that are created in day-to-day operations between the parties. Relational bonds were seen to have a more abstract character and to incorporate the continuity dimension of business relationships. This distinction also seemed both logical and relevant in the case. A number of specifications are needed, however, to clarify the distinction between bonds and the concept of the operational bond in particular.

First, it seems that the emerging 'operational bonds' not only form ties and interdependences between the parties but also – and even more apparently – an infrastructure for the relationship, an indispensable and concrete framework for interaction processes. Secondly, the use of the term 'bond' for two apparently different sets of factors is confusing. By introducing a new name for 'operational bonds' I wish to clarify further the distinction made in the *a priori* model. Thirdly, during this study a need emerged for adding some new concepts to the model and modifying some old ones in the category of operational bonds. These changes also call for a new identity for the entire set of concepts. *I therefore decided to introduce a new conceptual category, 'relational infrastructure', to the agency–client relationship process model.*

The relational infrastructure includes the social, functional and economic framework of an advertising agency–client relationship. In the case I identified *four major elements: personal relationships, inter-firm*

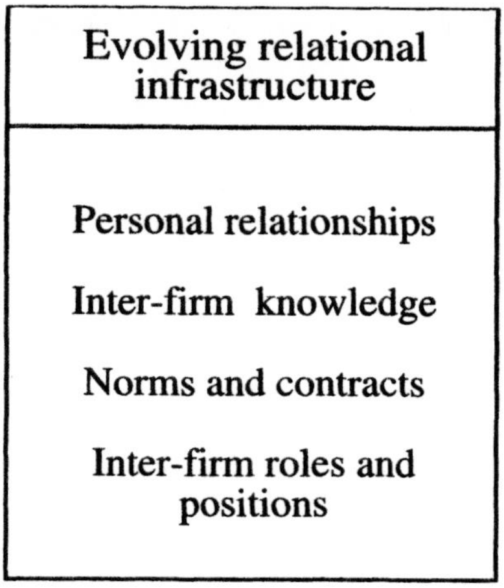

```
┌─────────────────────────────────┐
│      Evolving relational        │
│        infrastructure           │
├─────────────────────────────────┤
│                                 │
│    Personal relationships       │
│                                 │
│    Inter-firm  knowledge        │
│                                 │
│    Norms and contracts          │
│                                 │
│    Inter-firm roles and         │
│         positions               │
│                                 │
└─────────────────────────────────┘
```

Figure 6.3 The evolving relational infrastructure in an advertising
agency–client relationship

knowledge, norms and contracts and finally inter-firm roles and positions (see
Figure 6.3). On the basis of the case study evidence, I propose that *these
four elements form an infrastructure for advertising agency–client relationship,
that sets limits and creates opportunities for further interaction and the
development of a business relationship.*

The concept of relational infrastructure accentuates the prevailing
situation within an agency–client relationship in which interaction takes
place. It thus has an important influence on the character of interaction
processes and their outcomes (see arrows D and E, Figure 6.1, p. 180). The
elements of relational infrastructure also contribute to the development
of relational bonds between the parties (see arrow G in Figure 6.1).

Relational infrastructure evolves in interaction, as a result of interaction
processes (see arrow C in Figure 6.1). It is affected by the character and
intensity of interaction processes but it is also influenced by events and
changes in contextual factors (see arrows A in Figure 6.1). The elements of
infrastructure and the related empirical evidence will be dealt with in
detail in the following sections.

6.3.1 Personal relationships

*Personal relationships between the contact persons in interacting firms create the
most elementary part of a relationship's infrastructure.* The establishment of
personal relationships is a necessity for exchange. Agency-client relationships often start through personal acquaintances, and in order to realise
the exchange new personal relationships have to be created as well.

Any assignment but the smallest requires cooperation from several people on both sides. *Over the course of time an inter-firm network of personal relationships emerges, which includes both weak and strong relations between contact people* (see Cunningham and Turnbull 1982; Håkansson 1982).

On the one hand, the network of personal relationships is built up in interaction processes between the interacting firms. Some of the existing personal relationships may also have developed previously in other commercial or private interactions. On the other hand, the currently existing network of personal relationships forms an important part of the relational infrastructure that sets limits on and creates opportunities for further interaction and the development of an agency–client relationship. Personal relationships can be used to expand the business relationship into new task areas or the advertising of other products. For instance, the favourable personal contacts with Fiskars's top management helped Törmä in its attempts to broaden the relationship to other units of Fiskars (see e.g. section 5.2.6, p. 131 and section 5.4.1, pp. 163–4). Equally, the characteristics of contact staff in each company and their personal relationships may hinder the progressive development of an agency–client relationship. For instance, in the relationship with Billnäs, weak personal relationships aggravated the weakening of the whole business relationship on several occasions (see sections 5.2.5, p. 120 and 5.2.7, p. 137).

The nature of individual personal relationships, i.e. weak or strong, was revealed as important in explicating the development of the unit business relationships studied. On the basis of the interviewee's descriptions, three dimensions seem central in characterising personal relationships: interpersonal appeal, or synonymously interpersonal chemistry; interpersonal trust; and knowing the other person (see Table 6.6). Several types of personal relationships were identified with respect to knowing the other person. Some can be characterised as occasional business acquaintance-ships, where people know very little about each other, others as business partnerships, where they have already known each other for some time. Some of the personal relationships were good business partnerships or even friendships that had developed over a number of years, and which had their roots either in business life or in the individuals' private lives. By definition, the more the persons liked and trusted each other, and the better they knew each other, the stronger their personal relationship was considered to be. In characterising personal relationships, the adjectives 'unfavourable' and 'favourable' are used synonymously here with weak and strong.

At least two characteristics of the inter-firm network of personal relationships appeared to be relevant: the extent of the inter-firm network of personal relationships and its intensity. The latter combines the strength of single personal relationships and their extent into one

Table 6.6 Indicators of personal relationships

Indicator	Concept

Strength of personal relationship estimated by
• Interpersonal appeal, based on the parties' perception of
  – each other's personality
  – professional capabilities and viewpoints
  – interaction styles
  – demographic factors
• Interpersonal trust based on parties'
  – perceptions of each other's character as dependable and reliable
  – actions such as personal disclosure
• Knowing the other party based on
  – how long the persons had known each other
  – how intensive their contact had been
  – how personal their relationship was
	Personal relationships

Extent of the inter-firm network of personal relationships • Number of people involved in face-to-face contact • Number of personal relationships between the interacting firms • Number of hierarchical levels involved in interaction Intensity of the inter-firm network of personal relationships • Sum of personal relationships weighted by their strength • Number of hierarchical levels where strong and relatively strong personal relationship(s) exist	Inter-firm network of personal relationships

network characteristic. By the extent of the inter-firm network of personal relationships I mean the number of people and the number of different hierarchical levels involved in interactions. Three indicators were derived from the data as manifestations of the extent of the networks (see Table 6.6). The extent of personal relationships across different functions in the companies, as compared with hierarchical levels, appeared to be of less importance in the unit relationships studied.[2] Two combined indicators may be constructed for the intensity of the inter-firm network of personal relationships (see Table 6.6).

As the relationship develops, so potentially does the network of personal relationships into a stronger and more extensive inter-firm structure. This process is, however, not cumulative and deterministic but dependent on changes generated by events in the context of an agency– client relationship. The inter-firm network of personal relationships changes, for instance, as a result of organisation changes and personnel turnover. In these situations the network becomes at least temporarily thinner and weaker. New personal relationships have to be built in place of previous relationships. This takes time and requires adaptations from the parties. The building of an intensive network of personal relationships can be viewed as an investment in the business relationship.

Individuals and their links with each other form an essential force for change in agency–client relationships. The network of personal relationships has great potential for both innovative and destructive processes within the existing inter-firm connection (see Johannisson 1987: 11). The stability or change of people in a given business relationship clearly affects its overall development. In addition, a high degree of relational dynamics is dependent on interacting individuals, their will power, attitudes, perceptions and intentions. Inter-firm exchange primarily serves the economic goals of the companies, but it occurs through individuals, who also aim to satisfy their own needs and goals in the process. These individuals bring their own personalities, capabilities, experiences and working styles to the inter-firm interaction, all of which is apt to create tensions and changes in business relationships.

The role of personal relationships is revealed to be multi-dimensional. First of all, they have a strong instrumental role in exchanging necessary information, in negotiating terms of exchange and in assessing the outcomes of interaction (see also Cunningham and Turnbull 1982: 308). Favourable personal relationships proved to be conducive to open communication and thus yielded more satisfaction with the outcomes of assignment processes. When relationships were strong, it was also possible to give negative feedback to the partner and engage in corrective action within the exchange. An agency representative described the benefits of strong personal relationships as follows:

> In this relationship there are more channels through which to communicate negative things, too. So that we can kind of air them. If we don't meet on any other occasions apart from for the assignment, and the client is immature, then they hold everything back. And then all of a sudden they've had enough. It makes it a lot easier if you can communicate negative things as well in a safe fashion. Then the relationship usually stays healthy for much longer.

In addition to their crucial role in information exchange, personal relationships also played a significant part in resolving and avoiding problems and conflicts in business relationships. Cunningham and Turnbull (1982: 308) talk in terms of a crisis insurance role for personal contacts. In the unit relationships studied I identified several occasions where favourable personal relationships at upper hierarchical levels were used to solve problems that risked the smooth progress of an assignment and outcome satisfaction. In the relationship with Billnäs, favourable personal relationships both at top management level and at marketing manager/account supervisor level were used for this purpose (see section 5.2.3, p. 107). When the parties encountered problems in the planning of the company image for Head Office, the strong personal relationship at top management level was used in reconciliation (see section 5.4.1, p. 175). I also found examples of the reverse, where the absence of favourable personal relationships hindered conflict resolution and even put the progressive development of the relationship at risk. The organisational change at Fiskars Consumer Products Group in which Törmä lost its valued personal contacts with the group's management is a good example (see section 5.2.4, p. 121).

The study also showed the importance of favourable personal relationships as a source of personal rewards and satisfaction. Strong personal relationships seemed to make day-to-day work more congenial and enhanced perceived satisfaction with assignment processes and with the whole relationship (see section 6.4). The following describes the importance of favourable personal relationships from an agency perspective:

> It's measured, this credibility or friendship or whatever you call it, trust, it always comes up at a crisis stage. Then the role of this kind of chap and these kinds of people is important, when they say that, 'Hey, just a second, [this agency] has done a good job on us for this long, now let's wait and see for at least this long,' which means that you've got that time then to fix it ... Those agencies which can build some added value with a relationship, more of that credibility, those are the ones that grow at the expense of others ...
> There's a mental added value very strongly linked to this process which you can then call friendship or trust.

From the case study evidence of the role of personal relationships it is suggested that *the existence of strong personal relationships between parties to the relationship is likely to lead to satisfaction with assignment processes and with the whole business relationship* (see arrow E in Figure 6.1, p. 180). This proposition is also congruent with research findings regarding advertising agency–client relationships (see Wackmann *et al.* 1987: 25–6; Verbeke 1989: 23) and business-to-business relationships in general (see Mummalaneni and Wilson 1991: 15).

As noted earlier, individual personal relationships may also play a crucial role in the initiation of an agency–client relationship (see section 6.1). The influence of personal ties in the later phases of relationship development is also significant. The intensity of the inter-firm network of personal relationships, for example, seems to have an important impact on the continuity and commitment of agency–client relations. These results will be dealt with in greater detail in section 6.5.

6.3.2 Inter-firm knowledge

Inter-firm knowledge forms another important part of the relational infrastructure between agency and client, being each party's knowledge about the other. In the case studied, knowledge did not create particularly strong interdependences. Instead, it may be regarded as an element of the relational infrastructure that the parties had built during interactions, which was important in creating mutual outcome satisfaction from interaction processes.

Knowledge is an essential element in advertising service production and in the building and maintenance of a business relationship. Each party has to develop an understanding of the other's task environment. The client needs knowledge about the agency's philosophy, personnel and procedures in order to be assured of the agency's resources, capabilities and compatibility with client needs and preferences. The agency, on the other hand, needs knowledge about the client's business in general, about its markets, products, marketing and advertising strategies. Knowledge about the client's organisation, internal politics and the various roles and responsibilities of the decision-makers in the client company is also relevant to relationship development. The agency's needs for inter-firm knowledge seemed more significant than the client's.

Inter-firm knowledge forms part of the framework in which interactions take place. The client selects an agency on the basis of the knowledge it has of that and other agencies. Each assignment is executed within the limits of existing knowledge about the partner. The furtherance of the relationship via agency-initiated ideas and proposals is also dependent on the level of shared inter-firm knowledge.

Inter-firm knowledge is primarily created in communication between the parties and by purposely investing in personal relationships as channels of this communication (see arrow C in Figure 6.1, p. 180). In other words, the level of inter-firm knowledge depends mainly on the openness and intensity of communication and the strength of personal relationships. Part of the required knowledge may be created by direct communication between the parties, but on the whole is experiential in nature. It stems from personal interactions with the partner in question over time. The following nicely describes the two types of knowledge formation:

They can give assignments which are well considered, but not already laid out like some . . . They've got a clear vision of their own line of business which they then communicate to us so clearly that it makes an easy starting point. Then, for our part, we've had the same art director there and the same supervisor we can get information from. This gives [the relationship] some continuity and a kind of backbone.

The level of inter-firm knowledge is closely related to the understanding the parties can demonstrate towards each other. The importance of feedback information is a good example from the case. Open feedback information regarding the success of campaigns and other projects can help the agency form a realistic image of the client's markets and the role and scope for advertising as a marketing tool. Thus both the agency and the client need to invest in inter-firm knowledge.

It is evident that inter-firm knowledge and personal relationships are closely linked with each other. Several informants cited the need to build the knowledge base anew when people changed within the business relationship. The lack of relevant knowledge was especially manifested when the Consumer Product Group changed its organisation and the Marketing Director left the company. He had been an important information channel in the relationship between Törmä and Billnäs. In addition, the group management was transferred to the United States, which made it impossible for Törmä to maintain its knowledge about the company's international marketing and advertising strategy (see section 5.2.5, p. 123). The data also provided supportive evidence for the reverse, which showed how the level of inter-firm knowledge accumulated and remained high when the same people stayed with the business relationship for a longer period of time.

It was fairly difficult to isolate and evaluate the knowledge component in the unit relationships studied. Different types of data segment from the interviews were used to evaluate the level of people's inter-firm knowledge. Informants brought up the issue of knowledge purposely, or they imparted information about their level of knowledge more implicitly, between the lines. They mostly made remarks about the lack of knowledge. The dyadic research approach also helped to illuminate the important role of knowledge-building in an agency–client relationship. By comparing the informants' descriptions, I could see that client representatives often thought that agency personnel knew more than they actually did. Consequently, the client saw no reason to put any effort into informing the account team, which then caused dissatisfaction on the side of the agency.

One overall indicator – the number of individuals who knew the other party well – was used as an indicator of the level of inter-firm knowledge (see Table 6.7).

Table 6.7 Indicators of inter-firm knowledge

Indicators	Concept

Estimate of the level of knowlege each party had of the other party
• Number of people in each firm who knew the other party well, based on
  – level of knowledge of each individual according to the data
  – experience of each individual of the specific business relationship
	Inter-firm knowledge

In an ongoing business relationship, the parties have better opportunities to learn to know each other, which means that the level of inter-firm knowledge potentially increases. However, as in the development of an inter-firm network of personal relationships, the development of inter-firm knowledge seemed not to follow a pattern of incremental growth. Several events in the context of a business relationship are likely to create pressure for continuous communication and the reconstruction of inter-firm knowledge created in the past.

The study provided ample evidence of this. When giving the company image assignment to Törmä, Head Office expected the account team to already have a good knowledge of the Fiskars corporation (section 5.4.1, p. 174). Armed with this belief, the client made no special effort to inform the account team. Problems later arose during the assignment process that revealed the account team's insufficient knowledge. The lack of agency investment in acquiring the necessary information annoyed the client. The agency was equally dissatisfied with the client's passive mode as regards sharing that information. Changes in agency personnel and in the client's task environment created additional requirements for knowledge-building and aggravated the consequences of poor communication (see section 5.4.1, p. 171).

This evidence implies that inter-firm knowledge is only partly based on the parties' common history. *Both client and agency personnel constantly have to invest time and effort in acquiring and providing each other with the necessary information.* Inter-firm knowledge has to be rebuilt, in particular, when new or novel assignments are placed, when changes occur in the client's market situation or advertising strategy, or when new employees become involved in interaction.

The adopted interaction orientation, together with the level of intensity of business exchange, appears to influence the level of inter-firm knowledge in a relationship (see arrows A and C in Figure 6.1, p. 180). Interaction orientation describes how the parties view each other and handle the

216

relations between their respective interests. It determines whether the parties are willing to behave cooperatively – seeking common interests – or competitively – focusing on their own interests (see Ford *et al.* 1986: 30). When assignments are frequent, and the parties behave cooperatively, they are also more willing to share information with each other. Communication is intensive and open, often covering a broad range of issues. This is apt to create high levels of inter-firm knowledge between the parties. An agency representative described the situation in the following way:

> I must say that the clients are always at their best where we are a part of them, like a part of their advertising department. You can only get to this kind of relationship with big clients. We try to think with their brain. But it means that we know an awful lot about them and that we are in such [tight cooperation] that we know almost every month how last month's [sales] went and what went wrong, what to fix now and where to change direction.

Several comments by informants revealed the important role of inter-firm knowledge in achieving relationship satisfaction. Sound knowledge of the client company improved the agency's ability to produce mutual satisfaction with assignment processes. A high level of inter-firm knowledge seemed to offer the agency a better opportunity to adapt its service offerings to the needs of the client and demonstrate investment initiative, i.e. to suggest new business to the client and advance the development of the business relationship.

Other researchers have also been interested in this topic. Berry (1983: 26) has pointed out that by learning about the specific characteristics and requirements of individual customers, and then employing the data in the future, service firms can tailor their offerings more precisely to the situation at hand. When the agency understands the needs of the client better it can create advertising which is not only potentially effective but also better accepted throughout the client organisation (Beltramini and Pitta 1991: 158). Crosby *et al.* (1990: 76) have pointed out that continuity of interactions creates ongoing opportunities for the service provider to identify the customer's unmet needs and to propose new business.

Informants also brought up increased ease of briefing and decreased briefing costs as a consequence of sound inter-firm knowledge. It became evident that both parties can make savings in their interactions by dealing with the same partner for longer periods. This is especially so where the same individuals are involved who have already got to know the counterpart. Client representatives noted that sound inter-firm knowledge is a major advantage of a long-term agency–client relationship:

> [The benefit of a long-term relationship] is the ease of briefing, the ease of communication, the shared knowledge. You could even call

217

it a code language. We can refer to some old job, like 'You remember when we did that, shall we do the same again?' and so on. Us sharing the same background, it helps an awful lot.

[A long-term relationship] has the benefit that you don't have to start from the year 1649 every time and make them think the same way as we do, but they sort of know the bases of the job and thinking. And it saves mainly time, but some money, too. Well, it's a different issue that staff change quite a lot on the agency side ... but I think perhaps the knowledge is transferred more easily than if you changed your agency all the time.

To summarise, it is proposed that a high level of inter-firm knowledge is likely to lead to satisfaction with the outcome of assignment processes and with the whole business relationship (see arrow E in Figure 6.1).

6.3.3 Norms and contracts

As expected, institutionalisation was a relevant dimension of coordination processes in the unit relationships studied. *By institutionalisation, I mean the process through which various norms – patterns of behaviour and expectations of behaviour on the part of the other – become established* (see Heide and John 1993: 34). Norms and contracts that become established in the process of institutionalisation are an important part of the relational infrastructure. They set limits but also create opportunities for interaction processes and their outcomes.

Various norms develop during interaction, in order to help coordinate the activities of the participants and facilitate the exchange of advertising services (cf. Hassard 1991: 118). *The assumption of the primary importance of unwritten rules and customs as compared with contractual arrangements was supported in this study.* The parties to the three unit relationships never put their names to any written contracts, but different tacit agreements, unwritten rules, customs and standard operating procedures were identifiable. The compensation system, the pattern of personal contacts and certain customs in the division of work when similar tasks recurred have already been mentioned in connection with coordination processes (see section 6.2.2). The importance of norms also became evident in the pilot study interviews:

In an old relationship like this ... in order to make it confidential, functional, then you of course invest in it at the initial stages, and it probably needs investment from both sides, because there are many things you don't talk about on a daily basis, but they're behind everything that in the end is created as advertising, whether it's company culture or whatever.

Norms were not easy to identify, especially in the retrospective part of the study. Indeed, it seemed at first as though they did not exist at all. Informants found it difficult to say whether they had made any tacit agreements or conformed to unwritten rules in their relationships. This is probably due to the nature of norms themselves: they are socially created and implicit. They are created and learned little by little in interpersonal interactions, and people who have been in a relationship for some time easily lose sight of them. In the study, I tried to turn this problem to advantage. I asked about the norms of those people who had, in particular, become recently involved with the business relationship. It was thus possible to identify a number of norms in the business relationships (see Table 6.8).

Norms clearly developed over time: some remained the same during the investigated period, while others changed. For instance, in the Billnäs relationship the compensation system and the questions related to copyright in planned materials were at first actively discussed and negotiated but, once the parties had reached agreement, tacit customs arose which were not questioned any further. Exchange control and briefing styles did change, however. Briefs were at first relatively open and sometimes verbal (see section 5.2.3, p. 109), but invoice limits were later set and written briefs became the rule (section 5.2.5, p. 125).

The study showed that norms are primarily dependent on the interacting individuals (see arrows A in Figure 6.1, p. 180). It seems that most norms are created in day-to-day interaction between people, which implies that their nature is also dependent on contact persons, and on their experience of the relationship and style of interaction. This was spontaneously brought up by several informants:

> Well, it depends on whether the people remain the same. In that case conversation is like, you know yourself, that people you get on with and stick to – you don't have to say everything, it's enough when you start a sentence: the other already knows what it's all about, what you need to get and so on.

> I didn't find it difficult at all getting involved in that [cooperation]. There weren't any [set ways of working]. I don't quite know why. I think there's obviously been so much rotation all the time that they haven't had a chance to be set. People have been changing all the time, as you know.

In the unit relationships studied, the change of contact persons also led to changes in some norms. When the Marketing Director changed in the organisation shake-out, the formality of control increased in the relationship. Invoice limits for each assignment were set from there on in. The same thing happened when a new Product Manager was appointed to Billnäs in 1991 (see section 5.2.7, p. 137).

Table 6.8 Indicators of norms and contracts

Indicators	Concept
Existence and type of norms as perceived by the parties	
- established compensation system	
- patterns of personal contacts (e.g. 'the matched status, multi-level contact pattern', established meeting places)	
- customs in the division of work	
- tacit agreement on copyright questions	
- norms related to formality of control; strictly defined briefs, use of invoice limits	Norms
- norm related to style of briefing: verbal or written	
- established time perspectives for future planning and media campaigns	
Existence of institutionalised creativity, i.e. clinging to old ideas and thinking in creative planning	
Existence and importance of a written contract	Contracts
Explicitness of a written contract	

Aside from the personal factors, it became clear that company policy and even the economic situation in the country influenced the development and change of norms (see arrows A in Figure 6.1). The change of habit from acceptance of cost estimates to invoice limits, for instance, was related not only to the preferences of the new staff but also to the new economising policy of the client company. Cost control was stepped up for a long time and influenced patterns of behaviour irrespective of the person in charge of marketing management. In the relationship with Malmi, the economic recession in 1991 stopped almost all exchange between the parties and subsequently broke the habit of making annual plans. The well established pattern of running two media campaigns per year also ceased – at least for the period in question (see section 5.3.3, p. 158). Norms were, however, rather different in the three relationships, which supports the idea that personal factors play a significant role in their determination.

The institutionalisation of creativity appeared as a new and especially important dimension of institutionalisation in advertising agency–client relationships. This implies that people in the account team cling to their creative ideas and are thus unable to create something new when it is needed. They may eventually be able to launch a good campaign, but be unable to revive it because of personnel wear-out (Verbeke 1989: 26). It seems to be a common view in the advertising field that a team can easily get stuck in a rut, unable to come up with creative new ideas about products which they have previously planned advertising for. An agency representative told of his experience (see also Table 6.8):

> Then in practice this is what happens, that the big thinking, the new idea, starts turning into routine. It's like any marriage. And then of course you've got to watch out that everyday life is so good that it lasts. That everyday life has to produce new thinking, it has to renew itself. In this respect there is a sort of trump in the advertising agency business. Staff move regularly from one agency to another, so that not one client can say that you've always got the same old faces.

Institutionalised creativity needs to be distinguished from the intentional consistency of advertising messages and materials. It may be desirable for the basic ideas in visual and auditory communication to stay the same over time, e.g. where a consumer brand is being built up. In such a situation it may be beneficial if the people in the relationship do not change too much – if people remain who are influential enough to monitor the consistency of advertising communication. Institutionalised creativity, on the contrary, is perceived to be harmful and undesirable. It is likely to lead to dissatisfaction with the creative output of assignment processes (see arrow E in Figure 6.1, p. 180). Especially where innovative assignments are concerned, potential institutionalised creativity and the extent of creative talent at an agency become a major issue.

In the relationship with Billnäs, the institutionalisation of creativity seemed to become more and more relevant the longer the relationship lasted. In the most recent phase, the perceived risk of institutionalised creativity was so high that the client considered organising an agency contest for packaging redesign in order to activate the agency (see section 5.2.5, pp. 127–8 and section 5.2.7, pp. 138–9). The willingness to re-evaluate the current agency was, however, also related to the change of interaction orientation in the client firm. Client representatives put their arguments for the agency contest as follows:

> Then there's maybe Törmä, and an in-house [design team] who're going to compete, and maybe a third one. The [concept] will be made over from the beginning. And there is such a high product image *now* that Törmä may find it difficult, and we in the company may find it difficult to get done.

> They of course have got a certain picture of Fiskars products and that picture is quite difficult to get changed . . . I think it demands quite a lot from an advertising agency. But it's exactly in that sense, that if the [assignment] is given to another agency [as well], that's

when you sharpen up the output, and it's only then that you realise that you've really got to forget the old things and really concentrate on the new one. But of course you mustn't forget Fiskars's background, it mustn't be totally forgotten in that sense, but you've still got to get rid of what's been done before if you want something in a totally new style.

Institutionalisation of creativity could also be identified in the relationship with Head Office during the prolonged assignment process concerning company image planning. The team began to cling to its own ideas and conceptions of the client's needs and could no longer motivate itself to a new start (see section 5.4.1, p. 174). Finally, the team was changed in order to deliver what the client wanted.

The role of written contracts was very weak in the institutionalisation of the unit relationships studied. The parties negotiated a contract but it was never signed. From the client company's point of view, the potential benefits of a written agreement did not justify its costs.[3] Interpersonal trust and the functioning of the business relationship at the human level were seen to be stronger guarantees of outcome satisfaction than any written contract. Informants described the role of written contracts thus:

I've been on the agency side for such a long time that I know exactly how valuable a contract between the advertiser and the agency is. It's a totally useless piece of paper, because you can negotiate the fees but you can't negotiate how long a certain job takes . . . You can put the notice period in it and then you keep some minor part of [your advertising at that agency] and do something else elsewhere. So it's got to be based, on both sides, on the fact that things work, and if they don't, they don't . . . And [things working] and the trust in the agency are very much linked with people. They're linked with management's ability and the desire to get good people there . . . I've seen so many agencies where the management has changed and the agency gets the runs after that. That's the second reason why the contract is more or less a useless piece of paper, because the agency or the contract party may be somebody totally different in a year's time. The name remains, but that name is completely useless.

I'm quite happy with the sort of contract where somebody says that this is what we'll do. A written contract won't change it into anything else, not for better or worse. *Not one bit*. Even in older civilised countries a handshake is enough. It often holds better than contracts.

There seemed to be a clear connection between trust and the perceived need for a written contract. In research into inter-cultural business

222

negotiations, two approaches to contract negotiations have been identified (see Usunier 1993: 411). The first approach involves the parties to the relationship drawing up a written contract because they do not trust each other as people. Trust is built in the process of contract negotiation and is brought to its highest point when the parties sign the agreement. The second approach implies that the parties favour oral agreements because they have personal trust in one another. In that case the parties tend to consider the signing of a written contract an important step, but one among other important steps in a continuing negotiation process – which is itself seen as the best basis for maintaining trust.

In the studied case the latter approach was the rule, but the former also seems to exist in the advertising field. *The case showed that trust and social norms may become a vital supplement to contracts, and that they may even substitute for an explicit contract* (see also Macneil 1980: 8; Thorelli 1986: 41; Anderson and Weitz 1989: 320).

Aside from trust and favourable personal relationships, there seemed to be other reasons for oral agreement. The nature of advertising services was seen as a barrier to making specific agreements (see Mills 1986: 50 and 1990: 36). Some situation-specific reasons were also identifiable. Gottfredson and White (1981) have studied inter-organisational agreements, and state that difficulties in finding terms acceptable to all parties increase as the number and diversity of organisations increases. They also suggest that as a favourable history develops between parties to the relationship the attention that is paid to formal and explicit contracts between them diminishes. This proved to be the case in the relationship between Fiskars and Törmä. It appeared to be difficult to strike a common agreement with all three units (see section 5.2.3, pp. 109). At the time of contract negotiations, the parties had already experienced mutual outcome satisfaction and therefore felt no need for an explicit, written contract.

6.3.4 Inter-firm roles and positions

The role of the parties *vis-à-vis* each other emerged as an especially important factor in the development of agency–client relationships. The parties' roles in interaction and their positions within each other's intra-group and inter-firm networks proved an important element of the relational infrastructure. *The concepts of role and position were consequently added to the process model of advertising agency–client relationships.*

The role of the company determines to what extent it is involved in the business relationship and how much responsibility it has. The concept of role refers to the breadth of the relationship – to the range of activities undertaken within it.[4] Sociologists and social psychologists have used the concept of role in their attempt to understand individuals' behaviour. In

223

the context of inter-firm interaction, the concept of role can be similarly viewed, i.e. as a concept closely related to the behaviour of the parties to the relationship *vis-à-vis* each other. The concept of role has also been generally connected with change and dynamics (see Anderson and Havila 1993: 2). Roles are formed in interaction processes as a result of the parties' perceptions of their roles, their expectations and intentions concerning them, and their actual behaviour based upon their roles. In the course of time, business relationships often become fixed into a set of roles that each party expects the other to perform (Ford 1978: 410–11).

Network researchers have favoured the concept of position over that of role. Position has been used to describe how individual actors in the network are related to each other in terms of their function, importance and identity in a network structure (see e.g. Mattsson 1983; Johanson and Mattsson 1992). The concept has a broad meaning[5] and has been developed for studying network structures and companies' strategic behaviour within them. For the purposes of this study a narrower definition of position is required. *Thus I have defined position as the importance of the relationship for each party with respect to specific intra-group and inter-firm nets.*

The concepts of position and role are very closely related. They are actually different facets of the same phenomenon. Position has been treated mostly as a static and structural concept, whereas role and role behaviour involve the dynamics inherent in business relationships (Anderson and Havila 1993: 2). A firm's position *vis-à-vis* the other is to a great extent the result of the breadth of the role the other party allows the firm, and also the result of the firm's own role behaviour. The firm's position, on the other hand, sets limits for role behaviour but also creates opportunities for further interaction and broadening of the relationship.

It was possible to derive a number of indicators from the data as determinants of the inter-firm roles or breadth of the relationship (see Table 6.9). In the informants' assessments of their position in the current business relationship, both economic and strategic issues were raised. As to the importance of the relationship for the client, it seems to be essential to consider the significance of other advertising agencies the client uses, especially in the same markets and for similar tasks but also in terms of the proportion of work done in-house. The agency can be used, for instance, as a sole supplier or as a major or minor supplier for a specific brand or product group. According to the primary target group of the client unit's marketing operations, either the international intra-group nets or the role of distributor nets acquired relevance for the agency's position (see Table 6.9). The significance of advertising for the client affected the agency's position as well. As to the importance of the relationship to the agency, the client's position among the agency's clientele was obviously a relevant factor (see Table 6.9).

Table 6.9 Indicators of inter-firm roles and positions

Indicator	Concept
Breadth of the business relationship estimated by • Number of activities in the advertising and promotion process performed by the agency • Number of different task types performed by the agency • Number of products, brands or product groups the agency handles	Role (of the agency)

Importance of the business relationship to the client with respect to relevant nets
• Estimate of economic and strategic importance in relation to
  – other advertising agencies used for the same tasks and markets
  – the proportion of work done in-house
  – international intra-group net or distributor nets
  – significance of the client's advertising function
	Position
	(of the agency)

Importance of the business relationship to the agency with respect to relevant nets
• Estimate of the economic importance of the client based on
  – rank of the account by gross margin among the agency's clientele
  – percentage of the account of the agency's gross margin per year
• Estimate of the stategic importance of the client based on
  – realised or expected benefits for the agency's development
	Position
	(of the client)

In the unit relationships studied, the role of each party was primarily determined by the client, who gave out the assignment and paid for the service. The role determined the limits of the agency's behaviour and potential to develop and expand the relationship. This could be seen in the comments of informants on both sides:

> The way I see it is that, to a certain extent, the role of the agency is to respect the client's business framework, whichever client it's a question of, there are very many different types of clients. And I work in a different fashion with different clients, taking into account their different frameworks ... Also the activity of the agency towards the clients is defined according to the framework the client's given us.

225

The agency won't be brought in before the moment comes when it's been decided that this is what we'll do. The agency is not involved in the process [of product design and strategic planning]. They have no effect on planning and the future. But we take a new product to them and we say that here it is and this is what we're going to do.

The study revealed that a relationship can be broadened in three ways: first, by increasing the participation of the agency to cover activities in the earlier or later stages of the advertising and promotion process; secondly, by diversifying the types of task executed in the relationship; and thirdly, by including the advertising of new products or product groups in the existing relationship.

The expansion through the advertising process implies that the agency is given responsibilities over the usual area, which most commonly includes advertising planning and execution in the agency's area of specialisation (see Ray 1982: 61; cf. also Normann 1991: 33). The client may allow the agency to participate in marketing planning and product planning, in research activities concerning marketing concepts and advertising, or in the planning of distribution channel activities. Törmä was interested, for instance, in broadening its participation to product screening and in the planning of display materials for retail stores. Expansion, or at least attempts to expand, through new task types or products could be seen in the relationship with Head Office as well as with Billnäs. Törmä submitted tenders for the production of annual reports, which it has not yet done for Head Office (see section 5.4.1, p. 164). In the Billnäs relationship, Törmä showed interest in starting the display planning for household products and hand tools (see section 5.2.7, p. 139).

Situations and changes in the aforementioned intra-group and inter-firm nets determined how important the business relationship could become, as also how the parties could extend their interaction with respect to these nets. Billnäs first wanted Törmä to take the role of lead agency in the European markets, which would have increased the importance of Törmä to the Consumer Products Group. Later in the organisational change, however, the idea was dismissed and Törmä's position narrowed from even the previous position; only Scandinavian units were potential users of the packaging and advertising materials planned in cooperation between Törmä and Billnäs (see section 5.2.5, p. 123). Malmi, on the other hand, had preferred to focus more and more of its advertising resources on cooperation with major distributors, devoting correspondingly less attention to direct contacts with advertising agencies. In the initiation of the relationships with both Billnäs and Malmi, Törmä's intra-group net had played a role. The dealings of its sister company, AC-mainos, with Malmi and some other units of Fiskars prevented Törmä marketing itself actively to Billnäs and Malmi (see sections 5.2.1, p. 100 and 5.3.1, p. 141).

Thus I conclude that the roles and positions of the parties vis-à-vis each other form an important part of the relational infrastructure. They both set limits and provide opportunities for the parties' investment initiative and for the development of the relationship.

The position of the partner company in specific networks is significant, as it indicates inter-firm commitment. The stronger the position of the client, in an economic and strategic sense, the more dependent the agency is on the client, and vice versa. Inter-organisational power is also an attribute of position in the network structure (Thorelli 1986: 40; Johanson and Mattsson 1992). It came up in the study that an agency cannot allow any client to become too important, if it wishes to preserve objectivity in servicing the client and maintain its economic independence. These factors are central to the agency's ability to provide advertising services. In advertising literature objectivity, freedom to create and professional independence have been cited as important conditions in the successful provision of advertising services (see e.g. Ray 1982: 68; Belch and Belch 1990: 70).

Inter-firm roles and positions are important determinants of relationship satisfaction. When the actual role and role expectations of an agency are not congruent, the agency becomes dissatisfied and, consequently, considers the client less attractive. This happened, for instance, in the relationship with Billnäs after the restructuring (see section 5.2.5, p. 123). The client, on the other hand, is interested first and foremost in the performance of the agency in the given role. In addition, the position of the client within the agency's clientele, and that within the client company's own units that interact with the agency, both had some impact in this study on the client's satisfaction with the business relationship. Supported by the propositions of distribution channel and service encounter research (Frazier 1983: 709; Solomon *et al.* 1985: 109), *I propose that congruent role expectations and role behaviour are likely to lead to satisfaction with the business relationship* (see arrow E in Figure 6.1, p. 180).

6.4 PERCEIVED OUTCOMES OF INTERACTION PROCESSES

The assessment of interaction processes is an integral part of advertising agency–client relationships. *The parties to a relationship constantly evaluate their interactions and the outcomes of these interactions as they experience them* (see arrow F, Figure 6.1). All elements cannot be evaluated simultaneously, since the outcomes of interaction processes take different amounts of time to materialise. It is also typical of the assignment process that several evaluators, persons and firms take part in it.

The evaluation of outcomes forms the basis of the parties' decisions concerning their current behaviour and the future of the relationship. The perceived outcomes of interaction processes affect the continuity of the relationship and contribute to the development of relational bonds (see arrow H, Figure 6.1).

In the *a priori* process model I suggested three concepts to describe the reward–cost outcomes of interaction processes: the performance outcome of an exchange process; the performance outcome of a business relationship; and the psychosocial outcome of a business relationship. In other words, the perceived outcome of a relationship was divided into more specific concepts according to two dimensions: the nature of the rewards and costs (i.e. economic, functional or psychosocial) and, secondly, the unit of analysis, i.e. business relationship or exchange process (assignment).

To understand the development of agency–client relationships, it seems reasonable to treat the perceived outcome of an individual assignment process as a separate concept.[6] Satisfaction with the first assignment process is a necessary condition of the second one, and several successful assignment processes are needed for the progressive development of a business relationship (cf. e.g. Wilson and Mummalaneni 1986: 51). The assessment of individual assignments is an essential part of the evaluation process, in which the parties decide whether the business relationship will be continued and if so in what form. The perceived outcomes of assignment processes also have an important role to play in the development of trust and commitment between the firms (see section 6.5).

In fact, in the advertising agency–client relationship studied, it appeared very difficult to separate the economic or functional aspects of outcomes from the psychosocial aspects – at least, using the chosen research methods. As expected, individual and organisational goals, as well as individual and organisational reward–cost outcomes, appeared to be largely intertwined. The role of individuals and their personal preferences seemed so significant in judging what is economic and functional in advertising or in business relationships that it became questionable whether it was in fact possible to identify economic/functional and psychosocial outcomes as different concepts. A more general and temporally-oriented distinction seems appropriate to an understanding of the development of agency–client relationships. *I therefore propose to settle on two general outcome concepts, each of which incorporates both the economic and the social aspects. First, the perceived outcome of an assignment process and, secondly, the perceived outcome of a business relationship* (see Figure 6.4). Advertising agencies and clients assess their satisfaction with respect to both individual assignments and the entire relationship (see also the relationship quality model by Liljander and Strandvik 1995). This is done on the basis of their own

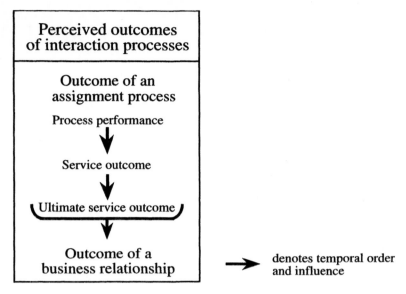

Figure 6.4 The perceived outcomes of an advertising
agency–client relationship

experience of agency–client interactions and their judgement of received
economic and social rewards and costs. The outcome concepts and their
elements are discussed in the following sections.

6.4.1 Perceived outcome of an assignment process

The evaluation of an assignment process was revealed to be a multi-stage
process that occurs over a long time period (see also Danaher and
Mattsson 1994; Iacobucci *et al.* 1994). *When the temporal dimension of an
assignment is taken into account, it seems necessary to distinguish between three
elements in the perceived outcome of an assignment process: process performance,
service outcome and the ultimate service outcome* (see Figure 6.4).

The distinction between the service production process (i.e. process
performance) and its output (i.e. the service outcome) has been common
in service quality research. Lehtinen (1983) separated process quality and
output quality, paying special attention to the temporal dimension of
service performances (see also Lehtinen and Lehtinen 1991). Grönroos
(1982) drew an almost similar distinction by separating functional
and technical quality in his service quality model. As already shown in
section 6.2.1, the exchange of an advertising service is an interactive
process that may take several months to complete. It is obvious that the
quality of this process becomes a focus of assessment in its own right.

Day and Barksdale (1992: 87–8) also raised this point in studying the selection of architectural and engineering firms. Since the effects of advertising are difficult to measure, it is also logical to assume that the quality of the process *per se* plays an important role in determining the parties' satisfaction with the service (cf. the results of Grönroos 1982: 70, 78).

The identification of the ultimate service outcome as a separate element in the evaluation of service quality has received far less attention. This ultimate outcome should be especially relevant in the exchange of professional business services, since such demand represents derived demand. Clients ultimately deal with advertising agencies in order to improve the company's performance and well-being, not to enjoy the service process or the quality of creative work as such. The ultimate service outcome refers to the final outcome of a service that cannot be evaluated until some time has passed after the completion of the assignment process (see Meyer and Mattmüller 1987). Szmigin (1993: 9) has pointed out that the ultimate outcome is often difficult for the parties to the relationship to control. An advertising agency may put together an advertising campaign that meets the brief in all particular, but may still not achieve the client company's objectives, e.g. sales targets. The ultimate outcome is susceptible to external pressures and environmental conditions, but it is still a part of overall outcome evaluation.

The process performance concept

The concept of process performance refers to the level of satisfaction the parties perceive with respect to the interactive service production process, i.e. all interaction episodes between the parties during an assignment process. The process performance involves the idea of functional quality, in other words, the way in which service is rendered to the client (Grönroos 1990b: 38). In addition, it includes the idea of process quality, which refers to the way the client participates in the service production process, and that of interactive quality, originating primarily from the characteristics and styles of interacting individuals (see Lehtinen and Lehtinen 1991: 289–91). In an advertising setting, interaction entails multiple elements and usually concerns several people, thus calling for a broad perspective on process performance.

Assignment processes take place in an inter-firm network of personal relationships as teamwork. This means that several people with their different personalities, capabilities and working styles have an impact on the interactive service process. In the case study it became clear that both a professional and a personal match between interacting people is necessary for the mutual satisfaction of process performance (cf. Gummesson 1981: 111). Agency personnel's appreciation of the client's advertising strategy needs to be in line with the client's own view.

Interpersonal appeal also seemed to foster satisfaction (cf. also Crosby *et al.* 1990: 76).

Interaction consists of exchange processes, i.e. business exchange and communication, and the coordination of activities between parties. Interaction also comprises mutual adaptations required during the process. Related to these elements, *the types of interaction style – the openness of communication, formality of control and investment initiative – appeared to have an important influence on perceived process performance* (see arrow F in Figure 6.1, p. 180). It seems indeed that an adequate fit between the interaction styles of the participants is a prerequisite of mutual satisfaction in service processes (cf. Lehtinen 1983: 308; Lehtinen and Lehtinen 1991: 292). Together with communication openness the clarity of assignment goals merited special attention in the informants' descriptions of service process satisfaction:

> The whole designing of the campaign actually went really well. When we'd got that brief, we knew what they were looking for, we knew what they wanted done with the product. We made a proposal which they accepted immediately. It went really smoothly. There were no complaints about costs . . . commercials and materials were made, they'd no complaints to make.

> Well, I really enjoyed it when the team started making that concept, how well it was thought right through . . . the international commercial . . . and then the packaging thinking which they developed . . . they've been great ideas, all of them. And the fact that it was set off so well, that's not at all just down to us but there was this one guy who knew an awful lot of stuff and our people understood what he was saying . . . When they presented the products and were building that [concept] our people always sparkled when they came back from those meetings. They got so much real knowledge, they got food for their creativity. And that's what all of it was born from. Those people knew what they wanted . . . and then our chemistries also worked at the practical level, and that's what creates this sort of thing.

Insufficient investment initiative was particularly noticeable. For instance, in the Head Office relationship, the lack of investment initiative caused dissatisfaction with the service process on both sides (see section 5.4.1, p. 170–1). Formality of control was also a frequently mentioned source of dissatisfaction. Invoice limits, for instance, were negatively perceived, as explained in the following extract from a client interview:

> When you go to the advertising agency and you tell them that we've got this [sum of money] to use, design that concept or we go elsewhere, then of course the relationship gets a bit infected. They

see it that we're putting pressure on them, but by the same token, they should have cost-effectiveness as their target, so the prices can't keep going up all the time.

A satisfying service process usually means, in practice, then (see Table 6.10), that the parties have achieved a common understanding of the goals of the assignment; they have clear responsibilities laid out within the process; that timetables and budgets are met; that the people involved have adequate access to required information and do not feel too controlled; that new ideas, suggestions and opinions are actively presented, and that quick feedback to proposals and requests is given.

Satisfaction with a service process also entails primarily personal costs and rewards (see Table 6.10). Delays, unexpected problems, a lot of travelling, frequent meetings and other factors that may require additional time and effort from the parties were perceived negatively. Above and beyond costs, the participants emphasised different personal rewards they received during service processes. People on both sides evaluated service processes where they enjoyed each other's company more favourably. Agency representatives were particularly satisfied when they felt their professional skills and knowledge were beneficial to the client or when the client showed respect for and confidence in their capabilities. The following descriptions from client and agency interviews further clarifies how the parties perceived service process satisfaction:

> Then [as the objectives were clear] the guys [at the agency] started developing and then they started getting really enthusiastic. It was fantastic to work, you didn't have to explain, but as I said, 'Use your imagination. I don't know how it should be done, but you do it, and this is the result [that we're aiming at]. We're going to turn this into the best product in the world, and you're going to do it, and it's got to be done in this framework.'

> This is an ideal client for me, quite the best client from the point of view [of the fluency of work] . . . It's nice to work for them. You've got to have such clients who have the skills and knowledge . . . and who are easy to get on with . . . You also need the feeling of success at work. And you get that feeling with good, skilful clients. We talk on the same wavelength and don't spend half an hour talking about how a girl is pictured on a bicycle, is she wearing trainers or is she wearing Ecco shoes, so inessential . . . Well, it's the art director who does that sort of thing.

Table 6.10 Indicators of the outcome of an assignment process

Indicator	Concept
Perceived satisfaction with the interactive service production process estimated for both parties separately and on the basis of - clarity of briefing, i.e. common understanding of the assignment goals - clarity of responsibilities - meeting timetables - keeping to budgets - openness of communication - informality of control - degree of investment intiative - personal costs and rewards (e.g. inconvenience, additional required effort, or having fun, feeling oneself capable, getting respect)	Process performance
Perceived satisfaction with the creative output - ideas and campaign plans developed for the client's marketing and advertising - tangible results; ads, packages, TV commercials Perceived satisfaction with the creative output in the relevant client networks Perceived satisfaction with the final price of the service - problems and debates over invoices - perceived value, i.e. reward–cost ratio	Service outcome (for client)
Perceived satisfaction with assignment profitability - gross margin received	Service outcome (for agency)
Perceived satisfaction with the market response - sales figures - success of the marketing concept in the target markets	Ultimate service outcome (for client)
Perceived satisfaction with the benefits for the agency's development - benefits for the agency's marketing - benefits for the agency's capabilities	Ultimate service outcome (for agency)

The service outcome concept

Service outcome refers to the level of satisfaction the parties perceive with respect to the immediate result of the service production process. In other words, it alludes to what a firm receives as a result of its interactions with another company (cf. Grönroos 1990b: 37; Lehtinen and Lehtinen 1991: 293).

From the client's point of view, I was able to identify three major elements in service outcome: creative output, reception of creative output in the relevant client nets and the final price of the service (see Table 6.10). *On the agency's side, assignment profitability was the most important service outcome.* These elements affected the assessment of assignment processes in all three unit business relationships (see Figure 6.5).

Creative output is an element that can be evaluated immediately in the course of the service process. As Comanor *et al.* (1981: 434) have pointed out, advertisers readily question the quality of the work submitted, owing to the lack of adequate measures by which to test advertising effectiveness. By creative output, I mean the new ideas and campaign plans developed for the client's marketing and advertising, and the tangible results of these ideas, e.g. the advertisements, packaging and TV commercials. The creative output sometimes aroused satisfaction, sometimes dissatisfaction amongst the client personnel:

> Well, I've been satisfied with this agency in principle and at least I've been satisfied with this creative solution and that in a way is what's most important.

> Visually they've got a very strong touch, a logical touch. It started when they created this Fiskars Classic line. And they've followed this visual line very logically in everything.

> Sometimes I feel that they're, like, running out of ideas. While we were making a brochure for instance, we even had to change the art director in the middle because we felt nothing was coming of it.

The reception of creative output in the relevant client nets constitutes another element of the service outcome. Malmi's media campaigns, for instance, were regarded as an important means of persuading the major distributors to buy the product. Consequently, distributor evaluations of the materials and campaigns produced were decisive for the total service outcome. In the case of Billnäs, the acceptance and feedback from the company's international marketing units, to whom Billnäs was supposed to market the concepts planned, turned out to be an important determinant of the total service outcome:

> I'm happy with this concept. It was launched with materials for sales managers in the Nordic countries in June, and everyone took it really well . . . Europeans too have admired this packaging of ours . . .

> Earlier, we used to sell all the concepts to the Europeans by hook or by crook, but when they got this autonomy they wanted to go ahead and develop their own things. The Germans didn't then want the Avanti or Roll-Sharp commercials. They wanted to do their own with McCann. The company felt it lost a lot of money that way.

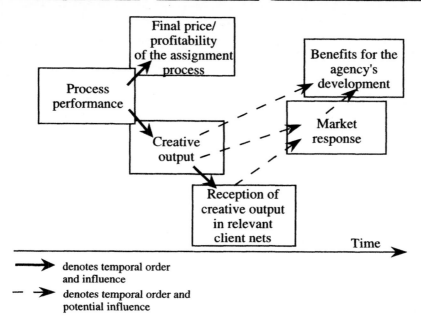

Process performance   Service outcome   Ultimate service outcome

Figure 6.5 The outcome elements of an assignment process and their relationships in time

The final price of the service is also an essential part of the service outcome concept. What amounts to an acceptable price for each service operation caused constant debate in the relationships studied, and seems to be a common problem in the advertising sector in general. When a service is a process and dependent on both parties' activities and decisions, it is extremely difficult to determine a fixed price for an assignment beforehand. Published hourly prices indicate the general price level of the agency but indicate little about the final price of an assignment. As a result, the parties typically negotiate about the costs afterwards, at the point of invoicing, when the costs are fully known.

The role of costs and the final price in service evaluation has also been noted by other researchers (Iacobucci *et al.* 1994: 31; see also Grönroos 1982: 76). Ultimately, the parties to the relationship evaluate the perceived value of the service, i.e. the rewards accruing in relation to costs incurred (see also Freeman and Dart 1993: 30; Liljander and Strandvik 1995: 144). A member of the advertising profession described the client's evaluation problem in the following way:

It's awfully difficult to measure the financial result like that ... if they'd given us a slightly better campaign, would we have

235

had more money coming in? This is not the sort of thing you can measure. But on the other hand, what you can say about Törmä that they're a kind of mid-price agency. Not the most expensive, but not the cheapest either. And then what is the right price for a campaign? It's 'in the lap of the gods' if anything! When you pay a Merc-style price for a campaign, then it feels incredibly valuable and I guess that's what it is. It's not expensive if the campaign is so good that you sell so much more of the product. But this is becoming all ifs and buts; you can never know what the true value of a campaign is.

The ultimate service outcome concept

The ultimate service outcome refers to the level of satisfaction the parties perceive with respect to the final and indirect results of an assignment process on each company's business (see Figure 6.5). For the client, the ultimate service outcome is embodied primarily in the effect of advertising on the selected target group, i.e. the market response in its various forms. For the agency, the potential benefits for its development could be derived from the data as indirect outcomes (see Table 6.10).

In principle, market response should be the most important outcome dimension for the client. This study revealed, however, that the client paid relatively little attention to it. This is probably due to the fact that it is extremely difficult to assess market response, because of the temporal carry-over effects and multitude of intervening variables in the marketing environment. The client representatives in fact placed more emphasis on the different elements of the service outcome.

The agency's own marketing benefited from the use of some of the planned marketing concepts and campaigns as credentials in acquiring new clients. The development of the agency's capabilities was also seen as a potential benefit. Planning international marketing concepts for a well known and internationally successful consumer product company was perceived as an important opportunity for the agency to gain experience of international advertising tasks.

Aside from organisational rewards and costs, personal values were also seen to be important in the evaluation of both service outcomes and ultimate service outcomes. Personal rewards can be considered as by-products of assignment processes. As such they can be connected with all three outcome elements. Personal satisfaction may arise during the service process or, for instance, as a consequence of positive feedback from the relevant nets. It may also result from good sales figures or from awards received in advertising competitions.

Several informants felt that they had been able to learn something from the assignment processes. Improvement in an agency's capabilities is also a very clear and direct result of the learning and development of its personnel. This shows how difficult it is in some cases to separate personal and organisational outcomes from each other. In addition, people on both sides emphasised the feeling of success they had experienced as a result of certain assignments. They felt that they had achieved something in their work and received other people's appreciation. Similar but contrary aspects manifested themselves as 'personal costs' and causes of dissatisfaction in some negatively perceived assignment processes.

Temporal considerations of assignment process outcomes

The temporal gap between the execution of an assignment and the realisation of its ultimate outcome in target markets makes the evaluation of an assignment process a continuous process rather than a one-off activity (see Figure 6.5). The relative importance of different elements of the outcome varies according to the moment of evaluation. The parties often have to act before they have a chance to evaluate an assignment process fully. They are compelled to base their decisions concerning the future of the relationship on partial outcome evaluations, i.e. on the first outcomes experienced, such as the process performance, creative output and price or profitability assessment. If these results are satisfactory, new assignments may be given, even though the client has not been able to assess the ultimate outcome of the current assignment process.

The long duration of the assessment process accentuates the important influence of the existing relational bonds on the future development of an agency–client relationship. When the evaluation of an assignment process is difficult the perceived attraction, preliminary impressions of the partner's trustworthiness, and early attitudinal commitment have an important impact on the parties' decisions concerning the maintenance and development of the business relationship (see section 6.5).

Because of the temporal gap it is difficult to show clear influence relationships between the different outcome elements over time. It is logical, however, to assume a strong correlation between process performance and service outcome, as by definition the service outcome, including creative output and the final price or profitability level, is a direct result of the service process. Therefore, by controlling the service process, the parties to the relationship may also control the service outcome (cf. Lehtinen and Lehtinen 1991: 293). The relationship between service outcome and ultimate service outcome is extremely difficult to show, however. The ultimate outcome cannot be controlled by the parties (see Figure 6.5).

In the case study, I was able to assess the level of satisfaction with the process performance, creative output and final price or profitability in seven assignment processes. In four of the assignments, all three elements were evaluated positively by both parties, who expressed either satisfaction or a great deal of satisfaction. All three elements were negatively evaluated in two assignments, while only one assignment had aroused a low degree of satisfaction with process performance and price/profitability, although a high degree of satisfaction was recorded for creative output. This could be explained by situational factors, especially by the simultaneous change of several people in an otherwise established and committed relationship. Current personal misfits, insufficient experience or poor communication in certain personal relationships were temporarily compensated for by adaptations on the part of the agency and a special effort by new personnel to give satisfaction in terms of creative output. This exception very clearly points up the important role of the existing relational infrastructure and bonds in explaining perceived satisfaction with assignment process outcomes (see sections 6.3 and 6.5).

6.4.2 Perceived outcome of a business relationship

Instead of the two concepts proposed in the a priori *model, the psychosocial outcome of a business relationship and the performance outcome of a business relationship, I now introduce a single but broader concept, the perceived outcome of a business relationship* (see Figure 6.4). The case study clearly shows that there is a need for a more general concept covering all aspects of satisfaction with the relationship. The outcome of a business relationship incorporates the economic/functional and psychosocial costs and rewards of a whole relationship. It refers to the extent to which the parties subjectively believe that each carries out its commitments and that the relationship is worthwhile, equitable, productive and psychosocially rewarding.[7]

The parties to a business relationship form their opinions of the relationship through their experience of individual assignment processes (cf. Liljander and Strandvik 1995: 144). Experience of an agency's invoicing or the work of the creative team gradually gives an idea of the agency's real price level and the quality of its creative work. Similarly, experience of the client's briefings and communication during assignment processes creates a conception of its capabilities in buying advertising services.

However, not all interactions, i.e. exchange, coordination and adaptation processes, relate directly to some assignment process; some relate, rather, to the relationship as a whole. They relate, for instance, to the construction of a relational infrastructure including personal relationships, inter-firm knowledge, norms and contracts, and the roles and positions of the parties *vis-à-vis* each other. The nature of these interactions and satisfaction with the evolving relational infrastructure also influence overall satisfaction with the relationship.

During the study, certain aspects characteristic of the whole business relationship turned out to be especially influential on the perceived outcome of an agency–client relationship (see Table 6.11).

The importance of the interaction styles in creating relationship satisfaction has already been discussed in connection with process performance (section 6.4.1) and in outlining the three types of inter-action style in section 6.2.4. On the basis of the case study evidence, it does indeed seem that open communication, informal control and investment initiative are important determinants of satisfaction in agency–client relationships. Recent findings from industrial supplier-buyer relationships also lend support to this idea (see Leuthesser and Kohli 1995). *It is proposed that open communication, informal control and investment initiative are likely to lead to satisfaction with the process performance and the outcome of the business relationship* (see arrow F in Figure 6.1, p. 180).

Satisfaction with inter-firm roles and positions was highlighted in the study. Both the role of the partner in the business relationship and the position of the partner in the relevant nets influenced the parties' satisfaction with the business relationship. The agency was typically satisfied with a broad role, since that afforded opportunities to take the initiative and expand the relationship. The agency's satisfaction with its role was also associated with the scope for it to use and develop its capabilities within the given role (see section 6.3.4).

Personal relationships were also raised as a source of overall satisfaction. In the production of advertising services, the role of the individual is so basic that the nature of personal relationships seems to impinge on every facet of an agency–client relationship. Favourable personal relationships are an important medium in exchanging information, resolving conflicts and producing personal rewards for the contact persons (see section 6.3.1).

The similarity of the parties' interaction orientations is also essential for relationship satisfaction. If the agency behaves cooperatively and the client competitively, the agency is likely to become dissatisfied with the relationship. Depending on the perceived attractiveness of the client, the agency either tries to accommodate the client's orientation or gives up the relationship. Respectively, the client might prefer a more cooperative orientation than the agency. In the growth phase of the relationship with Billnäs, both parties were cooperatively oriented and very satisfied with the business relationship (see section 5.2.3, p. 110). At the start of the Malmi relationship the parties had clearly differing orientations, which resulted in mutual dissatisfaction with the relationship (section 5.3.1, p. 144). Both parties adapted their behaviour and expectations, but the relationship still continued in the shadow of conflicting interaction orientations and a somewhat unsatisfactory atmosphere (section 5.3.2, p. 153). It appears that a fit between the parties' interaction orientations is necessary for mutual satisfaction with the relationship and thereby for the progressive development of the relationship.

Table 6.11 Indicators of the outcome of a business relationship

Indicator	Concept

Perceived satisfaction with the relationship in general estimated separately for both parties and based on
  - satisfaction with interaction style
  - satisfaction with inter-firm roles and positions
  - satisfaction with personal relationships
  - perceived similarity of interaction orientations
	Outcome of a business relationship

The outcome of the business relationship is a function of past time. In interaction processes, the parties gain experience of each other that makes it possible to evaluate the actual compatibility of the parties' needs, resources, capabilities and interests. The materialised experiences of these factors give the parties an idea of how well the counterpart will fulfil the prerequisites of a relationship (see arrows B in Figure 6.1). Relationship satisfaction grounded on past experience forms the basis of future exchange potential and the continuity and strength of the relationship.

A positive relationship outcome is not, however, a sufficient condition for the progressive development of a relationship. Future exchange is also dependent on the currently perceived strength of inter-firm attraction, trust and commitment. When new needs arise and new situations emerge, the parties assess their attraction and trust towards each other in the light of these future needs. Whether the prerequisites of relationship development existed in the past is not necessarily indicative of a relationship extending into the future.

6.5 EVOLVING RELATIONAL BONDS

Relational bonds incorporate the continuity dimension of business relationships between advertising agencies and their clients. *The three relational bonds – attraction, trust and commitment – that were distinguished in the a priori model were also identified as essential content elements in the development of the unit business relationships studied.* The strength of these bonds varied in different phases of the relationships' evolution, reflecting major changes therein (see Figure 6.6).

Relational bonds develop primarily in interaction processes, but they are also affected by various factors and events in the context of a business relationship (see arrows A in Figure 6.1, p. 180). Relational bonds strengthen or weaken depending on the perceived outcomes of inter-action processes and the strength of the relational infrastructure (see

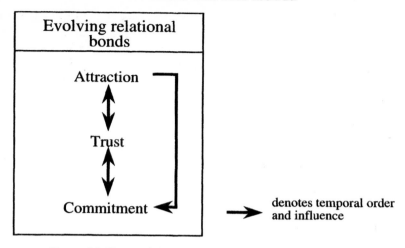

Figure 6.6 The evolving relational bonds in an advertising agency–client relationship

arrows H and G in Figure 6.1). The strength of relational bonds determines the stability of the whole relationship, whether interactions are continued or not (see arrow I in Figure 6.1) (see also Wilson and Mummalaneni 1988: 14).

6.5.1 Attraction

The attraction concept

Attraction turned out to be a key element in the unit business relationships studied. Other evidence from the field of advertising also supported the important role of attraction in the development of business relationships. This was somewhat surprising considering the scant attention that attraction has received in models of buyer–seller relationships to date. It is evident that advertising agency–client relationships differ in this respect from industrial buyer–seller relationships, which the existing models mostly describe. Judging by the descriptions and emphases of informants, attraction appeared to be even more important than commitment, which has usually been treated as the most elementary aspect of business relationships.

Attraction was defined as a company's interest in exchange with another, based on the economic and social reward–cost outcomes expected from a relationship over time. This definition also seems appropriate in the light of the empirical data. *Attraction appeared to be a future-oriented bond* that incorporates the conscious as well as the unconscious expectations towards the business relationship, and its important

241

role in agency–client relationships thus becomes comprehensible. The intangibility of service offerings and the ambiguity of many of the rewards resulting from interaction combine to force companies to place special emphasis on presumed and potential reward–cost outcomes of their relationship.

It is obvious that in competitive markets the agency has to market itself in order to create attractiveness in the eyes of its potential clients. The nature and level of agencies' attractiveness were broadly described by the informants. Some of them actually used the term 'attractive' in their descriptions. 'Keeping a certain agency on a short-list' or 'getting on to a buyer's short-list' appear to be common expressions in the field. They also tell us something about the importance of attraction in agency–client relationships.

Somewhat surprisingly the attractiveness of clients was even more pronounced in the data than that of agencies. Attraction proved to be a real relational bond that drew and kept the parties together. Agency representatives provided rich descriptions of the attractiveness of clients. The active role of the client in building this attraction was also noted. The agencies represented in the study actively assessed their clients' attractiveness. The study also provided examples of situations where an agency abandoned a client because it considered another client from the same industry to be more interesting.

The existence and strength of attraction were estimated on the basis of interview data. Various types of economic and social rewards came up in the interviews as a basis for attraction (see Table 6.12).

Sources and consequences of attraction

Inter-firm attraction is based on the prerequisites of a business relationship, i.e. on complementary needs and resources, on personal awareness of the other party's goals, needs and resources, and on common interest in building a business relationship (see arrows B in Figure 6.1, p. 180). In assessing the attractiveness of a counterpart, each party uses several different indicators of the other's goals, needs, resources and interests. Through these indicators they acquire information about the potential reward–cost outcomes of a business relationship and try to decrease the uncertainty and risk involved in service exchange.

Attraction to an agency is dependent on a number of company factors, as well as the infrastructure qualities of an existing business relationship (see arrows A and G in Figure 6.1). Agency capabilities as perceived by the client, and their potential compatibility with the client's advertising needs, appeared to be the most important determinants of attraction. Relevant factors emphasised by clients in respect of agency capabilities included the area of specialisation, high-quality work, creativity, vision and ideas.

242

Table 6.12 Indicators of attraction

Indicator	Concept

Estimate of the strength of the client's interest in exchange based on
• Perceptions of potential economic rewards and costs of a relationship
  – additional resources and capabilities for advertising tasks
  – new ideas for advertising
  – support for the client's image
  – appropriate prices
• Perceptions of potential social rewards and costs of a relationship
  – satisfied employees when they can work with people whom they like
	Attraction (to an agency)

Estimate of the strength of the agency's interest in exchange based on
• Perceptions of potential economic rewards and costs of a relationship
  – opportunity to earn economic benefit from the relationship
  – strategic benefits for the agency's own marketing (enhancing reputation, providing credentials and referrals)
  – strategic benefits for the development of the agency's and its employees' capabilities
• Perceptions of potential social rewards and costs of a relationship
  – motivating tasks for the employees
  – smooth and congenial interaction
  – satisfied employees when they can work with people whom they like
	Attraction (to a client)

The client's conception of agency capabilities was very much dependent on the agency's reputation in the market, i.e. on how highly the agency's clients and other actors in the field valued its work. A reputation for advertising expertise appeared to be a critical factor, affecting a potential client's willingness to include the agency on its list of potential suppliers (see also Belch and Belch 1990: 85; Dowling 1994: 234). Who are best in a market, who are creative or innovative, or lead in their area of specialisation – these are factors continually assessed by current and past clients, other agencies, advertising sector surveys, journalists and juries of award competitions. The study also lent support to the important role of referrals and credentials in building up agency reputation. Client representatives were typically aware of an agency's other clients and the type of advertising it planned for them. Some of the informants also followed these topics actively.

The price level of the agency turned out to be a third important determinant of attraction. Price and capabilities were considered in relation to each other. Both the agency's expertise and its price level had to be in keeping with the needs and preferences of the client. Agency size was also noted as an indicator of its attractiveness. A large agency was regarded as a provider of a broad range of services and resources, while a small one implied flexibility and lower prices.

The strength of attraction the client felt towards the agency was also dependent on the relational infrastructure between the parties. Strong personal relationships were typically viewed as sources of inter-firm attraction. If a client representative knew someone from the agency whom he liked and who he felt was professionally capable, he considered the agency itself to be more attractive. Examples to the contrary were also apparent: if the client representative did not like or trust the contact person, attraction to the agency remained low and no business relationship emerged. This is in congruence with what has been previously stated with regard to the important influence of personal relationships on the initiation of agency–client relationships (see section 6.1 and the findings of Cagley 1986 and Marshall and Bong Na 1994). Agency representatives were also well aware of the importance of personal relationships for agency attractiveness:

> When looking for a partner like this, then you've got to get along, you've got to appreciate the other as a professional, as a firm, but even more so as skilled professional people. And then the last point, that also as people, mates, you're on the same wavelength.

Client representatives also paid attention to the stability of contact persons, either to the benefits of stable personal relationships or alternatively to the rewards that might emerge from people changing in the account team. The appreciation of stable personal relationships is likely to be connected with higher levels of inter-firm knowledge between the firms. A good knowledge of the client was also explicitly mentioned by informants as one of the factors increasing an agency's attractiveness.

Attraction to the client company was based on a long list of factors related to the client company, task factors and the relational infrastructure (see arrows A and G in Figure 6.1).

Clients were perceived to be most attractive when they offered an agency the potential to derive economic benefit from the relationship. The potential for intensive business exchange and a large account were considered important to a client's attractiveness (cf. also Pels 1992: 6). Agencies felt a strong attraction to a client which was successful in its own business and which considered advertising as a relevant and effective competitive tool. Both these factors evidently increase agencies' earning potential. Agency representatives also emphasised the nature of a client's products and brands. High-quality product planning and sound products were appreciated because they created challenges for advertising planning and potential for impressive and effective advertising. An agency representative summarised his feelings of attraction thus:

> Yes, this is most definitely an awfully interesting client, and a nice one too. Their products are good, and this is the kind of client you can get results with. This is full of opportunities all round!

Innovativeness of assignments appeared to be a significant source of attraction. New products, marketing or creative strategies, and the planning of new materials, motivated creative personnel in their work and generated more invoicing and profitability for the agency as well. The importance of innovative tasks for maintaining agency interest in the relationship was manifested on several occasions and in several ways in the data. Routine tasks clearly decreased the client's attractiveness, whereas innovative tasks increased it. The following extracts from client interviews illustrate this dependence:

> And when there were no more of these interesting projects then of course you noticed it to some extent at Törmä, too, that they weren't that awfully interested any more. The design of an individual package, that doesn't interest an advertising agency so much, it's one job and then it's over. But then there were new products again – that children's scissors job interested Törmä tremendously . . . they got new impetus from that again. So if you've got a product and concept that are interesting enough, then the agency will be interested too, and they do all sorts of things. If you can't get them enthusiastic yourself then it turns into a matter of duty.

> Of course we brought money to Törmä because we had these media campaigns, and of course they got this media commission, but we weren't interesting to them from the point of view of creative work . . . because we didn't buy that off them, no ideas or things where their know-how is seen, but we only bought this media time off them, in which of course the know-how is equally visible, but I'm sure it's not that interesting from an agency's point of view or so visible. In that, it's difficult to show evidence of success or failure.

Beltramini and Pitta (1991: 153) have explained the effect of innovative tasks on attractiveness in terms of the strengthening of the agency's influence and role in the relationship. They point out that routine tasks are apt to minimise the influence and the role of the agency. This leads to less interaction and communication, and potentially to a weakening agency–client relationship. The attractiveness of a broad role and strong position were also manifested in this study. Both the breadth and the importance of the client relationship were identifiable as sources of attraction. This was to be expected, since a broad role and a strong position naturally generate intensive business exchange and probably also broad, important and innovative assignments. The agency's ability to demonstrate investment initiative and suggest new business is essentially strengthened when its role is broad and its position strong (see section 6.3.4). With relevance to other infrastructural elements, agency representatives – in the same way as those of the clients – considered favourable personal relationships to increase the attractiveness of the partner. Boström (1995: 158) has made similar findings when studying what architects value in their clients.

Task innovation attracted agencies further because the potential to develop capabilities occurred to a great extent in new and exciting assignments. Agency personnel had an opportunity to acquire experience and develop their professional skills through innovative tasks. Lindmark (1989: 11) has also noted this point. Innovative as well as novel tasks involve the seeking of new knowledge and solutions. They also provide the potential to make use of the client's knowledge during assignment processes (Lindmark 1989: 11). Challenging and knowledgeable clients are crucial to the development of agency capabilities. This is evidently one reason why agencies feel attracted to clients with sophisticated marketing capabilities (cf. also Pels 1992: 6 and Boström 1995: 157). Another reason is that capable clients seemed to make interaction much more congenial and fluent, as the following illustration of a client makes clear:

> That's an interesting client from the agency's point of view because there are people with know-how. There you don't have to, like, sell them on (or tell them) why this is a fine idea: they accept these semi-finished ideas and see their functionality, their potential, immediately. Their skills in marketing are distinctly better than with many other clients. So a challenging client . . .

Finally, agency representatives paid attention to the interaction orientation of their clients. Cooperative behaviour attracted agency personnel, since it made open communication and investment initiative possible and evidently contributed to the achievement of other agency interests.

The concept of attraction has to be separated from the outcomes of interaction processes. Satisfaction with the outcomes is based on materialised, past experiences, whereas attraction is based primarily on future potential and possibilities that have not yet been realised.

The link between satisfaction and attraction is, however, evident. Experienced outcomes of assignment processes and the whole relationship are easily taken as reliable and concrete evidence of the possible rewards of a relationship. While at the beginning of a relationship attraction is necessarily based on expected and presumed rewards alone, materialised experiences seem to affect the strength of attraction later as well. For instance, in the relationship with Billnäs the strong attraction Törmä felt to the client was partly based on intensive business exchange and past important and innovative assignments (see section 5.2.4, p. 121). Following earlier suggestions by Dwyer *et al.* (1987: 18) and Anderson and Narus (1984: 63), *it is also proposed here that satisfaction with the outcomes of assignment processes and the business relationship are likely to lead to a stronger perceived attraction between the parties to the relationship* (see arrow H in Figure 6.1, p. 180).

Attraction also has consequences for the development of agency–client relationships: it increases the potential for business exchange and also functions as an important impetus to investment initiatives and further adaptations. The sources of attraction actually indicate only a possibility of achieving different rewards from the relationship over time. Realising these rewards requires effort from the parties concerned. Attraction, with its future orientation, is thus very closely connected with investment initiative and the intensity of investments. Some of the factors that create attraction also create opportunities to demonstrate investment initiative (see for instance inter-firm knowledge and inter-firm role, section 6.3). On the basis of the case study evidence I propose that *attraction to the other party is likely to stimulate investment initiatives, and increase investments in the relationship* (see arrow I in Figure 6.1; see also Frazier 1983).

The proposed relationship is particularly relevant on the agency side and could be identified both in situations where attraction was low and in situations where it was high. In the initial and growth phases of the Billnäs relationship, attraction was very strong on both sides and both parties invested time and ideas in the relationship. The situation was similar in the active phase of the relationship with Head Office: the challenging corporate image campaign and the possibility of extending business with the Fiskars corporation as a whole led the agency to engage two teams for creative planning (see section 5.4.1, p. 169). After the organisational change, Billnäs's attractiveness decreased and routine tasks like the Classic scissors brochure did not inspire the team to sufficiently creative efforts (see section 5.2.5, p. 125, 127). In the new growth phase, the new product and changes in the agency's personnel activated the team anew (see section 5.2.6, pp. 128–9).

In discussing agency contests, some agency managers expressed lack of enthusiasm for them, but at the same time they emphasised that an especially attractive client would certainly lead to the agency taking the risk and investing resources in a contest. The following description concerning a former client of an agency also shows the dependence between attraction and investment initiative:

> We arranged many negotiations [to revive that relationship] to no effect, which of course meant that our interest ended again. The situation was such that it's not worth while us endlessly trying to get [business] from somewhere, especially if it looks as though what we'd get would be pretty minimal. We've got to, like, count what we use that time of ours on.

Strong attraction does not always lead to increased investment, however. Different situational factors, e.g. perceived risk and uncertainty, lack of resources, or a preference for using resources in other, more attractive relationships, may hinder the parties' efforts. Even though Törmä was greatly interested in the lead agency role Billnäs offered it, the turbulent situation inside the Consumer Products Group made it too risky to invest in the new role (see section 5.2.4, p. 118). Head Office felt attracted towards Törmä, but did not make much effort to advance the execution of the company image assignment because the need for the whole campaign had become uncertain. The recession in the Finnish economy and a number of other factors had altered the content of the assignment and its importance in relation to the client's other projects (see section 5.4.1, pp. 171).

Temporal considerations of attraction

In the a priori model, I suggested that some level of attraction is a precondition for a business relationship to start. In the light of the empirical evidence established it is, however, not necessarily required. For instance, in the case of Malmi, the internal power politics of the corporation significantly influenced the choice of the agency. The director of the sales unit did not feel any special attraction to Törmä (see section 5.3.1, p. 143). It seems that intra-group nets as well as inter-firm networks may in some cases dictate agency or client choices, decreasing the role of attraction in the initiation process. The reason for starting the relationship is then necessity based on authority, rather than a decision based on expected reciprocal benefits (see Oliver 1990: 245).

Mutual attraction seems, however, to be an especially important element for the progressive development of an advertising agency–client relationship. Attraction has to be built up consciously by both parties in order to estab-lish and maintain a business relationship. At the beginning, the burden of building attractiveness lies naturally with the agency. Later, however, when a relationship is established, the need to maintain attraction may become of interest to the client, too. In the Head Office relationship the client built attraction in the hope of increasing the agency's investment initiative and achieving better outcomes from interactions (section 5.4.1, p. 172). The deliberate building of attraction was also important when a business relationship was no longer new and there was a risk of creativity becoming institutionalised. The building of attraction was additionally perceived as necessary or beneficial on other occasions: for instance, when the client needed a new burst of creativity and special attention, as in the growth phase of the relationship with Billnäs (see section 5.2.3, p. 116).

However, it is more important for the agency to succeed in maintaining its attractiveness as a business partner. In the long run, the continuity of a business relationship seems to depend on the agency's flexibility in adapting its own resources and capabilities to fit the client's needs and preferences.

Building attraction means creating expectations of future rewards. This makes attraction building an especially challenging task in agency–client relationships. Communication about the client's future strategies and plans will evidently arouse expectations in the minds of agency personnel, for instance. *There may be a risk of overselling on the part of both the client and the agency, thus giving rise to unrealistic expectations, which may in turn lead to serious disenchantment in the relationship and subsequent weakening of the attraction.* The build-up of the account team's expectations in informing them about the launch of Roll-Sharp is a good example (see section 5.2.3, p. 105). In the Head Office relationship both companies had somewhat unrealistic expectations of their business relationship. The client expected the agency to know much more already about its business, and the agency raised its expectations on the basis of the client's new marketing strategy, among other things (see section 5.4.1, pp. 170, 174).

Unrealistic expectations may be unconsciously created in the imagination of the business partner by the other party. A history of outcome satisfaction may be internalised as a rule that is expected to continue in the future. What the parties have come to expect from their relationship becomes the determinant of attraction (cf. Anderson and Narus 1984: 63, 66). This means, however, that one party has been blinded by past outcome satisfaction and is unable to realise and anticipate the changes that may occur in the needs, resources or interests of the other party in the near future. Törmä found itself in this situation when the organisational change in Fiskars Consumer Products Group suddenly cut back the intensity of business exchange and considerably altered the nature of the interaction between Törmä and Billnäs (see section 5.2.4, p. 121).

6.5.2 Trust

The trust concept

The empirical findings of the case study supported the important role of trust in the development of agency–client relationships. As a consequence of the intangible, customised and people-intensive nature of advertising services, some level of trust seems to be necessary for exchange to occur and for a business relationship to exist. Trust also proved to be the key factor in advancing and maintaining a relationship.

Trust was defined as one party's belief that its needs will be fulfilled in the future by actions undertaken by the other party (Anderson and Weitz 1989: 312). In more explicit terms this means that the representatives of one firm believe that those of a partner company will perform actions resulting in positive outcomes for the firm, that they will fulfil their obligations in the business relationship, and that their word or promise is reliable (cf. Schurr and Ozanne 1985: 940; Anderson and Narus 1990: 45; Grönroos 1990a: 5–6). Each of these factors was supported by the empirical part of the study.

Two types of trust were distinguished on the basis of the case study. When considering the development of relationships it seems useful to separate *general trust – which depends on generally known characteristics of the other party – and specific trust, which is based on personal experience of the other* (for a related distinction see Young and Wilkinson 1989: 114). General trust is necessary in the initiation of new relationships, when the parties are unfamiliar with each other. Specific trust is crucial to the further development of a business relationship. It is in this latter sense – although implicitly – that trust is usually regarded in the literature of buyer–seller relationships. It is specific trust that is also referred to here, unless otherwise specified.

Trust clearly has its roots in the past, in the common history of a business relationship. *It is primarily built through past shared experiences but simultaneously directed towards the future of the relationship.* In the unit relationships studied past experiences were used in building current beliefs and expectations of the partner's trustworthiness in the future. The future perspective of the parties was revealed to be short-term, however. Possible changes and uncertainties in the parties' task environments restricted their belief in trust to the very near future alone.

Trust between an advertising agency and its client is essentially a social phenomenon. To have confidence in a firm is mainly a function of the confidence one feels in individual representatives of a firm. The majority of informants emphasised the role of individuals in building inter-firm trust. The trustworthiness of a company is not an irrelevant concept, however. People also trust companies because of their good reputation or resources in general, not just because they have confidence in some of the company's representatives. General trust is manifested primarily at the company level. Further, in cases where the parties have built an extensive network of personal relationships between each other it is difficult to attribute the feeling of trust to any person or persons in particular. Trust therefore relates to companies as well as persons (see also Wilson and Mummalaneni 1988: 10).

It also became evident that specific trust is a strongly reciprocal bond (see Young and Wilkinson 1989: 112). Behaving in a trustworthy way leads to perceptions of one's trustworthiness and encourages others into trusting responses and actions. The data also gave evidence of the necessity of mutual trust for the progressive development of a business relationship.

To trust another company or person to act beneficially means that one has confidence in the other's ability and intention to act so (Young and Wilkinson 1989: 112; Ganesan 1994: 3). In the case study, these two factors were identified as elementary but separate bases of trust. *Trust is grounded on one party's perceptions of the other party's professional capabilities as well as on its intentions as reflected in its interaction behaviour.*

The existence and depth of trust were inferred from the interview data. The informants were asked outright whether they trusted their partner or not, and what they meant by trust (see Appendix 5). They described in many instances how they felt about their counterpart's capabilities and in what way they perceived behaviour, whether it aroused trust or not (see Table 6.13). Trust and distrust were best manifested in connection with critical events, such as particularly satisfying or unsatisfactory assignment processes, personnel and organisation changes and economic recession. The strength of general trust was estimated separately.

When discussing trust the interviewees almost invariably considered the capabilities of the other party (see Table 6.13). This is congruent with other research findings from service settings, which have shown an association between perceived expertise and trust (Crosby *et al.* 1990: 76; Moorman *et al.* 1993: 92–3). Informants also emphasised the people-dependent side of the companies' capabilities. Advertising agency expertise, in particular was, perceived to depend on the professional skills and experience of its individual employees. One of the informants described agency capabilities as follows:

> That [trust] in these agencies in particular is very much down to people. The agency world is, like, tomorrow half the people may leave and start up their own agency, in which case the situation is totally new. At agencies there is no kind of permanent know-how: it all goes out of the door in the evening, and hopefully comes back in the morning.

The parties' intentions as reflected in their interaction behaviour formed another important basis of trust. Reliable behaviour fostered a feeling of trust, opportunistic behaviour a feeling of distrust. A partner that kept its promises, was fair in interactions and wanted to fulfil its obligations in the relationship was perceived as trustworthy. Several factors that were perceived as displays of trust on the part of the other also increased the evaluator's trust in the other. Giving new assignments, open communication and informal control in the form of open briefs and a 'free hand' in planning work were perceived as indicating trust by agency personnel (see Table 6.13). Reserve in communicating, by contrast, was quickly taken as hiding information and a sign of distrust. Trust was manifested even in the types of norms that emerged during interactions:

> We had a clear unwritten rule which everybody followed, that there's a group of professionals each of whom do their part, and then those parts are put together, as a new entity, and nobody messes up or interferes with the business of others. And we laid the strategies and everything openly on the table, not hiding anything.

Antecedents and consequences of trust

General trust seems to be built primarily on indirect personal contact and company reputation (cf. the findings of Ganesan 1994: 9). Mere awareness of the potential partner's specialisation tends to increase its perceived trustworthiness in that particular area. Other people's experience and referrals are used to build a preliminary idea of a company's trustworthiness when direct contacts have yet to be established.

Satisfaction with the outcome of previous assignment processes is the principal antecedent of specific trust. The parties gain experience of each other's capabilities and intentions through commonly experienced interactions. This connection, which has been emphasised by several researchers, also became apparent in this study (see e.g. Thorelli 1986: 41; Dwyer et al. 1987: 18; Anderson and Narus 1990: 54; Crosby et al. 1990: 70). At the beginning of the relationship with Billnäs the client was clearly testing the agency's capabilities and behaviour (see section 5.2.2, p. 104). The agency apparently earned the client's confidence by good creative work, a reasonable price-quality relationship and satisfactory service processes. For the agency, the client's trusting behaviour appeared to be an important antecedent of trust, besides the profitability of past assignments. The following description by an agency representative nicely illustrates how outcome satisfaction from previous assignment processes functions as an antecedent of trust, and new briefings as displays of trust:

> They were not very satisfied with this scissors packaging line and asked us if we could make counter-proposals to the Hall &

Table 6.13 Indicators of trust

Indicator	Concept

Estimate of each party's confidence in the the other party based on
• Perceived confidence in the agency's professional capabilities
  – in necessary advertising tasks
  – in the management of the agency
• Perceived confidence in the client's professional capabilities
  – in marketing
  – in briefing
  – in dealing with advertising agencies in general
• Perceived confidence in the other party's intentions regarding interaction reflected in opportunistic or reliable behaviour
  – keeping promises
  – being fair
  – being willing to fulfil obligations
  – giving new briefs
  – communicating openly
  – using informal control
  – types of norms
	Specific trust

Estimate of the confidence each party felt in the other before they came into contact	General trust

Cederquist proposals. That is what we did, and they then decided to test the packages both here [in Finland] and in Europe ... And one of our proposals won the test quite overwhelmingly ... And this is how we then got the engagement with Fiskars. Right after that, when we had shown them, it was a kind of 'apprentice's final exam piece', they trusted us to the extent that they brought us this totally new project, which was this knife sharpener Roll-Sharp.

I suggest that satisfying outcomes of assignment processes are likely to deepen trust between the parties to the relationship (see arrow H in Figure 6.1, p. 180).

During a long-term relationship, the parties are also able to build strong personal relationships and inter-firm knowledge, both of which seem to increase the trust instilled by the other. Sufficient knowledge of the client's industry and understanding of the client's needs and marketing conditions were perceived to be an important determinant of an agency's credibility. The ability of an agency to present relevant ideas with development potential for the client's marketing depends to a great extent on the level of inter-firm knowledge. Favourable personal relationships, which themselves involve interpersonal trust, strengthen the parties' belief that the other will act beneficially in future interactions (see also Thorelli 1986: 40). On the basis of this study, I propose that *strong personal relationships and a high level of inter-firm knowledge are likely to deepen trust between the parties to the relationship* (see arrow G in Figure 6.1).

The common clarified interests and inter-firm roles also seemed to contribute to the depth of trust, which equates with earlier results from a marketing channel context (see Anderson and Weitz 1989: 319; Young and Wilkinson 1989). Common interests involve trust that the other party will provide what is required (Ford 1982: 825). In the first phases of the Billnäs relationship, the parties discussed the client goals and the agency role, finding common interests. The relationship developed in an atmosphere of mutual trust. After the organisation change distrust began to creep in. Törmä was uncertain about its role in the new situation and felt an urgent need to clarify whether the parties still had a common interest in continuing the business relationship (see section 5.2.4, p. 121).

The establishment of the relationship with Malmi provides another example. The parties did not discuss their expectations at the beginning. Their difference of interests was soon discovered and a period of distrust ensued (see section 5.3.1, p. 144). A client representative described the initial conditions as follows:

> At the beginning we for instance had these competitive proposals put together, as we thought naïvely that we could give these kind of campaign assignments to others as well. And we discussed in, well, even quite heated tones, why we had had them drawn up, and at the beginning a kind of suspicion shadowed the relationship for about half a year . . . The expectations were different, that Törmä of course had an attitude such that we were a sure thing but we didn't know that that's what we were; we were being rather rebellious. But of course it wasn't about people but about things, and when our roles became clear then everything went fine.

A difference also persisted in the parties' interests in the later phases of the relationship, a fact which hindered the development of trust (see section 5.3.2, p. 153). Supported by research results from the marketing channel context, it is proposed that *common clarified interests are likely to deepen trust between the parties to the relationship* (see arrows B in Figure 6.1).

The parties' behaviour in interactions was dependent on their interaction orientation, on whether it was cooperative or competitive. For trust to develop, it is essential that one party can count on the other's fairness, good will and effort. The client should not feel that it is being made to pay too much for the agency's services, and, equally, the agency should not perceive that it is being made to invest in the relationship without fair compensation for its efforts.

A partner's own interaction orientation also appeared to function as an antecedent of its trust towards the other party. A cooperative orientation appeared to lead to trust. In contrast, a competitive interaction orientation appeared to be associated with distrust. For instance, at the beginning of the relationship with Billnäs, the client already had a cooperative orientation which then developed into highly cooperative behaviour, creating trust in the agency (sections 5.2.1, p. 101 and 5.2.3, pp. 110, 112). The client's orientation later developed into a more competitive one and confidence in Törmä's creative abilities also decreased (see section 5.2.5, p. 127). The relationship with Malmi, on the other hand, started in the shadow of competitive behaviour, which together with differing interests and the loss of personal confidence created suspicion and distrust on both sides (section 5.3.1, p. 144).

Several marketing channel or business relationship studies have also shown a clear relationship between trust and cooperative behaviour, but in these studies trust has been viewed as a determinant of the competitiveness or cooperativeness of behaviour and not vice versa (see e.g. Schurr and Ozanne 1985: 940; Holden 1990: 242; Young and Wilkinson 1992: 396). The empirical evidence of this study suggests rather the contrary, that interaction orientation is a determinant of trust. Anderson and Narus (1990) found a similar causal link in a study of channel relationships, contrary to their expectations. On the basis of this and the case study evidence, I propose that *a cooperative interaction orientation is likely to deepen trust and a competitive orientation to weaken it between parties to the relationship* (see arrows A in Figure 6.1).

Trust proved to be a key factor in the development of agency–client relationships and had several consequences for agency–client interactions. As also proposed by Anderson and Narus (1990: 45), trust in the other party enables a firm to respond trustingly or to take an action that renders it vulnerable to the other party's actions and to potential losses. Some researchers have recently even suggested that both the belief and the behavioural intention components must be present for trust to exist. Trust is limited if one party believes that the other is trustworthy but cannot be relied upon behaviourally (Moorman *et al.* 1992: 315; see also Young and Wilkinson 1992: 396).

When the client trusted the agency, it was willing to continue interaction and to give more assignments. When one party trusted the other it also seemed to be more willing to indulge in open communication. Interpersonal trust, in particular, appeared to foster personal disclosure and to open sharing of all sorts of business-related information (see also Cunningham and Turnbull 1982: 307; Etelä 1985: 75; Holden 1990: 242–3). Thus it is proposed that *trust is likely to increase openness of communication* (see arrow I in Figure 6.1). It should be noted, however, that openness also depends on other factors. How openly the parties actually communicate may depend on company culture, especially on the adopted disclosure policy, as well as on the personality of the interacting individuals.

When the client trusted the agency it saw no need to use formal control mechanisms in the relationship (see also Mills 1990). Open communication and a common understanding of the means and goals of cooperation substituted for the need of more formal control. This could be seen in the growth phase of the relationship with Billnäs (see section 5.2.3, p. 109) and also in starting the campaign image planning with Head Office (section 5.4.1, p. 169). Furthermore, personal trust allowed of an oral agreement rather than a written one. Thus it is proposed that *trust is likely to increase the informality of control* (see arrow I Figure 6.1).

A high level of mutual trust seemed to provide better opportunities for the agency to demonstrate investment initiative in interaction. At the beginning of the Billnäs relationship, for example, the agency had to prove its capabilities and learn to know the client. Later, when trust had deepened, the potential for the agency to propose new business, to suggest new ideas for the client's advertising, to influence the breadth of the relationship or even the position of the agency in the client's nets seemed to increase. Trust also allowed of disagreement between the parties, which often produces novel insights for creative planning (see also Moorman *et al.* 1992: 316). The following extracts from the agency interviews describe the relationship between trust and investment initiative:

> If it's a question of a client like this, then that gives us the opportunity to take the initiative and be active, especially in this case where we know . . . we have confidential relationships there, or we have access to inside information, which we don't have that often at all.

> The fact is . . . that by investing more in this client our position there now would be noticeably much better, because they believe in us already at certain levels, we know certain jobs . . . [We] have some kind of credibility.

On the basis of the study, it seems that a trusting relationship together with favourable personal relationships and a high level of inter-firm knowledge provide the necessary means for an agency to demonstrate initiative (see also sections 6.3.1 and 6.3.2). I propose that *depth of trust between the parties creates investment initiative opportunities for the agency and the chance to advance the development of the business relationship* (see arrow I in Figure 6.1).

The influence of trust on interaction styles generates greater potential to achieve process performance and relationship outcome satisfaction, as stated earlier (see section 6.4). *It therefore seems that trust is also likely to lead indirectly to process performance and business relationship outcome satisfaction, which further fosters the progressive development of the relationship* (see arrows I and F in Figure 6.1). Recent findings by Moorman *et al.* (1992: 322) support this proposition.

Temporal considerations of trust

Inter-firm trust develops gradually as the firms and their representatives perceive positive outcomes from their interaction (see also Wilson and Mummalaneni 1988: 10). Nevertheless, the evolution of an agency–client relationship cannot be regarded in terms of cumulative or incrementally increasing confidence between the parties. On the contrary, the depth of trust may change significantly during the relationship. Certain phases and events appeared to be more important for trust-building than others. *It seemed indeed that the depth of trust fluctuates over time and that trust has to be first achieved, then maintained and yet rebuilt continually in changing situations.* In a study of the electronics industry, depth of trust was found not to be positively associated with the length of the relationship (Holden 1990: 275). This lends further support to the above conclusion.

First contacts between parties and the first assignment processes proved to be important in building trust. In establishing a business relationship, the contact persons in the account team first needed to win the confidence of the client and then create opportunities for successful cooperation. It became clear that it takes time to win the client's confidence.

Certain events appeared to be especially influential in the development of trust during a business relationship. In the relationship with Billnäs, the packaging test for Classic scissors and Törmä's winning proposal acted as a turning point in the whole relationship. This event definitively convinced the client of the agency's capabilities and deepened its trust (see section 5.2.2, p. 104). The planning of the marketing concept and a launch campaign for the Roll-Sharp knife sharpener was another important trust-building event. Service process satisfaction and good service outcomes – even ultimate service outcome – created trust in the agency both at Billnäs and at Malmi. In the relationship with Billnäs the Roll-Sharp project developed into a success story, exerting a positive influence on inter-firm trust over a period of several years (section 5.2.3, p. 115).

As to the events that decreased trust between the parties, the restructuring of Fiskars Consumer Products Group was the most critical one. Törmä lost confidence in the client's marketing capabilities and future activities and later Billnäs lost its confidence in Törmä's integrity, suspecting it of opportunistic behaviour (section 5.2.4, pp. 121–2). Assignment process dissatisfaction was manifested in the planning of a new brochure for Classic scissors with Billnäs (section 5.2.5, p. 127) and the presentation of the company image campaign for Head Office (section 5.4.1, pp. 173–4); these events were identified as trust-decreasing. Their role was not, however, so critical as that of other events.

Confidence in the beneficiality of the other party's future activities was not very strong. Every new assignment was thus regarded as a challenge for the agency to earn the trust of the client. Distrust of the agency's capabilities or intentions easily gained ground as the business relationship aged. From the client's point of view, trust appeared to be based on some specific and tried area of expertise. When completely novel assignments were given and a new kind of expertise was needed, the client typically felt uncertain about the agency's ability to handle the task. This happened particularly in the last phase of the Billnäs relationship, for instance in the advertising of lawn and garden tools and the planning of point-of-sale marketing for tools and consumer products (section 5.2.7, p. 133).

Another factor which decreased the client's trust was the perceived risk of institutionalisation of creativity (see section 6.4.3). In addition, the client might simply be uncertain about the quality of work the agency provided, and therefore prefer to seek concrete reference points by asking for proposals from other agencies. Finally, the change of contact persons created distrust and uncertainty in the relationship. This is understandable, since trust is built primarily through personal relationships, and capabilities and interaction orientation are both heavily dependent on individual people.

Constant effort to maintain trust is clearly necessary in preserving the agency–client relationships. Assuring trust required investment from both parties, but from the agency in particular. When uncertainty and distrust gained ground in the business relationship, the agency made new business proposals or speculative presentations in order to restore the bond of trust (see e.g. section 5.2.7, p. 139). Favourable personal relationships were also used to rebuild trust in the agency's capabilities as well as in its positive intentions in interaction (see section 5.4.1, p. 175).

6.5.3 Commitment

The concept of commitment

Commitment was defined as an implicit or explicit pledge of relational continuity between the parties to the relationship. It represents the most developed state in a relationship, including the idea of increased interdependence between the firms (see Dwyer *et al.* 1987: 19).

Commitment has been viewed as a key component of long-term buyer–seller relationships (see e.g. Ford 1982; Wilson and Mummalaneni 1986; Dwyer *et al.* 1987; Han 1992; Morgan and Hunt 1994). *In the agency–client unit relationships studied, commitment did not, however, play such a significant role.* In describing and explaining the development of agency–client relationships the value of other relational bonds, attraction and trust, proved to be at least as important as that of commitment.

This is probably due to the nature of advertising services and the subsequent nature of adaptation processes. It was noted earlier that adapting and investing involves individual and intangible resources rather than organisational or physical ones (see section 6.2.3). As a consequence, the interdependence between companies is not so strong, concrete, and economically significant as in many industrial relationships, on which the existing models of buyer–seller relationships are based.

In the *a priori* model I identified two dimensions in commitment, attitudinal and behavioural; the former refers to the willingness of the parties to develop and maintain the relationship in the future, the latter to the actions and choices taken over time through which they have become committed to each other (see Hallén and Sandström 1988: 258; Morris and Holman 1988: 117; Anderson and Weitz 1992; Gundlach *et al.* 1995: 79). In the light of the empirical evidence of the development of agency–client relationships these definitions and distinctions appear highly relevant.

The study also revealed that commitment is a reciprocal phenomenon, so that each party's commitment to the relationship is based on its perceptions of the other party's commitment (see also Anderson and Weitz 1992). For instance, in the relationship with Billnäs, the proposal to use Törmä as lead agency could be interpreted as a sign of strong attitudinal commitment (see section 5.2.3, p. 112). When Törmä perceived no such committing behaviour on the part of the client in this respect, and in contrast noted a considerable level of turbulence within the client company, it felt it too risky to invest in the offered role. As the client did not seem to make any investments, Törmä did not increase its behavioural commitment through new investment either. On the other hand, Törmä's passive nature was remarked on by the client and created doubts about the agency's attitudinal commitment (see section 5.2.4, p. 118). Several instances in the unit relationships studied indicated that if the client is not responsive to the agency initiatives and shows no activity on its part, the agency can easily lose its willingness to invest in the relationship as well.

As is the case with the other relational bonds, commitment is intrinsically bound in time. The need to include the temporal dimension in the description of commitment has also been stressed by Fichman and Levinthal (1991: 445). *Commitment is strongly oriented towards the past; it reflects the history of the business relationship. However, it does connote a future orientation as well.* It acts as a constraint on future actions; it increases the resistance to change and fosters relationship continuity. A future orientation was visible, for instance, in the nature of the perceived switching costs, i.e. in the perceived risk of starting a new relationship and in the perceived loss of future business opportunities.

Three types of indicator could be used to estimate the existence and strength of commitment in the unit relationships studied: perceived switching costs, actions demonstrating commitment, and willingness to continue the relationship (see Table 6.14).

The potential switching costs perceived by the parties to the relationship appeared to be an important indicator of commitment. In an ongoing relationship it is difficult to grasp and assess commitment without examining the potential consequences of relationship dissolution. The various ties that bound parties together became clear only when the informants considered a potential break-up of their relationship and the subsequent starting of a new one.

Three types of switching cost were identifiable. First, the investments and potential losses of time, money and personal effort that the parties perceived inevitable in ending the old relationship and in starting a new one. These indicate behavioural commitment in particular and were described by informants in this way:

> Well, I at least would start from the point, when talking about branded goods that it's a question of an investment of millions of

Table 6.14 Indicators of commitment

Indicator	Concept
Perceived switching costs of each party separately - necessary investments and potential losses of time, money and personal effort in switching partner	Behavioural commitment
Perceived switching costs of each party separately - risks in starting a new relationship - loss of future opportunities	Attitudinal commitment
Actions demonstrating commitment by each party - investment initiative - promises and anticipation of future exchange - how passive in assessing alternative agencies; giving priority to the client	
Estimate of each party's willingness to continue the relationship in the future	

marks, that one should always aim at a more long-term relationship. It costs money to change an agency. A change takes about as much money as a campaign does.

The second type of switching cost, the perceived risks or exposure of making bad choices when starting a new relationship, indicate attitudinal commitment. The client representatives in particular brought up the uncertainties that the start of a new agency relationship would entail. A member of the advertising profession described:

> If there is a break of relationship it may well turn out that the next relationship will be short, too. In other words, the new advertising agency relationship doesn't work. The new agency hasn't got the experience of the previous one and you may be very impatient in your expectation for results, which can't be created overnight.

Jackson (1985: 124–5) also identified these two types of switching cost when considering changing the seller from a customer's perspective. In this study a third cost, that of losing future opportunities, was identified. It was interpreted as an indicator of attitudinal commitment (see Table 6.14). Agency representatives perceived the severing of an old client relationship in terms of losing future business possibilities and opportunities to develop the agency's reputation and capabilities:

> This client has brought in about half a million [marks' worth] in gross margin, in other words, that makes up only about three per cent of our margin. So that it wouldn't hurt so much financially, if the client relationship broke down, but in my view it'd be more painful in that we haven't utilised the potential there would've been in that relationship. It always annoys me if another agency then goes and does it.

Actions demonstrating commitment are essential indicators of attitudinal commitment and also form the basis of parties' perceptions of each other's commitment. Investment initiatives, especially those to advance the relationship, were seen as signs of a committed attitude. Whereas the intensity of adaptation processes in previous phases of a relationship shows the achieved level of commitment, investment initiative indicates the current positive attitude and willingness to develop a relationship further.

Some actions were intentionally taken to make one party feel that the other would stick by them. For instance, Billnäs's suggestion that Törmä should be used as international lead agency can be interpreted as a sign of the client's willingness to commit itself even more strongly to the agency (see section 5.2.3, p. 112). Some of Törmä's speculative offers were deliberately made to show that it wanted to maintain the relationship even if that required new capabilities and investment on the agency's behalf (see section 5.2.7, p. 139 and section 5.3.3, pp. 160).

Efforts to keep communication channels open also indicate investment initiative and thereby a committed attitude. It is the efforts that are made to stay in touch (Crosby *et al.* 1990: 71) and the investments made in developing information exchange (Hallén *et al.* 1987: 25) that create commitment and indicate commitment to the other party in particular (see also Dwyer *et al.* 1987: 19). Both the absence and the existence of this kind of activity could be identified in the unit relationships studied.

Besides the investment initiative, promises and anticipation of future exchange also showed commitment (see Table 6.14). Billnäs had already showed its willingness to cooperate with Törmä in the initial phase of the relationship, by giving the agency several interdependent assignments, signalling that other assignments would follow as soon as the new creative strategy was accepted (see e.g. section 5.2.2, pp. 102–3). When Malmi started to make annual plans for its media campaigns with Törmä, it could be interpreted as a sign of increased attitudinal commitment on the part of Malmi (see section 5.3.2, p. 145).

The active assessment of alternative advertising agencies indicates a low level of attitudinal commitment by the client. As pointed out by Dwyer *et al.* (1987: 19), committed parties maintain their awareness of alternatives but they do not test them actively and constantly. Conversely, giving priority to other clients and devoting more time and effort to servicing them could be perceived as low attitudinal commitment on the part of the agency.

Finally, in the real-time part of the study, the representatives of the client and agency parties were asked outright whether they were willing to continue the relationship in the future (see Appendix 5). This was used as an indicator of attitudinal commitment (see Table 6.14).

Antecedents of commitment

I was able to identify several factors in the case study that built commitment between parties to the relationship. The literature review revealed six potential antecedents of commitment: adaptations and investments in the relationship, contractual terms, the necessity of exchanging confidential information, intensive communication, social pressures to maintain a relationship, and satisfaction with the relationship. The case study revealed two additional commitment-building elements: the position of the partner and the client's adopted marketing and advertising strategy. The meaning and importance of the antecedents suggested in the *a priori* model were also specifiable in the empirical investigation.

In contrast with prior expectations, intensive communication did not appear to have a direct influence on commitment (cf. Hallén *et al.* 1987: 25; Michell 1987: 37; Anderson and Weitz 1992). The case study evidence seems to show, rather, that contact intensity creates commitment indirectly through the investments the parties make in inter-firm knowledge, and in personal relationships as communication channels. The time and effort devoted to facilitating communication serve to move the relationship to a more committed level.

Thus it was possible to identify seven antecedents in the case study:

1 Adaptation processes.
2 Personal relationships and the inter-firm network of personal relationships.
3 Inter-firm knowledge.
4 Contractual norms.
5 The position of the partner.
6 Outcome satisfaction from assignment processes and the business relationship.
7 The client's adopted marketing and advertising strategy.

The influence of adaptation processes on the parties' commitment was twofold. Organisational adaptations played no significant role in binding the parties together. It was difficult to find relationship-specific investments in the studied case, which are commonly viewed as a basis for commitment (see e.g. Ford 1982: 289; Wilson and Mummalaneni 1986: 52). The management of the partner companies might sometimes participate more in interaction; the agency might invoice less than its efforts would have justified; it could change its team or put some effort into broadening its role *vis-à-vis* the client, but such events were only occasional.

Individual adaptations turned out to be more important. Their influence on commitment can, in turn, be seen in the effect of personal relationships and inter-firm knowledge on commitment. It also appeared that people with a significant stakeholding in the outcome of the relationship tended to be more willing to maintain the relationship. The personal involvement of interacting people in the choice of the partner and the process of initiating and developing the relationship proved to be significant in building commitment. This could be seen in many instances in the studied case. Those who had not become committed personally to the current relationship were more inclined to criticise it and consider its dissolution or substitution with a new one. Those who had committed their time and effort to the business relationship showed more loyalty and countered the emerging pressures for change within their companies.

The existence of strong personal relationships and an intensive inter-firm network of personal relationships proved to be important antecedents of commitment. The importance of personal relationships on the continuity of unit business relationships was studied by examining the impact of permanent and long-term personal relationships and particularly by investigating the effects of broken personal relationships.

Several events in the unit relationships studied and several statements by informants emphasised the role of favourable personal relationships in creating commitment. For instance, a client informant described an agency relationship this way:

> It's very easy for me to note that at this point this relationship equates to a working relation with my account executive. If he walks out, then this time the advertiser definitely walks out with him. This is assuming that he goes to another agency. And if he doesn't then of course I've got to check whether there is someone at that same office who'd really know this same framework in which we've worked and would take care of the relationship as fluently and with the same sovereignty. But it surely wouldn't be very smooth.

In the case study, the favourable personal relationship at the top management level, and its stability, were crucial to the continuity of the three unit business relationships. Hedaa (1991: 120) has pointed out that friendship between two powerful decision-makers may be a better predictor of the strength of a business relationship than favourable personal relations at other levels. However, in the case there were other strong and stable personal relationships which contributed to relational continuity. In the relationship with Billnäs, favourable personal relationships could be found at every level, but especially at management level and amongst creative personnel. Consequently, the business relationship was characterised by relatively strong commitment. In the relationship with Malmi, the personal relationship between account executive and product manager was most pronounced. However, none of the personal relationships was especially strong, which could also be seen in the low commitment between the parties.

The changes of staff at important boundary positions proved to be a challenge to the continuity of agency–client unit relationships. None of the dissolved personal relationships alone was capable of producing any dramatic change in the business relationships. However, when several personal contacts were broken within a short period of time, the consequences for the strength of commitment and other relational bonds became more obvious. This happened for example in the second phase of decline in the relationship with Billnäs. The favourable personal relations at the management level that had developed over the previous years secured the continuity of the business relationship in this situation, where several personal relationships at the operational level were still weak and full of uncertainties (see e.g section 5.2.7, p. 133).

On the basis of the empirical evidence, it seems that the importance of one personal relationship and the consequences for commitment of dissolving it depend to a great extent on the intensity, i.e. the strength and extent, of the current network of personal relationships between the firms. Thus besides individual relationships, the broader social structure engenders commitment. It is proposed that *an intensive inter-firm network of personal relationships is likely to strengthen commitment between the parties to the relationship* (see arrow G in Figure 6.1, p. 180). When personal relationships are strong and their inter-firm network is extensive, it is more likely that the business relationship will continue even in changing circumstances.

Some researchers into industrial buyer–seller relationships as well as investigators of professional service relationships have recently found empirical support for this relationship. In a study of auditor–client relationships, Seabright et al. (1992: 152–3) found that individual ties between contact persons play a major role in building commitment. Mummalaneni and Wilson (1991: 20) arrived at similar results in an empirical investigation of business-to-business relationships. Wilson (1990: 4) has also suggested that social pressure to maintain a relationship is one of the structural elements that binds parties more closely together. Such social pressure is likely to increase as the number of individuals involved in the relationship increases within each organisation. Beltramini and Pitta (1991: 158) have proposed that the concern of an advertising agency for the client's whole buying centre can lead to an overall positive evaluation of the agency and reluctance to change it.

Inter-firm knowledge created in earlier interactions appeared to be one of the antecedents of commitment. Parallel to personal relationships, inter-firm knowledge may be regarded as a medium of outcome satisfaction in interaction processes and is therefore significant in keeping the parties together. Inter-firm knowledge is closely related to the individual investments made in agency–client relationships, to learning by doing. The acquired inter-firm knowledge exerts pressure for the continuation of the existing agency relationship, as the following extracts reveal:

> I guess it's so that once you build such [a relationship] . . . , when an advertising agency learns to know a client's entire history and products . . . , then of course it's easy to use that agency. Then on the other hand if you go to a new agency every time you do something, then you've got to teach them the same things all over again. And still you can never be sure they've got it right. And especially if you're doing something in a hurry, so there's no time to go into things . . . Well it could be a bit tricky to get somebody else all of a sudden who'd know all these strategies of ours as well as Törmä. It would take time – of course, things can be taught, but it takes time!

If we want to make something high-quality or, let's say, high-quality Fiskars branded concepts of household utensils, well, then we go to Törmä. As they've done for such a long period, they understand what we want. So now if we were to go to a new agency again, like, just like that, then we'd have to start it all right from the beginning.

I therefore propose that *a high level of inter-firm knowledge is likely to strengthen commitment between the parties to the relationship* (see arrow G in Figure 6.1).

It also became evident in the study that contractual norms *can form constraints and increase the level of commitment between the parties* (see also Anderson and Weitz 1992). The term of notice and copyright questions were mentioned as examples. In the unit relationships studied, however, legal and contractual ties did not play any role. Trust and established social norms were substituted for a formal contract.

The position of the client amongst the agency's clientele, and of the agency among the client's advertising service providers, were essential determinants of present commitment. A strong position in the other party's nets meant that the other party was more dependent and hence committed. For instance, by the end of 1987 Törmä had achieved the important position of the sole agency used for Fiskars' branded consumer products. At the same time, Billnäs had become significant for Törmä, ranking among its ten largest accounts. Both parties had become more dependent on each other (see section 5.2.3, p. 111). Ford (1982: 294, 296) has noted this factor. Perceptions of commitment are influenced by environmental factors such as the number and importance of the parties' other customers or suppliers. A company's actual commitment to a relationship is related to its assessment of the importance of that relationship within the context of its other dealings in the inter-firm network (see also Han 1992: 14) Thus it is proposed that *the parties' strong position in each other's nets is likely to strengthen commitment between the parties to the relationship* (see arrow G in Figure 6.1).

Outcome satisfaction from assignment processes and the business relationship are natural antecedents of commitment (see also Wilson and Mummalaneni 1986: 52; Dwyer *et al*. 1987: 19). It is evident that there has to be at least some satisfactory experience of interaction processes before the parties can commit themselves behaviourally. This could be seen at the beginning of the relationship with Billnäs. The first assignment processes and particularly the packaging test of Classic scissors created both trust and committed attitudes in the client (see section 5.2.2, p. 104), which then led to intensive business exchange and a much more committed business relationship by the end of 1987 (see section 5.2.3, pp. 111). Satisfaction with creative output, the final prices of assignments, the service process and with the relationship in general were given as the reasons for committed attitudes and for a long and stable business relationship. On the basis of the case study evidence, it is proposed that *satisfaction with assignment process and business relationship outcomes is likely to strengthen attitudinal commitment between the parties to the relationship; this in turn is likely to lead to behavioural commitment* (see arrow H in Figure 6.1).

The effect of the marketing and advertising strategy the client adopts on its commitment to the agency also became evident. This finding is congruent with Michell's proposition (1984b: 50) that commitment to current marketing and creative strategies fosters the maintenance of the existing agency relationship. In the relationships with Billnäs and Malmi, the advertising strategy adopted led to a series of assignments with Törmä. The commitment of Billnäs to the new creative strategy for Fiskars' branded products had already established a committed attitude towards Törmä in the early phases of the relationship. Long-term strategies also imply the realisation of results of marketing activities in the long term. Therefore, evidence of potentially incorrect choices does not emerge for some time, which also fosters the maintenance of the relationship. The following comment lends further weight to the commitment-building effect of permanent strategies:

> I've always preached in favour of long-term relationships because I believe in keeping a consistent line in advertising. Of course it has to be checked and improved and fixed every now and then. But a long line can only be maintained by having the same agency doing it for as long as possible. You see, agencies have such a besetting sin that at the point when they get a new client, they refuse to carry on the previous line because they have to show that they can do other things than imitate, so something totally new.

It is thus proposed that *a client's commitment to its current marketing and advertising strategies is likely to strengthen its commitment to the agency* (see arrows A in Figure 6.1).

The type of strategy depends naturally on the nature of the advertised product and on market conditions. It has to be remembered that in the unit relationships studied it was mostly a question of consumer brands advertised in mature markets, which typically require consistent marketing communication. In other industries and situations, advertising may not require such a long-term perspective (cf. the findings of Michell 1988: 64–5).

As potential antecedents of commitment, inter-firm knowledge and the marketing and advertising strategies adopted reveal that commitment is based on a certain type of assignment or specific brand or product group, to which the same advertising strategy is applied. A new or competing agency could be considered for other areas, but not for those where the current agency had carried out decisive planning work and had already acquired experiential inter-firm knowledge. The linkage between commitment and a specific area of expertise is also based on trust and its connection with the same area. When completely novel assignments were given and new expertise was needed, the agency had to earn the confidence of the client anew (see section 6.5.2). Only when trust had been built up, could the client also become committed to the agency in that new area.

Temporal considerations of commitment

The longitudinal analysis of relationship development highlighted the need to distinguish between attitudinal and behavioural dimensions of commitment. The case study evidence showed that in the evolution of commitment the emphasis on attitudinal and behavioural aspects does vary. Commitment evidently does exist in the early phases of relationship development but it is mostly of an attitudinal type. The firms have to have a desire and willingness at least to test the prospective partner if a relationship is to get started. In the relationships with Billnäs and Malmi, the adoption of the new marketing strategy and the centrally taken decision to use Törmä as Fiskars's principal agency clearly engendered attitudinal commitment in the early phases of the relationships. In the Billnäs relationship, a good fit between the client's needs and the agency's capabilities speeded up the development of attitudinal commitment. The client had an urgent need for advertising services, which advanced the development of committed attitudes towards the agency (cf. also Mills 1990: 37; Grønhaug and Venkatesh 1991: 26).

Behavioural commitment develops over time as a result of successful interaction processes and the emergence of commitment-building elements as listed above. To become interdependent and strongly committed, a longer period of intensive interaction is required. It takes time to develop strong personal relationships, inter-firm knowledge and a strong position in the partner's nets. Adaptations are made gradually in day-to-day operations and the outcomes of interaction processes materialise over time, even though there may also be intensive periods in interactions which speed up development. Thus it seems logical to suggest that behavioural commitment develops incrementally over time (see also Ford 1982: 289; Wilson and Mummalaneni 1986: 52; Levinthal and Fichman 1988: 348).

Conversely, it is tempting to assume that commitment also decreases incrementally. The case study lent only partial support to this proposition, however. Since rapid changes may occur in the main antecedents of commitment, its weakening is not likely to be incremental either – at least, not exclusively. Radical changes in client strategies, for instance, may erode the major foundation of inter-firm commitment.

The study provided an example of one major decline in commitment and a couple of occasions when commitment weakened gradually. The reorganisation of the Fiskars Consumer Products Group meant a rapid and sudden change in inter-firm commitment. It involved changes to several important antecedents of commitment (see section 5.2.5, pp. 123–5). A gradual weakening of commitment was identified in the renewed decline phase of the Billnäs relationship (see section 5.2.7, pp. 138–9). The study also supported the idea that a single unsatisfactory assignment process is insufficient to break a committed and trusting business relationship. Somewhat similar ideas have been presented in studies of both industrial and service relationships (see Hedaa 1991: 148; Liljander and Strandvik 1995: 153). A longer period of distrust or simultaneous changes in other commitment-building elements is required for a break-up. The following extract illustrates this:

> Yeah, sure, the relationship is questioned if we're not happy with the agency's work, but it's got to be some major blunder. We can't start breaking up relationships over some minor thing. There has to be a longer and pretty profound lack of trust, some fundamental incompatibility, like if for instance people's chemistry just simply doesn't go together.

Thus it seems *that behavioural commitment tends both to strengthen and to weaken incrementally, but major changes, or several simultaneously occurring changes, in the antecedents of commitment may cause a rapid weakening of behavioural commitment and even dissolve the business relationship.*

6.5.4 Interrelations between relational bonds

In this study I have identified three relational bonds in the content of agency–client relationships. The longitudinal research approach and emphasis on relationship development highlighted this distinction even more firmly. *The conceptual differences in attraction, trust and commitment became clearer and their intrinsic link with time was also highlighted.*

Figure 6.7 illustrates the temporal emphasis of the three concepts. Attraction is a future-oriented bond. It incorporates the expectations of each party concerning the potential rewards of the business relationship over time. However, attraction is also affected by the outcome satisfaction of past interaction processes. Trust has its roots clearly in the common history of the relationship, but is essentially also coloured by current expectations about the future. Trust is built through outcome satisfaction from interaction processes over time and directed towards the future

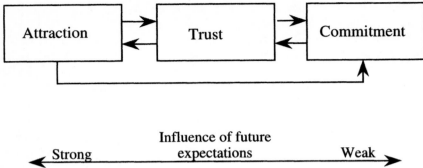

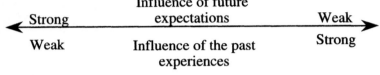

Figure 6.7 The development of relational bonds in an advertising
agency–client relationship

actions of the counterpart. Commitment is the most advanced bond and takes the most time to develop. It reflects, first and foremost, the prior history of the relationship. A future orientation is less significant for the proper understanding of its meaning, even though commitment also has a future aspect.

Regardless of their different temporal emphases, relational bonds seem to some extent to develop simultaneously and not only sequentially. The temporal succession arises primarily from their different development processes over time. Further conceptual specifications, the introduction of general trust and the separation of attitudinal and behavioural commitment were needed to describe the emergence of bonds in agency–client unit relationships.

Attraction is logically the bond that develops first. However, general trust appeared to occur simultaneously. Attitudinal commitment might also arise in the early phases of a relationship. Specific trust and behavioural commitment, on the contrary, required common experiences for their development. Behavioural commitment in particular required a longer period of intensive interaction before it emerged. The building of attraction and trust best describes the early phases of an agency–client relationship, whereas trust and commitment govern the development of its later phases.

The interdependences of relational bonds that were proposed in the a priori *model were supported and backed by specifying evidence in the case study* (see Figure 6.7). When a business relationship was initiated voluntarily by the parties, at least some level of attraction was found necessary for them to get in touch. A close link was discovered between one party's trustworthiness or trusting behaviour and the attraction felt by the other

270

(see also Schurr and Ozanne 1985: 941). As to trusting behaviour, the demonstration of trust in and respect for the work and capabilities of agency personnel proved to be an effective means of increasing the agency's attraction towards the client. This could be seen clearly in the growth phase of the Billnäs relationship (see section 5.2.3, p. 109). Opportunistic behaviour on the part of either party decreased the attraction felt by the other, as the following illustration by an agency representative indicates:

> It was a pretty bitter pill for us, as we'd done very thorough foundation work and analysis and really done a huge amount of work according to their wishes which we haven't been able to invoice. And then at the stage where there would've been advertising design which would have created income the client relationship was broken up, which wasn't even down to us. To us, the client turned into a kind of . . . that in the end there wasn't even any interest any more.

On the basis of the case study evidence, it is proposed that *attraction creates trust and vice versa*.

There also appeared to be a close relationship between trust and commitment. Depth of trust is apt to foster the continuity of the relationship and the parties' commitment to it. Conversely, weak trust was found to lead easily to dissolution of the relationship. This could best be seen in the informants' comments on the effects of outcome dissatisfaction on the development of relationships. An unsatisfactory assignment process was not perceived as sufficient cause to end an established relationship. A longer period of deepening distrust would be required to break the commitment. The relationship between trust and commitment as proposed here has also received support in empirical studies of professional services (see Etelä 1985; Moorman *et al.* 1992: 323) as well as in other buyer–seller contexts (see e.g. Schurr and Ozanne 1985; Anderson and Weitz 1992; Morgan and Hunt 1994).

The reverse link, i.e. from commitment to trust, could also be identified. Several actions that demonstrate commitment by the agency party, in particular, could be interpreted as measures taken to restore the client's trust (see also Wilson and Mummalaneni 1988: 9–10; Hallén *et al.* 1991: 30; Ganesan 1994: 12). It is thus proposed that *trust creates commitment, and vice versa*.

Finally, there also appeared to be a link between attraction and commitment. As proposed earlier, attraction is likely to stimulate investment initiatives, and increase investments in the relationship. Through such investment the parties are also likely to become more committed to each other behaviourally. Conversely, lack of attraction and effort was seen as a potential reason for low commitment and relationship dissolution:

Well, the relationship breaks up at the point where the agency starts dealing with your things indifferently. They've got no interest in your things any more, they're only interested in new clients, new things. An old relationship and what's done in it turn into routine. They don't go into what they do any more and how the advertising should be done. Meetings turn into squabbling on both sides.

The study provided evidence of the need to sustain and build attraction constantly in order to maintain the business relationship (see section 6.5.1). On the basis of the case study, it is proposed that *attraction creates commitment through its impact on investment initiative.*

The strongly reciprocal nature of trust and commitment was pronounced in the study. When one party perceived the other as behaving reliably or to be trustworthy in other ways, confidence in the other party tended to increase. The same phenomenon also applies to commitment. *Reciprocity thus creates a positive cycle of reinforcement, increasing the depth of trust and commitment in the relationship.* Both the development of trust and commitment, and the maintenance of attraction, occur in interaction between companies and their representatives – not in each company separately. These concepts cannot be understood properly without considering the interactive process behind their development and the setting within which they occur, i.e. the specific parties to the relationship.

6.6 CRITICAL EVENTS IN RELATIONSHIP DEVELOPMENT

In the *a priori* model, events were proposed as potential analytical tools for describing and structuring the development of advertising agency–client relationships. Critical events were defined as events that are decisive for the relationship and function either as driving or checking forces on its development (Elsässer 1984: 162–3; Liljegren 1988: 374). On the basis of the existing literature only two effects of critical events could be identified: changes in the perceived level of uncertainty concerning the continuity of the relationship (Liljegren 1988: 374), and changes in the intensity of adaptation processes (Edvardsson 1988: 434).

During the study, the concept of event turned out to be a particularly useful tool in understanding the development of agency–client relationships. Events that could be considered as critical affected the content and process of the relationship development in various ways. They either advanced or hindered the progressive development of relationships. Critical events could also function as turning points (or break points) in the unit business relationships studied, showing boundaries between different developmental phases in the relationships.[8]

Critical events were found to affect a broad range of elements in the content of unit relationships. Their influence could be seen particularly in: the intensity of the business exchange, the intensity of adaptation processes, the level of satisfaction with the business relationship, and the strength of the three relational bonds, attraction, trust and commitment. It was also typical of critical events that some types increased the perceived level of uncertainty regarding relationship continuity, while others decreased it.

An event that increased business exchange, adaptations and the level of satisfaction and, in addition, strengthened the relational bonds was regarded as a driving event. The reverse trends were interpreted as signs of a checking event. When changes in the listed elements were clear and significant, the event was considered as critical. To a great extent, of course, it was a matter of interpretation. The boundary between critical events and minor events involving incremental or smaller changes is not always clear in business relationships (see also Hedaa 1991: 140). Minor events may also pose challenges for the parties in their attempts to maintain and develop their relationship.

A list of potential critical events was presented in the theoretical part of the study, based on earlier studies of agency changes and success factors in advertising agency–client relationships. It included: each assignment process and interaction episode – particularly the unsatisfactory ones; changes in the client's marketing strategy; changes in the parties' personnel and organisation; changes in the companies' intra-group nets; and changes in macro-environmental trends (see Doyle *et al.* 1980; Cagley 1986; Michell 1987; Wackmann *et al.* 1987; Verbeke 1989; Michell *et al.* 1992).

The findings of this study mostly confirmed the list; a number of critical events could be identified in the unit relationships studied. As expected, critical events arose not only from the interaction itself, but also from the different levels of a relationship's context. Contrary to expectations, satisfying assignment processes were accentuated more than unsatisfactory ones as critical events. Certain particularly satisfying assignment processes functioned as driving forces for relationship development. When the events are examined in the context of the relationships, the reorganisation of the client company and the economic recession, as well as certain changes in personnel, functioned as checking events. Changes in the client's marketing strategy could have either a driving or a checking effect on the business relationship. Task factors then emerged as a new source of critical events: the need to give completely novel assignments was identified as a critical event, one that might have either a driving or a checking effect on the agency–client relationship.

Two assignment processes, the winning of the packaging test for Classic scissors, and the Roll-Sharp project, can be seen as critical for the relationship with Billnäs. The creative output in the packaging project convinced the client of the agency's capabilities and deepened its trust in the agency. As a result, business exchange intensified and an attitude of commitment developed between the parties. Moreover, both parties were satisfied with the relationship (see Figure 5.2 p. 103). The positive effects of the Roll-Sharp project were even more significant for the development of the relationship (see Figure 5.3 p. 106). The Roll-Sharp assignment became a success story owing to the high degree of outcome satisfaction on both sides. The trust-building effect of the assignment process could be felt several years later.

The organisational change in the Fiskars Consumer Products Group was a multi-faceted and checking critical event in the relationship between Törmä and Billnäs (see Figures 5.9–10). It was linked with the change in marketing management at Billnäs and with changes in the client's international intra-group nets. It resulted in target market shrinkage for the marketing concepts planned with Törmä. The establishment of five independent business groups to replace the centrally managed organisation resulted in a clear decline in the business exchange between the parties and also changed the type of assignments given. Uncertainty concerning the continuity of the relationship increased considerably. Turbulence within the client organisation and the agency's loss of important personal relationships with the client created uncertainty within the agency.

Attraction between the parties also decreased. Törmä experienced disappointment with regard to its future expectations and had to adapt to a minor role in the relationship. Billnäs regarded Törmä as an expensive and less suitable partner with regard to its future advertising needs. During the process of the organisational change the parties' trust in each other decreased as well. Törmä lost its confidence in the client's marketing capabilities and Billnäs, in turn, lost confidence in Törmä's integrity, suspecting it of opportunism. Finally, the organisational change also meant a rapid and sudden change with regard to inter-firm commitment. It involved changes in several important antecedents of commitment: in the position of the agency in the client's international intra-group net; in the network of personal relationships between the parties; and, consequently, at the level of inter-firm knowledge.

The deep recession in the Finnish economy proved to be a checking critical event for the relationship between Törmä and Malmi (see Figure 5.22, p. 156). The personal changes in the relationship reinforced the weakening effect of the recession. Business exchange diminished, some assignments were withdrawn and dissatisfaction with the relationship increased, at least on the agency's side. Recession aroused uncertainty in the markets which was also reflected in the business relationship as increased uncertainty about relationship continuity. Behavioural commitment was already low, and it weakened further as a result of the recession and changes in personnel.

Isolated personnel changes, however, did not appear as critical events alone. In the case study it was possible to investigate ten separate personnel changes that occurred either on the agency or the client side. The most influential changes occurred in connection with other events such as the organisational change, the recession, or other personnel changes.

Many of the personnel changes studied revealed that even though they were not critical they did nevertheless exert a checking or weakening force on the relationship. Changes of boundary persons caused at least a temporary weakening of trust and increased uncertainty about the continuity of the relationship. The interaction orientation of the new-comer and his or her earlier experiences of agency relationships aroused distrust on the agency's side. The risk of a weakening role *vis-à-vis* the client, or the risk of losing the client completely to competitors, was emphasised by the agency informants. Newly elected client managers were perceived to favour agency change, which confirms the earlier findings of Michell (1987: 31–2). The client, in turn, could not have confidence in the creative abilities of the new members of the account team who did not have experiential knowledge of the client company. There was also uncertainty on both sides concerning the compatibility of the contact persons and possible changes in the style of interaction between the companies.

When a member of the team changed, changes in the strength of attraction and commitment between the companies also occurred. Relational bonds could either weaken or strengthen, depending on the situation. Changes in personnel easily resulted in breaks or at least periods of low interaction volume in the business relationships. The newcomers typically needed time to learn their new jobs and to adapt to the existing business relationship. Each change also created a need for new adaptations and investments. New personal relationships had to be built and inter-firm knowledge rebuilt. Some of the personnel changes studied occurred during the assignment processes, causing new coordinating efforts, e.g. delays and changes in the plans, new adaptations and an increased need for communication.

The change in the client's marketing strategy appeared to be critical in initiating the relationships. The decision to invest in the global Fiskars brand and follow a standardised marketing strategy functioned as a critical event for the initiation of the business relationship between Billnäs and Törmä (see Figure 5.1). The new strategy also fostered the beginning of the relationship with Malmi (see section 5.3.1, p. 141). Similarly, the beginning of the active phase in the relationship with Head Office was connected with changes in the client's communication strategy. The brief for the company image campaign involved a change in the client's disclosure policy with investors and the general public (see section 5.4.1, p. 169).

The study also lent support to the reverse trend, i.e. to the weakening of an existing business relationship due to change in the client's marketing strategy. The adoption of new marketing strategies or decisions to implement new creative strategies generated clear pressure to re-evaluate the current agency. As Michell (1987: 31) has pointed out, every notable change in the client's marketing strategy, whether in the form of different marketing objectives or different policies, renders the relationship vulnerable, since the current agency is seen to be closely tied to the old marketing policies.

This could be seen in the relationship with Billnäs, when the changed focus of its marketing activities decreased its need for the former type of advertising services. Trust in Törmä and in its ability to satisfy the client's future needs decreased, as the client had no evidence of Törmä's capabilities in the new focus areas (see Figure 5.14, p. 134). Billnäs also doubted the account team's ability to change their pattern of creative thinking; it perceived a risk of institutionalised creativity. Trust as well as commitment were sustained only in the limited and shrinking area of past interactions.

The change of marketing strategy, in fact, created a need for completely novel tasks that had not previously been undertaken in the current business relationship. It may be concluded that novel tasks connected with changed marketing strategies are potential critical events in agency–client relationships.

In the final analysis, it seems that all critical events are somehow connected with the perceived needs of advertising and with the complementarity of needs and resources between the parties. *Events have critical consequences for the development of relationships because they affect the prerequisites of these relationships and entail new requirements for the complementarity of needs and resources in particular.* Some of the critical events caused clear changes in needs and resources (e.g. the organisational change, changes of contact persons); others seemed to prevent need satisfaction or deferred it to the future (e.g. the recession); and still others seemed to change preferences and the assessment of needs (e.g. changes of contact persons, change of marketing strategy). Moreover, the successful assignment processes were connected with the parties' needs and resources: assignment processes that showed an unexpectedly good fit between the client's needs and the agency's capabilities functioned as driving critical events. A recent study of the dissolution of auditor–client relationships also seems to support this idea (see Seabright et al. 1992: 152). The researchers found that changes in the client's resource needs increased the likelihood of their switching auditors.

The strength of the effects caused by a potential critical event seems to depend on the current state of the business relationship (see also Hedaa 1991: 148). By the 'state of the relationship' I refer here to the effects of common history, particularly the strength of relational bonds and the relational infrastructure between the parties. For instance, one unsatisfactory assignment process is not enough to jeopardise a committed and trusting relationship. Similarly, the break-up of one personal relationship, even a strong one, is not likely to dissolve the agency–client relationship when an intensive network of personal relationships exists between the parties. *Thus the effects of potential critical events are very much situation-specific. The state of the relationship, the depth of trust and commitment and its associated antecedents, in particular, determine to a great extent how strong the driving or checking influence of an event can be.*

6.7 PHASES OF RELATIONSHIP DEVELOPMENT

The different phases, or periods, of the development process could be identified in the unit business relationships studied. Each phase characterises a developmental trend that can be conceived of in terms of the content elements of agency–client relationships, and the temporal and logical relationships between these elements.

The identification of phases is connected with the events in the relationship development. As previously mentioned, *critical events marked the turning points in the relationship development and showed the boundaries between the different developmental phases.* Critical events functioned as driving or checking forces for relationship development and, simultaneously, as triggering factors for new phases. However, *different phases could also emerge slowly through minor events and incremental changes* without any visible connection with any major event as a turning point. Minor events often occurred in succession, supporting the same developmental trend and thus causing a transition from one phase to another.

As with the identification of critical events, the separation and existence of, for instance, growth and decline phases is very much relationship-specific. The kind of development considered as growth, and that which is considered as decline, depends on the earlier developments of each specific business relationship. In other words, there are no absolute measures to determine which phase a business relationship is in. The different phases only characterise the developmental trend of each relationship.

In addition, the time perspective of the investigation is likely to affect the separation of phases. When relationships are investigated retrospectively, over several years, more coherence and continuity in the development are likely to be perceived. Minor events and changes can be related to more significant ones, and will probably not be interpreted as critical events any more. In contrast, when relationships are young, or when they are investigated in real time, it is more probable that minor events will also be interpreted as turning points in a relationship.

Six different types of phase could be identified in the agency–client unit relationships studied: pre-relationship, initial, growth, decline, constant and troubled. Naturally, there is also a termination phase, which could not be investigated in this study (see Table 6.15).

The pre-relationship phase (cf. Ford 1982) proved to be important in understanding the reasons and motives for the establishment of a new business relationship. The investigation of the situation before the initiation of the business relationship provided essential cues and explanations for its further development. Three contextual factors were particularly important for understanding the situation: the nature of the client's marketing function, including its marketing strategies and organisation; the client's current and earlier contacts with advertising agencies; and both companies' key personnel, with their personal contact networks. Before initiating a business relationship, general trust and attraction emerged between the prospective parties. The parties became aware of each other, particularly through indirect and direct personal contacts (see section 5.2.1, p. 102).

In the initial phases the parties developed first contacts (see sections 5.2.2, p. 104; 5.3.1, p. 145; 5.4.1, p. 177). They familiarised themselves with each other, both as persons and as businesses, and started negotiations about terms of exchange. Intensive communication and coordination characterised the relationships, with the exception of the relationship with Head Office, which remained dormant for several years. In the initial phase, the parties started building the relational infrastructure. It was typical for all three initial phases that the parties clarified their roles *vis-à-vis* each other. The parties also evaluated each other as potential parties and tried to make sure of the attractiveness of the other party. When the agency proved to be attractive enough, or when the client felt the relationship necessary for internal reasons, as in the case of Malmi, first assignments were given.

Uncertainty still shadowed the relationships. Trust between the parties was only developing. First experiences of interaction and assignment processes created either satisfaction or dissatisfaction and functioned as tests of the other party, deepening or weakening the bond of trust accordingly. The first signs of attitudinal commitment could also be seen in the initial phase.

The growth phases involved intensive or at least intensifying business exchange: more assignments or economically and strategically more important briefs. Other interactions were intensive as well: communication, coordination processes and adaptation processes intensified. As interaction intensified, the parties' conditions for building their relational

Table 6.15 Characteristics of the developmental phases

Indicator	Pre-relationship phase	Initial phase	Growth phase	Decline phase	Constant phase	Troubled phase
Intensity of business exchange	None	Low First assignments	Increasing; potentially intensive	Decreasing	Established level with minimum of variations	Sudden decline
Intensity of communication, coordination and adaptation processes	Occasional communication	Potentially intensive communication and coordination	Intensive communication, and coordination; increasing adaptations	Decreasing	Established level with minimum of variations	First decreasing, later potentially increasing communication and adaptations
Strength of relational infrastructure	–	Building relational infrastructure; clarification of inter-firm roles	Strengthening of personal relationships, inter-firm knowledge, inter-firm roles and positions, emergence of norms	Weakening	Established personal relationships, level of inter-firm knowledge, norms, and inter-firm roles and positions	Sudden weakening in personal relationships, inter-firm knowledge and inter-firm roles and positions
Satisfaction with the outcome of the business relationship	–	From low to high	High	Low	Established level, relatively low	Low
Strength of relational bonds	Emergence of general trust and attraction	Checking attractiveness; developing trust; potentially some attitudinal commitment	Strong attraction deep trust; strong attitudinal commitment; increasing behavioural commitment	Weakening attraction, trust and attitudinal commitment; incrementally decreasing behavioural commitment	Relatively weak attraction, trust and commitment; minimum of variations in the strength of bonds	Potential weakening of attraction, trust and attitudinal commitment
Uncertainty about the continuity of the relationship	–	High	Decreasing and potentially low	Increasing and potentially high	Relatively low	Very high

infrastructure improved, particularly those parts of the infrastructure to do with personal relationships and inter-firm knowledge. Various norms began to become established in interaction. Increased business exchange tended to increase the importance of the relationship for the parties as well. Each party's position in the other's nets strengthened. The role of the agency could also broaden through new activities, types of task or products or by including completely new units in the cooperation as in the case of Malmi.

I could identify two growth phases in the unit relationships studied (see sections 5.2.3, p. 117, and 5.2.6, p. 133). These phases were characterised by strong attraction, which stimulated investment initiative in the development of the business relationship. In addition, the maintenance of the growth trend required mutual satisfaction with the business relationship. Outcome satisfaction from assignment processes deepened the bond of trust between the parties, committed attitudes became stronger, and behavioural commitment increased. Uncertainty about the continuity of the relationship decreased correspondingly.

The decline phases manifested opposite trends and characteristics of the growth phases. The three decline phases identified were distinguished by the client's decreased advertising needs or decreased advertising possibilities (see sections 5.2.5, p. 128; 5.2.7, p. 139, and 5.3.3, p. 160). As a result, business exchange declined and communication and other interactions decreased. This led to a weakening of personal relationships and inter-firm knowledge, and eventually also to changes in the established norms in the relationship. The inter-firm roles also tended to become narrower and the positions weaker. Interaction styles changed, which increased dissatisfaction with the relationship. The decline phases were also characterised by increased uncertainty about relationship continuity. Attraction weakened; the current agency was no longer the preferred partner in the light of new needs or preferences, nor was the current client preferred, with its decreased needs and potentially less innovative and less important assignments. Trust in the other party also decreased as a consequence of personnel changes and the perceived risk of institutionalised creativity. Attitudinal commitment to the other party decreased. The behavioural commitment that had developed during the parties' common history seemed to keep them together. Trust and commitment to the other party were limited only to familiar tasks and to areas of co-operation that still survived.

A constant phase can be regarded as a phase of steady development with a minimum of variations in the intensity of interactions or the strength of relational bonds. Only one constant phase could be identified in the unit relationships studied (see section 5.3.2, p. 155). In this phase, business exchange stabilised at a certain level. Certain norms had been established in the relationship: similar types of assignments followed each other at established time intervals, and the style of communication and briefings remained the same. These developments were related to the fact that the same persons were responsible for interaction for a relatively long time. Both parties could be fairly confident about the continuity of the relationship. When personnel changes occurred the parties were sufficiently committed to make the necessary investments in order to build up new personal relationships. In the constant phase identified, attraction, trust and commitment developed slowly and incrementally and remained at a low level. This was due to differences in interests and interaction orientations. No extensive changes occurred in the relational bonds, or in the degree of mutual satisfaction. Both parties were somewhat dissatisfied with the relationship.

A business relationship was considered to have entered a troubled phase when the parties felt strongly uncertain about the continuity of the relationship. This definition corresponds fairly well with the concept of the 'troubled state' used by Ford and Rosson (1982) and Rosson (1986), and also with the concept of 'uncertainty phase' introduced by Liljegren (1988: 374).

I could identify only one troubled phase in the unit relationships studied (see section 5.2.4, p. 122). A critical event, the organisational shake-out of the Consumer Products Group, which was also followed by personnel changes, caused great uncertainty, particularly in the agency. Uncertainty arose as a result of sudden changes in the client's activities even before the organisational change took place. It became even greater when the event and its consequences for the relationship became clear to the parties.

The business exchange declined suddenly in the relationship. Unexpected changes occurred in the type of assignment and in the role of the agency. Some favourable personal relationships were broken which, together with the organisational change, disrupted the working communication channels between the parties. Communication and investment in the relationship increased temporarily when the agency tried to clarify its role in the relationship and see whether the parties still had a common interest in continuing the relationship. Attraction and trust weakened. The planned investments for broadening the business relationship were not made, which hindered the growth of behavioural commitment as well. In short, the troubled phase was distinguished by great uncertainty caused by sudden and unexpected changes in the business relationship.

No termination phase was investigated in this study. The various examples given by the informants showed, however, that termination can also be viewed as a phase rather than an event in the relationship development, and that it includes specific processes of dissolution, and takes varying amounts of time. Relationships may terminate quickly as a result of some checking critical event, for example as a result of a change in an international partner agency's clientele. Alternatively, they may fade away slowly as a result of incrementally changing needs or other cumulatively affecting events. The client may have decided to change agency but, in order to reduce the risks of change, may prefer to maintain the current relationship while already initiating a new one. Termination may, logically speaking, occur in any phase of the relationship development after the initial phase (see also Rosson 1986: 211; Dwyer *et al.* 1987: 19; Hedaa 1991: 161).

As discussed in section 1.3, business relationships are not likely to follow any single, prescribed life cycle in their development. In this respect, the study supports the earlier findings of studies of industrial relationships (Ford and Rosson 1982; Rosson 1986; Liljegren 1988; Hedaa 1991). Figure 6.8 depicts the developmental paths from one phase to another through which the unit relationships studied developed. As the figure shows, phases occurred in an unpredictable way, and they could also occur repeatedly over the duration of a business relationship.

The case study findings further emphasised that the absolute time length of relationships cannot be used as a measure of their developmental phase (see also Ford 1989). Relationships can be in various phases: growth, decline, constant, troubled – almost irrespective of their age and irrespective of their previous phase of development. On the basis of the case study evidence and supporting results from other research settings, it is suggested that *agency–client relationships are not likely to develop according to the life cycle metaphor, which implies a prescribed order of developmental phases.*

Reasons for the idiosyncrasy of relationship development can be sought from contextual influences and the parties' own behaviour in developing their relationship. Each relationship emerges in its own specific context and has its own situations. The context of an agency–client relationship is vulnerable to continual changes; events and changes in the interacting companies and in the network of relationships surrounding them have an impact on the development of relationships. Relationship development is also dependent on the parties' behaviour in different situations. Relationships are developed intentionally by the interacting parties, but sometimes unintentional episodes may affect their evolution. In these circumstances, it is not logical to assume any single path of development in agency–client relationships. At most one may argue that it is possible to discern different phases in the development of relationships.

6.8 CYCLES OF DEVELOPMENT

The identification of phases is, first and foremost, an effective means of giving a simple and comprehensible description of relationship

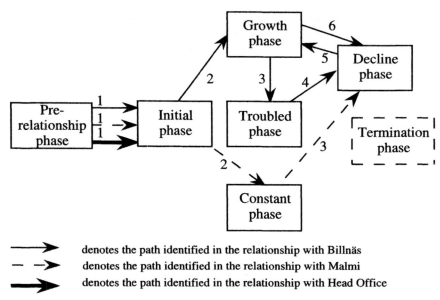

denotes the path identified in the relationship with Billnäs
denotes the path identified in the relationship with Malmi
denotes the path identified in the relationship with Head Office

The numbers indicate the chronological sequence of phases in the development paths

Figure 6.8 The developmental paths of the agency–client unit
relationships studied.

development. What actually happens during these phases, how the contents of relationships change and what kind of developmental processes are at work, are questions that have to be approached by other means. *The concept of a cycle proved to be a useful analytical tool for describing the development of relationships from a processual perspective. In the unit relationships studied I could identify three different and recurring developmental processes, which I shall call here cycles of development.*

A cycle is a recurrent pattern of activity (cf. Van de Ven 1987: 335). In the context of this study, *cycles of development are formed from chains of temporal and logical influence relationships between the content elements of agency–client relationships.* The cycles of development thus emerge directly from the conceptual relationships and empirical evidence presented in the previous sections 6.2 to 6.5. The three cycles of development emerged from the data as closely related to one or several types of phase in the relationship development. *They can be termed accordingly as cycle of growth, cycle of decline and cycle of maintenance.*

The cycle of growth was manifested in the growth phases of the unit relationships studied. Growth was triggered and later maintained by some driving critical event, such as a change in the client's marketing strategy, or by a particularly successful assignment process (see the relationship with Billnäs, section 5.2.3). Minor events such as offering an exceptionally innovative task or a change of contact person could also stimulate growth (see the relationship with Billnäs, section 5.2.6). The emergence of a cycle of growth required strong attraction between the companies. As proposed earlier, attraction is likely to stimulate investment initiatives in the relationship. Strong attraction thus provides a partial explanation for the cycle of growth (see also Hedaa 1991: 41).

Figure 6.9 illustrates the cycle of growth in advertising agency–client relationships. A driving event and existing sources of attraction (see Figure 6.9[a]) are likely to create mutual attraction between the parties [b].[9] When the client feels attracted to the agency it means that it is interested in exchange with the agency and is willing to give it assignments [c]. Giving an assignment, in turn, is potentially perceived as a display of trust [d], which further increases the agency's attraction to the client [e]. In addition, other factors connected with an assignment process, such as open communication and the use of informal control, may be seen as displays of trust.

Strong attraction stimulates investment initiative in the relationship [f], which, in turn, is likely to lead to outcome satisfaction from assignment processes and the relationship [g], and consequently, to increased trust between the parties [h]. Outcome satisfaction and trust are also likely to create mutually committed attitudes [i]. The client is ready to give more assignments [j], possibly novel tasks in new task areas or product groups, which broadens the relationship, or important and innovative tasks, which further strengthens the agency's attraction to the client [e].

Intensified and diversified business exchange leads potentially to further interactions: to intensive communication, coordination and adaptations, including investment in the relationship [k]. The relational infrastructure becomes stronger as a result of intensive interaction [l]. The inter-firm network of personal relationships is extended and strengthened, inter-firm knowledge increases, and different norms emerge in interaction. The relationship becomes more important to the parties; their position in each other's nets is likely to become stronger. Strong relational infrastructure creates possibilities for more satisfying outcomes of the assignment processes and the whole relationship [g]. It also builds behavioural commitment between the parties [m], which in turn paves the way to new assignments and further interactions [n].

In short, the cycle of growth involves an increase of interaction, an incremental strengthening of relational infrastructure and relational bonds. The reciprocal nature of the development of trust and commitment further reinforces the cycle of growth. Basically, the cycle is maintained, however, by continuously occurring and mutually satisfying outcomes of assignment processes.

In contrast to the cycle of growth, the cycle of decline is characterised

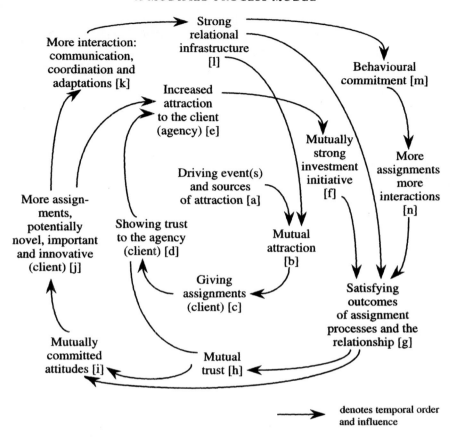

Figure 6.9 The cycle of growth in advertising agency–client relationships

by decreasing business exchange and other interactions, weakening relational infrastructure, dissatisfaction with the outcomes of interaction, and by weakening relational bonds. The cycle of decline was manifested in the decline phases of the unit relationships studied. This cycle was triggered by some checking critical event such as recession, or organisational change (see the relationship with Malmi, section 5.3.3, and the relationship with Billnäs, section 5.2.5). Similarly some minor events or incremental changes together, such as changes in the client's marketing strategy, personnel changes, an increase in routine tasks or institutionalisation of creativity, may start or at least reinforce the decline (see the relationship with Billnäs, section 5.2.7).

Figure 6.10 illustrates the cycle of decline. The checking events mentioned are likely to decrease the level of satisfaction with the relationship [b], and potentially decrease the perceived attraction between the parties to the relationship [c]. Possible changes in the sources of attraction naturally also decrease attraction. The checking events and decreased attraction will lead to reduced business exchange; the client will give fewer assignments, which are potentially less important and less innovative [d]. Decreased attraction is also likely to lead to diminished investment initiative on the part of the agency in particular [e]. As a result, dissatisfaction with the assignment outcomes and the relationship is likely to increase [f].

Distrust gains ground [g] and attitudinal commitment, i.e. the willingness of the parties to continue the relationship, weakens [h]. The client is reluctant to give new assignments. It is possible that at least more important and innovative tasks are given to other agencies [i]. When assignments decrease, other interactions also diminish, including communication, coordination and particularly investment in the relationship [j]. The relational infrastructure weakens [k]. The poor personal relationships, the low level of inter-firm knowledge, potentially institutionalised creativity and minor roles and positions similarly weaken attraction [c]. The weakening infrastructure gradually erodes the behavioural commitment built up in the past [l]. More time and effort will be devoted to a search for alternative partners [m], and termination of the relationship becomes easier for the companies [n]. Investment initiative expended in advancing and developing the relationship [e] will decrease further, which reinforces the cycle of decline.

The cycle of decline entails inertia. At least one of the parties begins to take the other for granted or realises that the relationship is no longer worth further investment. While the cycle of growth is based on the existence of strong attraction, the cycle of decline is basically the result of a low level of attraction. Together with checking events, either critical or minor ones, the lack of attraction gradually erodes the previously strong and well established relationship.

The third cycle of development, the cycle of maintenance, is somewhat different from the other two, because it recurs in various developmental phases. It refers to a process which is initiated deliberately by either or both of the parties in order to keep the relationship going. In the studied case, cycles of maintenance were initiated to shift relationship development from decline to growth, or at least from decline to constant development (see the relationship with Billnäs, section 5.2.7, and the relationship with Malmi, section 5.3.3). The cycle of maintenance was particularly apparent in the troubled phase (see the relationship with Billnäs, section 5.2.4).

The cycles of maintenance could be identified in connection with checking critical and minor events. Such events could be personnel changes, organisational changes, recessions, changes in marketing and advertising strategies, or briefings on completely novel tasks.

Figure 6.11 illustrates the cycle of maintenance. The checking events

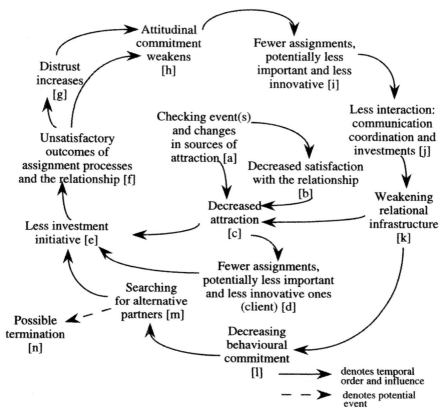

Figure 6.10 The cycle of decline in advertising agency–client relationships

lead first to reduced business exchange and other interactions; they potentially weaken the relational infrastructure, cause dissatisfaction, and also weaken relational bonds [b]. The declining trend in a relationship increases the perceived uncertainty about the continuity of the relationship in general [c]. When perceived uncertainty increases, the parties need to invest in the relationship in order to maintain it; immediate action may be needed (see also Hedaa 1991: 140). The partner who feels strong attraction to the other is likely to demonstrate investment initiative and engage in investments that are aimed at reviving the relationship [d]: management potentially participates in interactions, personal relationships are built, inter-firm knowledge is purposely gained or proposals are made for new business, for example. Checking events and the resulting uncertainty provide special opportunities to demonstrate attitudinal commitment to the other party (cf. also Ford 1989: 296; Hedaa 1991: 140).

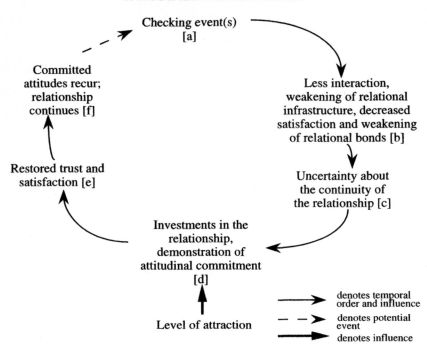

Figure 6.11 The cycle of maintenance in advertising
agency–client relationships

Investment and the demonstration of attitudinal commitment potentially restore trust and make the parties satisfied once more [e]. Trust can
be gained e.g. through outcome satisfaction from assignment processes in
new areas of cooperation or by investing in the building of new personal
relationships. Committed attitudes develop once more and maintain the
relationship [f].

The success of the recovery of the relationship depends on how the
situation is handled by the parties, and how seriously the relationship,
particularly the prerequisites of the relationship, have been affected by the
checking events. For instance, in the relationship with Billnäs, Törmä's
speculative presentation to the business gift unit of the Scandinavian
Business Group did not convince the client and the decline continued (see
Figure 5.9, p. 119). In the renewed growth phase the strengthening of personal relationships and satisfaction with the Junior scissors assignment
helped to restore trust in the agency (see Figure 5.12, p. 129). At best, the
way events are handled turns the relationship into growth. At worst, the
cycle of decline cannot be stopped in spite of the reviving investments,
and the relationship ends.

6.9 SUMMARY OF THE MODIFIED PROCESS MODEL AND RESEARCH RESULTS

On the basis of this study, a modified process model of the development of advertising agency–client relationships is presented (see Figure 6.12). In comparison with the *a priori* process model presented in the theoretical part of the study (see Chapter 3), a number of new concepts and one new conceptual category were added to the model.

First, the concept of interaction style, with its three dimensions – openness of communication, formality of control and investment initiative – proved to be an important element of inter-firm interaction between advertising agencies and their clients. Openness of communication and investment initiative proved to be particularly important factors in understanding the dynamics of business relationships, their initiation, development and maintenance.

Secondly, the evolving relational infrastructure was added to the model as a new conceptual category. It provides a more adequate description of the actual role of the earlier 'operational bonds', which form the concrete and necessary framework for interaction. The relational infrastructure sets limits and creates opportunities for further inter-actions. Inter-firm roles and positions were added to the model as an important part of the relational infrastructure. Thirdly, the distinction between different outcomes of interaction processes was changed to make it more applicable to a model of relationship development. Two outcome concepts, the perceived outcome of an assignment process, including three subconcepts, and the perceived outcome of a business relationship were introduced instead of the three previous outcome concepts, which emphasised the types of reward received over the temporal dimension of outcome assessment.

In addition, the meaning of both new and old concepts as well as the temporal and logical relationships between these concepts was defined and specified. New ideas and analytical devices such as events, phases and cycles were proposed for describing and understanding the process of relationship development.

Various critical events were identified in the unit business relationships studied. They originated from changes in the contextual factors or from the interaction itself, i.e. from assignment processes and their outcomes in particular (see symbols ✳ in Figure 6.12). Critical events functioned as turning points in relationship development and as potential boundaries between different developmental phases. Six types of developmental phases were separated and described by means of the content elements of agency–client relationships: pre-relationship, initial, growth, decline, constant, and troubled phases. In addition, three cycles of development emerged from the chains of temporal and logical influence relationships

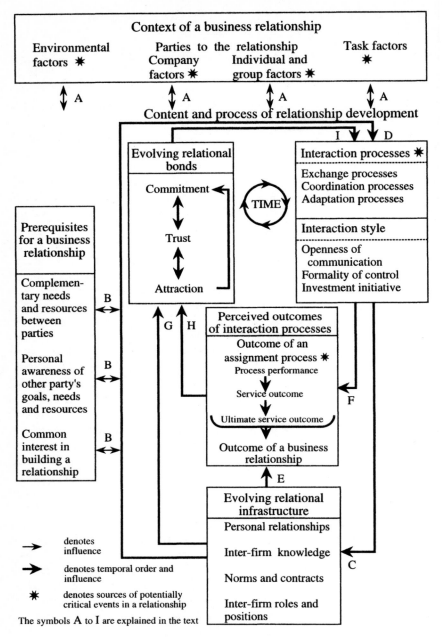

Figure 6.12 A modified processs model of the development of advertising agency–client relationships.

290

between the content elements: the cycle of growth, the cycle of decline and the cycle of maintenance.

6.9.1 The content and logic of the model

In short, the modified process model of the development of agency–client relationships can be understood through six conceptual categories, and the temporal and logical relationships between them:

1 The context of a business relationship.
2 The prerequisites for a business relationship.
3 Interaction processes and interaction styles.
4 An evolving relational infrastructure.
5 The perceived outcomes of interaction processes.
6 Evolving relational bonds.

First, agency–client relationships emerge and evolve in a context which is composed of three groups of contextual factors: environmental factors, factors related to the parties to the relationship, i.e. company factors; individual and group factors; and task factors. These three groups form a complex set of nested antecedents that influence the content and process of relationship development and the prerequisites for a business relationship (see arrows A in Figure 6.12). Interaction processes occur in specific situations determined by different contextual factors. The level of satisfaction with the perceived outcomes of interaction processes, the strength of the relational infrastructure and the strength of relational bonds are also vulnerable to contextual influences. The influence is not one-sided, however. The process of relationship development also shapes the various factors in the context of the relationship.

Secondly, there are three prerequisites for the existence of an agency–client relationship: the parties need to have complementary needs and resources, they need to be personally aware of each other's goals, needs and resources, and they have to have a common interest in building a relationship. These three prerequisites have to be met if a relationship is to start. Their existence is further required and assessed by the parties to the relationship on a continual basis. The three prerequisites are connected with the content and process of relationship development in several ways (see arrows B). They are formed and their existence is stated during the interaction processes and during the assessment of the outcome of a business relationship. Their existence also affects the evolution and strength of relational bonds.

Thirdly, advertising agency–client relationships are formed in a continuous process of interaction where three types of interaction processes can be identified: exchange processes, coordination processes and adaptation processes. These processes are firmly connected with each other. Exchange processes form the core of agency–client relationships. They involve business exchange, i.e. the exchange of a service for money, and communication – the sharing of information and meaning between the parties to the relationship. Coordination processes refer to the harmonisation of the parties' actions and decisions. Institutionalisation is an important dimension of coordination processes in which various norms become established. In adaptation processes the companies eliminate potential mismatches between their needs, resources and interests, their functions and procedures, and even between their attitudes and values. Adaptation processes include two dimensions: first, investing, i.e. the firm purposely adapts or changes its resources in order to make the relationship more beneficial, and secondly, adapting, i.e. the firm adapts itself to the requirements of the other party or to the demands of the contextual setting and eventual changes in it.

In advertising agency–client relationships, interaction occurs mostly in the form of assignments. The term assignment process is used to refer to individual assignments executed in a relationship. The execution of an assignment process occurs over a variety of time spans and involves episodes of exchange, coordination and adaptation.

The interaction style, defined as the manner in which inter-firm interaction is conducted, is an essential element of agency–client relationships. It includes three dimensions: openness of communication (connected with exchange processes), formality of control (connected with coordination processes) and investment initiative (connected with adaptation processes).

Openness of communication refers to how candidly and how widely the parties exchange information and meaning with each other. It is an important medium in building an agency–client relationship as well as in maintaining it in changing situations. The formality of control is also a relevant dimension of interaction style in agency–client relationships. It refers to how formally and strictly the parties control each other and the relationship. Investment initiative is an important medium in advancing assignment processes and the development of the agency–client relationship. It means that the company and its representatives take the initiative and make an effort to develop the relationship in the form of ideas, actions, time or money.

Fourthly, in interacting with each other, the companies create and build a relational infrastructure, i.e. a social, functional and economic framework for their relationship (see arrow C in Figure 6.12). This includes personal relationships, inter-firm knowledge, norms and contracts, and inter-firm roles and positions. These four elements form the concrete framework of interaction processes. They set limits to the interaction but they also create opportunities for further interaction and for the development of the relationship (see arrow D).

The personal relationships and the emerging inter-firm network of personal relationships form the most elementary part of the infrastructure. Moreover, inter-firm knowledge and norms are closely connected with people's interaction and thereby with personal relationships. Inter-firm knowledge refers to each party's knowledge about the other party. Norms are the patterns and expectations of behaviour that become established in coordination processes. Institutionalisation of creativity is peculiar to the advertising sector. Contracts refer to written contracts. They have potentially less importance in agency–client relationships than unwritten norms. Role refers to the breadth of the relationship and position to the importance of the relationship with respect to relevant intra-group and inter-firm nets. Roles and positions are related to the companies rather than to individuals.

The relational infrastructure has an important influence on the perceived outcomes of assignment processes and on the outcome of the business relationship (see arrow E). Favourable personal relationships and inter-firm knowledge are likely to lead to satisfaction with assignment processes and with the relationship as a whole. Different norms may have either positive or negative effects on perceived satisfaction. Institutionalised creativity was a particular cause of dissatisfaction. Finally, inter-firm roles and positions also influence satisfaction; congruent role expectations and role behaviour are likely to lead to satisfaction with the business relationship.

Fifthly, during interaction, the parties assess their relationship, particularly the associated reward–cost outcomes. On the basis of the perceived outcomes, i.e. the level of outcome satisfaction, the parties make decisions about the future of the relationship. The perceived outcome of an assignment process and the perceived outcome of a business relationship include the assessment of both social and economic rewards and costs. The perceived satisfaction with an entire business relationship is the result of all interaction episodes between the parties. It is influenced by the outcomes of individual assignment processes and other interaction, by the interaction styles and also the existing relational infrastructure (see arrows F and E in Figure 6.12). In addition, contextual factors or factors related to them, such as similarity of the parties' interaction orientations, are likely to affect it (see arrows A).

The evaluation of outcomes is a continuous and complex process. A number of people and companies assess the outcomes and, subsequently, several criteria are applied to evaluation. The assessment of an assignment process is a multi-stage process that occurs over a long period of time. The perceived outcome of an assignment process can be divided into three chronologically successive outcome elements, which take different periods of time to materialise. Process performance is used to refer to the level of satisfaction the parties perceive with respect to the interactive service production process, i.e. all interaction episodes between the parties during an assignment process. Open communication, informal control and investment initiative are likely to create satisfaction with the service process and also with the relationship as a whole. Service outcome refers to the level of satisfaction the parties perceive with respect to the immediate results of the service production process. The ultimate service outcome is the *raison d'être* of most assignment processes. It refers to the level of satisfaction the parties perceive with respect to the final and indirect results of an assignment process on each company's business. Ultimate service outcomes are very difficult to assess because of the temporal carry-over effects and the multitude of intervening variables in the parties' marketing environment.

Finally, the evolving relational bonds incorporate the continuity dimension of business relationships, i.e. the parties' bilateral expectation of future interactions. The three relational bonds of attraction, trust and commitment are basic content elements of advertising agency–client relationships. The development of these bonds makes the relationship strong and potentially long-lasting. Correspondingly, changes in these bonds reflect major changes in the relationship development.

Attraction refers to a company's interest in exchange with another, based on the economic and social reward–cost outcomes expected from a relationship over time. Attraction is a future-oriented bond which incorporates the conscious as well as unconscious expectations concerning the relationship. It is based on the three prerequisites of a business relationship (see arrows B). A number of company-related factors, task factors and qualities of the relational infrastructure also function as sources of attraction (see arrows A and G). They all indicate possibilities of gaining rewards from the relationship in the future.

An agency's capabilities, reputation, price level and size contribute to its attractiveness in the eyes of a client. In addition, favourable personal relationships with agency personnel and a high level of knowledge about the client company are likely to strengthen attraction to an agency. The attractiveness of the client in the eyes of the agency is influenced by the client's business success, the role of advertising in its marketing, and brand and product type. Innovative assignments, sophisticated marketing capabilities, and a cooperative interaction orientation are also likely to increase the client's attractiveness. In addition, favourable personal relations with the client's personnel, a broad agency role and a strong position in the client's nets potentially strengthen the bond of attraction.

The parties also use common past experiences as evidence of each other's attractiveness, which may sometimes create unrealistic expectations and consequently lead to disappointments. Satisfaction with the assignment and relationship outcomes is likely to lead to stronger perceived attraction between the parties to the relationship (see arrow H).

Attraction is a particularly important bond for the progressive development of advertising agency–client relationships. By definition, it increases the parties' interest in exchange. It is also likely to stimulate investment initiative in the relationship (see arrow I).

Trust is one party's belief that its needs will be fulfilled in the future by actions undertaken by the other. Trust has two dimensions: general trust, which depends on the generally known characteristics of the other party, and specific trust, which is based on the personal experience of the other. Specific trust – the crucial dimension – has its roots in the common history of a business relationship but is simultaneously directed towards the future of the relationship. It is essentially a social and reciprocal bond. Specific trust is grounded in one party's perception of the other party's professional capabilities as well as in its intentions, which are reflected in interaction behaviour.

General trust is based on indirect personal contacts and company reputation (see arrows A in Figure 6.12). In contrast, satisfying outcomes of earlier assignment processes are the principal antecedents of specific trust (see arrow H). With regard to the relational infrastructure, strong personal relationships and a high level of inter-firm knowledge are likely to deepen trust between the parties to the relationship (see arrow G). Furthermore, common clarified interests and cooperative interaction orientation are likely to deepen trust (see arrows A and B).

Trust is an important factor in the development of agency–client relationships. Trust in the other party encourages the company to adopt a trusting stance in return. Trust paves the way for further interaction and is likely to increase the openness of communication and informality of control (see arrow I). Deeper trust creates opportunities for the agency to demonstrate investment initiative and advance the development of the relationship.

Commitment is defined as an implicit or explicit pledge of relational continuity between the parties to the relationship. Commitment represents the most advanced state in a business relationship, including the idea of increased interdependence between the parties. It paves the way for further interactions and adaptations between the parties (see arrow I). Commitment also has two conceptual dimensions: it is behavioural when built up by the actions and choices of the parties over time. Attitudinal commitment refers to the parties' willingness to develop and maintain the relationship in the future. As is the case with other relational bonds, commitment is also intrinsically bound up with time: it reflects the history of the relationship, in particular, but connotes a clear future orientation as well. Like trust, commitment is also a strongly reciprocal bond.

There are several temporal antecedents that determine the current level of commitment. Adaptation processes and individual adaptations, in particular, build commitment. An intensive network of personal relationships, a high level of inter-firm knowledge and the other party's strong position in one's nets are all factors that are likely to strengthen commitment between the parties (see arrow G in Figure 6.12). Outcome satisfaction in assignment processes and the relationship are important antecedents of attitudinal, and thereby also of behavioural, commitment (see arrow H). In addition, the client's commitment to its current marketing and advertising strategies is likely to foster commitment to the agency (see arrows A).

Relational bonds develop partly simultaneously and partly in succession to one another. The chronological sequence of relational bonds arises mostly from the differences in their development. Attraction develops first, leading to the first assignment processes and to the emergence of trust through common experiences of interaction. General trust is likely to exist at the beginning of a relationship as well, and attitudinal commitment may also develop at an early stage. The strength of specific trust is likely to fluctuate over time. The maintenance of both attraction and trust requires continuous effort from both parties to the relationship. Behavioural commitment takes longest to develop. It tends to increase and decrease incrementally, but major or several simultaneously occurring changes in its antecedents may cause a rapid weakening of behavioural commitment and even dissolve the relationship.

The relational bonds are closely related to each other. Not only are attraction and trust likely to lead to commitment, but trustworthiness or the trusting behaviour of the other is also likely to increase attraction, and actions demonstrating commitment may be taken in order to restore trust between the parties. Attraction potentially leads to increased commitment through its positive impact on investment initiative.

6.9.2 Events, phases and cycles in relationship development

Events that arise from changes in contextual factors or from interaction itself are useful analytical tools for describing the development of advertising agency–client relationships over time. Critical events are decisive for a relationship and function either as driving or as checking forces in its development. They affect a broad range of elements in the content of agency–client relationships, particularly influencing the intensity of business exchange, intensity of adaptation processes, the level of satisfaction with the business relationship, and the strength of the three relational bonds: attraction, trust, and commitment. Critical events also affect the perceived level of uncertainty concerning the continuity of the relationship.

Satisfying outcomes of assignment processes may function as driving forces in the development of agency–client relationships, and organisational changes in the client company, economic recession and personnel changes as checking forces. Changes in the client's marketing strategy and the need to give completely novel assignments may also constitute critical events for a relationship, either checking or driving.

The strength of the effects driven by a potential critical event is situation-specific; it depends on the current state of the relationship. The depth of trust and particularly the depth of commitment, including its antecedents, determine to a great extent how strong the driving or checking influence of an event can be. For instance, one unsatisfactory assignment process or the dissolution of a single personal relationship is not enough to destroy a trusting and committed relationship. In the final analysis, the seriousness of the effects is dependent on the behaviour of the parties in the particular situation. The consequences of a critical event are also related to the type of the critical event itself. Critical events may affect the prerequisites for a business relationship to such an extent that they cease to exist and the relationship dissolves (see arrows A). This is particularly true of the complementarity of need and resources.

Different types of developmental phases can be identified in the development of agency–client relationships: pre-relationship, initial, growth, decline, constant and troubled. Critical events or a series of minor events and changes delineate the boundaries between developmental phases. Each phase characterises a developmental trend in a relationship. The developmental trends in the intensity of business exchange and other interactions, in the strength of the relational infrastructure, in the level of relationship satisfaction, in the strength of the relational bonds, and finally in the uncertainty regarding relationship continuity can all be used to describe the developmental phase of an agency–client relationship.

Phases are likely to emerge in an unpredictable way and they may also occur repeatedly over the duration of the business relationship. There seems to be no single, prescribed path of development for all relationships, which is due to the fact that relationships are developed intentionally by the parties to the relationship and that each relationship has its own specific context and situations which affect its development.

Cycles can also be identified in the development of agency–client relationships. Cycles of development are formed of chains of temporal and logical influence relationships between the content elements of agency–client relationships. Growth phases evolve through cycles of growth. It means that business exchange and other interaction increases, the relational infrastructure gradually strengthens, the level of satisfaction also increases, and the relational bonds become stronger. This development is likely to be triggered and maintained by some driving critical event or several minor events, together with strong mutual attraction between the parties.

Correspondingly, phases of decline develop through cycles of decline. They refer to declining business exchange and other types of interaction, to the weakening of relational infrastructure, the increase in dissatisfaction with the outcomes of interaction and to weakening relational bonds. The cycle of decline is likely to be started by some checking critical event or minor events and changes which lead to decreased satisfaction and weakened attraction in the relationship.

In addition, cycles of maintenance may occur. These cycles are purposely initiated by either party in order to maintain the relationship and to turn it from decline to growth or at least to a constant phase. Cycles of maintenance are thus likely to occur in phases of decline, although they may also occur in troubled phases. A cycle of maintenance is a reaction to some checking critical or minor event. It involves investment in the relationship in an attempt to revive it, restore satisfaction and trust and regain the committed attitudes of the other party. In the cycle of maintenance the role of attraction is also crucial. It determines who will engage in reviving investments and whether the cycle of maintenance will occur at all.

7

ASSESSMENT OF THE STUDY

The assessment of any study entails at least two related tasks: the assessment of its contribution and the evaluation of its validity. The reliability and validity of the collected data have already been discussed in section 4.5. In this chapter, I shall first assess the contribution by presenting the major theoretical and practical implications of the study. I will then address the issue of validity by taking the whole research process and the different meanings of validity into account. At the end of the chapter some avenues for future research will be proposed.

7.1 CONTRIBUTION AND CONCLUSIONS

When assessing a study which aims at theory construction one has to ask what can be considered a legitimate, value-added contribution to theory development. Whetten (1989: 492–3) has addressed this issue, in particular, and suggested various ways in which a contribution can be made. By applying an old model to a new setting, one may contribute improvements and indicate new ways in which the model functions. One may add to or subtract concepts from an existing model and demonstrate how the change affects the previously accepted relationships between the concepts. One may borrow a theoretical perspective from another field in order to encourage the change of current metaphors, and to challenge the underlying rationale supporting the accepted theories.

In this study, all these types of theoretical contribution are present in some form. The contribution culminates in the process model proposed for understanding the development of advertising agency–client relationships. *First, I have applied the IMP Group's Interaction Framework – which was originally designed for international and industrial business settings – to the context of professional business services and advertising in particular.* The value of this application depends very much on how appropriate and applicable the Interaction Framework has been in developing an empirically grounded process model for advertising agency–client relationships, which was the purpose of this study. In other words, one should ask whether the application created any new theoretical knowledge of agency–client relationships or professional business service relationships. The value of the application can also be looked at from the perspective of the applied Interaction Framework. In this respect, one should question how fruitful its application has been in generating new knowledge and understanding of the Interaction Framework, in other words, whether the findings changed earlier knowledge or raised any new questions.

In principle, the Interaction Framework seemed eminently suitable for the study of advertising agency–client relationships. The Interaction Model (see Håkansson 1982; Möller and Wilson 1988) and the related models of relationship development (see Ford 1982; Ford and Rosson 1982) also provided relevant concepts and useful ideas. These models could, however, be used only as a basis for the development of the process model.

When compared with most industrial products, advertising services are, first and foremost, very intangible and highly dependent on individual people, their personal characteristics and capabilities. The role of technology, physical materials and investment is much less significant than in typical manufacturing industries. The exchange of advertising services also entails strong ambiguities that concern both the advertiser and the agency. Consequently, somewhat different factors are accentuated in agency–client relationships than in typical industrial buyer–seller relationships:

1 The characteristics of individuals and their personal relationships had a strong influence on relationship development. Individual capabilities, including professional skills and knowledge, and people's personality and working style, all proved to be important individual factors. Personal relationships were seen in terms of three dimensions: interpersonal liking, trust and knowing. They were shown to play a significant role in creating the necessary awareness of the other party's goals, needs and resources, which is a prerequisite for a relationship's start-up and development. Favourable personal relationships also had an important role to play in maintaining business relationships, as they were crucial in resolving and avoiding conflicts and in providing satisfying outcomes of assignment processes and the business relationship as a whole. Much of the relational dynamics was revealed to be dependent on the characteristics of interacting individuals, their will-power, attitudes, perceptions and intentions.

2 The important role of individuals was also accentuated in the nature of adaptation and coordination processes. Adaptation processes occurred in day-to-day interaction between contact persons and particularly involved individual resources: learning by doing and individual sacrifices. In coordination processes, institutionalisation in the form of

various unwritten norms that were created and learned in interaction appeared to be more important than written contracts.

3 Instead of a continuous flow of exchange episodes, the role of individual assignments was accentuated in the development of agency–client relationships. Assignments also had a clear processual nature.

4 As a result of the intangible nature of advertising services and the considerable ambiguities related to their exchange, future-oriented relational bonds seemed to receive most weight in agency–client relationships, i.e. attraction and trust were seen to be more important than commitment. The low level of organisational and physical investment reduced the importance of commitment. While economic, technological and functional dependences are important antecedents of commitment in manufacturing industries (see e.g. Han 1992: 39), personal relationships and other human factors such as inter-firm knowledge and personal stakeholding in the outcomes of the relationship appeared to receive more emphasis in the advertising sector.

5 The interaction style appeared to be an important element in the development of advertising agency–client relationships. Openness of communication, informality of control and investment initiative proved to be essential factors in the production of advertising services and in creating satisfying outcomes from interaction.

6 The power relationship between the agency and its clients appeared to hold much less importance for the nature and development of business relationships than is commonly expected and also shown in studies of industrial or marketing channel relationships. This may be due to the nature of advertising services and advertising markets, although certain choices made in the research design have possibly influenced this finding as well. The case relationship was purposely selected from the agency's medium-sized accounts, which has potentially attenuated the manifestation of power in the unit relationships studied. The dyadic perspective may also have been too narrow for studying power effectively. Power is an attribute of larger structures and relative to other participants in the inter-firm network, as is emphasised for instance by Cook and Emerson (1978: 721) and Thorelli (1986: 40).

In the second area of theory contribution, the concepts of the original Interaction Framework and the related models of relationship development were modified and complemented in various ways in the study. During the construction of the *a priori* model, new concepts were added to the original Interaction Framework. I borrowed concepts such as attraction and trust from the American interaction studies; being more socially and psychologically oriented concepts, they seemed particularly applicable to the advertising context (see e.g. Anderson and Narus 1984, 1990; Wilson and Mummalaneni 1986; Dwyer *et al.* 1987). The service marketing literature was used to complement the Interaction Framework, especially when the nature of services and their evaluation were concerned.

During the empirical investigation, a number of new concepts also emerged as important elements of agency–client relationships. The nature of advertising services and the processual perspective on relationship development highlighted the need to add interaction style with its three dimensions to the model as a new concept. The evolving relational infrastructure, including the concepts of role and position, was introduced to the model as a new conceptual category. In addition, the perceived outcomes of assignment processes proved to be essential explanatory factors for the development of agency–client relationships. The perceived outcome of an assignment process and the outcome of a business relationship were conceptually distinguished from each other, and different, chronologically consecutive, elements were separated and defined in the outcome of an assignment process.

The meanings of both old and new concepts were defined and specified. The roles and meanings of various bonds, in particular, were clarified. 'Operational' bonds were conceptually separated from relational bonds and connected with the model as elements of the evolving relational infrastructure. The definitions of relational bonds, i.e. attraction, trust and commitment, were specified by paying special attention to their relation to time: to the past, present and future. In previous research, the conceptual differences between attraction and commitment, and trust and commitment, have sometimes remained blurred. Attraction has commonly been treated as an element or an indicator of commitment (see e.g. Wilson 1990; Fichman and Levinthal 1991), as has trust (see e.g. Dwyer *et al.* 1987). This is due to the fact that longitudinal research designs have been rare and, typically, only one of the relational bonds has been investigated at a time. The relational bonds are indeed closely related to each other, which has obviously increased conceptual ambiguities.

The most demanding analytical task in the study was to combine the concepts into a logical process model of the development of advertising agency–client relationships (see Figure 6.12). For this purpose, a number of theoretical propositions concerning the temporal and logical relationships between the concepts were drawn from the data. The model, including its conceptual relations, did not, however, reach data saturation point; it must therefore be considered a preliminary attempt to model relationship development. It should be viewed as a set of propositions rather than an empirically tested model.

The longitudinal examination of the development of agency–client relations in their real contextual setting yielded *a broader understanding of the process of relationship development.* Critical events that functioned as driving or checking forces in the development could be identified both in the context and in the content of relationships. Critical and minor events marked the beginning of new, and the end of previous, developmental phases. It was possible to separate six different phases: pre-relationship, initial, growth, decline, constant and troubled. Cycles of growth were identified in the growth phases and cycles of decline in the decline phases of relationship development. Cycles of maintenance were found in both decline and troubled phases.

The idiosyncratic and cyclical nature of relationship development became apparent; deterministic and cumulative evolutions were not present. Both critical and minor events continuously create challenges for the parties to the relationship in their attempts to maintain the relationship. Continuous efforts were needed to maintain the strength of the relational infrastructure and the strength of the relational bonds, particularly those of attraction and trust. Only commitment seemed to develop more incrementally. Agency-client relationships seem to be continuously shaped by contextual influences and by the intentional and unintentional actions of the parties with respect to their relationship and its context.

Deterministic and cumulative evolution does not seem possible in these circumstances. The criticism of the determinism of the life cycle metaphor found support in the study. No single, prescribed path for the development of all business relationships seems to exist. Different developmental phases, including recurrent cycles of development, are likely to occur repeatedly and in an unpredictable way throughout the duration of an agency–client relationship. The absolute time span of relationships cannot be taken as a measure of their developmental phase.

For the third contribution to theory, in applying the Interaction Framework to a professional business service sector, I challenged the particularly static nature of the existing models of buyer–seller relationships in the area of service marketing. I introduced a processual perspective for understanding the development of agency–client relationships and potentially also the development of other professional business service relationships. I also proposed *a dyadic approach* for studying service relationships, as it is particularly useful in facilitating understanding of how relationships are actually created, evaluated and maintained (cf. Brown and Swartz 1989). In addition, the Interaction Model provided *a framework for simultaneously dealing with the social and economic aspects of relationships,* which is particularly relevant in service contexts (see Czepiel 1990: 16).

A number of *managerial implications* can be drawn directly from the theoretical conclusions of the study. Only the most significant implications for the development of agency–client relationships will be presented here.

The idiosyncratic and cyclical nature of relationship development requires special attention from practitioners regarding at least two issues. First, one has to be aware which factors form the essential content of agency–client relationships and what is the current state of each relationship with respect to these factors. Secondly, one has to be aware of the contextual setting in which each relationship has evolved, operates at present and will potentially evolve in the future. *Periodically repeated, systematic appraisals of agency–client relationships should form the basis of relationship development and corrective action.* In order to be realistic and useful, these appraisals should be based on mutual discussions between the agency and the client. At best they can provide the client with positive opportunities to improve the perceived outcomes of assignment processes. The process performance and creative output may be enhanced and the final price of the assignment process is eventually lowered. With regard to the agency party, systematic appraisals are likely to increase its awareness of change and future business possibilities, thus improving the company's profitability and development potential.

The crucial role of personal relationships and human factors in service production implies that the development of agency–client relationships primarily concerns the management of personal relationships. Advertising practitioners need to have good communication and interaction skills. One has to know the right people in organisations, their intentions and preferences. One also needs to understand the importance of individual people and the likely risks and consequences of their leaving the relationship.

Personal relationships are significant for both the client and the agency. Strong personal relationships with the other party create satisfying assignment process outcomes and help to maintain the relationship over time. Clients need to be aware that the agency personnel's investment initiative depends very much on the attractiveness of the client, which in turn and to a great extent is based on expected personal rewards. Attraction needs to be consciously developed if one wishes to achieve satisfying outcomes from interaction. For advertising agencies, the development of personal contact networks and the strengthening of company reputation through referrals are effective marketing tools.

The intangibility of advertising services and the related ambiguities also mean that the management of people's expectations in agency–client relationships becomes crucial. Clearly communicated and commonly shared interests and expectations help to develop a business relationship and maintain it satisfactorily in changing as well as stable conditions. Clear briefings and open communication on both sides are essential elements of successful agency–client relationships.

It is often argued that during successive interactions the parties to the relationship develop clear expectations concerning each other. On the basis of the research findings I would, however, question the clarity of such expectations. It seems that expectations may also develop unconsciously and become unrealistic simply because the parties do not communicate intensively or openly enough. This is critical, since unrealistic expectations easily lead to disappointments and may jeopardise the continuity of the relationship.

The research findings also emphasise the reciprocity of agency–client relationships. In order to be a relevant option for an advertising agency and an advertiser, the development of a business relationship has to benefit both parties. The benefits may be economic or social and may manifest themselves, for example, in the form of cost savings in interaction, increased profitability, improved organisational capabilities or various personal rewards. The materialisation of benefits requires, however, investments from both parties to the relationship in the initiation, development and maintenance of the relationship. Attraction, trust and commitment as well as their potential benefits can be created only in cooperation between the parties, not by either party alone.

7.2 VALIDITY OF THE STUDY

The validity of a scientific study is a broader issue than just the quality of the collected data. *Validity concerns the whole research process, the adherence to generally accepted scientific values, the internal logic of a study and the external applicability of its findings.* Validity cannot be purchased with techniques. It is rather like integrity, character, or quality, to be assessed relative to purposes and circumstances (Brinberg and McGrath 1985: 13).

There is no generally accepted set of guidelines for the assessment of case studies that aim at model building (Eisenhardt 1989: 548). Scientific principles are, of course, common to all kinds of research, but it seems that many of the traditionally used concepts and measures of validity are not directly applicable to case studies that explore new knowledge (see Norén 1990: 6–8).[1] In the assessment of this study, I will use the framework of Brinberg and McGrath (1985) as the main guideline, since it takes a broad perspective on validity and seems to be applicable to a wide range of studies. *According to their ideas, validity can be viewed from three perspectives: validity as value, correspondence and robustness.*

Validity as value refers to the idea that different aims are regarded as valuable and desirable in different domains of research. In the conceptual domain, i.e. in any conceptual presentation, issues such as parsimony of concepts and conceptual relationships, the broad scope of the problem the conceptual presentation covers, and differentiation of detail are commonly viewed as desirable. In the methodological domain, the value criteria are generalisability with respect to populations, precision with respect to measurement, and realism with respect to the context of the phenomenon. In the substantive domain, three general criteria can also be distinguished: the well-being of the substantive system, the task performance effectiveness of the system and its costs. The criteria of each domain are mutually conflicting and cannot be maximised simultaneously, which poses a set of dilemmas for the researcher (Brinberg and McGrath 1985: 41–53).

The criteria set for conceptual presentations are the most significant for this study. In building the model I have primarily sought comprehensiveness, which means that I have valued the detailed differentiation of concepts and the broad scope of the research problem. Simultaneously, I have had to compromise with regard to parsimony (see Brinberg and McGrath 1985: 48; Bacharach 1989: 507; Whetten 1989: 490)

Another set of criteria is also relevant for conceptual presentations: they should be logically coherent, relevant and testable (Brinberg and McGrath 1985: 49; Eisenhardt 1989: 548). In other words, the proposed model should not contain mutually contradictory conceptual relationships or logical gaps. It should be adequate for describing and explaining the substantive phenomenon; relevant factors should be included and different details should be suitably balanced and placed in the whole. It should also be possible to falsify the model in empirical tests (Bacharach 1989: 501).

I have paid special attention to these criteria during the research process. The relevance and potential to test the model have been sought by means of an explorative and inductive research strategy. The creation of a testable and measurable 'theory' can be viewed as a special strength of theory-generating case studies (Eisenhardt 1989: 547). The demonstration of logical coherence, in turn, is very much an issue of how the conceptual analysis is reported and documented in the study. Its assessment ultimately remains the responsibility of the reader.

In the methodological domain, I have valued realism with respect to the empirical context of the study. This has been necessary, although at the cost of generalisability and precision in measurement (see Brinberg and McGrath 1985: 43; cf. Pettigrew 1990: 283). The exploratory and inductive research strategy particularly serves the aim of building an empirically realistic model.

The substantive domain involves ongoing, real-world systems, which in this study refer to the business relationships between advertising agencies and their clients. *By investigating relationships between companies, this study necessarily – although implicitly – places the highest priority on task performance effectiveness at company level.* The well-being of the members of the companies or the advertising sector, or the costs of the interacting companies, have also been taken into account, but only indirectly and as secondary criteria.

Validity as correspondence refers to how well the researcher has been able to bring together the elements and relations of the three research domains: conceptual, methodological and substantive (Brinberg and McGrath 1985: 94). The concepts and relations of the conceptual presentation have to match the methodological tools and procedures used and the substantive phenomenon, its elements and processes. 'Correspondence validity' refers to the logic of the entire research process and also includes the idea of construct validity.

The latter has traditionally been used to describe the match between theoretical and operational definitions of concepts (see e.g. Yin 1989: 40; Norén 1990: 18). In qualitative, theory-building research, construct validity means that one is concerned about whether the phenomena manifested in the data are properly interpreted and labelled; and whether one is collecting the right kind of data and asking the kinds of question conducive to revealing the essential nature of the phenomena (cf. Kirk and Miller 1986: 21).

In addition to the correspondence between the elements of conceptual, methodological and substantive domains, correspondence validity also refers to the fit between the relationships of different elements in each of the three domains (see Brinberg and McGrath 1985: 95–100). The whole idea of the study was to increase the validity of the *a priori* process model by comparing it with the empirical case from the advertising sector, and by using an appropriate longitudinal research design to reveal the processual characteristics of business relationships. The focus of the study was to explore the development of business relationships, and thus to examine the temporal order of relationships between theoretical concepts, different points of data collection (or 'measurements'), and phenomenon events and activities. Consequently, in evaluating the correspondence validity of this study the key questions are: Which temporal order does the conceptual domain specify for specific concepts? Can the methodological tools chosen distinguish temporal orders? Can the substantive materials display any temporal order?

Various steps were taken to increase the correspondence validity in this study:

1 Triangulation of evidence was used to increase construct validity (see section 4.3 and Norén 1990: 21; Yin 1989: 41).
2 Most informants were contacted several times and over a long period of time, which helped to create trusting personal relationships with the informants and achieve a better understanding of the agency–client relationships (see Norén 1990: 22).
3 The key informants read through the case description and gave feedback regarding accuracy and correspondence with their own understanding of events and the contextual factors affecting the relationship (see Hirschman 1986: 244; Norén 1990: 22).
4 The chain of evidence from the initial research questions to the ultimate case study conclusions was strengthened by various means (see Yin 1989: 41; Norén 1990: 22). First, the case study evidence and the research process were documented and saved in a database in order to facilitate the checking of the chain of evidence (see Appendix 4 and Yin 1989: 45; Norén 1990: 18). Secondly, different data display devices such as event–process–state charts (see Appendix 6), and other means such as analytical summaries of each developmental phase (see Chapter 5)

were used to illustrate the temporal and logical order of events and activities in the unit business relationships studied. Thirdly, the link between the empirical evidence and the theoretical conclusions was maintained by making reference to the case description as the findings were presented. Evidence for the theoretical conclusions was purposely sought from all three unit relationships, particularly from opposing and extreme situations that were manifested therein (see Miles and Huberman 1994: 270–1). Fourthly, the empirical indicators of each theoretical concept were also explicitly reported.

Finally, validity as robustness refers to the assessment of the scope and limits of research results, i.e. to the assessment of the external validity or generalisability of the findings. In assessing robustness, one needs to ask whether the findings could be replicated if the study was repeated, and whether the results would converge or differ if reproduced in different research settings, in varying contexts and using different methods and conceptual formalisations. In order to reduce the uncertainty associated with the research findings, they need to be evaluated with respect to each of the three domains of research: conceptual, methodological and substantive (Brinberg and McGrath 1985: 120–7).

Replication refers to the possibility of obtaining similar results and drawing similar conclusions when the study is repeated in the same manner (Yin 1989: 45). In its strict sense replication is never possible, since the passage of time and the prior exposure of the investigator to the research materials always change the research setting. Therefore, it is even more important for the researcher to determine the scope and boundaries of the findings, i.e. under what broader range of conditions the results will and will not hold (Brinberg and McGrath 1985: 121–2).

In the conceptual domain, the researcher needs to consider whether the model and concepts selected uniquely and adequately account for the set of findings under study or whether alternative models and concepts are equally effective in explaining the findings (Brinberg and McGrath 1985: 134). The starting point of this study was the failure of the existing models of business relationships to illuminate the process of relationship development. Alternative models are thus few. The *a priori* process model, which drew on existing models and the available knowledge of the advertising sector, was improved during the study. The specific nature of advertising agency–client relationships and the process of their development were integrated into the model. The modified model proposed at the end of the study may be viewed as a more effective description and explanation of advertising agency–client relationships than the earlier models.

Some researchers speak of analytical generalisations when referring to generalisation at conceptual level (see Yin 1989: 44; see also the discussion by Norén 1990: 9–10). In analytical generalisation, the investigator strives to generalise a particular set of results to some broader theory. This means that each case is viewed as a planned experiment selected on theoretical grounds.[2] The generated theory must be tested through theoretical replications of the findings in other contexts, where the theory has specified that the same results should occur (Yin 1989: 43–5).

In the methodological domain, one needs to consider what limits the method used, the data collection and analysis techniques, or the research strategy impose on the generalisability of the findings (Brinberg and McGrath 1985: 131–2). The qualitative case study method involves several reliability risks that have already been discussed in section 4.5. The researcher is the study instrument, which means that the given inter-pretation of data is always subjective and dependent on the researcher as a person (Hirschman 1986: 245; Norén 1990: 14). Many of the case study findings, however, received support from other studies that had used different methods. This increases the generalisability of the findings. One major strength of a case study is that it allows the triangulation of different data sets and accounts of the events and activities within the same study. With regard to the chosen research strategy, it always reflects the values of the researcher. As noted earlier, the inductive strategy is well able to provide realistic and comprehensive models, albeit at the cost of parsimony and generalisability.

In the substantive domain, one needs to explore the potential convergence or divergence of findings across different types of informants and different types of contexts, including the spatial, temporal and situational aspects of the environment within which interaction occurs (Brinberg and McGrath 1985: 128–9). In this domain lie the greatest weaknesses of the case method. In particular, when using a single case design, it is difficult to show whether the study's findings are gener-alisable to other contexts.

The selection of the case may significantly affect the research findings. In this study, the aim was to select a case representative of the advertising field. Two factors in the context of the selected agency–client relationship are proposed as relevant in terms of its representativeness. Instead of media campaigns, the assignments mostly consisted of the planning of product concepts, packaging and advertising materials. Moreover, advertising was mostly planned for international use. This means that creative planning and international aspects probably received more emphasis in the proposed model than is typical of the area in general.

In order to make industry-specific generalisations about the development of advertising agency–client relationships, the proposed model needs to be tested in other agency–client contexts. It should be noted that different types of relationships exist in the advertising sector. Even though the building of long-term relationships is common in the field, there are also clients who place emphasis on price and standardised services and prefer to switch agencies frequently. For these clients, relationship building is not a relevant option. For clients who value customised services and long-term satisfaction with service outcomes, the development of cooperative relationships is particularly relevant. The parties become interdependent because outcome satisfaction cannot be produced without some level of commitment between them.

Where case studies are involved, excessive emphasis should not be placed on the generalisation of particular findings, but rather on the transferability of an interpretation to another context, thus recognising that no two social contexts are ever identical (Hirschman 1986: 245; Norén 1990: 12). Norén (1990) calls this contextual generalisation and stresses that a case study researcher has to describe both the context and the theory in order to create understanding of the phenomenon for her readers. For contextual generalisation, thorough description of the phenomenon in its real-life context is valuable as such. To assess the transferability of an interpretation one must know not only the specifics of the context in which the interpretation was generated, but also the specifics of the context to which the interpretation is to be applied (Hirschman 1986: 245; Norén 1990: 13–14). In order to increase the possibility of contextual transferability, the case relationship has been described in detail in this study.

In the final analysis, it may be concluded that the findings of this study are also applicable and transferable to other professional business service sectors. Many of the findings were supported by the most recent research results from other professional service contexts. *The potential for both contextual and analytical generalisations is considered to be high.* The interpretation of the case and the derived theoretical conclusions are probably most applicable in those professional business service sectors where services are complex and customised, where their production requires the active participation of the client and where services are needed on a continuous or periodic basis. This study should therefore be of special interest to the buyers and sellers of marketing research services, legal services, financial services (e.g. bookkeeping and auditing) and training and consulting services.

7.3 AVENUES FOR FUTURE RESEARCH

The avenues for future research arise both from the need to verify and broaden the area of application of the proposed model and from the theoretical ideas that arose during the research process.

The study provides a good basis for planning empirical tests of the proposed model or parts of that model through quantitative inquiries. In addition to the important concepts, the study also provides ideas for possible operationalisation of the concepts. The testing of the model in the advertising sector would be a natural extension of the study. It would also be interesting to see how well the model applies to other professional business service sectors, which may differ from each other quite considerably.

More empirical evidence is further required for the proposed processual patterns of relationship development. The proposed cyclical and non-deterministic natures of relationship development are issues that should be addressed more thoroughly in future research. It would be interesting to investigate the paths of the developmental phases that agency–client relationships travel down and the underlying reasons for the existence of various paths. Systematic, longitudinal studies that collect data in real time from several relationships could be useful here.

Another topic that came up during the study was the dissolution of relationships. Remarkably little is known about this topic, about why and how relationships are dissolved. Such information could be valuable both to advertising agencies and to their clients in their attempts to make their existing relationships stronger and more beneficial.

The interaction orientation of the parties to the relationship proved to be one of the key determinants of relationship development. The evidence of its effects remained, however, weak. Which factors create and influence cooperative or competitive interaction orientation, how the interaction orientation of a company changes and how interaction orientations influence relationship development could all be rewarding questions to pose in future research.

8

SUMMARY

The aim of this study was to increase knowledge concerning the development of business relationships in professional business service sectors. The purpose was to build an empirically grounded process model for understanding the development of advertising agency–client relationships in particular. Three research questions were posed:

1 Which theoretical concepts are the most appropriate to describe the content of an advertising agency–client relationship?
2 What are the processes through which advertising agency–client relationships develop?
3 Which contextual factors have an influence on the development process of advertising agency–client relationships and how does this influence manifest itself?

In professional business service sectors, including advertising, economic exchange has typically been organised through long-term business relationships between service companies and their clients. The development of a business relationship is an important issue for both the buyer and the seller, in their attempts to do profitable business with each other and attain their respective goals through exchange. In order to manage business relationships to each party's benefit, professional service companies and their clients need to have an understanding of the dynamics of business relationships, how they evolve and what factors are likely to affect their development.

The lack of research knowledge in this area was the starting point of the study. No attempt had been made to conceptualise the development of business relationships in the advertising sector or in any other professional business service industries. Empirical studies of the process of relationship development have been particularly rare, even in other business contexts.

In this study, the development of agency–client relationships was examined from a processual perspective by studying, in particular, the nature, sequence and order of events and activities that unfold over the

312

duration of a business relationship. Relationship development was regarded as an evolutionary phenomenon involving potential ups and downs, not only progressive development.

Theoretically, the study was based on the IMP Group's Interaction Approach, together with certain interaction studies of American origin and the theoretical developments of service marketing research.

Building the process model of the development of advertising agency–client relationships occurred in three phases. First, in the theoretical part of the study, an *a priori* process model was developed on the basis of existing theoretical and industry-related literature and research results. Second, an empirical investigation was undertaken in the advertising field, in the form of a case study. One agency–client relationship and its development was investigated intensively. Third, a modified process model was developed by confronting the *a priori* process model with the empirical case description. New ideas and theoretical modifications were sought in this comparison.

In building the *a priori* model, the specific natures of advertising markets and advertising services were taken as starting points. The content and process of relationship development were viewed by means of three conceptual categories and the temporal relationships between them: interaction processes, the perceived outcomes of interaction processes, and evolving bonds. The prerequisites for starting a business relationship were separated as a distinct conceptual category in the model. Three broad groups of influencing factors were isolated in the context of advertising agency–client relationships: those related to the environment of relationships; those related to the parties to the relationship – companies, individuals and groups representing them; and finally those related to the tasks that are executed in relationships. The development process was also delineated in terms of events. The nature of critical events in the content and context of agency–client relationships was discussed.

A qualitative case strategy and single-case design were used in the study. The case relationship was chosen so that it would represent a typical business relationship in the field and be mature enough to study the development process. The case relationship was studied longitudinally; data were collected partly retrospectively and partly by following the events and activities in real time. Personal interviews and available company documents were used as primary sources of data. A total of 36 focused interviews and several shorter discussions were conducted during the study. The number of investigated documents amounted to several hundred. A dyadic approach was used in data collection; contact persons on both the agency and the client sides were interviewed and documents collected in both companies.

The agency–client relationship between a Finnish advertising agency, Markkinointi Topitörmä Oy, and its international client, Fiskars Oy

Ab, was selected for the study. The relationship included three unit business relationships: three business units of Fiskars cooperated with Törmä. The three unit relationships provided a fairly diversified picture of advertising agency–client relationships. It was possible to study various assignments in the unit relationships, including the planning of marketing concepts for international use, media campaigns for Finnish markets and a company image campaign. A detailed case description was produced in the study. The events and activities of the three agency–client unit relationships were described in chronological order and by paying special attention to the contextual setting and its influence on relationship development.

In the development of the modified process model, the case description and the inductively derived theoretical ideas were compared with the *a priori* process model and the most recent debates and findings in the literature. Each concept, conceptual relationship and processual pattern of the emerging model were discussed in the light of the empirical evidence. The development process was addressed by investigating the temporal and logical relationships between the distinguished concepts. A number of propositions were suggested concerning new concepts and new conceptual relationships.

As a result of the study an empirically grounded and modified process model was presented. The model was described using six conceptual categories: the context of a business relationship; the prerequisites for a business relationship; the content of a business relationship, including interaction processes and interaction styles; the evolving relational infrastructure; the perceived outcomes of interaction processes; and evolving relational bonds.

In the comparison with the *a priori* process model, a number of new concepts and a new conceptual category were added to the model. The interaction style with its three dimensions – openness of communication, formality of control and investment initiative – proved to be an important element of advertising agency–client interaction. Openness of communication and investment initiative appeared to be particularly relevant in understanding the dynamics of relationships.

The evolving relational infrastructure was introduced to the model as a new conceptual category. Relational infrastructure was defined to form the concrete and necessary framework for interaction and to include four elements: personal relationships, inter-firm knowledge, norms and contracts, and inter-firm roles and positions. Relational infrastructure was seen to set limits and create opportunities for further interactions.

The perceived outcomes of assignment processes were pointed out to be essential explanatory factors for the development of agency–client relationships. The perceived outcome of an assignment process and the outcome of a business relationship were conceptually distinguished from each other, and different, temporally consecutive elements were separated and defined in the outcome of an assignment process.

Three relational bonds – attraction, trust and commitment – were identified as essential content elements of agency–client relationships. Their meaning was specified by paying special attention to their differing temporal perspectives. The meaning of both new and old concepts as well as the temporal and logical relationships between the concepts were defined and further specified during the study.

New ideas and description devices were advanced for understanding the process of relationship development. Critical events arising from changes in the contextual factors or from interaction itself were identifiable in agency–client relationships. Critical events functioned as turning points in relationship development and as potential boundaries between different developmental phases. Six types of developmental phase were separated and described using the content elements of relationships: the pre-relationship phase and the initial, growth, decline, constant, and troubled phases. In addition, three cycles of development emerged from the chains of temporal and logical influence relationships between the content elements: a cycle of growth, a cycle of decline and a cycle of maintenance.

The implications for theory and for management practice were presented at the end. Owing to the intangible and ambiguous nature of advertising services, individual people and personal relationships appear to play an important role in the development of advertising agency–client relationships. The roles of future-oriented bonds, attraction and trust were also accentuated. The need for systematic appraisals of agency–client relationships by both parties to the relationship was highlighted as an important implication for management practice. The ability to manage the human element – personal relationships and people's expectations – was identified as a crucial skill in developing advertising agency–client relationships.

In conclusion, the issue of validity was addressed by taking the whole research process into account. A number of avenues for future research were proposed.

Appendix 1

ADVERTISING AGENCIES IN 1989

The lack of comprehensive statistics in the advertising sector makes it difficult to give an overview of advertising agency markets in Finland. The statistics of the Finnish Association of Advertising Agencies (MTL) were the best available data sources, but they only concerned the member agencies of the association, which had a market share of about 40–5 per cent in 1989 (see Kähkönen 1991: 24, 30). All the biggest advertising agencies were members of MTL. Other statistics were produced and published by the Association of Finnish Advertisers (ML) or by the trade journal *Mainosuutiset* (for references see Appendix 2).

The producers of statistics also used different definitions of an advertising agency, which made it difficult to get an idea of the number of advertising agencies operating in Finland. According to the Finnish Association of Advertising Agencies, there were about 100 full-service agencies in Finland in 1989 (Larres, 11 January 1990, see Appendix 3). The Association of Finnish Advertisers listed 305 advertising agencies, excluding media agencies, designers, advertising consulting companies, market research companies and so on from the total (see Mainostajan hakemisto 1990). The Central Statistical Office of Finland used a still looser definition. In 1988 its register of enterprises and establishments included as many as 860 advertising agencies (Kähkönen 1991: 24).

By structure of agency ownership, Finnish advertising agencies are commonly divided into three categories (Larres 11 January 1990; Kähkönen 1990: 19; Kerttula 1988: 10). First, local independents, owned by Finnish-owned groups and independent entrepreneurs; secondly, international agencies, which are owned partly by international chains, and thirdly in-house agencies, which are owned by advertisers themselves, typically by one of the major group wholesalers.

Of the aggregate gross margin reported by the 60 MTL member agencies in 1989, the 41 local independents accounted for 47 per cent, the four in-house agencies for 11 per cent and the 15 international agencies for 42 per cent (see Kähkönen 1990: 19). Of the 41 independent agencies, 21 were owned by agency groups. They accounted for over half the aggregate gross margin reported by all independent agencies.

316

In 1989, agency gross margins ranged from FIM 49.1 million to around FIM 0.1 million and the number of personnel from 142 to 1 (Mainostajan hakemisto 1990: 206–9). Among the 60 MTL member agencies and 60 non-associated advertising agencies, the median of gross margins was FIM 5.1 million and the mean FIM 8 million (Nevalainen 1990: 4–5). The median of personnel was 12 and the mean 22 employees. Nevalainen has not explained what criteria she used for including the non-associated agencies in the investigation. Among MTL member agencies, the respective figures were larger. The median of gross margins was FIM 9.2 million and the mean FIM 12.4 million, the median of personnel 25 employees and the mean 33 employees (Nevalainen 1990: 4).

Figures of the distribution of agencies' turnover were available only for MTL members (see Kähkönen 1990: 20–1). In 1988, 60 per cent of the total turnover was in media advertising, 27 per cent was purchased production and 14 per cent in own production. In the long term, the share of media invoicing has declined. As to the clients, MTL full-service agencies had 38 clients per agency on average (Kähkönen 1990: 20–1). Half of these clients cooperated with only one advertising agency.

Appendix 2

PUBLICATIONS AND INTERNAL DOCUMENTS USED IN CASE SELECTION AND CASE DESCRIPTION

SECONDARY DATA SOURCES

'Advisor luo uutta toimistoa'(1990) *Mainosuutiset* 15: 3.

Yearbook of the Finnish Association of Advertising Agencies, volumes 1990–92, Helsinki.

Artimo, R. (1992) 'Stig Stendahls Fiskars – ett amerikanskt företag med rötter i Finland', *Forum för ekonomi och teknik* 14–15: 6–8.

'Fiskars, Wilkinson, Montana. Oranssipäisiä saksia kolmella nimellä' (1990) *Kauppalehti Optio* 30 August 1990: 34–5.

Herlin, N. (1990) 'Kaukonen: kansainvälistyminen kuluttaa, myös Fiskarsissa on pulaa johtajista', *Kauppalehti* 3 April 1990.

—— (1992) 'Fiskarsin tulosta kaivetaan esiin', *Kauppalehti* 24 March 1992.

'Huhut puskivat Turkaman nurin' (1992) *Mainosuutiset* 8: 2.

Kervinen, J.-P. (1990) 'Törmä raskaaseen sarjaan', *Talouselämä* 27: 52.

Konttinen, H. (1993) 'Törmä kansainvälistyy kesään mennessä', *Mainosuutiset* 4: 24.

'Kultamuna' (1987) *Talouselämä* 1: 81.

Kähkönen, T. (1990) 'Balancing the Books', in *Yearbook of the Finnish Association of Advertising Agencies*, volume 1990, 16–27. Helsinki.

—— (1991) 'Balancing the Books', in *Yearbook of the Finnish Association of Advertising Agencies*, volume 1991, 20–31. Helsinki.

Laitinen, P. (1983) 'Fiskars fokusoi', *Talouselämä* 38: 124–5.

Linnanahde, A. (1986) 'Käsityökalut yhteiseen pakkiin', *Talouselämä* 11: 48–9.

Louhivaara, L. (1990) 'Advisor järjesteli Törmän suureksi', *Mainosuutiset* 13: 3.

Luotonen, J. (1987) 'Klipp', Talouselämä 11: 81.

Mainostajan hakemisto, Association of Finnish Advertisers (ed.), volumes 1981–90, Helsinki.

Malin, R. (1988) 'Wallenbergit voimalla Fiskarsiin', *Talouselämä* 15: 72.

—— (1992) 'Nurkkakiviksi kulutustavarat ja Metra', *Talouselämä* 29: 30–2.

Mikkonen, A. (1988) 'Iso Fisk hiljaisessa vedessä,' *Talouselämä* 41: 28–31.

—— (1991) 'Fiskarsin merkki on miinus', *Talouselämä* 15: 36.

Mård, A. (1990) 'Paljon vaihtohaluja, vähän vaihtoehtoja', *Talouselämä* 41: 44–7.

Nevalainen, E. (1986) 'Uuden odotusta', *Talouselämä* 10: 74.

—— (1990) 'BSB on suurin, Salomaa johtaa, Kuutoset nousevat', *Mainosuutiset* 4: 4–7.

—— (1993) 'Case Fiskars, Design muuttaa markkinat navettalapiosta puutarhan ergonomiaan', *Mainosuutiset* 15: 17.

Niemi, R. (1991) 'Fiskars-konsernin ongelmat kärjistyivät', *Kauppalehti* 11 April 1991.

Nyström, S. (1990) 'Advisorissa suursiivous – Byroo, Ilmo ja Artifex paketoidaan Linnunradaksi', *Kauppalehti* 12 October 1990.

—— (1991) 'Mainostoimistojen myyntikatteet putoavat noin 10–15 prosenttia', *Kauppalehti* 30 October 1991.

—— (1992) 'Suurten mainostoimistojen myyntikatteet romahtivat', *Kauppalehti* 31 January 1992.

Pelttari, S. (1990) 'Fiskarsista päämerkki', *Talouselämä* 29: 82.

—— (1992) 'Lintas, Topitörmä ja McCann perustivat mediatoimiston,' *Talouselämä* 24: 41.

'Publicis ei valtaa' (1991) *Mainosuutiset* 17: 11.

'Rahoituskulut painoivat Fiskarsin tulosta' (1991) *Kauppalehti* 14 March 1991.

Rantanen, E. (1981) 'Vanhan Fiskarsin nykyaikaiset pulmat: vastuu ja karsinta', *Talouselämä* 7: 20–39.

—— (1991) 'Fiskars Kaukosen jälkeen', *Talouselämä* 28: 60.

'Reijo Kaukonen ulos Fiskarsista' (1991) *Helsingin Sanomat* 22 August 1991.

'Sankarimyytit murtuvat' (1990) *Kauppalehti Optio* 29 March 1990: 30.

Sininen Kirja XXI. Talouselämän suurhakemisto (1989) Helsinki: Startel Oy.

Statistical Yearbook of Finland, Statistics Finland (ed.), volumes 1987, 1988, 1992, Helsinki.

'Suomi ja Ruotsi rokottivat Fiskarsia' (1992) *Kauppalehti* 12 March 1992.

'Tulosnäkymät heikentyneet, Fiskars nopeuttaa yhtiöittämistään' (1990) *Kauppalehti* 2 November 1990.

Vihma, P. (1987) 'Merkki tutki mainostoimistojen yrityskuvat – kärki kirkastuu, lahot hajoavat', *Talouselämä* 23: 38–41.

—— (1988) 'Mainostajien mielipide mainostoimistosta: hyviä yhä vähemmän', *Talouselämä* 39: 50–4.

Ydintietoa pätevistä mainostoimistoista, List of members of the Finnish Association of Advertising Agencies, volumes 1979–89, Helsinki.

'Yrjö Turkama luopumassa Advisorista' (1991) *Mainosuutiset* 14: 1.

INTERNAL DOCUMENTS

A draft of a contract between Markkinointi Topitörmä Oy and Fiskars Oy Ab, 1 October 1987.

Annual reports of Fiskars Oy Ab, volumes 1980–91, Helsinki.

Annual reports of Markkinointi Topitörmä Oy, volumes 1963–92, Helsinki.

Brand strategy overview of Fiskars consumer products, year 1991.

Briefs of Fiskars Oy Ab to Markkinointi Topitörmä Oy.

Company policy and strategy statement of Markkinointi Topitörmä Oy 30 January 1989.

Correspondence between Markkinointi Topitörmä Oy and the three units of Fiskars Oy Ab, including e.g. cost estimates for briefs, various versions of the planned advertising materials, cost estimates and orders for printing and repro work, packaging texts in various languages, media plans, etc.

Fiskars Fokus. Bulletin of Fiskars Oy Ab, volume 1991, Helsinki.

Fiskars tekee terää. A brochure of the company's consumer product operations in Finland.

Fiskars Toimii. Bulletin of Fiskars Oy Ab, volume 1988, Helsinki.

Invoicing between Markkinointi Topitörmä Oy and Fiskars Oy Ab, years 1986–91.

List of major clients of Markkinointi Topitörmä Oy, years 1985–89.

List of personnel of Markkinointi Topitörmä Oy, 14 February 1990 and 26 March 1990.

Markkinointi Topitörmä Oy's profitability calculations of the accounts of Fiskars Oy Ab , years 1986–91.

Media plans.

Memos of media campaigns.

Minutes of meetings between Markkinointi Topitörmä Oy and Fiskars Oy Ab.

Notes made by Account Executives of Markkinointi Topitörmä Oy and Product Managers of Fiskars Oy Ab.

Organisation chart of Advisor Oy.

Organisation chart of the Scandinavian Business Group of Fiskars Consumer Products Group, 13 December 1989.

Product brochures for the consumer products of Fiskars Oy Ab.

Toimiva Fiskars. Bulletin of Fiskars Oy Ab, volumes 1989–90, Helsinki.

Appendix 3

INTERVIEWS AND DISCUSSIONS

CASE STUDY INTERVIEWS

Bensky, Roni, Deputy Managing Director, Markkinointi Topitörmä Oy, Helsinki, 22.5.1990, 19.6.1990, 17.10.1991, 18.8.1992.

Carlander, Hans, Product Manager, Fiskars Oy Ab, Billnäs, 17.9.1990, 20.8.1991.

Falck, Gunnel (past Account Executive of Markkinointi Topitörmä Oy), Helsinki, 13.11.1990.

Hellberg, Thommy, Managing Director, Ixxi Marketing Oy (past Marketing Director of Fiskars Oy Ab), Helsinki, 8.2.1991.

Hällfors, Rolf, Account Supervisor, Markkinointi Topitörmä Oy, Helsinki, 22.5.1990.

Jaakkola, Eira, Administrative Manager, Markkinointi Topitörmä Oy, Helsinki, 31.10.1990.

Kahila-Bergh, Leena, Communications Manager, Fiskars Oy Ab, Helsinki, 29.1.1990.

Kaksonen, Asser, Account Executive, Markkinointi Topitörmä Oy, Helsinki, 17.10.1991.

Kalliala, Eija, Marketing Manager, Lindström-yhtiöt, (past Product Manager of Fiskars Oy Ab), Helsinki, 25.6.1991.

Lindberg, Ingmar, Corporate Vice President, Fiskars Oy Ab, Helsinki, 31.10.1990, 11.8.1992.

Nummelin, Klara, Product Manager, Fiskars Oy Ab, Billnäs, 20.8.1991.

Rajamäki, Tuija (past Product Manager of Fiskars Oy Ab), Espoo, 31.7.1990.

Ranta, Matti, Sales Director (Finland), Fiskars Oy Ab, Helsinki, 22.2.1991, 28.7.1992.

Tuunanen, Marja, Account Executive, Markkinointi Topitörmä Oy, Helsinki, 5.9.1990, 14.9.1990, 3.10.1991.

Yrjölä, Erkki, Managing Director, Markkinointi Topitörmä Oy, Helsinki, 9.5.1990, 13.11.1990, 17.8.1992.

Österman, René, Marketing Manager and Marketing Director, Fiskars Oy Ab, Billnäs, 14.6.1990, 20.8.1991, 18.8.1992.

CASE STUDY DISCUSSIONS

Bensky, Roni, Deputy Managing Director, Markkinointi Topitörmä Oy, Personal discussions, Helsinki, 3.10.1991, 25.6.1992. Telephone discussion, 24.9.1991.

Carlander, Hans, Product Manager, Fiskars Oy Ab, Telephone discussion, 13.10.1992.

Falck, Gunnel (past Account Executive of Markkinointi Topitörmä Oy), Telephone discussion, 6.10.1992.

Hellberg, Thommy, Managing Director, Ixxi Marketing Oy (past Marketing Director of Fiskars Oy Ab), Telephone discussions, 16.1.1991, 16.9.1992.

Jaakkola, Eira, Administrative Manager, Markkinointi Topitörmä Oy, Personal discussions, Helsinki 6.9.1990, 2.10.1991, 3.10.1991.

Kahila-Bergh, Leena, Communications Manager, Fiskars Oy Ab, Telephone discussion, 14.12.1992.

Kalliala, Eija, Marketing Manager, Lindström-yhtiöt, (past Product Manager of Fiskars Oy Ab), Telephone discussion, 9.11.1992.

Lindberg, Ingmar, Corporate Vice President, Fiskars Oy Ab, Personal discussion, Helsinki 18.6.1992.

Nummelin, Klara, Product Manager, Fiskars Oy Ab, Telephone discussions, 1.4.1992, 14.04.1992.

Rajamäki, Tuija, Product Manager, Fiskars Oy Ab, Personal discussion, Billnäs 14.6.1990

Ranta, Matti, Sales Director (Finland), Fiskars Oy Ab, Telephone discussion, 5.6.1992.

Tuunanen, Marja, Account Executive, Markkinointi Topitörmä Oy, Personal discussions, Helsinki 31.10.1990, 29.1.1991. Telephone discussions, 24.9.1991, 18.12.1992.

Yrjölä, Erkki, Managing Director, Markkinointi Topitörmä Oy, Personal discussions, Helsinki 17.10.1990, 29.1.1991, 25.6.1992.

Österman, René, Marketing Manager, Fiskars Oy Ab, Telephone discussion, 25.3.1992.

OTHER INTERVIEWS IN THE INDUSTRY

Bensky, Roni, Deputy Managing Director, Markkinointi Topitörmä Oy, Helsinki, 17.10.1990.

Home, Niilo, Acting Professor, University of Helsinki, Helsinki, 14.12.1989.

Kaartinen, Pekka, Marketing Manager, Oy Esso Ab, Espoo, 19.6.1990.

Kuusniemi, Kaarina, Marketing Manager, Silja Line Oy, Turku, 24.1.1990.

Larres, Matti, Managing Director, Finnish Association of Advertising Agencies, Helsinki, 11.1.1990.

Nummela, Uolevi, Managing Director, Adax-Mainos Oy, Turku, 18.4.1990.

Siukosaari, Asko, Managing Director, Ogilvy & Mather Oy, Helsinki, 25.1.1990.

Suhonen, Kristiina, Managing Director, Association of Finnish Advertisers, Helsinki, 18.12.1989.

Appendix 4

CONTENTS OF THE CASE STUDY DATABASE

CASE STUDY PROTOCOL

- purpose of the research and research questions
- theoretical framework
- research strategy and design
- case study questions
- plan for data analysis
- research schedule

MATERIALS CONCERNING DATA COLLECTION

- list of interviews and discussions (Appendix 3)
- letters for the informants
- list of interview themes and questions for each interview
- documentation from interview situations
- interview transcripts on paper and electronic media
- copies and summaries of documents
- list of publications and internal documents used in case selection and case description (Appendix 2)
- list of Törmä's clients and their basic characteristics
- comparison of Törmä's client relationships as potential cases for the study

MATERIALS CONCERNING DATA ANALYSIS

- list of codes used in data analysis (Appendix 7)
- list of files, i.e. stacks used in organising data
- coded data stacks on paper and electronic media (produced by the HyperQual program, designed for qualitative data analysis)
- diary of data analysis
- memos of data analysis
- list of data display devices (Appendix 6)

Appendix 5

INTERVIEW THEMES AND EXAMPLES OF INTERVIEW QUESTIONS

QC = Question posed to the client. QA = Question posed to the agency

THE INFORMANT'S PERSONAL BACKGROUND

Work experience, education, professional skills

Tell me about yourself. How long have you worked for this company? What other places have you worked? What is your education?

JOB DESCRIPTION

What are your duties in your job? What are your duties in this specific agency–client relationship and what are the duties of the other team members?

Experience of the studied agency–client relationship

How long have you been involved with this specific agency–client relationship? What have your duties and responsibilities been in this relationship?

Experience of advertising agency–client relationships

QC: Do you have experience of other agency relationships? What kind of experiences?
QA: What other client relationships do you take care of? Why these kinds of clients?

FACTORS RELATED TO THE CLIENT COMPANY, ITS MARKETING FUNCTION AND ADVERTISING

Advertised products, marketing strategy, type and role of advertising

QC: What product categories do you market? What kind of marketing/image strategy do you follow? How has the strategy changed? How important a role has advertising in relation to other means of competition? What kind of advertising is carried out?

Other advertising agencies used, experience of other advertising agencies, policy towards advertising agencies

QC: What other agencies does your company use and for which purposes? What kind of experiences do you have of them? Do you plan advertising in-house and if so to what degree? How important is the Törmä relationship for you? Do you have any guiding principles in your dealings with advertising agencies? What were you told about dealing with Törmä when you started as a new product manager?

Marketing organisation and personnel

QC: What is the role of your unit within the Consumer Products Group? What is its market area? How is marketing organised? Which specific people are working and have been working with Törmä?

Marketing and buying capabilities

QA: How good is the client's marketing know-how? How capable is the client in buying advertising services?

Interaction orientation

QC: Do you purposely aim for long-term agency relationships? How often should the agency be changed? Does your company invite agencies for contests? Do you personally favour this process?
QA: How cooperative has the client been? Have you found common interests in cooperation?

FACTORS RELATED TO THE ADVERTISING AGENCY AND ITS MARKETING FUNCTION

Advertising capabilities, reputation

QC: What do you think of Törmä, what kind of an agency it is? How capable is it in advertising and marketing? What kind of reputation does Törmä have?

Agency organisation and personnel

QA: How is the agency organised? What is the role of the Adviser Group and which companies belong to it? How does it affect Törmä's activities?

Company policy towards clients, marketing efforts, philosophy of creative planning

QA: Does the agency have any principles in dealing with its clients or is the account executive free to choose its own way? What kind of marketing methods are used in marketing the agency to potential and current clients? What kind of ambitions has the agency with respect to its clients? Does the agency have some principles in creative planning, some ideology as to how good advertising is done?

Interaction orientation

QA: Have there been periods when you have neglected Fiskars because there have been other, more interesting clients? What do you think as a new account executive: does the agency invest in this client or is the client rather taken for granted?
QC: How cooperative has Törmä been? Do you feel that you have found common interests in cooperation?

MAIN EVENTS IN THE DEVELOPMENT OF BUSINESS RELATIONSHIPS

Initiation of business relationships

Tell me how the business relationship was started. What was the situation in the client company/agency?
QC: Why was an agency needed? Why wasn't the earlier agency relationship continued?
What was expected from the business relationship and the partner? Who took the initiative in starting the relationship? What actually happened? Why was the client/agency an interesting partner, a good alternative? Were other alternatives considered? What intentions did you have in starting the relationship? Did you seek a partner for a long period or just for a particular project (cf. interaction orientation)?

Assignments

Tell me what has happened in this business relationship. What assignments have been executed during the time you have been involved with the relationship? What kinds of assignment? Have there been assignments that you particularly remember as being especially satisfying or dissatisfying, or especially important?

Changes of personnel and organisation

When did you/a specific person start working with the agency-client relationship? When and why did you/a specific person leave the company? How did you feel about the change of this specific person? How did it affect the business relationship?
QC: What happened in the organisation change? Tell what happened before it, what events led to the change of the organisation? How did Törmä's role change?

Quiescent periods, intensive periods, conflicts

Have there been any especially quiescent or intensive periods in the business relationship or has exchange been continuous and regular? Have there been any difficult phases, some major conflicts ?

Other events in the relationships and in their context (a merger, international acquisitions, trial of a competing agency, recession)

What other notable events in the business relationship are worth mentioning? Have any other companies, i.e. competitors sometimes affected the business relationship and how?

QC: Why did you try another, competing agency? What was it like compared with Törmä (cf. attraction)? Did you plan to switch Törmä (cf. commitment)?

TOPICS CONCERNING EACH SPECIFIC ASSIGNMENT (FIRST, MOST IMPORTANT, MOST SATISFYING, LEAST SATISFYING BRIEFS)

Communication

How was the assignment given and when? What topics were negotiated? Who was responsible for the assignment on each side? How intensively were you in contact during the assignment?

Planning and norms

What kind of marketing plan and marketing concept did the client have? Where the plans already fixed or did the agency take part in the planning? What kind of plans were made in connection with the assignment? Were they written or verbal? Were there already established habits or unwritten rules that were followed without a separate agreement?

Goals and outcomes of assignments

What kind of goals were set for the assignment? Did you personally have some goals or ambitions concerning the assignment? How can one describe a successful assignment in general? How well did the assignment succeed? Were the goals met? Were you satisfied with the way the client/agency worked with you?

Progress of the assignment process, potential adaptations

How did the assignment advance? What is the situation now? Were there any problems or changes? How were the problems solved? Did the agency affect the content of the assignment? How did it affect it?

TOPICS CONCERNING THE BUSINESS RELATIONSHIP AS A WHOLE

Communication, personal relationships and knowledge of the other party

With whom are you in contact when you deal with the client/agency? How do you keep in touch? How often do you meet the representatives of the client/agency? Have there been changes in the intensity of communication? How well do you know the contact persons? Do you like them? Do you like to work with them? How well do you know the partner company? Do you get any information from them that you would not get from somewhere else?

Contract negotiations and invoicing principles

What kind of contract do you have? Why did you not have a written contact, what is your opinion? How are invoicing principles agreed upon?

Planning and norms

Do you make common plans regarding the relationship? At which time intervals are the plans made? Are there established habits or unwritten rules in the relationship? Are there any habits regarding briefing, are the briefs verbal or written? Are they strictly specified or open? What kind of distribution of work do you have?

Adaptations and investments in the business relationship

How well has your company handled the business relationship? Have there been any phases or situations where you have had to invest considerably in the relationship? Have you had to adapt or change your organisation or working habits because of the partner? Have you been compelled to teach the partner company's personnel? How much personal effort have you had to put into the business relationship?

ASSESSMENT OF THE RELATIONSHIP AND ITS FUTURE

Satisfaction with the relationship

How can an agency relationship be assessed in general? How would you assess this specific business relationship? Has the relationship been economically profitable? Have you had common interests? Have there been any conflicts? Has the relationship been personally rewarding?

Attraction, the business relationship compared with other relationships

How would you assess the partner compared with other potential partners? How is it better/worse than the others? Is this agency/client also a promising and interesting partner for you in the future? If so, why?

Trust

What do you think, is trust important in agency-client relationships? What does trust mean? Have there been periods of low trust in the business relationship? Why was trust low? In which factors do you have confidence and in which factors do you not? Is trust connected with some specific person or to the whole company?

QC: Do you trust the agency, its ability to produce the kind of advertising you need?

QA: Do you believe that the client will give you further assignments in the future?

Commitment

Is your company willing to continue the relationship with this agency/client? Why? Is it also willing to invest in continuing it? Would you personally continue the relationship if it was up to you to decide? How easy would it be to switch the agency/lose the client? What would the consequences be for the company/for yourself? Why do you think this relationship has lasted this long? Do you already have any plans concerning future cooperation?

Appendix 6

DATA DISPLAY DEVICES

- calendar of events in the agency–client relationship (see Miles and Huberman 1994:110)
- event–process–state charts for each unit business relationship (see Miles and Huberman 1994: 115)
- list of interaction episodes
- list of invoices
- list of documented meetings and other meetings between the parties in each unit business relationship
- calculation of invoicing per brief
- matrix of the characteristics of each brief
- calculation of invoicing per quarter for each unit business relationship
- account-specific profitability calculations per quarter for each unit relationship
- calculation of the economic importance to the agency of the three unit relationships over time
- chart of briefs and personnel changes on a time dimension for each unit relationship
- charts of inter-firm networks of personal relationships in each unit relationship over time
- table of personal relationships and their strength between the parties over time
- time-ordered matrix of the concepts of the model and their dimensions (see Miles and Huberman 1994:119)

Appendix 7

CODES USED IN DATA ANALYSIS

THEORY-RELATED CODES

Content elements of agency–client relationships

PREREQ (1.2.91; 1.9.93) Prerequisites for a business relationship
•NEED   Needs of the parties and complementarity of needs, resources and know-how
•GOALS   Similarity and difference of the parties' interests and expectations
•EXBUS   Basic conflict between the buyer and seller: cost control of the client, agency's willingness to sell more

EX   Exchange between the parties
•BUS   Business exchange: exchange of money and the type of the task
•COM   Communication
/SOC   Social exchange
/KNOW   Information exchange
/ASSES (14.1.91)   Assessment of the results of assignment processes between the parties
/GOALS (14.5.91)   Communicating the goals of an assignment
/CONFI (14.5.91)   Confidential communication, including the exchange of strategic information
•IMP (9.10.90)   Importance of an assignment: economic, strategic and personal importance
•INNO (14.1.91)   Innovativeness of an assignment

EXPRO (14.5.91)   Nature of an assignment process: e.g. length, changes and other temporal aspects

COOR   Coordination between the parties
•FORM   Institutionalisation through norms: established rules, customs, clear expectations
•CONT (14.1.91)   Contract negotiations and nature of the contract
•DECI   Locus of decision-making, responsible persons
•PEOP (1.2.91)   Information concerning contact people or people working with the assignment
•BILL   Invoicing negotiations
•EXPRO (1.2.91)   Temporal harmonisation of the assignment process
•WORK (14.1.91)   Division of work between the parties in an assignment process

331

•FUT	Planning future exchange
•ROLE (14.1.91)	Coordination concerning the roles of the parties
/POSI	Their position in the network of interacting companies
/WREL	Their role with respect to the range of services exchanged, variety of tasks executed, number of products and product groups advertised
AD	Adaptations by one or both parties concerning
•MSTR (14.1.91)	The marketing strategy of the advertised product, or the product itself
•TASK (14.1.91)	The assignment, its content or payment conditions
•EXPRO (1.2.91)	The assignment process *per se*
•ROLE (1.2.91)	The role and position of the parties
•ORG	Interacting organisations
•PEOP	Interacting people
MODE (1.2.91)	Interaction style
•ACT	Activity/passivity of the interacting parties in
/INV	Making investments in the relationship
/INI	Taking the initiative
/ARG	Putting forward arguments, suggestions, etc., concerning the client's advertising and marketing
/MSTR	Marketing the agency to the client
•OPEN	Openness of communication
•FORM (21.5.91)	Formality of control
GOAL (9.10.90)	Goals of the parties
•EX	Set for an assignment process
•REL	Set for the business relationship
EXPECT (9.10.1990)	Expectations concerning
•EX	A specific assignment process
•REL	The business relationship
PEROUT (1.2.91)	Outcomes of a specific assignment process
•EX	The outcomes of an assignment in general
•IND	Individual rewards from an assignment
•EXPRO	The outcome related to the working process itself: efficiency, smoothness, comfort
/CONFLI	Conflicts during the process
	Agency-specific codes (1.2.91)
•ECON	Profitability of an assignment
•REF	Referrals and other marketing-related outcomes
	Client-specific codes (1.2.91)
•CREA	Outcome of the creative work
/CONFLI	Conflicts concerning the creative work
•BILL	Costs of an assignment: price and invoicing
/CONFLI	Conflicts in invoicing
•MARK	Market response and other market-related outcomes: sales volumes, brand awareness etc.
•NET	Feedback from the client's intra-group nets and inter-company networks, distributors and subsidiaries

SAT (1.2.91; 1.9.93)	Outcome of a business relationship concerning
•REL	The business relationship in general
/ECON	Economic outcomes of the relationship
•ROLE (30.3.92)	The roles of the parties
•MODE (30.3.92)	Interaction style
KNOWB	Inter-firm knowledge between the parties
SOSB	Personal relations between the parties
•EXT	Extent of personal relationships
ATTR	Attraction between the parties
•IND	Individual attraction, object of attraction is an individual
•FIRM	Firm level attraction, object of attraction is a firm
TRUST	Trust between the parties
•IND	Individual; object of trust is an individual
•FIRM	Firm level; object of trust is a firm
•OPPORT	Opportunist behaviour
•UNCERT	Uncertainty concerning the beneficiality of the relationship in the future
COMM	Commitment between the parties
•ATT	Attitudinal commitment; willingness to maintain the relationship
•BEH	Behavioural commitment built up through choices and activities over time
/IND	Personal level involvement in the relationship
•SWCOST (1.2.91)	Costs of switching the partner
/AD/PEOP	In form of adaptations concerning people
/MSTR/BRAND	Related to the client's marketing strategy
/ECONB	Related to economic ties/losses, etc.
/SOSB	Related to the personal relationships
/FUT	Related to the future possibilities of the relationship
•IND	Individual; object of commitment is an individual
•FIRM	Firm level; object of commitment is a firm

Individual factors

EXP	Experience
•WORK (5.12.90)	Work experience
•REL (5.12.90)	Experience of the specific relationship
•RELS (14.1.91)	Experience of other agency-client relationships
COMP	Education, professional skills
CAP	Individual capabilities: experience, education and professional skills together
CHAR (9.10.90)	Character of a person as estimated by other informants
JOB (14.1.91)	Job description

Company factors

IMP	Importance of the partner, economic and strategic
REPU (14.1.91)	Reputation of the company in the market
MODE (1.2.91) •INTOR	Favoured interaction orientation: cooperativeness/competitiveness of behaviour
/ALT	Arranging agency contests, using other agencies
/CLOSE	Closeness of cooperation
/POWER	Use of power in the relationship
ECON (14.1.91)	Economic situation of the company
MORG (14.1.91) •CONAG •CONCL	Marketing organisation of the company Structure of the agency group Structure of the client group
HIST (14.1.91)	History of the firm
CULT (14.5.91)	Organisational culture

Client-specific codes

ATTADV	Attitude towards advertising and conception of it
CAP	Marketing capability and capability in buying advertising services
MSTR (14.1.91) •BRAND •IMAGO •ADV	Marketing strategy Brand strategy Company image strategy Advertising strategy and expenditure
COPO (1.9.93)	Company policy towards advertising agencies

Agency-specific codes

COPO (14.5.91)	Company policy concerning advertising ideology, management of client relationships and the development of the agency
PROC •PRICE	Working procedures Pricing and invoicing
ASSES (14.5.91) •CLS	Assessment Of client relationships
MSTR (14.1.91)	Marketing strategy
CAP (14.1.91) •TASK •ARG	Agency know-how related to A specific task area The ability to argue a case and to make good proposals

Environmental and network factors

NET	Network structure or its influence on the relationship
•AG	Agencies used by the client
•CL	Clientele of the agency
•SUPP	Suppliers of the parties: media, press, market research agencies, etc.
ENV	Influence of macro environment: economic situation of the country, trends in society, etc.

GENERAL CODES (9.10.1990)

-T	Related to Törmä
-F	Related to Fiskars
-C (14.5.91)	Related to Fiskars–Headquarters
-B (14.5.91)	Related to Fiskars–Billnäs
-M (14.5.91)	Related to Fiskars–Malmi
/IND	Related to an individual actor
/FIRM	Related to a firm, to the whole organisation
/CH (5.12.90)	Change of something or transformation of some phenomenon
/STAB (5.12.90)	Stability of something
/FUT (5.12.90)	Future of something
/PAST (5.12.90)	Past of something
/CUR (1.2.91)	Current happening of something
/TIME (21.5.91	The absolute time dimension of some phenomenon
/BTIME	The other dimensions of time

PATTERN CODES (9.10.1990)

PATT:	Relationship between concepts or phenomena
SIT:	Situation at one time
POINT: (14.5.91)	Break point in relationship development

Appendix 8

THE DEVELOPMENT OF FISKARS OY AB IN 1980–91 IN TERMS OF TURNOVER, PERSONNEL AND PRE-TAX EARNINGS

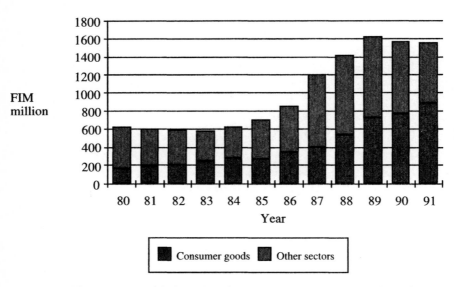

Figure 8.1 The turnover of Fiskars Oy Ab, 1980–91, at 1991 prices, adjusted by the wholesale price index (1980 = 100). The figures are not fully comparable from year to year owing to changes in accounting principles.
Source Annual Reports of Fiskars Oy Ab, 1980–91

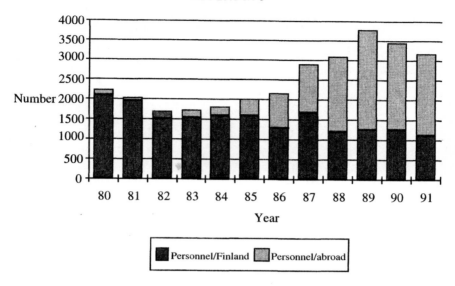

Figure 8.2 The personnel of Fiskars Oy Ab, 1980–91
Source Annual Reports of Fiskars Oy Ab, 1980–91

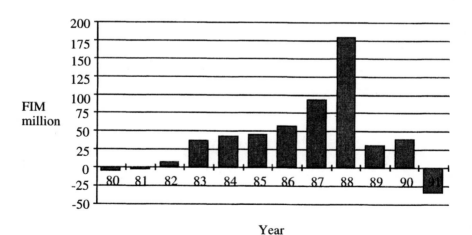

Figure 8.3 The pre-tax earnings of Fiskars Oy Ab, 1980–91, at 1991 prices, adjusted by the wholesale price index (1980 = 100). The figures are not fully comparable from year to year owing to changes in accounting principles.
Source Annual Reports of Fiskars Oy Ab, 1980–91

Appendix 9

THE DEVELOPMENT OF MARKKINOINTI TOPITÖRMÄ OY IN 1980–91 IN TERMS OF GROSS MARGIN, PERSONNEL, PRE-TAX EARNINGS AND MARKET POSITION

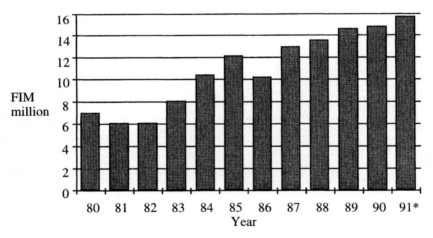

Figure 9.1 The gross margin of Markkinointi Topitörmä Oy, 1980–91, at 1991 prices, adjusted by the wholesale price index (1980 = 100).
*The figures for 1991 are unofficial because of the extended financial year 1 January 1991 to 30 June 1992.
Source Annual Reports of Markkinointi Topitörmä Oy, 1980–92

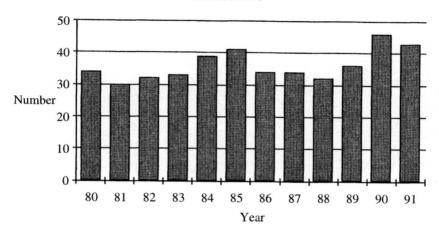

Figure 9.2 The personnel of Markkinointi Topitörmä Oy, 1980–91.
Source Annual Reports of Markkinointi Topitörmä Oy, 1980–92

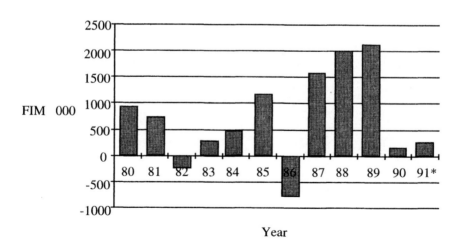

Figure 9.3 The pre-tax earnings of Markkinointi Topitörmä Oy, 1980–91, at 1991
prices, adjusted by the wholesale price index (1980 = 100). The figures are not
fully comparable from year to year owing to changes in accounting principles.
*The figures for 1991 are unoffical because of the extended financial year
1 January to 30 June 1992.
Source Annual Reports of Markkinointi Topitörmä Oy, 1980–92

Table 9.1 The position of Markkinointi Topitörmä Oy in the advertising sector

Year	Clients, turnover FIM 50,000 or more	Market share % of MTL members*	Rank by gross margin among MTL members
1980	25	n.a.	n.a.
1981	30	1.4	25
1982	40	1.4	25
1983	53	1.7	20
1984	46	1.9	18
1985	42	2.1	16
1986	36	1.6	22
1987	35	1.8	19
1988	33	1.8	19
1989	38	1.9	17
1990	50	2.0	16
1991	n.a.	2.8	10

* MTL refers to the Finnish Association of Advertising Agencies.
Source Annual reports of Markkinointi Topitörmä Oy 1980–92

NOTES

1 INTRODUCTION

1 The concept of relationship marketing involves relationship building with both internal and external stakeholders in a company, although its primary focus is on customer relations (see e.g. Christopher *et al*. 1991 and Morgan and Hunt 1994).
2 By transition, Eneroth means the change of an object into something else, and by transformation he means that an object is changing with respect to its form, strength and so on.
3 For the concept of time see especially Halinen and Törnroos (1995).
4 This definition of evolutionary models is used here. There are, however, various types of evolutionary theory (see especially Van de Ven and Poole 1995).

2 THE RESEARCH SETTING

1 For instance, Layder (1993) has recently advanced a less restrictive Grounded Theory Approach in order to build better theories of social phenomena.
2 For the concept of local causality and causal analysis in qualitative research, see Huberman and Miles (1985).
3 For more about analytical generalisation and theoretical sampling, see also Glaser and Strauss (1967: 45–7) and Layder (1993: 137).

3 AN INTERACTION FRAMEWORK FOR THE DEVELOPMENT OF ADVERTISING AGENCY–CLIENT RELATIONSHIPS

1 According to Gummesson (1978: 90), the following criteria are needed in identifying professional services: (1) the service should be provided by qualified personnel, should be advisory and should focus on problem-solving; (2) the professional should have an identity, i.e. should be known in the market for his specialities and under a specific name such as architect or management consultant; (3) the service should be an assignment given by the buyer to the seller, and (4) the professional should be independent of suppliers of other services and goods. Gummesson has also analysed the concept of a professional service and identified three groups of components within it: (1) resources of the professional firm to carry out assignments, i.e.

341

specialist know-how, individual professionals, methods, etc.; (2) the organisation of the assignment, i.e. the diagnosis and formulation of the problem and the goal of a specific assignment, as well as how to operate the assignment, and (3) the outcome of an assignment, i.e. the solution to the problem, the implementation of a solution and the result of the implemented solution. Gummesson treats professional services broadly, to include both the resources used and assignment outcomes. His analysis is valuable particularly because it shows both the processual nature of professional services and the multiplicity of their outcomes.

2 Research results are somewhat different, depending on the research methods used and national differences. In the United States, personal factors seem to play a more important role than e.g. in the Netherlands (see Verbeke 1989: 23).

3 One has to be careful in generalising these findings to the Finnish advertising market, where clients and their advertising budgets are usually smaller than in the United Kingdom, Michell's study only involved accounts of more than £250,000 per year, and the top 50 advertisers included in the study all spent more than £9 million on advertising.

4 Lehtinen and Leivo (1982) discuss the concept of buying ability, especially as an individual property, and relate it to the personality, experience and information reserve of the buyer.

5 Cf. Campbell (1985), who uses the term interaction style when he refers to the competitive, cooperative and command orientation of interaction. In this study, I have identified interaction style and interaction orientation as separate concepts (see company factors).

6 Common goals and common interests have to be separated. Common expectations of outcomes are necessary for a business relationship, common goals are not (see the discussion of Ford 1989: 825). In fact, the specific goals of a buyer and a seller may be very different but, simultaneously, the parties may share common interests with respect to their relationship.

7 The concept of the service encounter is close to the concept of the exchange process. A service encounter has been defined as 'a period of time during which a consumer directly interacts with a service' (see Bitner *et al.* 1990: 72). The concept is, however, too limited for the purpose of this study. Service encounters have been treated above all as social face-to-face interactions (Danet 1981: 384; Solomon *et al.* 1985: 100; Czepiel 1990: 14). In addition, they have been studied as discrete, individual transactions rather than as processes that occur in the context of a buyer–seller relationship.

8 The concept of formalisation, often used in studies of inter-organisational relationships, is very close to this concept. Formalisation has been defined as the degree to which inter-organisational contractual arrangements, fixed policies or standard operating procedures are used to govern the relationship (Van de Ven 1976: 26; Ruekert and Walker 1987: 6; Hyvönen 1988: 12).

9 For further evidence and discussion of this point see Spekman and Wilson (1990: 1007–8). See also Mills (1990: 39), who suggests that the existence of unwritten rules decreases the likelihood of monitoring behaviour.

10 Williamson (1981: 555) uses the term 'transaction-specific assets' and Wilson and Mummalaneni (1988: 18) the notion of 'irretrievable investments' in the same manner.

11 See Williamson (1981: 555), who divides transaction-specific assets into three categories – site-specificity, physical assets specificity and human asset specificity – or Håkansson (1982: 18), according to whom adaptations may be made in the elements exchanged, in the process of exchange or even in the organisation itself.

12 On the basis of the work of Kelley and Thibaut (1978), Anderson and Narus (1984: 63) have posited two constructs as bases for the evaluation of outcomes: the comparison level (CL) and the comparison level for alternatives (CLalt). In the current context CL can be defined as a standard representing the quality of outcomes the agency or client has come to expect, based upon the strength of present and past experience, from a given kind of relationship. The outcomes obtained from a relationship, compared against this standard, determine the attractiveness of the relationship and the degree of satisfaction the participant derives from the relationship. CLalt, by contrast, is a standard that represents the average quality of outcomes that are available from the best alternative business relationship.

13 Dwyer *et al.* (1987) have suggested a five-phase model for the development of buyer–seller relationships. These phases are awareness, exploration, expansion, commitment and dissolution (see Table 1.2).

14 See also Johnston *et al.* (1990: 334) for the commitment of an employee to the employer organisation.

15 The term 'critical event' or 'critical incident' has been used with somewhat different meanings in both service quality literature and in studies of industrial buyer–seller relationships. For the former see e.g. Edvardsson (1988), Bitner *et al.* (1990) and for the latter Elsässer (1984).

4 EMPIRICAL RESEARCH DESIGN

1 By the chain of evidence I refer to the principle prescribing that an external reader of the study must be able to follow the derivation of any evidence from the initial research questions and collected data to the ultimate case study conclusions (Yin 1989: 102).

5 DEVELOPMENT OF THE ADVERTISING AGENCY–CLIENT RELATIONSHIP STUDIED

1 Figure 5.1 and the subsequent figures showing the development of individual business relationships in their various phases illustrate the events, processes and states of the business relationship. Events refer to occurrences in the relationship and its context. Processes refer to chains of events and activities. Something in the relationship's content or context changes, increases, continues, moves or becomes something, for example. States indicate more stable characteristics of the relationship or its context, i.e. certain prevailing conditions, e.g. the strength of a relational bond, a state of satisfaction or dissatisfaction, prevailing expectations, feelings, needs and so forth. Events, processes and states on the left side of the figure are related to the client party. Those on the right side relate to the agency party, and those which are more or less in the middle area relate to both parties and their interaction. Alphabetical symbols ([a], [b], etc.) used in the text when referring to the figure indicate specific event, process and state 'boxes' in that figure.

6 A MODIFIED PROCESS MODEL OF ADVERTISING AGENCY–CLIENT RELATIONSHIPS

1 For the indicators of personal contact see Cunningham and Homse (1986).

2 Cf. the measurement of personal contact by Cunningham and Homse (1986).

3 Cf. Gottfredson and White (1981: 478) about reasons for not achieving an agreement.
4 Ford (1989: 823) discusses the width of the relationship and Larsson and Bowen (1989: 225) the size of the role, essentially in the same sense.
5 Network theorists have, for instance, distinguished between a company's micro- and macro-positions, where the former refers to the relationship with an individual counterpart and the latter bears on the company's relations to a network as a whole (see Mattsson 1983: 9; Johanson and Mattsson 1986: 245–6). The micro-position is characterised by (a) the role of the firm in relation to the (other) firm(s), (b) its importance to the other firm, and (c) the strength of the relationship with the other firm. The macro-position is characterised by (a) the functions performed by the firm for other firms, (b) by the relative importance of the firm in the network, (c) the strength of relationships with other firms, and (d) the identity of the other firms with which the firm has direct and indirect relations.
6 In accordance with the earlier discussion in section 6.2.1 the term 'outcome of an assignment process' will be used here instead of 'outcome of an exchange process.'
7 See also the definition of Van de Ven (1976: 33) regarding the effectiveness of inter-organisational relationships.
8 For the concept of break points in the study of processual phenomena see Van de Ven (1987: 335)
9 Symbols [a], [b], [c] and so on indicate specific elements of the cycle in the figure.

7 ASSESSMENT OF THE STUDY

1 There are conflicting views on this topic (see Norén 1990). Some scholars argue for the universality of assessment criteria (see e.g. Bacharach 1989: 512; Yin 1989: 40), others for the need to create one's own criteria for each research paradigm (see e.g. Hirschman 1986 on Humanist Inquiries).
2 See also Glaser and Strauss (1967: 45–7) and Layder (1993: 137) for theoretical sampling.

REFERENCES

English-speaking readers should note that alphabetical order is sometimes affected by the fact that in Scandinavia accented vowels are alphabetised last, e.g. å comes after z and has nothing to do with a. Thus Hyvönen precedes Håkansson, for instance.

Aaker, D. and Myers, J. G. (1987) *Advertising Management*, Englewood Cliffs, NJ: Prentice-Hall Inc.

Abrams, P. (1982) *Historical Sociology*, Bath: Open Books.

Achrol, R. S., Reve, T. and Stern, L. W. (1983) 'The Environment of Marketing Channel Dyads: A Framework for Comparative Analysis,' *Journal of Marketing* 47, 4: 55–67.

Alvesson, M. (1993) 'Organizations as Rhetoric: Knowledge-Intensive Firms and the Struggle with Ambiguity,' *Journal of Management Studies* 30, 6: 997–1020.

Alvesson, M. and Köping, A.-S. (1993) *Med känslan som ledstjärna. En studie av reklamarbete och reklambyråer*, Lund: Studentlitteratur.

Anderson, E. and Weitz, B. (1989) 'Determinants of Continuity in Conventional Industrial Channel Dyads,' *Marketing Science* 8, 4: 310–23.

—— (1992) 'The Use of Pledges to Build and Sustain Commitment in Distribution Channels,' *Journal of Marketing Research* 29 (February): 18–34.

Anderson, H. and Havila, V. (1993) 'Role and Position – Understanding Dynamics in Networks,' paper presented at the ninth IMP Conference, September 1993, Bath.

Anderson, J. C. and Narus, J. A. (1984) 'A Model of the Distributor's Perspective of Distributor–Manufacturer Working Relationships,' *Journal of Marketing* 48, 4: 62–74.

—— (1990) 'A Model of Distributor Firm and Manufacturer Firm Working Partnerships,' *Journal of Marketing* 54, 1: 42–58.

Arndt, J. (1979) 'Toward a Concept of Domesticated Markets,' *Journal of Marketing* 43, 4: 69–75.

Bacharach, S. B. (1989) 'Organizational Theories: Some Criteria for Evaluation,' *Academy of Management Review* 14, 4: 496–515.

Bagozzi, R. P. (1974) 'Marketing as an Organized Behavioral System of Exchange,' *Journal of Marketing* 38, 4: 77–81.

—— (1975) 'Marketing as Exchange,' *Journal of Marketing* 39, 4: 32–9.

Barnes, J. G. (1994) 'Close to the Customer: But is it Really a Relationship?' *Journal of Marketing Management* 10, 7: 561–70.

Belch, G. E. and Belch, M. A. (1990) *Introduction to Advertising and Promotion Management*, Homewood, IL: Richard D. Irwin Inc.

Beltramini, R. F. and Pitta, D. A. (1991) 'Underlying Dimensions and Communications Strategies of the Advertising Agency–Client Relationship,' *International Journal of Advertising* 10, 2: 151–9.

Berry, L. L. (1983) 'Relationship Marketing,' in L. L. Berry, G. L. Shostack and G. D. Upah (eds) *Emerging Perspectives on Services Marketing*, Chicago: American Marketing Association.

Berry, L. L. and Parasuraman A. (1991) *Marketing Services: Competing through Quality*, New York: Free Press.

Bitner, M. J., Booms, B. H. and Tetreault, M. S. (1990) 'The Service Encounter: Diagnosing Favorable and Unfavorable Incidents,' *Journal of Marketing* 54, 1: 71–84.

Bonoma, T. V. (1985) 'Case Research in Marketing: Opportunities, Problems, and a Process,' *Journal of Marketing Research* 22, 2: 199–208.

Bonoma, T. V. and Johnston, W. J. (1978) 'The Social Psychology of Industrial Buying and Selling,' *Industrial Marketing Management* 7: 213–24.

Boström, G.-O. (1995) 'Successful Cooperation in Professional Services. What Characteristics should the Customer Have?' *Industrial Marketing Management* 24, 3: 151–65.

Bowen, D. E. and Jones, G. R. (1986) 'Transaction Cost Analysis of Service Organization-Customer Exchange,' *Academy of Management Review* 11, 2: 428–41.

Brinberg, D. and McGrath, J. E. (1985) *Validity and the Research Process*, Beverly Hills, CA: Sage Publications.

Brown, S. W. and Swartz, T. A. (1989) 'A Gap Analysis of Professional Service Quality,' *Journal of Marketing* 53, 2: 92–8.

Cadotte, E. R., Woodruff, R. B. and Jenkins, R. L. (1987) 'Expectations and Norms in Models of Consumer Satisfaction,' *Journal of Marketing Research* 24 (August): 305–14.

Cagley, J. W. (1986) 'A Comparison of Advertising Agency Selection Factors: Advertiser and Agency Perceptions,' *Journal of Advertising Research* 26, 3: 39–44.

Campbell, N. C. G. (1985) 'An Interaction Approach to Organizational Buying Behavior,' *Journal of Business Research* 13, 1: 35–48.

Campbell, N. C. G., Graham, J. L., Jolibert, A. and Meissner, H. G. (1988) 'Marketing Negotiations in France, Germany, the United Kingdom and the United States,' *Journal of Marketing* 52, 2: 49–62.

Cardozo, R. N. (1980) 'Situational Segmentation of Industrial Markets,' *European Journal of Marketing* 5, 6: 264–75.

Chase, R. B. (1978) 'Where Does the Customer Fit in a Service Operation?' *Harvard Business Review* 6: 137–42.

Christopher, M., Payne, A. and Ballantyne, D. (1991) *Relationship Marketing: Bringing Quality, Customer Service and Marketing Together*, Oxford: Butterworth-Heinemann.

Comanor, W. S., Kover, A. J. and Smiley, R. H. (1981) 'Advertising and its Consequences,' in P. C. Nyström and W. H. Starbuck (eds) *Handbook of Organizational Design* 2, London: Oxford University Press.

Cook, K. (1977) 'Exchange and Power in Networks of Interorganisational Relations,'*Sociological Quarterly* 18, 1: 62–82.

Cook, K. S. and Emerson, R. M. (1978) 'Power, Equity and Commitment in Exchange Networks,' *American Sociological Review*, 43 (October): 721–39.

Crosby, L. A. (1991) 'Building and Maintaining Quality in the Service Relationship,' in S. W. Brown, E. Gummesson, B. Edvardsson and B. O. Gustavsson (eds) *Service Quality*, Toronto: Lexington Books.

Crosby, L. A., Evans, K. R. and Cowles, D. (1990) 'Relationship Quality in Service

Selling: An Interpersonal Influence Perspective,' *Journal of Marketing* 54, 3: 68–81.

Cunningham, M. T. and Homse, E. (1986) 'Controlling the Marketing–Purchasing Interface: Resource Development and Organizational Implications,' *Industrial Marketing and Purchasing* 1, 2: 3–25.

Cunningham, M. T. and Turnbull, P. W. (1982) 'Inter-organizational Personal Contact Patterns,' in H. Håkansson (ed.) *International Marketing and Purchasing of Industrial Goods: An Interaction Approach*, Chichester: John Wiley & Sons.

Czepiel, J. A. (1990) 'Service Encounters and Service Relationships: Implications for Research,' *Journal of Business Research* 20, 1: 13–21.

Danaher, P. J. and Mattson, J. (1994) 'Customer Satisfaction during the Service Delivery Process,' *European Journal of Marketing* 28, 5: 5–16.

Danet, B. (1981) 'Client–Organization Relationships,' in P. C. Nyström and W. H. Starbuck (eds) *Handbook of Organizational Design* 2, London: Oxford University Press.

Dawes, P. L., Dowling, G. R. and Patterson, P. G. (1992) 'Factors Affecting the Structure of Buying Centers for Purchase of Professional Business Advisory Services,' *International Journal of Research in Marketing* 9, 3: 269–79.

Day, E. and Barksdale, H. C., Jr. (1992) 'How Firms Select Professional Services,' *Industrial Marketing Management* 21: 85–91.

Dowling, G. R. (1994) 'Searching for a New Advertising Agency: A Client Perspective,' *International Journal of Advertising* 13, 3: 229–42.

Doyle, P., Corstjens, M. and Michell, P. (1980) 'Signals of Vulnerability in Agency–Client Relations,' *Journal of Marketing* 44, 4: 18–23.

Dunkerley, D. (1988) 'Historical Methods and Organizational Analysis: The Case of a Naval Dockyard,' in A. Bryman (ed.) *Doing Research in Organizations*, London: Routledge.

Dwyer, F. R., Schurr, P. H. and Oh, S. (1987) 'Developing Buyer–Seller Relationships,' *Journal of Marketing* 51, 2: 11–27.

Dyer, W. G., Jr., and Wilkins, A. L. (1991) 'Better Stories, Not Better Constructs, to Generate Better Theory: A Rejoinder to Eisenhardt,' *Academy of Management Review* 16, 3: 613–19.

Edgett, S., Cullen, C. and Egan, C. (1992) 'Customer Orientation: The Development of a Measurement Scale for the Professional Services,' in *Marketing for Europe – Marketing for the Future*, proceedings of the twenty-first Annual Conference of the European Marketing Academy, May 1992, Aarhus: Aarhus School of Business.

Edvardsson, B. (1988) 'Service Quality in Customer Relationships: A Study of Critical Incidents in Mechanical Engineering Companies,' *Service Industries Journal* 8, 4: 427–45.

Edvinsson, L. (1985) 'The Export Sales Life Cycle,' in C. Grönroos and E. Gummesson (eds) *Service Marketing – Nordic School Perspectives*, University of Stockholm, Department of Business Administration, Report 2-1985. Stockholm.

Eisenhardt, K. M. (1989) 'Building Theories from Case Study Research,' *Academy of Management Review* 14, 4: 532–50.

Ekstedt, E. (1988) *Human kapital i brytningstid – kunskapsuppbyggnad och förnyelse för företag*, Stockholm: Allmänna Förlaget.

Elsässer, M. (1984) *Marknadsinvesteringar. Två fallstudier av etablering på utländsk marknad*, Stockholm: Liber Förlag.

Eneroth, B. (1984) *Hur mäter man vackert? Grundbok i kvalitativ metod*, Stockholm: Akademilitteratur.

Etelä, K. (1985) 'Is the Advertising Agency Market-oriented or Production-oriented? A Study of Agency–Client Interaction,' in C. Grönroos and E.

Gummesson (eds) *Service Marketing – Nordic School Perspectives*, University of Stockholm, Department of Business Administration, Report 2-1985. Stockholm.

Evans, F. B. (1963) 'Selling as a Dyadic Relationship – A New Approach,' *American Behavioral Scientist* 6, 9: 76–9.

Fichman, M. and Levinthal, D. A. (1991) 'Honeymoons and the Liability of Adolescence: A New Perspective on Duration Dependence in Social and Organizational Relationships,' *Academy of Management Review* 16, 2: 442–68.

Fielding, N. G. and Fielding, J. L. (1986) *Linking Data: Qualitative Research Methods* 4, Beverly Hills, CA: Sage Publications.

Ford, D. (1978) 'Stability Factors in Industrial Marketing Channels,' *Industrial Marketing Management* 7: 410–22.

—— (1982) 'The Development of Buyer–Seller Relationships in Industrial Markets,' in H. Håkansson (ed.) *International Marketing and Purchasing of Industrial Goods: An Interaction Approach*, Chichester: John Wiley & Sons.

—— (1989) 'One more Time, What Buyer–Seller Relationships are all About,' in D. T. Wilson, S.-L. Han and G. W. Holler (eds) *Research in Marketing: an International Perspective*, proceedings of the fifth IMP Conference, September 1989, University Park, PA: Pennsylvania State University.

—— (ed.) (1990) *Understanding Business Markets. Interaction, Relationships, Networks*, London: Academic Press.

Ford, D. and Rosson, P. J. (1982) 'The Relationships between Export Manufacturers and their Overseas Distributors,' in M. R. Czinkota and G. Tesar (eds) *Export Management: An International Context*, New York: Praeger.

Ford, D., Håkansson, H. and Johanson, J. (1986) 'How do Companies Interact?' *Industrial Marketing and Purchasing* 1, 1: 26–41.

Frazier, G. L. (1983) 'Interorganizational Exchange Behavior in Marketing Channels: A Broadened Perspective,' *Journal of Marketing* 47, 4: 68–78.

Frazier, G. L., Spekman, R. E. and O'Neal, C. (1988) 'Just-in-Time Exchange Relationships in Industrial Markets,' *Journal of Marketing* 52, 4: 52–67.

Freeman, K. D. and Dart, J. (1993) 'Measuring the Perceived Quality of Professional Business Services,' *Journal of Professional Services Marketing* 9, 1: 279–46.

Ganesan, S. (1994) 'Determinants of Long-term Orientation in Buyer–Seller Relationships,' *Journal of Marketing* 58, 2: 1–19.

Gillette, J. (1985) 'History in the Here and Now: the Development of a Historical Perspective,' in D. Berg and K. K. Smith (eds) *The Self in Social Inquiry*, Beverly Hills, CA: Sage Publications.

Glaser, B. G. and Strauss, A. L. (1967) *The Discovery of Grounded Theory: Strategies for Qualitative Research*, Chicago: Aldine Publishing.

Golden, B. R. (1992) 'The Past is the Past – or is it? The Use of Retrospective Accounts as Indicators of Past Strategy,' *Academy of Management Journal* 13, 4: 848–60.

Gottfredson, L. S. and White P. E. (1981) 'Interorganizational Agreements,' in P. C. Nyström and W. H. Starbuck (eds) *Handbook of Organizational Design* 1, London: Oxford University Press.

Grønhaug, K. and Venkatesh, A. (1991) 'Needs and Need Recognition in Organizational Buying,' *European Journal of Marketing* 25, 2: 17–32.

Grönroos, C. (1980) 'Designing a Long Range Marketing Strategy for Services,' *Long Range Planning* 13, 2: 36–42.

—— (1982) *Strategic Management and Marketing in the Service Sector*, Swedish School of Economics and Business Administration, Research Reports 8. Helsinki.

—— (1990a) 'Relationship Approach to Marketing in Service Contexts: The Marketing and Organizational Behavior Interface,' *Journal of Business Research* 20, 1: 3–11.

—— (1990b) *Service Management and Marketing: Managing the Moments of Truth in Service Competition*, Toronto: Lexington Books.

—— (1994) 'Quo Vadis Marketing? Toward a Relationship Marketing Paradigm,' *Journal of Marketing Management* 10, 5: 345–60.

Guillet de Monthoux, P. B. L. (1975) 'Organizational Mating and Industrial Marketing Conservatism – Some Reasons why Industrial Marketing Managers Resist Marketing Theory,' *Industrial Marketing Management* 4: 25–36.

Gummesson, E. (1978) 'Towards a Theory of Professional Service Marketing,' *Industrial Marketing Management* 7: 89–95.

—— (1979) *Models of Professional Service Marketing*, Stockholm: Marknadstekniskt Centrum.

—— (1981) 'The Marketing of Professional Services – 25 Propositions,' in J. H. Donnelly and W. R. George (eds) *Marketing of Services*, Chicago: American Marketing Association.

—— (1987a) *Marketing – A Long-Term Interactive Relationship. Contributions to a New Marketing Theory*, Stockholm: Stiftelsen Marknadstekniskt Centrum.

—— (1987b) 'The New Marketing – Developing Long-Term Interactive Relationships,' *Long Range Planning* 20, 4: 10–20.

Gundlach, G. T., Achrol, R. S. and Mentzer, J. T. (1995) 'The Structure of Commitment in Exchange,' *Journal of Marketing* 59, 1: 78–92.

Hajba, S. (1982) *Yritysjohdon ammatillistuminen ja valikoituminen osana yritysten institutioitumista*, Publications of the Turku School of Economics and Business Administration, Series A–5. Turku.

Halinen, A. (1989) 'Stability and Instability of Agency–Client Relationships in the Advertising Industry,' in D. T. Wilson, S.-L. Han and G. W. Holler (eds) *Research in Marketing: an International Perspective*, Proceedings of the fifth IMP Conference, September 1989, University Park PA: Pennsylvania State University.

Halinen, A. (1996) 'Service Quality in Professional Business Services: A Relationship Approach,' in T. Swartz, D. Bowen and S. Brown (eds) *Advances in Services Marketing and Management* 5, London: JAI Press.

Halinen, A. and Törnroos, J.-Å. (1995) 'The Meaning of Time in the Study of Industrial Buyer–Seller Relationships,' in K. Möller and D. Wilson (eds) *Business Marketing: An Interaction and Network Perspective*, Boston: Kluwer Academic Publishers.

Hallén, L. and Sandström, M. (1988) 'Relationship Atmosphere in International Business,' in P. W. Turnbull and S. J. Paliwoda (eds) *Research Developments in International Industrial Marketing*, proceedings of the fourth IMP Conference, September 1988, Manchester: University of Manchester Institute of Science and Technology.

Hallén, L., Johanson, J. and Mohamed, N. S. (1987) 'Relationship Strength and Stability in International and Domestic Industrial Marketing,' *Industrial Marketing and Purchasing* 2, 3: 22–37.

—— (1991) 'Interfirm Adaptation in Business Relationships,' *Journal of Marketing* 55, 2: 29–37.

Hammarkvist, K.-O., Håkansson, H. and Mattsson, L.-G. (1982) *Marknadsföring för konkurrenskraft*, Malmö: Liber.

Hammersley, M. and Atkinson, P. (1989) *Ethnography: Principles in Practice*, London: Routledge.

Han, S.-L. (1992) *Antecedents of Buyer–Seller Long-Term Relationships: an Exploratory*

349

REFERENCES

Model of Structural Bonding and Social Bonding, Institute for the Study of Business Markets, Report 6-1992. University Park, PA: Pennsylvania State University.

Hassard, J. (1991) 'Aspects of Time in Organization,' *Human Relations* 44, 2: 105–25.

Hedaa, L. (1991) *On Interorganizational Relationships in Industrial Marketing,* Copenhagen School of Economics and Business Administration, Ph.D. Series 3-1991. Copenhagen.

Heide, J. B. and John, G. (1990) 'Alliances in Industrial Purchasing: the Determinants of Joint Action in Buyer–Supplier Relationships,' *Journal of Marketing Research* 27 (February): 24–36.

—— (1992) 'Do Norms Matter in Marketing Relationships?' *Journal of Marketing* 56, 2: 32–44.

Hirschman, E. C. (1986) 'Humanistic Inquiry in Marketing Research: Philosophy, Method, and Criteria,' *Journal of Marketing Research* 23 (August): 237–49.

Hirsjärvi, S. and Hurme, H. (1991) *Teemahaastattelu,* Helsinki: Yliopistopaino.

Holden, R. K. (1990) *An Exploratory Study of Trust in Buyer–Seller Relationships,* Ann Arbor, MI: UMI Dissertation Information Service.

Homans, G. C. (1958) 'Social Behavior as Exchange,' *American Journal of Sociology* 63, 6: 597–606.

Houston, F. and Gassenheimer, J. B. (1987) 'Marketing and Exchange,' *Journal of Marketing* 51, 4: 3–18.

Huberman, A. M. and Miles, M. B. (1985) 'Assessing Local Causality in Qualitative Research,' in D. Berg and K. K. Smith (eds) *The Self in Social Inquiry,* Beverly Hills, CA: Sage Publications.

Hyvönen, S. (1988) 'Coordination in Contractual Marketing Channels: Some Empirical Findings,' paper presented at the EIASM Workshop on Distribution Channels, October 1988, Brussels.

Håkansson, H. (1982) 'An Interaction Approach,' in H. Håkansson (ed.) *International Marketing and Purchasing of Industrial Goods: An Interaction Approach,* Chichester: John Wiley & Sons.

— (ed.) (1982) *International Marketing and Purchasing of Industrial Goods: An Interaction Approach,* Chichester: John Wiley & Sons.

Håkansson, H. and Snehota, I. (1995a) 'Analysing Business Relationships,' in H. Håkansson and I. Snehota (eds) *Developing Relationships in Business Networks* London: Routledge.

—— (1995b) 'Relationships in Business,' in H. Håkansson and I. Snehota (eds) *Developing Relationships in Business Networks,* London: Routledge.

Hägg, I. and Johanson, J. (1982) 'Företag på heterogena marknader – en teoretisk analys,' in I. Hägg and J. Johanson (eds) *Företag i nätverk – ny syn på konkurrenskraft,* Kristianstad: Studieförbundet Näringsliv och Samhälle.

Iacobucci, D., Grayson, K. A. and Ostrom, A. L. (1994) 'The Calculus of Service Quality and Customer Satisfaction: Theoretical and Empirical Differentiation and Integration,' in T. Swartz, D. Bowen and S. Brown (eds) *Advances in Services Marketing and Management* 3, London: JAI Press.

Iltanen, K. (1986) *Mainonnan suunnittelu,* Markkinointi-Instituutin kirjasarja 34, Espoo: Weilin & Göös.

Jackson, B. B. (1985) 'Build Customer Relationships that Last,' *Harvard Business Review* 63, 6: 120–8.

Johannisson, B. (1987) 'Beyond Process and Structure: Social Exchange Networks,' *International Studies of Management and Organization* 17, 1: 3–23.

Johanson, J. and Mattsson, L.-G. (1986) 'International Marketing and Internationalization Processes – A Network Approach,' in P. W. Turnbull and S. J. Paliwoda (eds) *Research in International Marketing* London: Croom Helm.

350

REFERENCES

—— (1987) 'Interorganizational Relations in Industrial Systems: A Network Approach Compared with the Transaction Cost Approach,' *International Studies of Management and Organization* 17, 1: 34–48.

—— (1992) 'Network Positions and Strategic Action – An Analytic Framework,' in B. Axelsson and G. Easton (eds) *Industrial Networks – A new View of Reality* London: Routledge.

Johnston, J. W. and Bonoma, T. V. (1981a) 'Purchase Process for Capital Equipment and Services,' *Industrial Marketing Management* 10: 253–64.

—— (1981b) 'The Buying Center: Structure and Interaction Patterns,' *Journal of Marketing* 45, 3: 143–56.

Johnston, M. W., Parasuraman, A., Futrell, C. M. and Black, W. C. (1990) 'A Longitudinal Assessment of the Impact of Selected Organizational Influences on Salespeople's Organizational Commitment during early Employment,' *Journal of Marketing Research* 27 (August): 333–44.

Kelley, H. H. and Thibaut, J. W. (1978) *Interpersonal Relations: A Theory of Interdependence*, New York: Wiley.

Kerttula, R. (1988) *Mainosalan rakenne Suomessa*, Helsinki School of Economics and Business Administration, Working Papers F-196, Helsinki.

Kimberly, J. R. (1976) 'Issues in the Design of Longitudinal Organizational Research,' *Sociological Methods and Research* 4, 3: 321–47.

—— (1980) 'The Life Cycle Analogy and the Study of Organizations: Introduction,' in J. R. Kimberly, R. H. Miles and Associates (eds) *The Organizational Life Cycle: Issues in the Creation, Transformation and Decline of Organizations*, San Francisco: Jossey-Bass.

Kirk, J. and Miller, M. L. (1986) *Reliability and Validity in Qualitative Research: Qualitative Research Methods* 1, Beverly Hills, CA: Sage Publications.

Kotler, P. (1986) *Principles of Marketing*, Englewood Cliffs, NJ: Prentice-Hall Inc.

Kotler, P. and Levy, S. J. (1969) 'Broadening the Concept of Marketing,' *Journal of Marketing* 33, 1: 10–15.

Kähkönen, T. (1990) 'Balancing the Books,' in *Annual of Finnish Association of Advertising Agencies*, volume 1991, Helsinki.

Larsson, R. and Bowen, D. E. (1989) 'Organization and Customer: Managing Design and Coordination of Services,' *Academy of Management Review* 14, 2: 213–33.

Layder, D. (1993) *New Strategies in Social Research: An Introduction and Guide*, Cambridge: Polity Press.

Lehtinen, J. R. (1983) *Asiakasohjautuva palvelujärjestelmä – käsitteistö ja empiirisiä sovelluksia*, University of Tampere, Acta Universitatis Tamperensis, Series A: 160, Tampere.

Lehtinen, U. and Lehtinen, J. R. (1991) 'Two Approaches to Service Quality Dimensions,' *The Service Industries Journal* 11, 3: 287–303.

Lehtinen, U. and Leivo, V. (1982) 'Buying Ability and Its Implications in Consumer Policy,' in *Social Responsibility in Marketing*, publications of Turku School of Economics and Business Administration, Series A–2, Turku.

Leuthesser, L. and Kohli, A. K. (1995) 'Relational Behavior in Business Markets. Implications for Relationship Management,' *Journal of Business Research* 34, 3: 221–33.

Levinthal, D. A. and Fichman, M. (1988) 'Dynamics of Interorganizational Attachments: Auditor–Client Relationships,' *Administrative Science Quarterly* 33, 3: 345–69.

Lilja, K. (1983) 'Types of Case-Study Designs,' in *Proceedings of Seminar on Methodology in Management and Business Research*, August 1983, Espoo.

Liljander, V. and Strandvik, T. (1995) 'The Nature of Customer Relationships in Services,' in T. A. Swartz, D. E. Bowen and S.W. Brown (eds) *Advances in Services Marketing and Management* 4, Greenwich, CT: Jai Press Inc.

Liljegren, G. (1988) *Interdependens och dynamik i långsiktiga kundrelationer. Industriell försäljning i ett nätverksperspektiv*, Stockholm: Stockholm School of Economics.

Lindmark, L. (1989) *Kunskapsföretagens individberoende. En studie av avknoppningsföretag i reklambranschen*, Umeå Universitet, FE-publikationer 114, Umeå.

Lovelock, C. H. (1983) 'Classifying Services to Gain Strategic Marketing Insights,' *Journal of Marketing* 47, 3: 9–20.

Lynn, S. A. (1987) 'Identifying Buying Influences for a Professional Service: Implications for Marketing Efforts,' *Industrial Marketing Management* 16: 119–31.

Macneil, I. R. (1980) *The New Social Contract: An Inquiry into Modern Contractual Relations*, New Haven: Yale University Press.

'Mainonnan kustannukset Suomessa 1988' (1989) *Mark* 5: 1–8.

Marshall, R. and Bong Na, W. (1994) 'The Advertising Agency Selection Process,' *International Journal of Advertising* 13, 3: 217–27.

Mattsson, L.-G. (1983) 'An Application of a Network Approach to Marketing – Defending and Changing Market Positions,' paper presented at Scandinavian–German Symposium on Empirical Marketing Research, September 1983, Kiel.

McQuiston, D. H. (1989) 'Novelty, Complexity and Importance as Causal Determinants of Industrial Buyer Behavior,' *Journal of Marketing* 53, 2: 66–79.

Metcalf, L. E., Frear, C. R. and Krishnan, R. (1992) 'Buyer–Seller Relationships: An Application of the IMP Interaction Model,' *European Journal of Marketing* 26, 2: 27–46.

Meyer, A. and Mattmüller, R. (1987) 'Qualität von Dienstleistungen. Entwurf eines praxisorientierten Qualitätsmodells,' *Marketing Zeitschrift für Forschung und Praxis* 3 (August): 187–95.

Michell, P. C. (1984a) 'Accord and Disaccord in Agency–Client Perceptions of Creativity,' *Journal of Advertising Research* 24, 5: 9–24.

—— (1984b) 'Agency–Client Trends: Polarization versus Fragmentation,' *Journal of Advertising Research* 24, 2: 41–52.

—— (1986/1987) 'Auditing of Agency–Client Relations,' *Journal of Advertising Research* 26, 6: 29–41.

—— (1987/1988) 'Point of View: Advertising Account Loyalty – a Segmentation Approach,' *Journal of Advertising Research* 27, 6: 61–7.

Michell, P. C., Cataquet, H. and Hague, S. (1992) 'Establishing the Causes of Disaffection in Agency–Client Relations,' *Journal of Advertising Research* 32, 2: 41–8.

Miettilä, A. and Möller, K. (1990) 'Interaction Perspective into Professional Services: A Conceptual Analysis,' in *Marketing Operations and Human Resource Insights into Services*, proceedings of the First International Research Seminar in Service Management, June 1990, Aix-en Provence.

Miles, M. B. and Huberman, M. (1994) *Qualitative Data Analysis: An Expanded Sourcebook*, Thousand Oaks, CA: Sage Publications.

Miller, D. and Friesen, P. H. (1982) 'The Longitudinal Analysis of Organizations: A Methodological Perspective,' *Management Science* 28, 9: 1013–34.

Mills, P. K. (1986) *Managing Service Industries. Organizational Practices in a Postindustrial Economy*, Cambridge: Ballinger Publishing Company.

— (1990) 'On the Quality of Services in Encounters: An Agency Perspective,' *Journal of Business Research* 20, 1: 31–41.

Moorman, C., Zaltman, G. and Deshpande, R. (1992) 'Relationships between

REFERENCES

Providers and Users of Market Research: The Dynamics of Trust Within and Between Organizations,' *Journal of Marketing Research* 29 (August): 314–28.

Moorman, C., Deshpande, R. and Zaltman, G. (1993) 'Factors Affecting Trust in Market Research Relationships,' *Journal of Marketing* 57, 1: 81–101.

Morgan, N. A. (1990) 'Communications and the Reality of Marketing in Professional Service Firms,' *International Journal of Advertising* 9, 4: 283–93.

Morgan, R. A. and Hunt, S. D. (1994) 'The Commitment–Trust Theory of Relationship Marketing,' *Journal of Marketing* 58, 3: 20–38.

Morris, M. H. and Holman, J. L. (1988) 'Source Loyalty in Organizational Markets: A Dyadic Perspective,' *Journal of Business Research* 16, 2: 117–31.

Mummalaneni, V. and Wilson, D. T. (1991) *The Influence of a Close Personal Relationship between a Buyer and a Seller on the Continued Stability of their Role Relationship*, Institute for the Study of Business Markets, Report 4–1991, University Park, PA: Pennsylvania State University.

Möller, K. (1992) 'Research Traditions in Marketing: Theoretical Notes,' in H. C. Blomqvist, C. Grönroos and L. J. Lindqvist (eds) *Economics and Marketing Essays in Honour of Gösta Mickwitz*, publications of the Swedish School of Economics and Business Administration Nr 48, Helsinki.

— (1994) 'Interorganizational Marketing Exchange: Metatheorical Analysis of Current Research Approaches,' in G. Laurent, G. L. Lilien and B. Pras (eds) *Research Traditions in Marketing*, Boston: Kluwer Academic Publishers.

Möller, K. and Anttila, M. (1987) 'Marketing Capability – a Key Success Factor in Small Business?' *Journal of Marketing Management* 3, 2: 185–204.

Möller, K. and Laaksonen, M. (1986) 'Situational Dimensions and Decision Criteria in Industrial Buying: Theoretical and Empirical Analysis,' in A. G. Woodside (ed.) *Advances in Business Marketing*, 1 Greenwich, CT: Jai Press Inc.

Möller, K. and Wilson, D. T. (1988) *Interaction Perspective in Business Marketing: An Exploratory Contingency Framework*, Institute for the Study of Business Markets, Report 11–1988, University Park, PA: The Pennsylvania State University.

—— (1995a) 'Business Relationships – an Interaction Perspective: Basic Elements and Process,' in K. Möller and D. Wilson (eds) *Business Marketing: An Interaction and Network Perspective*, Boston: Kluwer Academic Publishers.

—— (1995b) 'Introduction: Interaction and Networks in Perspective,' in K. Möller and D. Wilson (eds) *Business Marketing: An Interaction and Network Perspective*, Boston: Kluwer Academic Publishers.

Norén, L. (1990) 'Fallstudiens trovärdighet,' paper presented at the eleventh Nordic Business Administration Conference, August 1990, Vaasa.

Normann, R. (1973) *A Personal Quest for Methodology*, Scandinavian Institutes for Administrative Research, 19, Stockholm.

—— (1991) *Service Management. Strategy and Leadership in Service Business*, Chichester: John Wiley & Sons.

Odén, B. (1989) 'Tiden och periodiseringen i historien,' in P. Heiskanen (ed.) *Aika ja sen ankaruus*, Helsinki: Oy Gaudeamus Ab.

Oliver, C. (1990) 'Determinants of Interorganizational Relationships: Integration and Future Directions,' *Academy of Management Review* 15, 2: 241–65.

Parasuraman, A., Zeithaml, V. A. and Berry, L. L. (1985) 'A Conceptual Model of Service Quality and its Implications for Future Research,' *Journal of Marketing* 49, 4: 41–50.

Parvatiyar, A. and Sheth, J. N. (1994) 'Paradigm Shift in Marketing Theory and Approach: The Emergence of Relationship Marketing,' in Proceedings of the Relationship Marketing Conference, June 1994, Atlanta: Emory University.

Payne, A. (ed.) (1995) *Advances in Relationship Marketing*, London: Kogan Page.

Pels, J. (1992) 'Identification and Management of Key Clients,' *European Journal of Marketing* 26, 5: 5–21.

Pettigrew, A. M. (1987) 'Introduction: Researching Strategic Change,' in A. M. Pettigrew (ed.) *The Management of Strategic Change*, Oxford: Basil Blackwell.

—— (1990) 'Longitudinal Field Research on Change: Theory and Practice,' *Organization Science* 1, 3: 267–92.

Pfeffer, J. and Salancik, G. R. (1978), *The External Control of Organizations: A Resource Dependence Perspective*, New York: Harper and Row.

Ray, M. L. (1982) *Advertising and Communication Management*, Englewood Cliffs, NJ: Prentice-Hall Inc.

Ripley, M. L. (1991) 'What Kind of Companies Take their Advertising In-House?' *Journal of Advertising Research* 31, 5: 73–80.

Rosson, P. J. (1986) 'Time Passages: The Changing Nature of Manufacturer-Overseas Distributor Relations in Exporting,' *Industrial Marketing and Purchasing* 1, 2: 48–64.

Ruekert, R. W. and Walker, O. C. Jr. (1987) 'Marketing's Interaction with other Functional Units: A Conceptual Framework and Empirical Evidence,' *Journal of Marketing* 51, 1: 1–19.

Savitt, R. (1980) 'Historical Research in Marketing,' *Journal of Marketing* 44, 4: 52–8.

Schurr, P. H. and Ozanne, J. L. (1985) 'Influences on Exchange Processes: Buyers' Preconceptions of a Seller's Trustworthiness and Bargaining Toughness,' *Journal of Consumer Research* 11 (March): 939–53.

Seabright, M. A., Levinthal, D. A. and Fichman, M. (1992) 'Role of Individual Attachments in the Dissolution of Interorganizational Relationships,' *Academy of Management Journal* 35, 1: 122–60.

Sharma, D. D. (1994) 'Classifying Buyers to Gain Marketing Insight: A Relationships Approach to Professional Services,' *International Business Review* 3, 1: 15–30.

Sheth, J. N. (1976) 'Buyer–Seller Interaction: A Conceptual Framework,' in B. B. Anderson (ed.) *Advances in Consumer Research* 3 B: Cincinnati, Ohio: Association for Consumer Research.

Sills, D. L. (ed.) (1972) *International Encyclopedia of the Social Sciences*, 7, 11 and 16, London: Collier-Macmillan Publishers.

Simmons, V. M. (1985) 'Reconstructing an Organization's History: Systematic Distortion in Retrospective Data,' in D. Berg and K. K. Smith (eds) *The Self in Social Inquiry*, Beverly Hills, CA: Sage Publications.

Solomon, M. R., Surprenant, C., Czepiel, J. A. and Gutman, E. G. (1985) 'A Role Theory Perspective on Dyadic Interactions: The Service Encounter,' *Journal of Marketing* 49, 1: 99–111.

Spekman, R. E. and Wilson D. T. (1990) 'Managing Strategic Partnerships: Towards an Understanding of Control Mechanisms and their Impact on Partnerships Formation and Maintenance,' in R. Fiocca and I. Snehota (eds) *Research Developments in International Industrial Marketing and Purchasing*, proceedings of the sixth IMP Conference, September 1990, Milan: Graduate Business School of Bocconi University.

Strauss, A. L. (1987) *Qualitative Analysis for Social Scientists*, Cambridge: Cambridge University Press.

Surprenant, C. F. and Solomon, M. R. (1987) 'Predictability and Personalization in the Service Encounter,' *Journal of Marketing* 51, 2: 86–96.

Szmigin, I. T. D. (1993) 'Managing Quality in Business-to-Business Services,' *European Journal of Marketing* 27, 1: 5–21.

Thorelli, H. B. (1986) 'Networks: Between Markets and Hierarchies,' *Strategic Management Journal* 7, 1: 37–51.

REFERENCES

Tuominen, R. (1981) *Organisaatioteoreettinen tutkimus koordinoinnista*, publications of Turku School of Economics and Business Administration, Series A–4: 1981, Turku.

Twedt, D. W. (1964) 'How Stable are Advertiser-Advertising Agency Relationships?' *Journal of Marketing* 28, 3: 83–4.

Usunier, J.-C. (1993) *International Marketing: A Cultural Approach*, London: Prentice Hall.

Van de Ven, A. H. (1976) 'On the Nature, Formation, and Maintenance of Relations Among Organizations,' *Academy of Management Review* 1, 4: 24–36.

—— (1987) 'Review Essay: Four Requirements for Processual Analysis,' in A. M. Pettigrew (ed.) *The Management of Strategic Change*, Oxford: Basil Blackwell.

—— (1992) 'Suggestions for Studying Strategy Process: A Research Note,' *Strategic Management Journal*, Special Issue 13 (summer): 169–88.

Van de Ven, A. H. and Huber, G. P. (1990) 'Longitudinal Field Research Methods for Studying Processes of Organizational Change,' *Organization Science* 1, 3: 213–19.

Van de Ven, A. H. and Poole, M. S. (1995) 'Explaining Development and Change in Organizations,' *Academy of Management Review* 20, 3: 510–40.

Van Maanen, J. (1979) 'The Fact of Fiction in Organizational Ethnography,' *Administrative Science Quarterly* 24, 4: 539–50.

Verbeke, W. (1988/1989) 'Developing an Advertising Agency–Client Relationship in the Netherlands,' *Journal of Advertising Research* 28, 6: 19–27.

Wackman, D. B., Salmon, C. T. and Salmon, C. C. (1986/1987) 'Developing an Advertising Agency–Client Relationship,' *Journal of Advertising Research* 26, 6: 21–8.

Wheiler, K. (1987) 'Referrals between Professional Service Providers,' *Industrial Marketing Management* 16: 191–9.

Whetten, D. A. (1989) 'What Constitutes a Theoretical Contribution?' *Academy of Management Review* 14, 4: 490–5.

Williamson, O. E. (1981) 'The Economics of Organization: The Transaction Cost Approach,' *American Journal of Sociology* 87, 3: 548–77.

Wilson, A. (1972) *The Marketing of Professional Services*, London: McGraw-Hill.

Wilson, D. (1990) *Creating and Managing Buyer–Seller Relationships*, Institute for the Study of Business Markets, Report 5–1990, University Park, PA: The Pennysylvania State University.

Wilson, D. T. and Mummalaneni, V. (1986) 'Bonding and Commitment in Buyer–Seller Relationships: a Preliminary Conceptualisation,' *Industrial Marketing and Purchasing* 1, 3: 44–58.

—— (1988) *Modeling and Measuring Buyer–Seller Relationships*, Institute for the Study of Business Markets, Report 3–1988, University Park, PA: Pennysylvania State University.

Yin, R. K. (1989) *Case Study Research. Design and Methods*, Applied Social Research Methods Series, Beverly Hills, CA: Sage Publications.

Yorke, D. A. (1988) 'The Development of Client/Supplier Relationships over Time in the Area of Professional Services – An Empirical International Comparison,' in P. W. Turnbull and S. J. Paliwoda (eds) *Research Developments in International Marketing*, proceedings of the fourth IMP Conference, September 1988, Manchester: University of Manchester, Institute of Science and Technology.

—— (1990) 'Developing Interactive Approach to the Marketing of Professional Services,' in D. Ford (ed.) *Understanding Business Markets: Interactions, Relationships, Networks*, London: Academic Press.

Young, L. C. and Wilkinson, I. F. (1989) 'The Role of Trust and Co-operation in

Marketing Channels: A Preliminary Study,' *European Journal of Marketing* 23, 2: 109–22.

—— (1992) 'Towards a Typology of Interfirm Relations in Marketing Systems,' in R. Salle, R. Spencer and J. P. Valla (eds) *Business Networks in an International Context: Recent Research Developments*, proceedings of the eigth IMP Conference, September 1992, Lyon: Institut de Recherche de l'Entreprise, Lyon Graduate School of Business.

Zeithaml, V., Parasuraman A. and Berry, L. L. (1985) 'Problems and Strategies in Services Marketing,' *Journal of Marketing* 49, 2: 33–46.

INDEX